THE PANAMA RAILROAD

Railroads Past and Present

H. Roger Grant and Thomas G. Hoback, editors

THE
PANAMA
RAILROAD

PETER PYNE

INDIANA UNIVERSITY PRESS

This book is a publication of

Indiana University Press
Office of Scholarly Publishing
Herman B Wells Library 350
1320 East 10th Street
Bloomington, Indiana 47405 USA

iupress.org

Manufactured in the United States of America

First printing 2021

Library of Congress Cataloging-in-Publication Data

Names: Pyne, Peter, author.
Title: The Panama Railroad / Peter Pyne.
Description: Bloomington, Indiana : Indiana University Press, [2021] | Series: Railroads past and present | Includes bibliographical references and index.
Identifiers: LCCN 2020005970 (print) | LCCN 2020005971 (ebook) | ISBN 9780253052070 (hardback) | ISBN 9780253052087 (ebook)
Subjects: LCSH: Panama Railroad Co.—History. | Railroads—Panama—History.
Classification: LCC HE2830.P2 P96 2021 (print) | LCC HE2830.P2 (ebook) | DDC 385.097287/5—dc23
LC record available at https://lccn.loc.gov/2020005970
LC ebook record available at https://lccn.loc.gov/2020005971

TO MY PARENTS,

Paul Pyne and Mary Freyne,

AND TO

Joan Magee

Contents

Foreword

SPECIAL CHALLENGES CONFRONT ANYONE WHO SEEKS TO WRITE the history of a small place with global significance. The virtues of the biographer and microhistorian must be balanced with those of a world historian, including the capacity to draw connections and make comparisons across oceans, continents, and the frontiers of empire and nation. Peter Pyne has met these challenges admirably in a book that will be of interest not only to historians of railroads or Panama but to anyone with a stake in the broader histories of capitalism, working people, and migration in the nineteenth century.

The construction of the Panama railroad ranks among the great feats of capitalism in the nineteenth century. The first interoceanic rail link in world history, the railroad served as a vital bridge between the Atlantic and Pacific worlds in the mid-1800s and was also instrumental in the building of the Panama Canal. The Panama Railroad Company's business and political strategies, including the foundation of the enclave port of Colón, were among the earliest manifestations of the United States' informal empire in Latin America. Similarly revolutionary was the company's formation and reliance on a divided workforce composed of workers from different continents. The consequences of the railroad's completion, intended and otherwise, continue to reverberate in Panama and elsewhere in the region into the present.

This book represents the first comprehensive scholarly history of the Panama railroad's construction. The story told here includes several titans of nineteenth-century capitalism, including figures such as William Aspinwall, George Law, and Cornelius Vanderbilt. But more significantly for me, it gives an entirely new account of the workers whose labor was essential to the success of the enterprise, whose lives and stories have been almost entirely ignored or unknown until now. Readers who have enjoyed Julie Greene's classic history of working lives and the building of the Panama Canal, *The Canal Builders*, will undoubtedly want to turn to this book, not only because of the importance of the railroad for the later canal but also because of the differences between the two enterprises, particularly concerning workers' health and mortality.

The difficulty of researching and writing any history of Panama in the nineteenth century cannot be overstated. The railroad may have been less than fifty miles long, but the list of conceivably relevant archives and libraries reaches across oceans. Pyne has done a remarkable job of tracking down unique and rare sources over the course of an odyssey that included Ireland, Panama, the United States, the United Kingdom, and Canada. I can only marvel at his ability to weave a compelling narrative from sources that are scattered, incomplete, and frequently cryptic.

It is not just the sources but also the methodological innovations that make this book important. As Pyne explains, the spinning of tales was inherent to the business of building railroads in the mid-nineteenth century. The challenge of separating fact from fiction was worsened in the twentieth century by authors who blended information drawn from historical sources with flights of their own fancy—some of which have sadly infiltrated even academic accounts of the railroad's construction. The author's careful dismantling of these myths is a model of evenhanded and sober truth telling. His book provides the first accurate estimates of the size and composition of the railroad's workforce, including startling new information about workers' origins. The author's careful analysis and estimates of worker mortality are pathbreaking and offer a model for future historians seeking to reconstruct the demography of nineteenth-century railroad building and other large-scale works.

As a historian who is himself of Irish descent and who has written about Panama in the mid-nineteenth century, I was startled to learn from Pyne about the extent of the Irish presence among the workers on the railroad and elsewhere on the Isthmus in the late 1840s and 1850s. His book has successfully managed to reclaim the place of Panama in the making of a global Irish diaspora during the devastating decades of the mid-1800s. As Pyne shows, Panama was not only a destination but also a confluence of different streams of migration emanating from Ireland, including American Irish who set forth to Panama from New York City and New Orleans.

Peter Pyne's efforts to recover the history of Irish immigrants who departed from Cork aboard a ship named the *Ben Nevis* in 1853 are nothing short of heroic. In the end, Pyne tells us he was unable to pinpoint any of the names of the

133 men who were chosen by Poor Law Commissioners to receive assistance for their emigration from Cork to Panama. Mindful as ever about the limits of his sources, Pyne quotes an admonition from two fellow historians in the conclusion of the book: "Histories, then, are never final because some historical conclusions must always be speculations built on mere patches of evidence." No doubt this admonition is true. But the author's own humility should not blind readers to what he has accomplished in these pages.

I, too, wish to know the names of the 133 men from Cork's workhouse who departed aboard the *Ben Nevis* in the early morning of December 3, 1853. But one need not know the names to sense the presence of their lives in these pages or to recognize the significance of the lives that were subsequently lost. Peter Pyne's years of research and writing have recovered that presence and much more.

Dr. Aims McGuinness
Associate Professor, Department of History
University of Wisconsin–Milwaukee

Preface

MOST PEOPLE ARE AWARE OF THE EXISTENCE AND IMPORTANCE OF the Panama Canal, the strategic waterway that bisects the Isthmus of Panama, the narrow neck of land connecting North and South America. Far fewer know of the existence of the Panama railroad, the iron highway that, like the Canal, connects the Atlantic and Pacific. This railroad, started in 1849 and completed in 1855, was the first in the world to provide an interoceanic link, fourteen years before the opening of the Union Pacific–Central Pacific railroad across the United States. It predates the Panama Canal by over half a century and is still in operation today almost 170 years after it was built.

Conceived and planned in the late 1840s, the Panama railroad represented an audacious initiative to shorten the travel time between America's east and west coasts. Its timing was brilliantly fortuitous, coinciding with the discovery of gold in California and the commencement of an immense migratory flow to the Pacific coast territories of the United States. The railroad played a major role in the growth and development of the United States in the latter half of the nineteenth century. It helped to populate the distant lands of the Pacific seaboard and aided their integration into the rest of the nation.

By facilitating the transport of valuable gold and silver shipments from California and Nevada to New York, the Panama railroad helped to power the mid-nineteenth century American economy and strengthened the creditworthiness of the Union government during the Civil War. The railroad's role in moving men and materiel of the Union armies between the east and west during the war that tore America apart helped the Union forces to victory. Then, half a century after its opening, this short stretch of rails played a pivotal part in the construction of the Panama Canal, one of the greatest engineering projects in modern history. In fact, the Canal could not have been built without the assistance of the railroad to remove millions of tons of excavated rock and earth.

I first became aware of Panama's transoceanic rail link when I joined commuters and tourists on the short but memorable train journey from the Pacific to the Atlantic coast while on holiday some years ago. Prompted by my trip to learn more about the history of this rail link, one of the first to be built in the tropics, I was surprised to find references to Irish laborers as well as to workers from distant parts of the globe in its construction. My interest in the history of South and Central America dates to the early 1970s, when I was a postgraduate student at the Institute of Latin American Studies of the University of Glasgow. My enthusiasm for Latin American history was renewed by research on modern Ecuador for my doctoral thesis for the University of Ulster.

Not surprisingly, then, the topic of the Panama railroad and the men who built it gripped my imagination and stimulated my interest in an undertaking whose story is almost unknown in this part of the world. Why did it take an American company five years and millions of dollars to complete a railroad less than fifty miles long? Just how difficult was it to build this short stretch of line through Panama's equatorial swamps and dense rain forests? What prompted large numbers of North American, Irish, South and Central American, Asian, and Caribbean workers to labor on this project in the early 1850s? How many of these laborers came to the Isthmus to work on the railroad, and what happened to them? What began as a holiday pastime gradually developed into a much larger investigation as I sought to piece together details of the railroad's construction.

My search for information led me on a lengthy and intriguing journey of discovery to libraries and archives in Panama City; Washington, DC; New York; Toronto; London; Dublin; and Cork. However, work commitments in my postretirement career as a B and B provider in Northern Ireland's hospitality sector constrained my research activities to two or three winter months per year. As a result, this book has taken much longer to complete than I would have wished. I can only hope that it has improved with time.

I began my research by returning to Panama on two further occasions to continue working on a topic that I had accidentally stumbled on and that has absorbed a good deal of my attention in the intervening years. I soon discovered that much of the railroad's early history, and particularly the role of the men who built the line, is obscure, uncertain, and subject to guesswork. Documents and records have been lost or simply were never kept in the first place. Attempting to record the story of the railroad's construction is akin to assembling a giant jigsaw puzzle with many of the pieces missing.

During my stays in Panama, I visited the Biblioteca Nacional and examined the files of the *Panama Star* and the *Panama Herald*, the two principal English-language newspapers of the Isthmus for the 1849–55 period. I did not have the opportunity to research the contents of another English-language paper, the *Panama Echo*, which ceased publication in May 1853, nor to ascertain to what extent its files survive. Unfortunately, the holdings of the *Star* and the *Herald* in Panama's National Library are not complete. This prompted me to go to Washington, DC, where I was able to fill some of the gaps at the Library of Congress. I discovered, however, that neither Panama's National Library nor the Library of Congress have copies of the *Aspinwall Courier* (1853–57), the first newspaper to be printed on Panama's Atlantic coast. This newspaper, potentially a valuable source of information, was published at the railroad's Caribbean terminus. I have been unable to locate its files; they may not still survive. Items from the *Courier* quoted in this work are taken from reports reprinted in other newspapers.

The following year I returned to Washington, DC, to consult the surviving records of the Panama Railroad Company held in the U.S. National Archives. These records include correspondence, annual reports, and legal and fiscal documents from 1848 onward. By far the best source of information on the day-to-day progress of the railroad's construction is the correspondence of George Totten, the project's chief engineer. However, these letters cover the 1849–53 period only. There is also an unexplained gap of almost nineteen months (February 1854–October 1855) in the reports of the company's executive and finance committee, which handled day-to-day operations. This forced me to rely on the often terse minutes of the board of directors for information during the final year of the railroad's construction. The National Archives also contain dispatches from the U.S. consuls in Panama City and Colón (formerly Aspinwall) that provide valuable insights into the political situation on the Isthmus of Panama during the 1850s.

While in Washington, I also accessed the extensive digital collection of a wide range of American newspapers held in the Library of Congress. The manuscript division of this institution houses the Panama collection of the former Canal Zone Library-Museum, which contains some useful material relating to the railroad's construction. My next research visit was to New York's excellent public library, where I was able to examine the extensive digital and microfilm holdings of Irish-American and American newspapers and periodicals of the 1850s. The Science, Industry, and Business Library, associated with the New York Public Library, holds a miscellaneous collection of pamphlets, circulars, newspaper clippings, and maps relating to the Panama Railroad Company. While in North America, I also used the digital resources of the Robarts Library of the University of Toronto.

My quest for further details of the railroad's construction took me to the British National Archives at Kew, which holds the correspondence of the British consulate in Panama. These letters contain useful insights into British-American relations on the Isthmus and some information on the railroad and Irish laborers involved in its construction. While in London, I also availed myself of the British Library's extensive collection of nineteenth-century travelers' accounts of Panama, which provide useful eyewitness descriptions of life on the Isthmus at the time the railroad was under construction.

Closer to home, I spent time at Dublin's National Library, which houses a comprehensive collection of nineteenth-century Irish newspapers, books, and pamphlets. These yielded additional background material on Irish involvement in building the railroad. Also in Dublin, I visited the national archives to examine the papers of the chief secretary's office and the Poor Law commissioners for information on the inmates from the Cork City workhouse who volunteered to work on the Panama railroad in 1853. A visit to Cork, Ireland's second city, followed where the city and county archives yielded additional information on the workhouse emigrants to Panama. I am indebted to the staff of all of the above institutions for the help and assistance they gave me during my research.

Despite my search over a number of years for the elusive details of the railroad's construction and for information on the laborers who actually built the line, this account is not as complete as I initially hoped it would be. Many details appear to have vanished in the mists of time. The loss of records or the failure or disinclination of the railroad company and other agencies to compile them in the first place means that much of what I have written—particularly in relation to where the workers came from and the numbers who died in Panama, or who perished shortly after leaving the Isthmus as a result of injuries or diseases contracted there—is to a considerable extent guesswork and surmise. There is a strong temptation for a researcher in this situation to continue the

quest for more information and greater certainty. There are manuscript collections, archives, and libraries that I have not visited and newspaper files I have
not read, but I have decided at this point to heed the axiom that "the perfect
is the enemy of the good." I can only plead in my defense that I have tried to
be comprehensive in my search for that most elusive of targets, the truth. Any
errors and omissions remain my sole responsibility.

Acknowledgments

I WOULD LIKE TO ACKNOWLEDGE THE ASSISTANCE AND HOSPITAL-ity given to me over the past few years by many individuals and institutions. Among these I want especially to single out my daughter, Lucy Pyne, in Dublin and my good friend Charlie Nurse of Cambridge, who read earlier drafts of this work and made numerous and invaluable suggestions for improving it. I also want to thank Ed and Linda Goff, now living in New Mexico, for putting up with me for weeks on end in their Washington, DC, home. I am grateful to Derek and Mary Keaveney for letting me use their Manhattan apartment while I stayed in New York. I also want to express my thanks to my sister Helen Hogan, who looked after me while in Toronto; to Harry and Mary Dunleavy for their warm welcome during my visits to New Jersey; to Karen Kerr for the use of her apartment in Panama City; and to Colette and Surender Sukhija for their hospitality during my visits to London.

Among others who went out of their way to help was Jim Phelan, who took my wife and me in his camper van on a memorable journey into Panama's Darien region. Juan David Morgan of Panama City, author of *El Caballo de Oro*, a novel dealing with the building of the railroad; Marilyn and Jerry Johnson; Barbara Tuan Yu Dove; and Mary Roush were all very kind during our stays in Panama City. Bruce D. Phelps showed me around the immaculately kept Corozal American Cemetery. Pedro Masoliver, one of Panama's foremost chefs, entertained us in his Chiriquí retreat and cooked us some memorable meals. Lewis Childs, formerly sublibrarian, and other members of staff of Ulster University's Magee campus library were most helpful, as were Frank Cassidy of the IT Department of Ulster University; Cork historian Colman O'Mahony; Colette McKenna, director of library services, University College, Cork; and Julie Coimbra, librarian at the Centre of Latin American Studies, Cambridge

University. Simon Lang, Darina Wade, and Paul Ferguson guided me through the Early Printed Books and Special Collections of Trinity College, Dublin. Following a serendipitous meeting with my wife and daughters in Romania's Carpathian Mountains, Kevin Busath, vice president of Iowa Pacific Holdings pointed me in the right direction when I was looking for a publisher, for which I am most grateful. I am obliged to Philip Schwartzberg of Meridian Mapping in Minneapolis for the maps. My thanks are also due to the National Portrait Gallery, Smithsonian Institution, the Peabody Essex Museum of Salem, and the British Library Board, London, for permission to reproduce images of paintings and illustrations in their collections. Ashley Runyon, acquisitions editor of Indiana University Press; Anna Francis, assistant acquisitions editor; and Stephen Matthew Williams patiently answered my queries and provided me with much-appreciated help and assistance in preparing this volume for publication. I am also indebted to Megan Schindele, Amnet editorial project manager, and to Nancy Lila Lightfoot for preparing and editing the electronically copyedited manuscript files. My sisters, Helen, Mary and the late Margaret provided support and encouragement during the book's gestation period. Finally, I would like to thank my wife, Joan; my daughters, Sarah, Jane, and Lucy; and my grandchildren, Rose, Nora, Daniel, and Oliver, for their forbearance and patience while the Panama railroad distracted me from my domestic, paternal, and grandparental duties in recent years.

THE PANAMA RAILROAD

Introduction

THE DECISION BY A GROUP OF AMERICAN ENTREPRENEURS IN 1848 to build a railroad across the Isthmus of Panama in Central America took place during a significant period of change in Panamanian, American, Irish, Jamaican, and Asian history. Developments in distant parts of the globe would link the destiny of thousands of men from widely different locations in the jungles and swamps of a little-known tropical region lying between Central and South America. In 1848, Panama—a neglected province of the country then known as Nueva Granada (New Granada) and later as Colombia, and largely unknown outside of its borders—was in the economic doldrums.[1] The prosperity it had enjoyed during the heyday of the Spanish empire had long given way to abandonment and decay. Trade with the outside world was minimal, condemning the mass of the population to want and penury. The imposing colonial buildings and churches of Panama City, the province's capital, crumbled and decayed in the heat of a tropical sun. Grass grew in once busy streets and plazas.

The United States in 1848 was undergoing the largest territorial expansion of its history, having just seized immense territories to the west and southwest from Mexico. The populating of these distant and sparsely inhabited regions and the establishment of reliable communication links between them and the rest of the country now became increasingly urgent. Meanwhile, Ireland in the late 1840s was undergoing the ravages of the last great famine to strike western Europe. A significant proportion of the island's population was brutally displaced by this cataclysm, and over a million of its inhabitants opted to risk the hazards of the Atlantic passage and the uncertainty of life in North America rather than face disease and death in their homeland.

While these events were taking place, the need for cheap labor following the abolition of slavery in the British Empire triggered a flow of migratory workers from the West Indies, as well as men from China and India, to distant countries that offered them the prospect of economic improvement. The building of the Panama railroad emerged from the momentary confluence of the shifting currents of mid-nineteenth-century history, briefly bringing together thousands of men of different nationalities, colors, religions, and languages in a humid wilderness of equatorial swamps and rain forests.

This bold and innovative railroad-construction enterprise was one of the first major projects undertaken by a U.S. corporation on Central American soil. Its completion in 1855 was celebrated as proof of the effectiveness of American technology, competence, determination, and organization. The credit went to a small group of white North American entrepreneurs, investors, and engineers. The part played by the men who actually built the railroad and who hailed from a surprisingly wide array of countries was largely ignored, both at the time and subsequently. I hope to broaden the narrative of the construction of one of the world's first tropical railroads by recounting, to the extent that records permit, the experience of ordinary railroad builders whose story has not been fully told before.

While Ireland has a long history of emigration resulting in a widespread diasporic population, historians of this topic have tended to concentrate on the so-called white settlement zones of North America, South Africa, and the antipodes. Comparatively little is known about Irish migrations to Latin America, Argentina being the principal exception, and almost nothing about Irish involvement in the building of the Panama railway.[2] In addition to a few hundred Irishmen who sailed directly from Cork, I contend that close to four thousand Irish-born laborers came to the Isthmus from the immigrant ghettoes of New York City, Boston, New Orleans, and other parts of the United States to risk their lives and health in the swamps and jungles. These American Irish were mostly unskilled laborers who—due to necessity born of poverty or desperation or from a sense of adventure—found themselves in a country few would have previously heard of or known much about. Although their stay in Panama was brief in most cases, their experience deserves mention in the growing literature on the Irish diaspora.[3]

The Irish were not the only group of migrant workers to labor on this audacious project. Other men from North America and Europe, together with workers from New Granada and adjoining Central and South American states, as well as laborers from Jamaica, China, India, and the Malay Peninsula, formed

Figure 0.1. View of the City of Panama, Nineteenth Century. iStock Stock Illustration.

part of one of the modern world's first multinational labor forces. For five years this international band of workers engaged in a tenacious battle against climate, disease, and geography to complete a daring and ambitious engineering feat. The Chinese laborers, perhaps because of their exotic origin and the novelty of their presence on the Isthmus at that time, have attracted the attention of writers and historians.[4] The West Indian workers on the railroad have also been the subject of several scholarly inquiries.[5]

The story of the remainder of the crew of international workers has been largely ignored. This contrasts with the attention paid by historians to the laborers who attempted the excavation of the Panama Canal under French leadership in the 1880s and who successfully completed this task under American direction just over a century ago.[6] Although I was initially interested in the Irish laborers who went to Panama, I have attempted to incorporate their narrative into a more inclusive account that involves workers of other nationalities, all of them engaged in a valiant, though now almost unknown, engineering venture. This study, then, represents an attempt to remember the forgotten workers of many nationalities who braved heat, humidity, disease, and other hardships of the Isthmus of Panama to complete one of the world's first railroads in the tropics.

The building of the Panama railroad has attracted comparatively little academic attention despite being one of the great infrastructural accomplishments of the mid-Victorian era. The gargantuan scale of the construction of the Panama Canal half a century later and its strategic, economic, and geopolitical importance have completely overshadowed the railroad in the popular and scholarly imaginations. While a number of journal articles and chapter-length accounts of this project have been written, few detailed histories of its construction have appeared in the almost 170 years since the railroad began operations, and some of these suffer from deficiencies of one sort or another.

Most historians of this enterprise use Tomes's book on Panama, written in 1855, as a primary source of information.[7] This work, apparently based on a stay of about two weeks in the country and paid for by the railroad, has been the source of fallacies and misconceptions that have had widespread acceptance up to the present.[8] A review of Tomes's book in the *Spectator* shortly after publication perceptively described it as "lively and telling, but very superficial . . . with the uncomfortable doubt, continually intruding, *how much of this is really true?*"[9] With a ready pen and a considerable facility with words, Tomes did not let dreary details spoil a good story. Wanting, no doubt, to capitalize on the public's interest in an exotic province of distant New Grenada that had become newsworthy following the California gold rush, he tended to embellish his account with extravagant and erroneous details.

The first detailed account of the railroad's construction was published in 1862, seven years after the project's completion. Engaging and well-written, Otis's brief history admirably captures the flavor of the period.[10] But the author did not have access to the archival sources that are now available, and much of the content appears to be based on oral accounts collected by Otis some years after construction had been completed. The author's objectivity may also be open to challenge because of the modest subvention he received for the publication of his work from the railroad's owners.[11]

No further detailed accounts of the building of the railroad appeared until Castillero's 1932 study, *El Ferrocarril de Panama*. This work treats the topic in a somewhat legalistic fashion and relies heavily on Otis for historical information. The railroad also attracted little attention from students seeking a dissertation topic, the exception being Sheldon's brief but informative 1933 study.[12] More recent attention in the anglophone world dates from Minter's

1948 book on Panama's Chagres River, which includes details of the railroad's construction. Unfortunately, the author blends historical facts with fictionalized or imagined conversations. Minter conceded that he set out to satisfy his readers' taste for entertainment as well as their sense of history and admitted frankly that "it weakens a story to acknowledge all its variations."[13] His account of the early years of the railroad contains factual errors, some of considerable importance.

Joseph L. Schott wrote the most recent extensive history of the Panama railroad, published in 1967. This fast-paced and entertaining work, although much more extensive than Otis's, reads like a novel and should be regarded as one. As a work of history, *Rails across Panama* suffers from fatal flaws, and its reliability has been called into question on several grounds. The author's admission years after the publication of this work that he had discovered one of his key sources was fraudulent, followed by his claim to have destroyed the spurious documentation, does little to inspire confidence in his work.[14] Schott, like Minter, also fails to substantiate numerous statements of fact with documentary evidence and neglects to provide the source of anecdotes and conversational material.[15] According to a recent authority, *Rails across Panama* is so full of fabrications and false statements that it is best considered "as a work of historical fiction."[16] Consequently, Schott's book does not provide a reliable narrative of the building of the railroad and should be read with considerable caution. Unfortunately, this work has misled later authors and websites dealing with the history of the railroad.

Several other published works contain incidental material on the early history of the railroad. Kemble's scholarly study, while containing a valuable and informative account of the railroad's construction, focused mainly on steamship services on America's Atlantic and Pacific coasts in the nineteenth century.[17] McCullough, the author of an impressive history of the Panama Canal, provided a short though illuminating overview of the Panama railroad in his book and also in a 1976 article for the *American Heritage Magazine*.[18] Grigore, in two more recent publications, added to our knowledge of this project, particularly its financial aspects, but did not furnish a comprehensive account of the railroad's construction. Parker's 2008 account of the building of the Panama Canal included a brief chapter on the railroad. McGuinness's *Path of Empire* contains an illuminating and perceptive section on the building of the railroad, but the main focus of his scholarly study of 1850s Panama lies elsewhere. Senior devotes a chapter of her recent book on the Panama Canal to the railroad but concentrates largely on the role of Jamaican laborers in its construction.[19]

I hope to remedy the deficiencies in some of these accounts, to fill in the gaps in others, and to furnish a more complete picture than that currently available. My focus will be on the social and organizational aspects of this undertaking, leaving the technical and engineering details of the railroad's construction to others more qualified. Any attempt to uncover what happened to thousands of workers employed on building a railroad in Central America almost 170 years ago would clearly be a challenging task even if abundant sources of historical data had survived. In the absence of personal documentation such as letters, diaries, or extensive firsthand narratives from laborers, I have endeavored to provide a tentative account based on the available records of the railroad company, newspaper sources, travel writings, consular reports, and other fragmentary evidence.

This approach inevitably skews the focus toward the railroad company as a corporate entity and its literate upper-echelon employees at the expense of ordinary, largely uneducated laborers whose voices are infrequently heard in documentation of this kind. Despite the limitations of the sources currently available, I have tried wherever possible to include and describe the experiences of ordinary workers. Nevertheless, the view expressed by the editors of a study on New York's Irish immigrants that "histories, then, are never final because some historical conclusions must always be speculations built on mere patches of evidence" is quite apposite in this case.[20]

This work, then, has a number of objectives. It aims to provide a more comprehensive account of the railroad's construction than that currently available and to explore the extent of Irish involvement in this undertaking. It also attempts to tell the story of the other nationalities that composed the project's international labor force and to estimate the number of lives lost in this daring attempt to link two of the world's great oceans. It throws some light on aspects of the United States' early involvement in Panamanian affairs, an involvement that helped to lay the foundations of that country's informal empire in Latin America in the second half of the nineteenth century. Finally, it hopes to make a modest contribution to our knowledge of modern Panamanian history.

Despite its rich colonial past and emergence in recent decades as a leading Central American nation with a dynamic economy, Panama's nineteenth-century history has been largely neglected by past and present-day scholars, particularly those in the English-speaking world. According to one reviewer writing in 1968, "The history of Panama is replete with legends, fables, and outright falsehoods."[21] The claim by two academics in 1986 that "Panama remains virtually unstudied by contemporary historians" still holds largely true despite some recent, welcome advances.[22] A dearth of scholarly research has led to the persistence of myths and fictions surrounding the building of the Panama railroad. These misrepresentations distort our understanding of aspects of Panama's nineteenth-century history. The present work will hopefully contribute to establishing a more accurate and objective understanding of this neglected period of the country's past.

I have divided the book into four sections. The first section includes early attempts to establish transport links across the Isthmus, culminating in the decisive initiative by a New York–based shipping magnate and his associates to construct a railroad in 1848. The remainder of this section follows a broadly chronological pattern, detailing the progress of construction from 1849 to 1855.

The second part of the book deals with the international labor force that built the railroad. The backgrounds of the workers from various countries and continents who were involved in the course of the five-year construction project are described and their numbers are estimated. This section also examines the conditions faced by the laborers and the limited amenities available to them while they struggled to lay tracks across Panama's inhospitable terrain. It tackles the controversial issue of workers' mortality and attempts to arrive at a more balanced assessment of the likely number of fatalities.

The third section deals with Irish involvement in this pioneering project. It estimates the size of the Irish-born contingent of laborers hired in the United States and examines the background of their decision to work in Panama. This section also looks at the recruitment of laborers from Cork and discusses their probable fate after arriving in Panama. Allegations that the Irish displayed an aggressive and hostile attitude to their Chinese coworkers are also scrutinized.

The concluding section of the book begins by assessing the relationship between an American corporation—determined to complete a costly though potentially profitable enterprise, despite powerful obstacles—and New Granada's authorities, who sought to uphold the sovereignty of their country and the rights of their citizens. It goes on to briefly outline the history of the railroad from its opening in 1855 to the present. The final chapter assesses the consequences of the line's completion at both the local and international levels. It reflects on the achievement of the men of many nationalities involved in this epic construction project. Despite many setbacks, the engineers, craftsmen, and laborers of the Panama railroad managed to overcome staggering odds and extreme circumstances in a valiant feat now largely forgotten and overlooked. The telling of their story provides the principal justification for this book.

PART I

Construction

ONE

The Grand Design

THE ISTHMUS OF PANAMA'S UNIQUE GEOGRAPHICAL POSITION AS A pivotal point between two oceans and two continents has focused attention on it since the discovery of the Americas by Europeans over five centuries ago. The dream of a shortcut from Europe to the Pacific and the Far East through the narrow Isthmus in Central America—one that would avoid the lengthy voyage around the tip of Africa, or the more dangerous one around Cape Horn—dates to the time of the Spanish conquistadores. In parts of Panama, the Atlantic and Pacific oceans are kept apart by a sliver of land only thirty to fifty miles wide. A canal between the two oceans was the obvious solution, but technological limitations and the scale of capital investment and logistical support required meant that serious consideration could not be given to a project of that magnitude until the early nineteenth century. Once Central America had broken free of Spanish rule in the 1820s, American, British, and French entrepreneurs began considering a communications link across Panama, at that time part of Bolivar's new state of Gran Colombia, to benefit from the growing trade between Atlantic and Pacific nations.[1] There would be many false starts, however, before a railroad would be built.

The first initiative to establish a railroad across the Isthmus was apparently made as early as 1828 by Wolwood Hislop, a Jamaican businessman and associate of Bolívar. Hislop failed to secure a concession from the government of New Granada.[2] In 1828 and 1829, two engineers in the Colombian service, L. A. Lloyd of Britain and Captain Falmarc of Sweden, surveyed jungle-covered central Panama and suggested two possible railroad routes.[3] The government of Gran Colombia then offered a concession for building a railroad but found no takers. Not long afterward, the United States became interested, and in 1835 Congress sent an agent, Colonel Charles Biddle, to the Isthmus to investigate possible railroad routes. Biddle obtained a tentative grant to build a line but died before he could report back to Washington. Nothing further came of this concession.[4] A letter from the secretary of the Baron de Thierry, who carried out another survey of the Isthmus in the early 1830s, listed the numerous difficulties of building a railroad across it—impediments that would plague and delay its American builders over fifteen years later.[5]

In 1841 a Frenchman called Sablá—first name unknown—carried out another survey of railroad routes and persuaded a group of French capitalists and some British investors to form the Compagnie de Panama in 1845.[6] Matthew Klein, agent and attorney for this corporation, journeyed to Bogotá, where he secured an agreement from the government in May 1847 to build a railroad across the Isthmus. The contract, approved by New Granada's legislature in June 1847, specified that the Compagnie de Panama would pay the government 600,000 gold francs within twelve months as security for its fulfillment.[7] Political instability and economic upheaval in continental Europe and revolution in France in 1848 prevented the company from raising the necessary capital. Consequently, the New Granada Congress declared the French contract forfeited in June 1848.[8]

A British proposal to build a road across the Isthmus also surfaced around this time. Captain W. B. Liot of the West India Royal Mail Steam Packet Company and Edward McGeachy, the crown surveyor of Jamaica, began surveying the Isthmus of Panama in 1845.[9] They recommended the construction of a macadamized road, fifty to fifty-five miles long, between Portobelo and Panama, at an estimated cost of £400,000 ($2 million). Liot and McGeachy did not anticipate any difficulty in hiring the two thousand laborers needed for the project in Panama. They hoped the British government would support the construction of this transit route, which they calculated would generate annual revenue between £60,000 and £70,000.[10] This innovative proposal failed to receive the backing of the British government sought by London investors, leaving the way open for another American initiative.

On January 24, 1848, James Wilson Marshall discovered gold in the tailrace of Sutter's Mill at Coloma, California, then one of the most remote regions of America's new territories. By the end of that year, the news had spread throughout the United States, and the search for the precious metal quickly assumed the character of a fever. The *New York Tribune* proclaimed, "We are on the brink of the Age of Gold."[11] A tidal wave of eager gold diggers headed for California from all parts of the United States, Europe, and many other regions of the globe, lured by the chimera of instant and immense riches.[12] One of the most remarkable migrations in recent history had begun, described by one journal as "the grandest drama of modern times."[13]

The gold rush raised the stakes for providing a safe and convenient route between the east and west coasts of the United States. Gold-seeking argonauts had three ways of getting to the gold fields: "the Plains across, the Horn around or the Isthmus over."[14] The dangerous westward trek across the plains from the Missouri River took at least four months and could not be attempted during winter. The second option, a fifteen-thousand-mile ocean voyage from New York to San Francisco around Cape Horn, could easily require four to six months and was also expensive. The final possibility was to sail to a convenient crossing point in Mexico or Central America, travel overland to the Pacific coast, and then undertake a second voyage north to San Francisco.

Three main overland routes emerged: Mexico, Nicaragua, and Panama. The closest to the United States was via the Isthmus of Tehuantepec in Mexico, but this option involved a potentially hazardous journey across a country that had recently been at war with the United States. American citizens and mail were not officially permitted to cross this isthmus until 1853 when the Gadsden Purchase was signed between Mexico and the United States.[15] Journeying across Mexico in the late 1840s and early 1850s was thus a risky enterprise, attempted only by a minority of independent travelers.

The second crossing point was through Nicaragua, which was closer to the United States than Panama and therefore required shorter voyages on the Atlantic and Pacific. However, this route involved a 180-mile transit across Nicaragua by river, lake, and land, and the overall traveling time was usually only a week or so shorter than via Panama. The Panama route, approximately fifty miles in length, offered the shortest overland journey between the Atlantic and the Pacific. For this reason it became popular with travelers from the late 1840s onward, despite its alarming reputation for tropical diseases. A journey via this route involved a voyage from New York or New Orleans to the port of Chagres on Panama's Caribbean coast, followed by a boat trip up the Chagres River, an overland crossing to Panama City on the Pacific coast, and a further voyage north to San Francisco. This journey could be accomplished in six weeks if conditions were favorable.[16]

However, the trip from east to west via Panama was far from straightforward. Steamers from New York took from ten to twelve days to reach Panama's Caribbean coast; steamers from New Orleans took less than seven. These ships

Map 1.1. Map of Central America and the United States, 1850, by Philip Schwartzberg.

disgorged their passengers and cargos at the open roadstead opposite Chagres, a small port at the mouth of the river of the same name. The *Camino Real*, the old Spanish colonial road across the Isthmus, had become impassable by this stage, so travelers had to hire canoes or small boats known as *bongos* that were rowed and poled up the Chagres River as far as seasonal water levels allowed.

During the early years of the gold rush, passengers had to negotiate their transport arrangements across Panama with local boatmen and muleteers at each stage of the journey. Because of the multiplicity of carriers and the high demand for transport, the cost of crossing the Isthmus could amount to as much as one hundred dollars per person.[17] During Panama's dry season, between December and April, small river craft could navigate as far as Gorgona, a village about twenty-six miles from Panama City. The arduous boat trip to Gorgona usually required three days or more. During the rainy season, higher water levels made it possible for boats to continue to Cruces, four and a half miles above Gorgona. This short distance by boat added an additional day's travel, however, because of the increasingly rapid current.

From Gorgona or Cruces, travelers headed overland to Panama City by rough trails suitable only for travelers on foot or muleback. The Gorgona trail was the better of the two but was impassable during the long rainy season. Travelers then had to rely on the twenty-two-mile Cruces trail, a neglected and deteriorated track built in the colonial period. Centuries of heavy rains and wear and tear caused by the passage of innumerable iron-shod mules had destroyed most of its surface. By leaving Gorgona or Cruces early in the morning, Panama City could, with luck, be reached by nightfall. An American traveler described his journey during the rainy season of 1850 as follows: "We found the 'road' in a horrible condition, the mud being 4 or 5 feet deep in some places, and at frequent intervals were dead mules in different processes of decomposition, which were now being torn and devoured by vultures. . . . We arrived at Panama [City] covered with mud from head to foot, our clothes torn into shreds, our feet blistered, and our bodies exhausted by over-exertion and exposure."[18]

Once tickets to San Francisco had been procured or endorsed in the capital, travelers and their luggage were carried through the surf by native porters to the small boats that would ferry them to steamships anchored far out in Panama Bay, as there were no deep-water berths at the port. Having boarded their steamers, the migrants could finally complete the last leg of their journey to the California or Oregon coasts.

Even prior to the acquisition of California by the United States in 1848 and the subsequent onset of the gold rush, arrangements had to be made for communicating with distant settlements in Oregon. The 1846 Webster-Ashburton Treaty, which defined the boundary between the United States and British North America, had opened up America's Pacific Northwest for settlement. The territories of Oregon and California were as remote as many overseas colonies, however, and were difficult to access and defend. They were separated from the towns and cities of the East by thousands of miles of uninhabited plains, deserts, and mountains watched over by often hostile native people. The government sought to address this isolation by encouraging the establishment of steamship services from the eastern United States to ports on Panama's Atlantic coast and on the Pacific from Panama City to Oregon.

Prior to the start of the gold rush in 1849, however, shipowners saw little profit in sailing thousands of miles to deliver letters and supplies to a small number of settlers in sparsely populated Pacific territories. Congress was forced to intervene by offering public funds, in the form of mail contracts, to private steamship operators. In March 1847, the legislature offered contracts to deliver and receive mail on both the Atlantic and Pacific coasts of the Isthmus of Panama. The mail would be transported by canoe and mule over the narrow strip of land separating the two oceans. The Atlantic contract was acquired by Albert Sloo, a speculator and lobbyist, in April 1847. The Pacific contract was advertised in May 1847, but there were no takers until November, when it was acquired by Arnold Harris, another speculator. Neither of these men had the financial resources to carry out the contracts they had secured.

At this point William H. Aspinwall, the principal figure behind the establishment of the Panama railroad, and George Law, his major shipping rival for the next five years, made bids for the Pacific and Atlantic mail contracts. Aspinwall, "a merchant at the pinnacle of New York society," was a major figure in the city's capitalist pantheon, with wealth estimated at about $2 million in 1855.[19] An influential figure in the American shipping industry, he and William Edgar Howland, his partner and cousin, owned one of the finest fleets of clipper ships in the world. Aspinwall purchased the Pacific mail contract from Harris on November 19, 1847.[20] Law had purchased the Atlantic mail contract from Sloo, and in March 1848, he and a consortium of wealthy investors formally established the U.S. Mail Steamship Company to carry American mail from New York to Panama's Atlantic port of Chagres. A month later, Aspinwall—along with two other wealthy investors, Gardiner Howland (his uncle) and Henry

Chauncey—established the Pacific Mail Steamship Company to carry the mail and whatever passengers it could find between Panama City and ports in California and Oregon.[21] Contracts for building suitable vessels were entered into shortly afterward by both companies.[22]

Investors and speculators wondered why a shrewd businessman like Aspinwall had put money into what promised to be an unprofitable shipping line serving the thinly populated territories of California and Oregon. The number of travelers crossing Panama at this time was insignificant.[23] The government's subsidy for the transportation of mail would not come close to meeting the running costs of a new shipping company. What commentators failed to realize was that Aspinwall had devised an ambitious transport plan combining sea and rail travel. He envisioned a rail link across Panama as the crucial pivot in a much bigger plan to stimulate, and benefit from, the long-term growth of trade and passenger traffic on the Atlantic and Pacific. Once he had established a rail connection across Panama, it would link up with his steamers on the Pacific in an integrated transport system that would prove profitable in the long term.

Aspinwall's plan was radical in the context of the time, as railroads were unknown south of the Rio Grande apart from those in Cuba and Jamaica.[24] His failure to bid for the government mail contract on the Atlantic, allowing it to fall into the hands of his rival, George Law, remains puzzling. Aspinwall may not have fully formulated his transport strategy at the time the mail contracts went to tender in April and May 1847. It is also conceivable that a comprehensive shipping plan embracing both the Atlantic and Pacific was too ambitious and far-reaching to have won the substantial financial support required from his partners and other investors. A biographer suggested more mundane reasons: Aspinwall may have been preoccupied with administering his late father's estate and with the forthcoming marriage of his brother and allowed his aggressive rival to snap up the lucrative Atlantic contract.[25]

Nevertheless, Aspinwall's timing was doubly fortunate. First, his scheme had been conceived and planned over a year before the news of the California gold discovery reached New York. Second, the Compagnie de Panama had by then failed to lodge the deposit required by New Granada's government, and the French company's railroad contract was forfeited. The way was now open for the New York tycoon to reach a new agreement with Bogotá's politicians to build an American-financed railroad across Panama. The shipowner's first step, however, was to dispatch a friend and business associate, John L. Stephens, who was also a well-known travel writer and explorer, together with J. L. Baldwin, an engineer, to Panama to ensure that the rail project was viable.[26] While carrying out a preliminary survey early in 1848, Baldwin discovered a pass in the continental divide no higher than three hundred feet and concluded that a railroad was feasible.[27]

After discussions with New Granada's government, a modified form of the Compagnie de Panama's concession was signed in Washington on December 28, 1848, by Aspinwall, Stephens, Henry Chauncey, and General Pedro Alcantara Herrán, New Granada's ambassador to the United States.[28] The term assigned to the Americans to run the railroad was forty-nine years, though the government of New Granada had the option to purchase it after twenty for $5 million. This clause was later to cost the Panama Railroad Company dearly. Aspinwall and his associates then deposited 600,000 francs ($120,000) with the New York Life Insurance and Trust Company as a guarantee for the contract's fulfillment.[29] The contract was forwarded to Bogotá for approval by New Granada's executive power.

While negotiations to secure the transfer of the French concession were being finalized, Aspinwall, Stephens, and Chauncey presented a memorandum to Congress seeking government assistance for the railroad in the form of a contract for the transportation of American troops, supplies, and mail. There was considerable pressure on the federal administration to support railroad schemes at this period. The government's hands were tied, however, as the Constitution appeared to preclude direct funding for infrastructure projects. This caused railroad entrepreneurs, aided by sympathetic congressmen, to lobby for indirect financial support in the guise of government land grants and mail contracts.[30] This was the approach followed by Aspinwall and his colleagues when they presented a proposal to Congress on December 11, 1848. They offered the secretary of the navy a twenty-year contract to transport troops, munitions, provisions, naval stores, and U.S. mail across Panama in return for an annual government payment.[31] The memorandum was referred to the Senate Committee on Military Affairs, but it failed to prosper because senators from southern and western states were opposed to any contract that did not benefit their constituents. George Law, the millionaire shipowner and business rival of Aspinwall, also lobbied against Senate approval of the contract.[32]

Aspinwall's proposal initially appeared to have better prospects in the House of Representatives. Its Committee on Naval Affairs requested Colonel J. J. Albert of the Army Corps of Topographical Engineers to prepare a report. He estimated that a single-track railroad across Panama would cost $3.8 million,

Figure 1.1. Portrait of William Henry Aspinwall. Oil on canvas, by Daniel Huntington, 1871.
Courtesy of National Portrait Gallery, Smithsonian Institution.

but the committee concluded that $5 million would be "the probable ultimate
cost of the work." The committee consequently recommended in February 1849
that an annual payment of $250,000, or 5 percent of the projected cost, be made
to the railroad for twenty years in return for transporting, free of charge, the

U.S. mail, troops, and munitions of war. However, the House, like the Senate, failed to support proposals for federal subvention.[33] The first attempts to secure government backing for the Panama railroad had failed.

Undeterred, Aspinwall and his colleagues pressed ahead. They commissioned a detailed survey of the railroad's route between January and June 1849 at a cost of over $80,000.[34] An exploratory party of eighty engineers and surveyors, headed by Colonel Hughes of the U.S. Topographical Corps, completed the survey without formidable difficulties and located a pass in the continental divide, which, at 275 feet, was lower than the one discovered by Baldwin a year earlier. Nevertheless, the surveyors suggested that a tunnel through the hills of the continental divide would make it easier for the low-powered locomotives to tackle the gradients involved.[35] The use of horse-drawn carriages had also been contemplated should steam locomotives prove unsuitable for some or all of the terrain.[36] Engineers subsequently concluded that replacing the tunnel by a long cutting would sufficiently reduce the gradient to enable steam trains to operate without difficulty.[37]

The discovery of the low pass through the hills led the 1849 surveying team to predict that the Isthmus could be crossed by train in two hours.[38] A company pamphlet optimistically pronounced that "the difficulties, instead of being greater, are less than on the average of railroads [sic] in the northern states of the Union."[39] In fact, the obstacles facing the railroad were far more difficult than those normally encountered in the United States, as the company and its shareholders were to discover over the next five years.

Aspinwall, Stephens, and Chauncey now embarked on the next step of their project. On April 7, 1849, an act to legally register the Panama Railroad Company as a body corporate in the state of New York with power to raise capital of up to $5 million was approved in the state legislature at Albany.[40] This charter was unusual, as it was one of the few at that time that permitted a U.S. corporation to own and operate a railroad in a foreign country.[41] Furthermore, although not specified in the charter, capital invested in the company could count on a degree of American government protection. Under the terms of the 1846 Bidlack-Mallarino Treaty between the United States and New Granada, the United States had been granted a right of way across the Isthmus of Panama, and Washington was obliged to protect this access against any foreign incursions.[42] This was one of only a handful of instances in which the U.S. government could be counted on to protect the investment of American shareholders in a foreign state.[43] With its legal formation completed, the company acquired an office at 78 Broadway in lower Manhattan. One of its first actions was to purchase the 1848 concession, which Aspinwall, Stephens, and Chauncey had negotiated with the Republic of New Granada. In return, each of the three grantees received $50,000 in company stock.[44]

Shares totaling $1 million were now offered for sale at $100 each.[45] The company had confidence that this sum could be raised because of the stimulus that the recently announced gold finds in California had given to emigration to the Pacific territories. However, an unenthusiastic public bought less than half this amount, and "Messrs. Aspinwall, Stephens, and Chauncey, and their immediate associates, were obliged themselves to take the residue, to enable the company to be legally organized."[46] Investors' reluctance to buy shares came as a shock to the company's founders. Their new enterprise had gotten off to a shaky financial start. With initial funding in place, the company elected Stephens vice president; he became president shortly afterward. The company then selected a board of directors, consisting of thirteen stockholders who would meet quarterly. Some of these, including Aspinwall, also sat on the board of the Pacific Mail Steamship Company. An executive and finance committee, composed of the president, vice president, and three directors, was appointed to manage day-to-day operations in the intervals between board meetings.[47]

Although the company's initial capital amounted to $1 million, $200,000 of this was immediately drawn down to cover the cost of the $120,000 deposit to the New Granada government and the $80,000 incurred on the topographical survey. The remaining balance of $800,000 would have to suffice to get the project started. Aspinwall and his fellow directors had concluded by December 1849 "that the total cost of the road, built in the best manner, with the necessary machinery, piers and depots for commercial purposes, will amount to five millions of dollars."[48] Completion would be dependent on securing further funding—hence the presentation of a second proposal to Congress at the end of 1849. Following the pattern of their earlier petition, Aspinwall, Stephens, and Chauncey sought a commitment from the federal administration to use the railroad for public service and to reimburse the company accordingly. Such a pledge would enhance the company's credibility in the financial markets, making it easier to raise the additional $4 million of capital it required.[49] Congress once again rebuffed Aspinwall and his colleagues by failing to commit federal support to the company's enterprise. The directors realized that they would have to dispense with federal support in raising capital. Nonetheless, they retained an expectation that it might be possible to reach an agreement with the government once the railroad became operational and Washington found its services to be indispensable.

The final piece in the political, legal, and financial jigsaw that constituted the Panama railroad was put in place when Stephens signed an amended contract in Bogotá on April 15, 1850, with Victoriano de Diego Paredes, New Granada's secretary of state for foreign affairs. This contract superseded the 1848 undertaking, which was based, in turn, on the lapsed French agreement of the previous year. The deal negotiated by Stephens was approved with a few minor modifications by the Congress of New Granada on May 29, 1850, and by the republic's president on June 4, 1850. The more salient provisions of this document are as follows:

1. The company had the exclusive right to build and operate a railroad across the Isthmus for forty-nine years, with the proviso that New Granada might purchase the railroad at the end of twenty for $5 million; after thirty for $4 million; or after forty for $2 million.[50]
2. The railroad should be complete within six years of the contract's ratification, though the company could ask for a two-year extension after one-third of it had been built.
3. The government of New Granada would not permit any other person or entity to open a road, railroad, or canal across the province of Panama without the consent of the Panama Railroad Company.
4. The railroad would enable travelers and freight to transit from ocean to ocean in twelve hours or less.
5. Panama City was to be the Pacific terminus. The location of the Atlantic terminus was left to the company's discretion.
6. The company was to deposit $120,000 as a guarantee for fulfilling the terms of the contract.[51]
7. The company was given extensive property grants, including a right-of-way across the Isthmus, land for a terminus at Panama City, Manzanillo Island in Navy Bay on the Atlantic side, and between 100,000 and 150,000 *fanegadas* of vacant public land in the provinces of Panama and Veraguas.[52]
8. The company could acquire land in private ownership provided it indemnified the owners following a fair valuation of the property.
9. The railroad would carry New Granada's troops, government supplies, and mail free of charge.
10. The company would pay the Republic of New Granada 3 percent of its annual net profits as well as 5 percent of the receipts from

its foreign mail contracts, an amount that was not to be less than $10,000 per year.

11. The railroad and its imports, equipment, and users were exempt from all taxes.

12. The company could propose regulations for the policing and security of its property, which would come into effect following approval by New Granada's executive.[53]

Once gold had been discovered, Aspinwall and his colleagues were not the only American entrepreneurs to cast covetous glances at the lucrative possibilities generated by the explosion of demand for passages to California and Oregon. Two self-made millionaires entered the fray for a share in the highly profitable transport market between the east and west coasts. George Law, an aggressive businessman of Ulster parentage, became, for a period, Aspinwall's competitor for control of the remunerative Panama route to the American West. The formidable "Commodore" Vanderbilt, who promoted the rival Nicaragua route, was another major contender in the shipping wars of the 1850s. The schemes of both these men had the potential to undermine the viability of the Panama railroad.

Born in New York, the son of a County Down immigrant, George Law worked his way up from early employment as a laborer in canal construction. A self-made man, Law epitomized the new breed of railroad and shipping tycoons who fought their way to the top echelons of American capitalism during an era of rapid industrialization. A powerfully built individual, six feet three, he enjoyed little formal education but made up for that with enormous energy, ambition, and ruthlessness. In appearance he resembled a prizefighter and apparently spoke like one too. Engaged as a contractor in a number of major construction projects, he later extended his business interests to steamships and railroads and amassed enough wealth to build a mansion on New York's fashionable Fifth Avenue. "It is impossible for outsiders to estimate his worth, and it is doubtful if he can do it himself."[54] A masterful lobbyist and dealmaker, who was alleged to bribe government officials, Law was regarded with suspicion by New York's patrician elite.[55] Rumors that Law planned to use his private yacht to smuggle guns to Cuba to aid anti-Spanish rebels made him popular among those who subscribed to an expansionist American nationalism. This also enhanced his political appeal to supporters of the American Nativist, or Know-Nothing, Party in the mid-1850s.

The U.S. Mail Steamship Company, established in 1848 by Law and his associates, enjoyed a government subsidy of $240,000 by carrying the mail on the commercially attractive run between New York, New Orleans, Havana, and Chagres. The timing of Law's shipping initiative, like that of his rival Aspinwall, could not have been better. Law purchased an old steamship, the *Falcon*, which left New York on her initial trip to Chagres on December 1, 1848, just four days prior to the president's message to Congress announcing the discovery of gold in California. This ship carried some of the first passengers from the East to California in the wake of the gold discovery. Two more of Law's ships, the *Ohio* and the *Georgia*, commenced sailing to Chagres in January 1849. The gold rush gave a tremendous impetus to Law's shipping line, which soon had nine large steamships on the Atlantic run.

Law had an adversarial relationship with Aspinwall throughout the early 1850s. Having previously lobbied Congress against granting financial support to the Panama railroad, Law dispatched a small steamer to the Chagres River for the purpose of transporting migrants in 1850. "It was a pioneer adventure of Mr. Law."[56] Aspinwall would have regarded this intrusion as competition to his own plan for a transport system across the Isthmus. For a short period in 1850–1851, Aspinwall competed with Law's ships in the Atlantic, and Law responded by putting some of his vessels on the Pacific run. Law continued his offensive against his rival in 1852 and 1853, seeking ways to wrest control of the Panama railroad from its founder.

The third major player in the struggle to dominate the transit trade between the American east and west coasts was the redoubtable Cornelius Vanderbilt, frequently dubbed the "Commodore." Tall, powerfully built, and ruthless in his business dealings, he was described as "a man of power, unquestionably.... Many fear, but few love him."[57] From late 1848 onward, a flood of prospectors descended on Panama on their way to California attracted by news of the vast quantities of gold allegedly available for the taking in its rivers and mountains. Vanderbilt aimed to break the near monopoly of the California transit enjoyed by Law on the Atlantic coast and Aspinwall on the Pacific side by opening up a new link between the East and California via Nicaragua. He realized that if a faster route could be established by means of a ship canal through Nicaragua, it would capture most, if not all, of the lucrative traffic of migrants heading to California and the gold shipments coming back East. "He planned to divert that golden torrent from Panama to a channel of his own making: a canal across the republic of Nicaragua."[58]

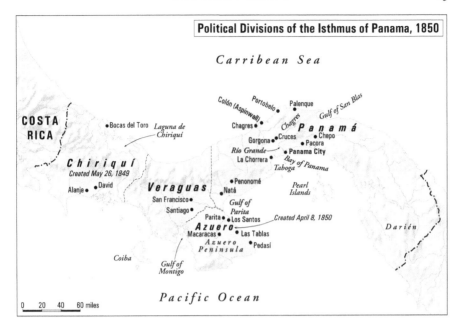

Map 1.2. Map of Political Divisions of the Isthmus of Panama, 1850, by Philip Schwartzberg.

Early in 1849 Vanderbilt, together with other New York financiers, formed the Compañía de Tránsito de Nicaragua and dispatched an agent to Nicaragua to negotiate the construction of a canal with its government. By August 1849 he had secured a contract giving his company the exclusive right to build a waterway across the country in return for a down payment of $10,000, as well as $10,000 a year while the canal was being constructed and 10 percent of its annual net profits.[59] Vanderbilt commenced operations by opening a transport service across Nicaragua linked to his shipping line on the east and west coasts, while simultaneously planning to excavate a canal large enough to accommodate oceangoing vessels.[60] Vanderbilt's promotion of the Nicaragua route posed a serious threat to both the Panama railroad and the U.S. Mail Steamship Company. An intense rivalry developed between Law's and Vanderbilt's shipping lines with each side trumpeting its own services and belittling the alternative route of its competitor. Faced with competition from Vanderbilt and hostility from Law, the prospects of the newly established Panama railroad looked distinctly uncertain.

TWO

A False Start

THE PLAN TO BUILD A SINGLE-TRACK RAILROAD ACROSS THE ISTH-mus of Panama had been decided on by mid-1849. Construction would take place in two phases: from Gorgona to the Pacific terminus at Panama City, followed later by the section from Gorgona to the Caribbean. Gorgona was a village almost at the head of the navigable section of the Chagres River and just over halfway across the Isthmus.[1] The directors expected that the first stage, slightly over twenty miles long, would be quickly built at a cost of $1 million. Work would then commence on the section to the Atlantic. Revenues generated by passenger and freight traffic on the completed section of rail, together with those accruing from the company's projected steamboat service on the Chagres, would help finance the costs of the remaining section of the line. The company's founders estimated that the entire railroad, from Atlantic to Pacific, could be completed within two to three years of the starting date.[2]

Before construction could begin, however, a contractor had to be selected. In July 1849 the company began taking proposals for the project, but the deadline had to be extended from September 15 to October 1, probably because of a lack of interest. The executive and finance committee worried that the company might be forced to construct the railroad itself if no contractors appeared. Their fears were dispelled on October 12, 1849, when a tender submitted by two prominent American engineers, George Muirson Totten (1809–1884) and John Cresson Trautwine (1810–1883), was approved. Totten had previously expressed an interest in being appointed chief engineer.[3] Other proposals were not mentioned and no details of the tender's provisions were disclosed. The *Panama Star* reported that the contract from Gorgona to Panama City was worth approximately $400,000.[4]

On November 27, the executive and finance committee formally approved the contract, which specified that the first phase of construction should be completed in just over two years.[5] Totten is unlikely to have been happy with this deadline, as he had previously expressed the view that a two-year time frame was too short.[6] Events were to prove him right. The contractors expected to begin work on December 1, toward the end of Panama's long rainy season.[7]

The Panama project arrived at an opportune time for Totten and Trautwine. For the previous four years, they had been engaged as contractors on the Canal del Dique, connecting the Magdalena River, New Granada's main fluvial artery, with the smaller Dique River, which flowed into the Caribbean Sea just outside the large port city of Cartagena.[8] The two men were prominent members of the American engineering profession and were well qualified for the task at hand. They had experience in managing construction projects in challenging tropical environments and dealing with New Granada's authorities. They had molded a body of local men into a skilled and low-cost workforce, and they hoped to persuade some of their former employees to transfer to their new undertaking several hundred miles away in Panama.[9] Events would show that recruiting a cheap labor force during the gold rush era proved to be unrealistic.

We know little of Totten the man, except for occasional insights into his personality gleaned from his correspondence with company officials. Totten, who had attended a military academy but had never served in the army, was frequently referred to as Colonel Totten. According to a colleague, Totten—a small, dark man who wore spectacles—had a quiet and reserved manner. "He was a superior man without being great, looked up to and respected by all."[10] He was a classic example of early railroad pioneers.[11] "To force through a railway against all the inevitable obstacles generally requires an element of obsession, bordering on fanaticism."[12] Totten was a driven man, and events would show that despite occasional bouts of pessimism and disillusionment, he had an obstinate determination to complete this new project against every obstacle, natural and man-made. Tough as leather, he was attacked by yellow fever some years after the railroad was completed and was not expected to survive. A coffin and a funeral train were prepared, and a tearful group "stood around the dying man, with the confident expectation that each breath would be the last." But Totten rallied and lived for over another twenty years.[13]

Totten may also have had a softer side. The *New York Herald* described him as "a gentleman of most amiable manners and kind disposition." A decade later, a

British visitor considered him to be an excellent employer. "I was particularly struck with the thoughtful care bestowed by that gentleman and his amiable lady on the comfort and happiness of those employed on the Colonel's working staff . . . they messed together just like the officers of a regiment."[14] Although his official title was chief engineer, throughout much of the project's lifetime, he, like many early railroad men, had to be a jack-of-all-trades. We know even less about Totten's colleague, Trautwine, as he had only a short-lived connection with the railroad. After leaving Panama at the end of 1850, Trautwine went on to have an outstanding career as an engineer and published his *Engineer's Pocket Book* in 1871; this became a standard reference work in the profession for many years.[15]

Preliminary work on the Pacific section of the railroad began in December 1849. Trautwine established a depot at the riverside town of Gorgona for the construction materials that were expected from the United States. Totten, his fellow contractor, was absent during early 1850, possibly completing work on the Canal del Dique and recruiting laborers in Cartagena.[16] Problems did not take long to appear. There were few roads in this part of Panama, and the Chagres became the main transportation artery by default. Using the river, however, proved difficult and expensive. During the short dry season that started in January, the water level fell. This made it impossible even for shallow-draft steamboats to contend with the river's rapids, submerged rocks, and acute bends. The transport of heavy equipment and supplies was feasible only when the water level was high.[17] Even then, as the previous wet season had demonstrated, the river was unpredictable, unruly, and subject to sudden enormous increases in volume. Riverboats lacked sufficient engine power to fight the currents and occasional floods common on the Chagres during the rainy season. Tropical wood-boring teredo worms, which attacked the timbers of river steamers, were another problem. Iron-plating a ship's hull offered some protection, but this increased the vessel's weight and hence its draft, thus restricting its ability to navigate the shallower upper reaches of the river.

The fact that river steamers could not provide reliable transport as far upstream as Gorgona throughout the year quickly became evident. Furthermore, the small native bongos and canoes that plied the Chagres were not suitable for carrying heavy and bulky railroad equipment. Even the transport of passengers required great exertions by the crews. The cost of river transport had also increased substantially. The volume of river traffic generated by the explosive growth of California-bound migrants led boatmen to inflate their costs for freighting men and supplies. The contractors also confronted the increased cost of hiring local laborers as well as the difficulty of retaining them. They had priced their contract on the assumption of having a large pool of cheap local labor to draw on, which had been the case with their previous project at Cartagena. Only a few years earlier, a traveler to the Isthmus had announced that "labor is abundant and cheap; the usual wages not exceeding four reals, or two shillings [50 cents] per day."[18]

The chance discovery of gold in California, which inflated labor costs in Panama, had destroyed the possibility of a low-paid local labor force. Not only did workers cost the contractors more, they also had a propensity to desert the team. The proximity of the Chagres River, Panama's main transportation artery, proved an irresistible enticement to men fatigued by long hours of heavy labor to abandon their tasks. The river provided an easy escape route for these employees, allowing them to seek easier and more remunerative employment elsewhere on the Isthmus—or, if they had the means, to abandon Panama altogether and head, like the hordes of forty-niners, for the goldfields of California.

By late February 1850, Totten and Trautwine realized that the initial project plan was no longer feasible. They recommended that construction be switched to the Caribbean end of the line, which was more easily accessible from the ports of New York and New Orleans. Equipment, manpower, and materials could be unloaded at the site of the railroad's Caribbean terminus, as yet undetermined, before being moved up by rail as it progressed across the Isthmus toward Panama City. The two engineers also relinquished their role as contractors.[19] The reasons were never made public but are not hard to guess. Now that the initial construction plan had proved impractical, their tender bid became irrelevant. Furthermore, they could no longer operate within the agreed contract price.[20] On March 12, 1850, the executive and finance committee relieved Totten and Trautwine of their contract, and the company assumed responsibility for managing the project. The company retained Totten and Trautwine not as contractors but as salaried engineers, at an annual stipend of $7,500 each. James Baldwin, who had surveyed the route with Stephens in 1848, was appointed principal assistant engineer.[21]

The decision to initiate construction at the fever-stricken Caribbean end of the line did not meet with unanimous approval. The company's decision to undertake construction itself, rather than appoint another contractor, was also not universally welcomed. The *Panama Star* later claimed that the company should have stuck with its original plan.[22] The *American Railroad Journal* criticized the move but may have had its own agenda; it had been advocating the merits of the Mexican and Nicaraguan routes in its pages.[23] Responding to criticism that the company should have entrusted construction to another American contractor, Trautwine delivered a prophetic warning to prospective railroad builders in Panama. "No matter how extended their experience in the United States may have been, it will not serve to secure them against failure in that country [Panama]."[24] Although the company had now assumed responsibility for construction, the directors in distant New York could rely on the presence in Panama of their president, John L. Stephens, to oversee proceedings. Over the next three years, Stephens supervised progress on the Isthmus.

After the first three months of 1850 had passed, the dry season, the only reliable working period for the railroad's builders, was almost over, and little progress had been made. American newspapers published gloomy assessments.[25] The London *Times* was equally pessimistic and predicted that "the less fatiguing, less distant, and perfectly salubrious route" through Nicaragua would now attract most of the traffic crossing Central America and would obviate the need for the Panama railroad.[26] It failed to mention that the Nicaragua route was subject to potential British influence because its Atlantic terminus, Greytown—or San Juan del Norte—was located on the border of the British Mosquito Coast protectorate.[27]

Unfavorable reports about the railroad's construction came early from London. "Impediments had occurred which were never contemplated, and, if the work is not entirely abandoned—as it is supposed it must be—it will at all events be many years before it can be completed, at a cost, too, compared with which the original estimates are trifling. Such is the publicly avowed opinion of those who are best informed on the subject."[28]

While the contract with New Granada's government designated Panama City as the Pacific coast terminus, no location had been specified for the Atlantic end. Trautwine now began surveying the coast between Chagres and Portobelo to locate a suitable spot for the Caribbean terminus. He eventually chose Manzanillo Island, in Navy (or Limón) Bay, which Colonel Hughes had also recommended in his survey the previous year.[29] The island, a low coral formation about one mile in length by three-quarters of a mile in width, lay several hundred yards from the Caribbean shore. Some quarters expressed surprise that an area of dense mangrove swamps and pestilential marshes had been selected as the Atlantic terminal rather than the colonial town of Portobelo—or even the port of Chagres.[30]

Figure 2.1 Landing Passengers at Chagres, 1849–1851. Hand-colored woodcut. North Wind Picture Archives / Alamy Stock Illustration.

Several factors appear to have influenced the selection of Manzanillo Island. The terrain there and on the adjacent mainland was flat, while both Chagres and Portobelo were surrounded by hills that would make access by rail more difficult. Navy Bay offered better protection to shipping than the open road-stead at the mouth of Chagres and had sufficient water depth for large vessels to berth, regardless of tidal conditions. Rivalry between Aspinwall and Law, the millionaire owner of the U.S. Mail Steamship Company, may also have played a role in the selection of this site. Throughout 1850, Aspinwall's Pacific Mail competed with Law's U.S. Mail on the New York–Chagres run, and Law retaliated by placing some of his steamers on the Panama–California route.[31]

It has been claimed that Law, on hearing rumors that Portobelo would be the likely rail terminus, bought up land around the town with the intention of reselling it to the railroad at a vast profit.[32] If these assertions are true, Law's gamble failed when the company opted for Manzanillo Island as its Caribbean terminus. The island had been granted gratis to the railroad by the New Granada government, and the adjacent coastal swamps were public lands and would cost the company nothing. Law's combative relationship with Aspinwall was far from over, however, and will be referred to again.

By this stage, almost halfway through 1850, months of planning and effort, as well as scarce capital, had been expended with little to show in return. William Perry, the British consul, reported that construction had not yet properly started "and I am of the opinion that the directors would throw it up if they could do so without the sacrifice of the money deposited with this [New Granada] government as a guarantee for the due performance of the work."[33] The consul clearly underestimated the steely determination of Aspinwall and Stephens. The radical change in construction plans was the principal reason for delay, together with the slowness of communications between Panama and the company's New York headquarters. It could take a month to six weeks for Totten and Trautwine to receive answers to queries and requests.

It would have been difficult to pick a more inauspicious and inhospitable site for the Caribbean terminus. Manzanillo Island was barely above sea level. The mainland, several hundred yards away, was covered with dense mangroves partly submerged at high tide. Behind those, a swamp stretched inland for two miles, leading to a short patch of high ground, inhabited by colonies of monkeys. Beyond this spur, initially named Monkey Hill, lay several more miles of deep swamp and a sea of glutinous mud before firm ground emerged once more. Somehow, tracks would have to be laid across this challenging terrain. Work finally began at the Caribbean end of the line in May 1850. The timing, after the monsoon rains had started, could not have been worse. Otis graphically recounted the event: "No imposing ceremony inaugurated the 'breaking ground'. Two American citizens, leaping, axe in hand, from a native canoe upon a wild and desolate island, their retinue consisting of half a dozen Indians, who clear the path with rude knives, strike their glittering axes into the nearest tree; the rapid blows reverberate from shore to shore, and the stately cocoa crashes upon the beach. Thus unostentatiously was announced the commencement of a railway, which, from the interests and difficulties involved, might well be looked upon as one of the grandest and boldest enterprises ever attempted."[34]

Despite the slow start and initial setbacks, the New York–based directors optimistically predicted that locomotives would run from Navy Bay to Gorgona within a year and that the entire line would be in operation in two years. "It is confidently believed that by the end of the dry season of 1852, a temporary railroad will be completed to Panama [City], ready to transport passengers with their luggage and light freight from ocean to ocean in not exceeding six hours. The perfecting of the work can then be carried on at leisure."[35] A quantity of crossties and six steam-powered pile drivers had been purchased, four locomotives had been ordered from American suppliers, and fifteen hundred tons of iron rails from Britain had been delivered to the Isthmus by early September 1850. The company obviously expected to start laying tracks soon.[36] Progress, however, proved to be far slower than the railroad's directors and investors envisioned.

In 1849, Totten had proposed building a temporary wagon road across the Isthmus to facilitate the transport of equipment, provisions, and stores until the railroad's completion, a measure also favored by Trautwine.[37] Highways of this kind, made of boards and logs, enabled nineteenth-century Americans to use wagons to cross swampy or marshy land. The two engineers may also have been influenced by a recent British publication that argued that a toll road from Portobelo to Panama City was the most practical way of connecting the two ports.[38] A road of this kind had also been discussed in the U.S. Congress during the inconclusive debates on subsidizing the Panama railroad in early 1849.[39] Once the decision to commence operations at Navy Bay had been made, the executive and finance committees gave the go-ahead for a wagon road.[40]

Given the nature of the terrain over which the railroad had to be built and the primitive construction technology available, most of the work would have to be undertaken by laborers supplemented, where conditions permitted, by the use of horses and mules and a few steam-powered machines. The company had to have an adequate supply of manpower in what was bound to be a labor-intensive operation. During the early stages of the project, references appeared in the company's documents and in the press to the employment of New Grenadian troops, but this deployment never took place.[41] The source of these statements was article 20 in the 1847 French concession, which had been transferred, with some modifications, to Aspinwall and his colleagues in 1848, pledging the New Granada executive to provide up to three hundred sappers to assist in the railroad's construction.[42] But the June 1850 contract, which superseded the 1848 concession, made no mention of the supply of troops by New Granada.

At the start of construction, the provincial government of Panama may have provided some convict labor to the company, but it is likely that the supply of prisoners was too small, unreliable, and unsuitable for the railroad's needs, because this source of labor was soon dropped.[43] The railroad's use of slave labor was equally brief and inconsequential.[44] The company abandoned this source of labor almost immediately, partly because of its desire to avoid adverse publicity in New York, where proabolition sentiment was strong, and partly because the reservoir of slave labor available in New Granada had almost dried up by 1850. Panama's slave population amounted to less than half of 1 percent, and all of New Granada's five hundred remaining slaves, including fifty in Panama City, were emancipated shortly afterward on January 1, 1852.[45]

The use of military, slave, and convict labor from New Granada was, therefore, either not possible or had been ruled out as impractical or inadequate at an early stage of construction. From the middle of 1850 onward, the railroad company opted to rely on the labor of waged employees, the only exception being the use of Chinese indentured laborers for part of 1854. Totten knew it would be difficult to recruit all the workers he required while at the same time keeping labor costs low. "I have ever considered that one of the greatest difficulties this company would meet with would be that of securing laborers at a reasonable rate of wages."[46] Local workers provided an obvious solution, but they were not available in sufficient numbers or at the right cost.

The first waged laborers on the railroad most likely consisted of Panamanians recruited in the towns of Chagres and Portobelo and their environs; some men hired by Totten came from Cartagena, the scene of his previous construction project. In early May 1850, between forty and fifty workers started the formidable task of clearing Manzanillo Island under the direction of Trautwine and Baldwin, the chief assistant engineer. Overwhelmed by the obstacles facing them and with the prospect of easier and better paid work nearby, many deserted. Totten made frequent trips to Cartagena in the ensuing months to recruit additional workers. It was claimed that Totten and Trautwine "drummed the New York waterfronts for workmen with the slogans of 'girls, adventure, good pay'" in 1850, but the timing of their movements casts doubt on this claim.[47]

The first mention of Irish workers occurred on May 30, 1850, when the executive and finance committee received a letter from David Rogers, a New Orleans contractor, offering to build a wagon road from the Chagres River to Panama City by November 1. The plan called for using Irish laborers from New Orleans.[48] The proposal was accepted, and the committee allocated $20,000 to cover the cost of Rogers's salary at $250 to $300 per month, as well as the purchase of tools, material for building shanties, provisions for one hundred men, transportation from New Orleans to Chagres, and the men's pay for four months. Rogers was instructed to reduce the number of recruits if he found that $20,000 proved insufficient for these purposes.[49] Economic refugees from an impoverished and famine-stricken homeland created a large pool of Irish laborers in New Orleans at this time, and Rogers would have hired men for Panama from among them.

The executive and finance committee appointed Messrs. Paradise Lawrason and Co., the company's agents in New Orleans, to administer the contract with Rogers.[50] This agency was paid $8,100.15 between August 12 and December 16, 1850, presumably to cover some of the expenses incurred by Rogers. Further payments of $4,632.92 were made directly to Rogers between August 10, 1850, and February 24, 1851.[51] The following month the committee authorized a second labor contractor, Colonel Baker of Illinois, to bring down fewer than one thousand men from St. Louis, "of whom as many as possible shall be mechanics and at least ten per cent familiar with the use of tools."[52] In return for working for one hundred days, the men would obtain a free passage to California with a gratuity of $20 each.[53] Company accounts show that Baker was paid a total of $22,434.50 between July 24, 1850, and July 12, 1851.[54]

Lack of suitable accommodation on Manzanillo Island inhibited the employment of large numbers of men at this stage. Trautwine would not accept more laborers until the island was sufficiently cleared to enable houses to be erected. By July a temporary depot for storing materials had been built and two hundred Carthaginian laborers had been engaged. Totten intended to place Rogers's Irishmen on the mainland, near Navy Bay, once they had arrived, "as they will not be able to work on the island in the water."[55] About one hundred white workers left New Orleans on the brig *Delta* bound for Navy Bay in August, and a much larger force was shortly expected to follow.[56] Many, if not most, of these men would have been Irish, given their preponderance among the city's unskilled labor force.

Otis, who wrote the first history of the railroad, provided a graphic description of working conditions on the island. "In the black, slimy mud of its surface alligators and other reptiles abounded; while the air was laden with pestilential vapors, and swarming with sand-flies and mosquitoes."[57] Workers had to cover their faces with gauze veils because of the numerous and annoying insects. Trautwine reported "that it was with difficulty we could induce the laborers to continue at their work—and that only by remaining with them in person, and aiding them during the whole day."[58] As residence on the island was impossible, the construction crew lived on an overcrowded old ship anchored in the bay. Conditions in the vessel's hold were so intolerable—because of the heat, mosquitoes, sand flies and cockroaches—that most workers preferred to sleep on deck even though this exposed them to drenching rains. In an effort to reduce overcrowding, the company subsequently purchased a condemned steamboat as a second waterborne residence for its workers.[59]

By August the island had been partially cleared of its dense mangrove thickets. This reduced the annoyance from mosquitoes and other insects. "The sand flies have so far left the island that the men are desirous of taking up their residence upon it."[60] A large storehouse for provisions and materials had been completed and other buildings were in progress. However, there was to be no proper accommodation for the workmen until the close of the year.[61] Between three and four hundred men, hailing from Panama, Cartagena, and the United States had been hired, though not all had arrived. Sickness caused by exposure to the incessant rains, the frequent need to work waist-deep in water, and vulnerability to diseases endemic to the locality soon reduced the number of workers by half. Many of the remainder frightened by fever or seduced by the prospects of less exhausting work and better conditions elsewhere deserted.[62]

Workers from Panama and Cartagena, referred to as "natives" by Totten and Trautwine, proved unreliable. These men were mostly mestizos or mulattoes, people of mixed race, *gente de color*, the result of several centuries of miscegenation.[63] They understandably abandoned their arduous and unpleasant employment whenever an opportunity to make more or easier money presented itself. This led some commentators to conclude that local men did not make good laborers. Otis, for example, maintained that "the native population . . . were too indolent and unaccustomed to labor to be depended on to any great extent."[64] However, William Wheelwright, founder of the Pacific Steam Navigation Company, had been impressed by the strength and endurance of Panamanian laborers, saying, "The natives are . . . patient of fatigue . . . they are . . .

Figure 2.2. Mangrove Swamps, Panama. Lucien N.B. Wyse, *Le Canal de Panama* (Paris: Hachette, 1886). Courtesy of the British Library Board.

strong athletic men, accustomed many of them to carry burdens of 150 pounds weight across the isthmus upon their backs, performing the whole journey of twenty-one miles in a day."[65] A journalist from the *Panama Star* commented on the stamina of the boatmen on the Chagres: "I could not help noticing the immense exertion of these men; they can stand more heat and labor than the European or North American; the fact is, we would sink under the burden very soon; our physical abilities would soon give way under such circumstances."[66]

Local laborers impressed Trautwine, but he had some reservations. The "native" workers, "when treated with a proper degree of kindness and firmness, are tractable and willing to work; yet when brought into contact with a stream of travel, such as that which now flows to and from California, they become altogether depraved, as I fully experienced on the Isthmus of Panama."[67]

Totten had earlier referred to the difficulty in recruiting and retaining Panamanians. "It is impossible to procure laborers on the Isthmus for the work of the Rl.Rd. Not only are wages so exorbitant as to make the work very costly, but the laborers will not work steadily, nor do they wish to do any other work than that of transporting the baggage of the immigrants, by which they gain in a few days sufficient to maintain them for a month."[68]

Totten accepted that many of the workers recruited from the Cartagena area would inevitably desert and go into the business of transporting migrants. The company's white workers could also not be depended on to remain at their posts. Two consecutive gangs of carpenters, hired to erect storehouses and workers' accommodations on Manzanillo Island, soon downed tools and headed for California.[69]

By August, about two miles of the route across the mainland's coastal swamps had been cleared of trees and vegetation, but the active workforce had been reduced to forty men. "The rest, having deserted, are running about here without having it in our power to take them." Totten asked the company to use its influence with the Panamanian authorities to make desertion by the railroad's workers a criminal offence. In the meantime, he prepared to return to Cartagena to recruit more men. So pressing was his need to hire and retain laborers that he was willing to allow these workmen, whose level of cultural advancement he did not rate highly, to bring their womenfolk with them. "We cannot expect the men—savages as they are—to be happy without their women."[70]

During these first months on the island, fever frequently prostrated Totten, Trautwine, and their colleagues. Their modus operandi was simple: whenever one member of the team got sick, another would take his place until he, too, fell ill, by which time the first man would have hopefully recovered sufficiently to resume his tasks. Working conditions were atrocious. "We meet a great deal of water in every direction. Sometimes we pass successive days wading over our boot tops. Not only ourselves, but the men also, fall sick from the exposure."[71] One of Totten's subordinates referred to the "impenetrable marshes too deep to ford" in the vicinity of Gatún camp.[72]

D. J. Rogers, the labor contractor, left New Orleans on the brig *Bella del Mar* for Navy Bay on July 31, reportedly accompanied by about one hundred men. A much larger force of five hundred was expected to follow soon.[73] According to Totten, however, when Rogers reached Panama on the slow-moving vessel on September 1, he headed a contingent of only forty-five Irish laborers and nine mules and carts.[74] The newly arrived Irishmen "were immediately set to work on the mainland to clear about 2,300 running feet of marsh thickly covered with bushes. They had cleared and made 1,500 feet of log and brush road in five days, and hope by the end of the week to get prepared to go into camp [the interior] on the following Sunday."[75] By mid-September more Irish had arrived. A New York newspaper reported that "there is a large number of Irish laborers employed on the Panama railroad" but gave no further details.[76]

The plan to construct a wagon road across the Isthmus using Irish labor was abandoned after a short section had been completed.[77] Its construction across extensive swamps during the deluges of the rainy season proved to be far more difficult and expensive than had been expected. A traveler's description of the dense, jungle-covered terrain illustrates the difficulties of building such a road across Panama. "All outline of the landscape is lost under this deluge of vegetation. No trace of the soil is to be seen; lowland and highland are the same; a mountain is but a higher swell of the mass of verdure. . . . What shape the land would be if cleared, you cannot tell."[78] According to Schott, "The plan [to build a plank road] was short-lived, however, as were most of the laborers. The Irishmen died so rapidly from fever that only two miles of road were completed before the survivors decided to escape with their lives."[79] Schott failed to cite a source for his information, and Totten's correspondence did not support his allegation about numerous Irish deaths. The *Panama Star* also confirmed in November that plans to build a plank road had been abandoned but made no mention of Irish deaths.[80]

The rains continued, and Totten reported that it was not possible to abandon the hulks in the bay and sleep under canvas on the island. "We cannot live in tents at this season of the year. Mr Baldwin tried it and fell sick with fever within a week. We are in the water all day and every day and can only keep our healths [*sic*] under it by taking care of ourselves at nights."[81] He now reversed his earlier decision not to place his Irish workers in the swamps—probably because he was short of men. Dissatisfaction with their new, semiaquatic working environment led some to desert. "The Irishmen are not pleased at being placed to work in the water; but as they expect to get through it this week, they do not complain as much as when they first commenced. Five or six of them have already deserted, while three of my negro deserters have returned of their own accord. On this score—desertions—I do not think there will be much difference between them."[82]

Evidence of the fate of these early Irish arrivals appears contradictory, but given the unhealthy nature of their working environment, a number of them likely perished, though probably not on the scale alleged by Schott. The chief engineer reported in September that some of the Irishmen had fallen ill three weeks after their arrival, though their condition was not critical. "A number of Dr. Rogers' men are also on the sick list, but none seriously ill—fevers and agues."[83] Totten's correspondence three months later suggests that while some of Rogers's men might have died, the remainder had survived the rigors of these early months: "The remnants of Dr. Rogers' force are now on Mansanillo Island. . . . Dr Rogers's men whom you thought had better be sent home are now at work on the Island. They are good men, excepting one, who I shall return, and now that they are recovering, will be useful."[84]

Trautwine reported that there had been at least ten deaths among the Irish workers. "Dr. Rogers made an attempt, with about forty picked men, to clear the trees from a short portion of the route that had been staked out by Mr. Totten. The result was, that himself, and every one of his men were almost immediately disabled by sickness, and their number reduced about one-fourth by death."[85] On the other hand, Dr. Gage, the railroad's surgeon-in-chief, informed New York in January 1851 that there were few men on the sick list and that only one death had occurred since his arrival the previous September. This man, a member of Rogers's Irish contingent, died in December 1850.[86] The Reverend Richard Waters, who arrived in Panama early in 1851 and who acted temporarily as an unofficial Catholic chaplain to the railroad workers, claimed there had been no sickness or deaths among the Irish who had arrived shortly before him, though he was probably not referring to Rogers's men but to a group from Pennsylvania hired by a labor contractor called Truesdale.[87]

One of the many problems confronting the engineers in the initial phase of construction was how to provide a solid base for the tracks on the spongy mudflats of the mainland adjacent to Navy Bay. These marshes would flood to a depth of several feet at high tide and remained wet even when the tide went out because of poor drainage and frequent heavy rainfall. To make matters worse, the swamplands were covered with "thick tangled underbrush, impenetrable except with the axe or machete, through which 1000 or 1200 feet made a good day's work."[88] It could take a team of six men laboring for the better part of a week to clear a narrow path through one mile of this scrub-covered swampland. The abundance of mangrove trees had one positive benefit; the intertwined roots formed a mat that provided some support for the men's feet in the soft mud.[89]

In some places, solid ground lay twenty or more feet beneath the surface. This led the railroad to advertise in New York in August 1850 for the supply of forty thousand spruce piles to underpin the track. The following month Totten asked for thousands of thirty-foot-long timber piles to provide a foundation for the railroad in this waterlogged terrain.[90] An American visitor was told, probably incorrectly, that timbers had to be driven sixty feet deep in some places to secure a foundation for the tracks.[91] A London journal made an exaggerated

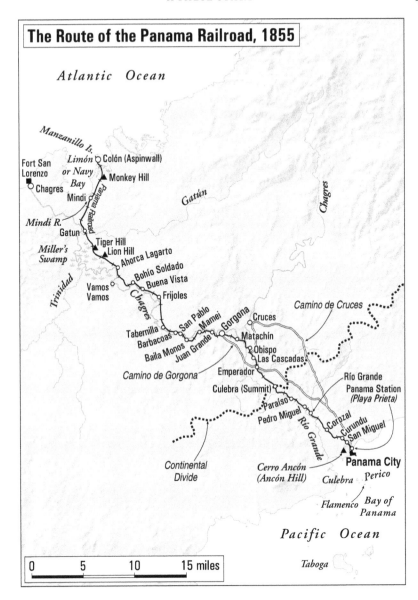

The Route of the Panama Railroad, 1855

Atlantic Ocean

Manzanillo Is.

Fort San Lorenzo
Chagres
Limón or Navy Bay
Colón (Aspinwall)
Monkey Hill
Mindi

Gatún

Chagres

Mindi R.
Gatun
Miller's Swamp
Tiger Hill
Lion Hill
Ahorca Lagarto
Bohío Soldado
Buena Vista
Vamos Vamos
Frijoles

Trinidad

Chagres

Tabernilla
San Pablo
Mamei
Gorgona
Cruces
Barbacoas
Juan Grande
Matachín
Baila Monos
Obispo
Las Cascadas

Camino de Cruces

Camino de Gorgona
Emperador
Culebra (Summit)
Paraíso
Pedro Miguel
Río Grande
Panama Station (Playa Prieta)

Corozal
Curundu
San Miguel

Continental Divide
Cerro Ancón (Ancón Hill)
Culebra
Perico
Panama City

Flamenco
Bay of Panama

Pacific Ocean

Taboga

| 0 | 5 | 10 | 15 miles |

Map 2.1. Map of the Route of the Panama Railroad, 1855, by Philip Schwartzberg.

claim that in parts of the marshes "three sixty feet piles were driven atop of each other, before a solid way could be formed for the road!"[92] Minter alleged that an Irish foreman dumped three thousand tons of rocks into the mire at one particular location with no apparent effect.[93]

Despite these improbable claims, when a section of the track across this swamp subsided in the early twentieth century, the scale of the problem facing the railroad's builders revealed itself. Soundings by U.S. engineers indicated that solid ground lay between 100 and 185 feet below the surface of the mud.[94] The difficulty of the terrain can be gauged from Totten's request at the start of 1851 for an additional twelve thousand wooden piles of 30 feet in length and for a thousand piles 40 feet long.[95] Six steam-operated pile drivers were placed at different points on the line, and much of the first section of the railroad was constructed with their assistance.[96] This initial stretch of track, from Manzanillo Island over a causeway to the mainland and across the coastal marshes along the lower Chagres basin, was the most difficult of the entire railroad to be built.

According to the *New York Times*, "The first seven miles of the road . . . run through an almost impenetrable swamp, the water being from one to three feet deep the whole distance. The soil at the bottom is composed of blue mud, soft and miry."[97] Trellis bridges made of wood and earthen embankments, ranging in height from two to twelve or more feet, raised the tracks above the mire in the worst low-lying areas. An apprehensive traveler wrote in 1852, "The road appeared to me to be rather insecure, being constructed on piles and always in water."[98]

Heavy rainfall aggravated the problem of track subsidence. Embankments were prone to collapse and had to be constantly topped up with gravel, stones, and earth. Wooden ties from the United States began decaying after a few months and had to be replaced with ties of lignum vitae (black guayacán) from the Cartagena region. Totten placed an order for two thousand crossties of this timber early in 1851.[99] In addition to overseeing the construction of the railroad across the coastal swamps, the engineers had to raise the level of Manzanillo Island from its original height of just above sea level by using thousands of tons of earth and rocks excavated along the line's route. This enormous task took several years.[100]

Trautwine's resignation as joint chief engineer in November 1850 came out of the blue. He remained in post for another month before leaving for the United States.[101] Trautwine was coy about the reasons for his departure. "I resigned, chiefly because I found that there did not exist between the board of directors and myself, that unanimity of opinion on certain points involved in the construction of the work, which I considered not only desirable, but absolutely necessary to a harmonious co-operation."[102]

Trautwine never clarified the reasons for his disagreement with the directors. He may have had doubts about the advisability of starting work at the unhealthy Caribbean end of the line, preferring instead to begin construction on the Pacific side at Panama City.[103] He might not have been happy with the decision to abandon the plank road, or he may have resented the oversight exercised by Stephens, the company's president, who was now spending several months each year on the Isthmus. His designation as "associate chief engineer" could have irked him, and difficult working conditions may have undermined the earlier spirit of cooperation and partnership between himself and Totten, the chief engineer.

Following Trautwine's departure, Totten assumed sole charge of construction. He became responsible for day-to-day operational decisions in the engineering, logistical, financial, and human resource aspects of a multimillion-dollar project located two thousand miles from its headquarters in an era of slow communications. He was, however, able to avail of the assistance of Stephens, the company's president, during the latter's sojourns on the Isthmus from 1850 to 1852. Totten, probably aware of Trautwine's impending resignation, asked New York in late October to send him one good principal engineer and five or six assistants, presumably to compensate for his colleague's departure. Aware of the challenge awaiting the new recruits, Totten stressed the need for men with physical and mental stamina, as well as technical ability. "Let them be sturdy working fellows, willing to go through everything."[104]

Physically exhausting labor, together with almost daily soakings from torrential downpours, took a toll on the laborers. They had to contend with energy-sapping humidity while wading through the mud and water of the swamps, wearing clothes that were rarely dry. Mosquitoes attacked them at night, making them tired and itchy in the mornings; these mosquitoes helped spread malaria.[105] The debilitating effects of the disease were described by a traveler who suffered an attack in Panama during the gold rush years. "One who has never been prostrated by fever in a burning tropical clime, when it was utterly impossible to obtain ice or cool water, can scarcely conceive of the torture and agony endured."[106] The dense tropical foliage formed a vault over the men's heads, shutting out air and converting their working environment into something resembling a jungle-enclosed steam bath, in which their arms and legs felt as heavy as lead.

Sickness was no respecter of social or occupational status, and laborers were not the only employees to fall ill. Captain Maunsell, a civil engineer and former

British officer, left New York on November 13, 1850, to join the railroad's engineering corps, but his stay in Panama was tragically brief, as he died on December 20. "His illness was of five days duration, produced by exposure to the climate, and being obliged to work in swamps up to his waist."[107] Dr. Franklin Gage, the company's senior surgeon, also succumbed. Forced by ill health to leave Panama within a few months of his arrival, Gage died shortly after being invalided home to the United States. He was replaced by Dr. Masters.[108]

Until October 1850, only white employees from the United States, and *gente de color*—mixed-race workers from Panama and the Cartagena region of New Granada—had been hired by the railroad. The employment pool now extended to the recruitment of black laborers from Jamaica. Stephens wrote to Mr. C. Armstrong of Jamaica in September, requesting him to send twenty to thirty laborers to the Isthmus "that an early trial may be made of the value of their labor." By October, thirty islanders had arrived to work for six months at one dollar per day, half to be paid weekly and the remainder at the end of their contract.[109] A second batch of fifty-seven Jamaican laborers landed in November 1850, and they were joined by another group of fifty-two men in late December.[110] Totten did not form a favorable opinion of these workers for reasons that will be discussed later, and the number of Jamaican laborers employed on the railroad remained relatively small until the latter part of 1853.

By mid-October between three and four hundred men worked at Navy Bay, some hailing from Cartagena and Jamaica, "but most of them Irish from New Orleans."[111] Company policy from this time onward was to maintain a steady stream of white recruits from the United States, together with workers from the region around Cartagena, supplemented for a time by a number of Jamaicans, to replace men who had completed their contracts or who were ill, had died, or had deserted. The Royal West Indian Mail Steam Packet Company shipped laborers from Cartagena and the interior provinces of New Granada. Cartagena was about 270 miles by sea from Chagres.

During the early stages of construction, the company also took advantage of the gold rush to hire Americans who lacked the resources to get to the goldfields. Their contract specified a passage to California usually in return for one hundred days labor on the railroad.[112] The supply of migrants heading west who were prepared to subsidize their travel costs with a spell of labor on the Isthmus was, by its nature, uncertain and fluctuating. The company discontinued this policy in 1851, possibly because of a lessening demand for assisted passages to San Francisco or because of dissatisfaction with the caliber of men recruited in this fashion. Henceforth, white laborers and tradesmen were generally hired in the United States for a period of six months at an agreed daily rate of pay and provided with a return passage to New York or New Orleans at the end of their contract, or if they became unfit for work through illness in the meantime.

As 1850 drew to a close, the flow of workers hired by the railroad increased. William Truesdale or Truesdail, of Erie, Pennsylvania, sailed from New York with a hundred mechanics and laborers on November 27.[113] He had initially been contracted to bring three hundred men from Pennsylvania to work for six months at one dollar per day or alternatively for a free passage to California plus a cash payment of twenty dollars.[114] A letter to a Panama newspaper suggested that some of his men were Irish.[115] The company appointed Truesdale superintendent of construction at the Gatún section of the line, a few miles inland.[116]

As noted previously, the directors had agreed that English-born Colonel Edward Dickinson Baker should raise a labor force of one thousand men in Illinois.[117] The colonel had succeeded in recruiting only about four hundred by October, and they were ordered to proceed to the Isthmus by way of St. Louis, traveling down the Mississippi on an old cotton barge to New Orleans.[118] There were some Germans and Dutch among Baker's men, but no mention was made of Irishmen, although it is possible that some were present given their growing numbers in the Midwest's laboring class at the time.

An advance party of 150 of Baker's men under the charge of a Dr. Henry arrived in Chagres in December. Totten was unhappy with these new arrivals. He described them as "western river boatmen, gamblers, etc., whose one desire is to pass the hundred days of their engagement in the easiest manner possible to ensure their passage to California. On their arrival they gave us a great deal of trouble. We had no cots, blankets or mosquito nets for them, and they refused to work until they were provided." Totten had on hand only 182 cots and 189 blankets for approximately four hundred white laborers and mechanics. He appealed to the company for beds and bedding for all his workers.[119]

The newly arrived men continued to cause trouble and may have been joined by some of the Irish and other workers on the island. While at the nearby port of Chagres, one of Totten's foremen warned him that the belligerent newcomers had passed resolutions not to work until they were provided with better food. "This dissatisfaction has been fomented by Dr Henry's men. . . . Dr Henry's commissary gave us warning this day that the [company's] superintendents on this island had better look out for their own safety." The chief engineer received a similar report from another of his supervisors.[120]

This strike, led by a surveyor's assistant called Gridly, paid off, as the company quickly yielded to their demands.[121] Totten reported on Christmas Eve that all of the men had now been provided with mosquito nets and good food "which should put an end to their troubles." He complained that the U.S. Navy was negligent in patrolling the coast, presumably not just to show the flag but also to control unruly American workers. His statement that "I do not fear the revolvers or bowie knives of Dr Henry's men" indicated the mettle of the man who was to supervise construction for the next five years.[122] The company's ledger recorded the purchase of a stock of Colt pistols for fifty dollars in 1851 but did not indicate their purpose.[123]

By the end of the year, building supplies arrived weekly from New York. An iron-hulled steamer had been placed on the lower reaches of the River Chagres "hauling construction materials and tools to the various sites along the river that had been selected for railroad way stations." Three barges were also pressed into service for this purpose.[124] The steamship *Philadelphia* left New Orleans on the first day of 1851 with 246 men bound for the Isthmus under Baker's charge.[125] By this stage a small village of frame houses had been erected on Manzanillo Island and log roads laid over its marshy surface.[126] Nevertheless Totten complained that he was still short of laborers accustomed to wheelbarrow work. He had offered Hugh Dougherty, who had experience of this kind, and who was most likely Irish, a position as foreman at fifty dollars per month.[127] The first year of work on the railroad had now drawn to a close with few significant results to show to the directors, shareholders, and general public.

THREE

Slow Progress

JANUARY 1851 SAW THE START OF THE DRY SEASON IN PANAMA, AND there was optimism that the previous slow pace of progress could now be accelerated. Hundreds of laborers on steamers from New York had arrived at Chagres in the course of the previous forty-five days, and hundreds more were expected shortly.[1] The chief engineer acknowledged the existence of the hurdles facing him but remained optimistic. "Although I have not complained of difficulties, I have nevertheless not been without them; but seeing nothing insurmountable I have made the best of them. Difficulties are to be expected."[2] Nevertheless, diseases and illnesses associated with Panama's tropical climate continued to enfeeble the workforce.[3] Fever took a toll on the workmen who had arrived the previous month. "Dr. Henry's men have suffered greatly from fevers—100 out of 150 were down at one time, 7 or 8 have died, and 6 will return by the first New Orleans steamer. They are now improving. Climate, of course, is the main cause of their illness."[4]

By late February, the effective strength of this group of 150 was down to about 80 men. The remainder had to be sent back to New Orleans, and their fate provoked the following reflection from Totten: "Disease has taken hold of the men sooner than I anticipated. I never did suppose white labor would stand this climate any length of time; but I did think they would be able to stand it three or four months at least. In this I am thrown back in my calculations. The last three weeks has diminished our workforce more than 100 men."[5]

Some of Baker's recently arrived workforce of 250 men from Illinois also succumbed to fever. Baker himself almost died and had to be taken back to the United States by his brother to recuperate. An American journal reported in February that half of the workers at one location were unable to work because of sickness. A New York newspaper agreed that there was considerable sickness.

"Shortly after the men arrive at their stations many are taken sick, and are entirely useless to the company; numbers are at present sick on their hands; notwithstanding this it looks very lively, very like a railroad."[6] Illness continued to exact its toll on the workforce, especially after the rains began again in April. Totten informed the company president in August that "the white [labor] force is diminishing as fast as those composing it become incapable of duty.... Since my last [letter] we have had a great deal of sickness on all parts of the work." He predicted that sickness would decline as the line moved away from the swamps of the low-lying Caribbean area.[7] A company engineer told an American woman who crossed the Isthmus in 1852 that men could work only for a week at a stretch before requiring time off to recuperate, dosing themselves with large amounts of quinine to combat fever.[8]

Dr. John Lidell, an American physician who worked for the company in 1851, agreed that illness and disease posed a major problem: "At the present time, the greatest obstacle in the way of constructing the Panama Rail-Road is the unhealthiness of the country through which it passes." Over 70 percent of the 382 hospital patients, all Americans or Europeans, whom he treated during a four-month period, suffered from fevers of one kind or another.[9]

It was now becoming clear that the services of laborers from the United States or Europe could not be relied on for the full period of their six-month contract. These men were usually able to work well during their first month or two in Panama. By the midpoint of their stay, however, a considerable number had either died or had to be invalided home as unfit for further labor. The value of the services of those who remained was substantially reduced, with some being placed on the sick list, while others, enfeebled by illness, were not as productive as they had been on arrival. Nevertheless, the laborers' output must have been enough to convince the railroad of the efficacy of a six-month contract period, because it continued to operate this system for the remaining four years of construction.

Lidell downplayed references to a high death toll by admitting that most of the diseases contracted by workers were not fatal, at least in the short term. "Of more than one thousand cases of disease treated either by myself or under my immediate observation in the valley of Rio Chagres, but ten patients died; and I have understood that some physicians present even better results than mine."[10] Commentators who were critical of working conditions on the Isthmus or hostile to a railroad across Panama selectively seized on some of Liddell's more disquieting observations. Liddell's conclusions, however, were derived from a time when workers still battled their way through the pestilential swamps of the coastal area. Conditions improved somewhat once the low-lying marshy areas bordering the Caribbean had been left behind and the railroad began its ascent to the hills of the continental divide.

Only occasional brief press references can be found on the deaths of railroad workers during 1851. The number of reported fatalities was small, and most reports were of men who died at sea on their way back to the United States.[11] Newspapers, however, were probably unaware of the actual number of deaths. Laborers were not the only category of workers to succumb. N. B. Putnam, the railroad's Panama agent, died on board the steamer *Crescent City* en route to New York in March 1851.[12]

The *American Railroad Journal* declared that white laborers heading for Panama from the United States were ignorant of conditions there. "Most of those going out in the service of this company have little idea of what they will be called upon to endure." According to the article, this would change once workers returned home and reports of working conditions in Panama began to circulate more widely. The periodical correctly predicted that these accounts would eventually make it more difficult for the company to continue recruiting laborers in the United States.[13] An early indication of this occurred in June 1851 when Totten recounted that a group of twenty-five ships' carpenters had been on their way to enlist at its New York office "when they encountered somebody who gave such terrible accounts of this place as to cause a retreat of the whole party." No member of this contingent sailed for Panama.[14]

Six-month contracts, together with the hemorrhaging of men through illness, desertion, repatriation, or death, meant there was a constant need for fresh workers. Stephens stressed to his fellow directors "the propriety of keeping up a continued supply of men to provide against sickness and desertion."[15] At its meeting on May 19, 1851, the executive and finance committee "decided to continue sending down from 40 to 50 [men] per [weekly] steamer including some ships carpenters if to be had on the best terms." Totten's correspondence was replete with requests for additional men.[16] Either because of recruitment difficulties or the need to keep payroll costs under control, the company was frequently unable or unwilling to comply with the chief engineer's insistent demands. As well as requesting more men, Totten frequently complained about the inferior quality of those sent to him. "We are not able to keep up with the work on hand, especially as some of our number are good for nothing . . . for heaven's sake, do not send me poor devils of no experience." Some months later,

Totten again criticized the poor quality of workers recruited by the company's labor contractors.[17]

Desertion became a recurring topic in the chief engineer's correspondence in the early stages of the project. Not long after the arrival of 250 men of Colonel Baker's force in January 1851, seventy-two of them headed for Panama City in an attempt to reach the California goldfields. Baker went in pursuit of the defectors, but with what success we do not know. Desertion lost some of its attraction after it became a criminal offence in Panama from February 1851 onward. Following representations by the railroad to the province's governor, a proclamation was issued ordering the arrest and imprisonment of deserters from the company's employment. This decree checked the stampede of absconders, and desertion became less frequent.[18]

American laborer George Bartholomew, who described his experience in the *New York Tribune* in 1851, provided one of the few testimonies from an ordinary worker. A total of 380 men were working for the company in January: 260 of them at Navy Bay, including 75 Jamaicans and "southern men" from New Orleans. The remaining 120 workers, described as "northern men" from the United States, German-speaking states, and Ireland, were based at Gatún. Bartholomew had a poor opinion of the Jamaicans, alleging that they were lazy and indolent and, somewhat surprisingly, that they were the first to fall sick. They were about to be shipped home, possibly because their contracts had come to an end. The "southern men" from New Orleans, most of whom were likely to have been Irish, allegedly lacked discipline and were dissipated, disorderly, and ruffianlike. Many of them had also fallen sick.

Bartholomew had a more positive view of the "northern men," possibly because he was from the north himself. The best axe men, according to Bartholomew, were Americans from the forested western states, while the best excavators were Irish and Germans with previous construction experience. "With such men this road can be built and with no others. They will endure fatigue longer and enjoy better health from their habits of sobriety and submission to discipline." However, not all the Irish at Gatún were models of sobriety. Three got drunk in violation of company regulations. "The next morning they were discharged; they repented, and returned to work, except the leader, who was obliged to leave as a disorderly person, whose presence was dangerous to the peace of our little community."[19]

During the early stages of construction, the company bought two 4-4-0 locomotives from the Philadelphia and Reading Railroad, and three grade-climbing

Figure 3.1. Primeval Forest: Preparing for the Iron Road. Bedford Pim, *The Gate of the Pacific* (London: Lovell Reeve, 1863). Courtesy of the British Library Board.

locomotives from George Sellers of Cincinnati. The railroad subsequently purchased additional locomotives from the Portland Company in Maine. The first locomotive, from the Philadelphia and Reading Railroad, was unloaded on Manzanillo Island on February 22, 1851, and two days later, the first rails of the Panama railroad were laid down.[20] These rails may have consisted of strap iron laid on top of wooden strips that were fastened to the crossties. In 1853, this initial section of track was replaced by bridge rails that resembled an inverted U, weighing forty pounds per yard. This type of rail required stub switches.[21] There is some confusion about the track gauge that appears to have been changed several times in the railroad's early years, from four feet, eight and a half inches, to five feet six inches and then to five feet—the same used by southern U.S. railroads prior to 1886.[22]

As soon as track laying started, Totten sent one of his senior foremen, a former Scottish railroad contractor called Miller, to the United States to recruit men experienced in railroad construction. The previous decade had witnessed a huge increase in railroad building in North America, and Totten wanted to quickly recruit laborers with experience of this kind of work.[23] Miller was instructed "to bring young, hearty Irishmen, from works where he has been engaged and is well known." Totten stressed that Americans were not suitable for laboring and that Irish or German workers would be more appropriate. "We want what we have not yet had—good graders—diggers and wheelbarrow men—with a proper set of foremen to direct them. . . . Let the graders be Irish or Germans, from New England or New York."[24] What Totten was looking for were select members of the laboring corps, men referred to in Britain as "navvies"—short for "navigators"—who were able to shovel tons of earth a day. Many of the early railway laborers in both Britain and the United States were Irishmen of this kind, and American construction foremen sometimes recruited them straight off the ships on which they had arrived from the old country.[25]

Notwithstanding his endorsement of Irish and German workers, Totten's experience of using local laborers, and specifically those from the Cartagena region, had convinced him of their superiority as workers in Panama's challenging climatic conditions, despite their lack of technical skills, their inability to speak English, and a propensity to desert. He informed Stephens, "I am anxious to get together a strong native force, not only for the [forthcoming] wet season, but because they are in every respect the most effective common laborers we have."[26] By August, about six hundred of these men were working on the railroad, and a further two hundred were expected.

Totten maintained his high opinion of these tough and hardy workers throughout the lifetime of the project. This did not stop him banning, from August onward, the arrival of women and children from Cartagena who wished to accompany their menfolk. On July 26, a British steamer had landed about 220 laborers on the Isthmus "and a large lot of women and children the importation of which I shall now stop, as I do not find the majority of them of any particular utility."[27] Totten had revised his earlier view that workers from New Grenada could not be happy without their women, possibly because the company was liable for payment of the fares of dependents who had accompanied their menfolk from Cartagena.

In January 1851, an Irish Catholic priest, the Reverend Richard Waters, unexpectedly appeared on the Panamanian scene.[28] Waters arrived from Spanish Town, Jamaica, where he had been exercising his ministry. Prior to that, he had been a chaplain at the court of Faustin I, the self-styled emperor of Haiti. The priest celebrated Mass at various locations along the railroad, which suggests that much of the workforce at this point was Roman Catholic and probably Irish. The soothing effect the clergyman had on the workforce pleased Totten. "The Irish Catholic missionary, Revd. Walters [sic], has officiated at our different stations on the river a number of times, and his preaching has a happy effect upon a large portion of our laborers, quieting them and reconciling them to their duties. Yesterday he held mass here, and gave us a short discourse on our duties to God and the Rl.Rd.Co. [underlined in original], and all, white and black, seemed to enjoy the first religious worship on Mansanillo Island."[29]

According to Totten, Waters "is a far better man than the New Granadian priests in general." The clergyman had requested a small fee as remuneration for his services, and Totten sought permission to pay him.[30] The *Panama Star* referred to the priest as "a missionary pastor, engaged as chaplain among the operatives on the railroad."[31] In a letter to this paper, Waters described himself as a "missionary apostolic."[32]

The priest's letter conveyed a favorable impression of the workers' conditions. Stating that he had been invited by Truesdale, the labor contractor, to afford the workers "religious consolation," he went on: "I never knew so large a body of men so contented and happy. I found that since the commencement of operations there have been only three deaths, and that those three men had been sick before they left the United States. As to the Irish laborers there has not one been sick since the commencement; all are perfectly contented and happy, owing to the wise, humane and judicious treatment of Mr Truesdale."[33] Waters was referring to the men who had arrived with Truesdale in December 1850, not the Irish who had come from New Orleans some months earlier. Ironically, Fr. Waters fell sick, quite likely from malaria, shortly afterward. Totten reported in March that the priest was convalescing from an illness that had put him out of action for two weeks.[34] Waters remained in Panama, possibly as unofficial chaplain to the railroad's Catholic workforce, though there are no further reports of his activities in either the press or Totten's correspondence. The priest's stay on the Isthmus did not last long. He died there on October 9, 1851.[35]

Miller, Totten's trusted foreman, returned to Navy Bay on March 8 with 153 men, presumably the Irish and German laborers he had been ordered to recruit some weeks earlier. He had managed to sign up a total of 250 men for Panama, but the steamer could not accommodate them all.[36] Meanwhile construction work advanced slowly. Company documents and American and Panamanian newspapers reported a constant stream of workers arriving by almost every steamer from the north during 1851. In April the executive and finance committee authorized payment for the passage and expenses of 148 men from New Orleans. These may have been additional Irishmen recruited by Rogers. By the following month, this group of New Orleans laborers began work at Bohío Soldado, one of the upper stations on the Chagres River.[37]

The steady stream of arrivals from the United States did not lead to a large increase in the workforce's size. The influx of workers was counterbalanced by an outward flow of men from the Isthmus—some having completed their contracts while others had died or been invalided out. According to one report, a total of about one thousand men were employed during the course of 1851, but this appears to be an understatement. Stephens estimated that there were nine hundred men working for the company during the month of April alone.[38] The *New York Tribune* maintained that there were about one thousand men at work in May, stationed in six construction camps along the line of the railroad.[39]

Occasional references to German and Dutch employees make clear that the railroad employed more Europeans than just the Irish. There was also evidence of a French presence in the workforce. In May 1851, a group of French laborers downed tools and refused to work, reportedly the result of an overseer's intemperance and bad conduct. The workers sang "La Marseillaise" and raised the French flag. Stephens, who received surly looks when he met the strikers, refused to listen to their complaints until the flag was taken down and they went back to work. In the meantime, he ordered that their food supply be cut off. The strikers soon gave way, and the stoppage ended.[40] Not long afterward, a *New York Tribune* correspondent reported seeing a procession of about fifty French laborers at the Bohío Soldado construction camp bearing the body of one of their dead companions for burial on a nearby hillside.[41]

It became obvious during 1851 that construction was falling behind schedule. This did not prevent the executive and finance committee from issuing an optimistic progress report in May, probably with the aim of attracting investors in a forthcoming bond sale. The committee claimed that twenty miles of the railroad would be in operation by July and that the twenty-seven-mile section from Navy Bay to Gorgona would be completed by September.[42] An American journal enthusiastically declared, "This great work under Col. Totten is proceeding rapidly towards completion."[43]

In June, the company advertised the sale of bonds to the value of $900,000 at 7 percent, convertible into stock at the expiration of five years. The bond sale was successful, raising $1,171,000, well over the initial offer.[44] Among the successful bidders were George Law ($100,000) and the Royal West India Mail Steam Packet Company of Southampton ($150,000).[45] Law, who had recently ended his brief shipping war with Aspinwall's steamship company, remained determined to undermine his rival. Law invested hundreds of thousands of dollars in Panama Railroad stocks and bonds. He became a major shareholder in the Panama Railroad Company in 1851, and for a while was reported to own about one-quarter of the stock, worth about $500,000.[46] Law's investment got him a seat on the railroad's board of directors not long afterward, putting him in an ideal position to challenge Aspinwall for control of the company.

Until 1851, the small coastal town of Chagres served as Panama's main Caribbean port. Hordes of California-bound prospectors scrambled ashore there during the early gold rush days. Bartenders, gamblers, and prostitutes, as well as cooks, waiters, barbers, innkeepers, porters, and boatmen, tended to their needs. During the course of 1850 and 1851, fifty-eight vessels freighted with stores and materials for the railroad docked at Chagres, in addition to ships carrying iron rails from Britain and the regular steam packets from New York, New Orleans, and Southampton.[47] Travelers arriving at Chagres were universally disillusioned and repelled by what, for most, was their first experience of a tropical port. Robert Tomes referred to Chagres as a "shore infected with pestilence and vice."[48] Fabens graphically described it as a "truly wretched old town" and referred to "its present filthy, dilapidated condition . . . its mean kennel-like hovels, its putrid streets, its stagnant pools, its slimy pavements, its hairless dogs, its sick carrion-fed pigs."[49]

Chagres's economic boom was short-lived. From 1851 onward, its role as Panama's principal Atlantic port was superseded by the new settlement spring-ing up around the railroad's terminus on Manzanillo Island. Once the island had been cleared of trees and vegetation, construction of a new town, later called Aspinwall after the railroad's founder, proceeded rapidly.[50] About fifteen buildings had been built, including two spacious warehouses, by May 1851. Deep-water wharves were nearing completion, and British freighters availed of these to unload rails and machinery for the railroad.[51] A causeway, built on piles, carried the railroad across the channel separating the island from the mainland.

Despite progress at Aspinwall, sickness, climatic conditions, and the physical obstacles posed by the terrain slowed the pace of the railroad's construction in 1851. According to one account, "The nature of the country through which the line of road had to be carried, was calculated to strike the hardiest specu-lator with dismay. The first thirteen miles from the Atlantic led through deep swamps covered with jungle, full of reptiles and venomous insects."[52] A Brit-ish engineer who had worked in Ireland confirmed the difficult nature of the terrain and was impressed by what had been achieved. "The first ten or twelve miles of the line is supported on timber piles, driven into swampy land of far worse description than I ever saw *even in Ireland* [my italics] . . . the execution of the railway . . . is one of the most difficult engineering operations that I have ever seen or read of."[53]

As a consequence, Totten had little progress to report for over a year after the start of the project. He apologized to the company's president early in 1851. "I regret I cannot say that we have rails actually laid. We are ready to lay down about two miles. . . . What with sickness, laziness, and other ills peculiar to this climate . . . the work is not progressing as rapidly as it should." Later the same month he explained, "My position would be good now for work if the [labor] forces were not diminishing so fast." It was not until March 6, 1851, that Totten was able to take a short ride on the railroad at Gatún.[54] On June 24, a locomo-tive that had been shipped in earlier that year got up steam and began running on a short stretch of completed line from Navy Bay to the mainland.[55] Progress remained painfully slow, and the chief engineer expressed his dissatisfaction in a letter to Stephens in July. "When I think of the amount of labor and money we have expended—how all my most reasonable estimates have fallen short—I am mortified at the result."[56]

By August 1851, Totten was coming under pressure from his directors in New York because of a lack of headway despite considerable expenditure. The difficulties undergone took their toll not just on the workforce but also on the hard-bitten and experienced chief engineer. In a rare disclosure of his personal feelings Totten confessed his despondency and anxiety. "This country does not admit of fixed ideas. One is obliged to adapt himself to circumstances. . . . I believe there are more causes for discouragement here than on any other work in the world. Sometimes I almost despair, and nothing but my most sanguine temperament keeps up my spirits." Later that month, Totten again referred to his failure to advance, this time transferring some of the blame to the work-force. "You will be astonished at our slow progress . . . and yet I do not know where we could have done better than we have. . . . I am exceedingly mortified at the slow progress of the work for the past three months, and at the expense we have incurred in maintaining and sending home worthless vagabonds."[57]

Following Trautwine's resignation at the end of 1850, Totten had assumed the role of chief engineer at a stipend of $12,000 per annum.[58] The failure of the railroad to advance as rapidly as planned called into question his generous salary, and Totten felt it necessary to defend his remuneration as the company's highest paid functionary. "I do not think my salary is out of proportion with the others . . . my duties here comprise far more than that of engineer—and my responsibilities are tenfold greater than they would be on any line in the U. States."[59]

Totten reported in early September that the railroad was now advancing at three hundred feet per day, an improvement on the rate earlier in the year, when construction averaged one mile per month.[60] Schott described the arrival of the rails close to Gatún some months earlier in his usual imaginative anecdotal fashion. "According to railroad legend, this event was celebrated only by an Irish construction foreman and his gang who got drunk on native rum and fired off a rusty old arquebus left over from the pirate days."[61] It was not until October 27, however, that the first train traveled from Navy Bay to Gatún.[62] After twenty-two months, a very considerable expenditure of capital, and the exertions of well over a thousand workers, the rails extended only eight miles from their starting point on Manzanillo Island. The local population was

RUNNING THE LINES.

Figure 3.2. Running the Lines, Panama. F. N. Otis, *Illustrated History of the Panama Railroad* (London: Sampson Low, 1862). Courtesy of the British Library Board.

amazed at their first sight of trains running over the short stretch of completed line "flying over the land like a bird."[63]

While the rails reached only as far as Gatún, considerable progress had been made in clearing a path through the rain forest as far as Barbacoas, sixteen miles or so farther on.[64] The worst of the swamplands had now been crossed, but Totten and his engineering colleagues knew that they still faced formidable obstacles. The line would have to be laid across more marshland and almost forty miles of rugged jungle-covered country. It would have to cross the wide Chagres River and then cut through the crest of the continental divide nearly three hundred feet above the Pacific before rapidly descending to sea level at Panama City. Almost a hundred watercourses, from small streams and rivulets to mountain torrents and turbulent rivers, still had to be traversed, requiring bridges from under ten feet to one over six hundred feet in length, as well as the construction of countless culverts and drains.

Totten's poor health contributed to his disillusionment at his failure to make faster progress. Illness in May prevented him from sending dispatches to New York. Two months later his health had deteriorated again, and he feared that he might be forced to return home to regain his well-being. "I have suffered severely for the last four days from the second attack of diseased bowels since you left us." He added that many of his skilled workers were also sick and that others were being invalided home. He became unwell again in August. "I have really been too ill to do anything but fret and scold." To add to his worries, another civil war had broken out in Nueva Granada, and Totten feared that laborers from the Cartagena region, his main source of local workers, might be pressed into military service by the opposing factions.[65]

Beset by health problems, conscious of his failure to meet construction targets, and mindful of the formidable obstacles still to be surmounted, Totten came to a difficult operational decision, one in which he virtually admitted defeat. He concluded in a letter to the company's president on August 9, 1851, that it would be in the railroad's interest to transfer construction to an outside contractor. A few weeks later, he again advised the company to contract out the remaining work "at any prices at which responsible contractors can be obtained."[66] His advice was eventually accepted, though it was not until the middle of the following year that a contractor assumed responsibility for completing the railroad.

As 1851 drew to a close, the railroad's progress lagged far behind the optimistic reports disseminated by the company. Furthermore, its finances had entered a critical phase. Most of the initial capital of $1 million had been expended on clearing Manzanillo Island and laying the track as far as Gatún. The company's share price slumped during 1851. Its financial fortunes were at low ebb despite a successful bond issue, and the directors were allegedly forced to borrow on their personal credit to continue the work.[67] The company's request for a loan of £25,481 (almost $130,000) from the Royal West India Mail Steam Packet Company in October confirmed its shaky financial situation at this time.[68] This shipping line ferried laborers between Cartagena and Panama, and the loan sought by the railroad may have been required to cover the cost of transporting some of these workers.[69]

A report by Captain Chappell, secretary of the West India Steam Packet Company, provided an insight into the state of the project in November 1851. The captain was presumably sent to assess the railroad's creditworthiness before his company authorized the loan requested by the directors in New York.

He reported that the railroad had three locomotives in operation, with another three under construction, together with a number of freight wagons. Five hundred workmen were employed. Parts of the line had cost £30,000 ($150,000) per mile to build; other sections had been constructed for considerably less. Chappell correctly forecasted that the remainder of the work would be handed over to a contractor.[70]

The company's financial situation improved dramatically following the arrival at Chagres of the *Georgia* and the *Philadelphia*, two large American steamers crammed with California-bound passengers at the end of November 1851. Stormy weather prevented the ships from disgorging their passengers at the mouth of the Chagres River. After days had passed and several lives had been lost in trying unsuccessfully to land passengers in small boats through heavy surf, both ships diverted to the nearby sheltered harbor at Manzanillo Island. Over a thousand impatient gold seekers swarmed ashore, saw the railroad, and demanded to be transported to the railhead at Gatún, about eight miles distant, which was as far as the tracks extended. Stephens and other company officials initially resisted the clamor. Passengers had hitherto been perceived as an inconvenience that would interfere with construction. Further, company policy was not to accept passenger traffic until the line reached the crossing point over the Chagres River at Barbacoas.[71]

Forced to give way against their better judgement by the demands of these impatient migrants, the railroad's officials decided to charge an exorbitant fare to deter future passenger travel. Undeterred by the high cost and the absence of passenger cars, the eager migrants crammed onto freight wagons. The first train conveying passengers on the Isthmus carried them to Gatún on December 8, 1851.[72] From Gatún they followed the established practice of hiring canoes to take them up the Chagres River to Cruces, before proceeding overland to Panama City by mule or on foot.

A precedent for using the railroad for passenger purposes had been established. Not long after, the railroad published its first timetable, announcing daily departures between Aspinwall and Bohío Soldado, some miles beyond Gatún, to where the rails now extended, at a fare of two dollars.[73] Henceforth, the company benefitted from a steadily growing and previously unplanned income of transporting passengers, even though the line was far from finished. The inflated fares paid by travelers during the remainder of the construction period contributed significantly to financing the project.[74] Furthermore, as soon as the *Georgia* and *Philadelphia* returned to New York with the news that the railroad had begun passenger operations, investor confidence was restored, the company's share price rose, and credit became easier to secure. In the view of one historian, the transportation of a thousand migrants by rail over the short distance between Navy Bay and Gatún, in December 1851, "probably saved the whole railroad project from disastrous failure."[75] President Millard Fillmore's premature announcement in his address to Congress at the end of 1851, that a considerable part of the railroad had been completed, also helped to boost the company's financial standing.[76]

The directors realized, possibly for the first time, their extraordinary good fortune in having secured a railroad concession across Panama just before the gold rush had started. What had previously been seen as a long-term speculative investment now had the potential to generate immediate revenue thanks to the demand for transportation from thousands of migrants heading to, or returning from, California, and the company's ability to transport them part of the way by rail. The railroad "from an enterprise which looked far into the future for its rewards . . . became one promising immediate returns from the capital and labor invested."[77]

Now that trains had started to run over part of the route, Stephens announced his company's readiness to transport the U.S. mail across the Isthmus from December 1, 1851. His offer was quickly accepted by the postmaster general.[78] The directors' hopes of an indirect government subsidy, dashed by Congress in 1849, were finally realized in January 1852 when the railroad was authorized to carry the U.S. mail across Panama and to charge for it by weight.[79] This agreement proved to be a source of considerable income for the railroad and a growing burden for the postmaster general because of the increasing volume of west coast mail. This led to the contract terms being revised some years later when the railroad accepted an annual payment of $100,000 for this service, an arrangement that lasted until 1860.[80]

The railroad's outlook remained uncertain at the end of 1851, despite the growing revenues from passenger receipts now flowing into the company's coffers and the certainty of additional income from the postmaster general. The climate, disease, problems in retaining manpower, and difficulties in laying the tracks across swamps and mudflats had delayed progress and added to construction costs. Expenditure to date had exceeded estimates. The executive and finance committee concluded that railroad costs on the Isthmus were four or five times higher than in the United States. Totten believed the differential was even greater, calculating the expense of building a railroad to be "about six times the value of that kind of work in the United States."[81]

Although the company's financial position was slowly improving, the directors decided to accept their chief engineer's earlier advice and began looking for a contractor who would complete the line at a lower cost and a faster pace. A New York newspaper hinted that investors were becoming impatient with the railroad's slow progress, and pressure from this direction is likely to have played a role in the decision to contract the remainder of the work to an outside agency.[82] The company's president blamed a lack of confidence—what he termed "the sin of unbelief"—that the project would ever be completed for holding the enterprise back.[83]

As 1851 gave way to the early months of 1852, sickness continued to impede progress. Totten complained that he had been forced to replace his assistants at Gatún five times in the previous six months because of illness. As a result, he frequently took the place of his subordinates while they were prostrated by fever or incapacitated for some other reason. The shortness of technical staff in the early months of 1852 forced him to promote several unqualified workers to the rank of engineer. "Most of them were young men, of very little experience." Asked to provide a timetable for the erection of the bridge to carry the line across the Chagres River at Barbacoas, he replied: "sickness spoils all calculations."[84] Work-related accidents, however, were not a factor in delaying progress. The local press reported only one fatality of this kind.[85] Many accidents were likely never publicly acknowledged.

While malaria and other jungle fevers took their toll on the workforce, the mortality rate at this period was not as horrendously high as some writers have claimed. Minter, for example, alleged that one in five workers died every month in 1850 and that during 1851 a daily funeral train ran directly from the company's hospital on Manzanillo Island to the cemetery at Monkey Hill, "where a crew of carpenters and painters worked full time at turning out white crosses."[86] A frightening mortality rate of this level, with little likelihood of employees surviving a six-month stint on the Isthmus, could not have remained hidden from the local and American press for long and would have effectively undermined the company's campaign to recruit new workers in the United States and elsewhere.[87]

Illness and the country's difficult topography were not the only obstacles delaying the advance of the rails. Heavy downpours early in the wet season of 1852 damaged parts of the completed track. On May 25 and 26, torrential rain caused embankments to subside and considerable time and effort were required to rebuild them. Some months later, Totten again referred to the damaging effects of Panama's tropical downpours. "The repair gangs are so small, and it rains so constantly, it is almost impossible to keep the tracks in running order."[88] By this stage a disillusioned Totten in Panama and anxious company directors in New York were committed to adopting a radically different approach to completing the railroad, and negotiations had already started with a prospective contractor.

FOUR

A New Departure

EARLY IN 1852, THE RAILROAD ENTERED INTO NEGOTIATIONS WITH Minor C. Story of Poughkeepsie, New York, who was "one of the largest railroad contractors in the world." He employed six thousand men during construction of the Portland and Montreal Railroad. Story, nevertheless, remains a shadowy figure.[1] Most of what we know of him stems from his business relationship with George Law, the politically ambitious, self-made millionaire of County Down parentage, who was challenging Aspinwall's control of the Panama railroad. Story was a business associate and probably a personal friend of Law; he nominated the latter to be the executor of his estate.[2] Although his background was in construction, Story had been appointed a director of Law's U.S. Mail Steamship Company in 1851.[3] The connection between the two men dated to 1850, if not earlier, and could be described as an informal partnership. Law acted as financial guarantor for Story's compliance and completion of a number of major construction and engineering projects.[4] Minor C. Story also wielded influence in New York's political circles, and this would have appealed to George Law, who harbored political ambitions of his own.[5]

By early 1852, Story and Law had become interested in tendering for the completion of the Panama railroad, and in February they visited the Isthmus, accompanied by Stephens, the company president.[6] Story and Law may also have had an ulterior motive to temporarily absent themselves from the United States. Not long after they had left for Panama, news broke linking the pair with New York's attorney general in a financial scandal. It was alleged that the latter, "under highly suspicious circumstances, had lobbied the board that was awarding contracts to widen the Erie Canal to set aside $1 million for Law."[7] Allegations that the proper procedures had not been followed resulted subsequently in a legal case.[8] Law was apparently in no hurry to hasten back to New York. He visited Portobelo, Havana, San Juan, and New Orleans before reaching home in April.[9]

In February 1852, Panama reached a milestone in urban development when the burgeoning settlement on Manzanillo Island was named Aspinwall in honor of the man who was the inspiration behind the railroad. However, the New Grenada authorities insisted on calling the settlement Colón to commemorate Columbus, who had explored the neighboring coastline. This controversy over the town's title persisted for decades. Story and Law were among the notables present at the naming ceremony. The population of the new settlement at this time was about eight hundred.[10] The small railhead grew in importance as it quickly developed into Panama's main Atlantic port, with freight and passenger ships docking there from early 1852 onward. The new port offered relatively safe berthing facilities, and passengers could avoid the danger and expense of having to transfer to small boats as had been the case at Chagres, its predecessor.[11]

While Aspinwall blossomed, Chagres declined as it reverted to its earlier status as a small fishing port. Many of its wooden houses were removed and rebuilt in Aspinwall. By April 1852, one hundred masons, bricklayers, and joiners hastened to complete the railroad's brick-built office. Several large warehouses, three or four hotels, and numerous private dwellings had either been constructed or were in the course of erection. Docks had been built where vessels drawing twenty feet or more of water could be moored safely.[12] Almost one hundred more houses were added in the next twelve months.

Messrs. Schuyler of New York also dispatched a surveying party to Panama to estimate the cost of completing the railroad. Robert and George Schuyler, Alexander Hamilton's illustrious nephews, were prominent railroad moguls, but their bid was not accepted.[13] Following his return from Panama, Minor C. Story met with members of the railroad's executive and finance committee in April 1852 to discuss the terms of a contract to complete the project.

By this stage, the rails approached the hamlet of Barbacoas, the designated crossing point over the Chagres River, about halfway across the Isthmus. "This village consists of a few huts in the rude Indian style, formed of bamboo and covered with palm leaves. Here are refreshment shops, retailing of spirits, with their accompanying gambling rooms."[14] Here, the contractor would have to erect a bridge across the wide and sometimes turbulent river before completing the line from the opposite bank to the Pacific terminus at Panama City.

Figure 4.1. View of Aspinwall (Colón), Mid-nineteenth Century. Classic Image / Alamy Stock Illustration.

At the April meeting, the contractor agreed to be paid on a per-mile basis, and negotiations on the precise amount continued over the following weeks. Story apparently asked for $75,000 per mile, and the committee countered by offering $70,000. However, as an incentive to finish the railroad by June 1, 1853, two months earlier than the specified contract date, the committee offered a bonus of $5,000 per mile. Story declined to accept these terms and submitted a written offer on April 29, 1852, which was accepted by the board.[15] On May 20, 1852, Story signed a contract to complete the railroad by August 1, 1853, and this agreement was ratified by the directors on June 1, 1852.[16] The press published few details of the contract, and little information about it appeared in the company's documentation. It seems likely that the directors agreed to pay Story $75,000 per mile to finish the remaining twenty-odd miles of the project.[17]

News that the contract had been signed was made public at a dinner in honor of George Law in New York's Astor House Hotel on May 20. Stephens informed the three hundred guests that the fact Law was acting as surety for the fulfilment of Story's contract was the best possible guarantee for the railroad's completion in just over a year's time.[18] Law might have seen the completion of the railroad by his associate as part of a longer-term plan to wrest control of the company from his old rival, Aspinwall. It was later alleged that Law had agreed to act as guarantor on condition that he received a share in Story's proceeds from the deal as his fee.[19]

The *American Railroad Journal's* verdict on the contract was favorable: "With the work under the charge of such a man [Law], its rapid progress was no longer a matter of doubt." The company's share price rose.[20] Rumors that the Cunard Line was considering a steamship route between London and Australia using the Panama railroad for the land transit between Atlantic and Pacific would also have boosted the share price.[21] The *New York Herald* announced that the "Panama Railroad has recovered from the recent depression, and is selling now at a very extravagant premium. Within the last twelve months, this stock went a begging in Wall Street. . . . At that time no one would touch it. . . . Now there are plenty of buyers . . . and very little stock offering at that."[22]

A new chapter in the railroad's construction had commenced. The paucity of information on the terms of the contract meant that the demarcation between the company's responsibilities and the duties and obligations assumed by the contractor was not clear. According to Totten, "The [contract] price is high and the company is to do a great deal towards assisting the contractor in fulfilling his agreement." He referred cryptically to "the peculiar nature of the contract" but failed to elaborate on this.[23] He may have been alluding to some form of collaborative arrangement between the company and the contractor.

While the contract lasted, Totten, who retained his title as chief engineer, devoted most of his energies and resources to improving and repairing the existing section of the railroad, which now reached almost halfway across the Isthmus. He may also have been engaged in acquiring land for the Panama City terminus.[24] The contractor made his own arrangements for recruiting workers, and no details of these appeared in the company's documentation. The chief engineer, however, continued to press for additional laborers, mechanics, quarrymen, and masons for repair and maintenance purposes.[25] William Clarke Young, former president of the Hudson River Railroad, was appointed consultant engineer for the contractor.[26]

The company employed about twelve hundred men in April 1852, prior to transferring construction to Story.[27] Workers continued to arrive from the United States throughout the rest of the year, but newspaper and company reports did not, as a rule, distinguish between men recruited by the railroad and those hired by Story. The company mainly recruited skilled workmen to improve and upgrade the existing track, while most of the laborers were hired by the contractor for new construction. Francis Spies, the company secretary, reported in August that the railroad had only a small workforce directly in its employ.[28]

The contractor did not move to Panama to personally direct his new railway project. Instead he devolved responsibility to a manager, William Miller. This was almost certainly the same man who had previously worked as a supervisor for Totten. Story paid at least two further visits to the Isthmus, one in June 1852, shortly after his contract had started, and another in February of the following year.[29] His failure to spend more time on the Isthmus would cost him dearly. At the same time, an assessment of him as "an incompetent contractor" was at odds with his prior record of successfully completing major projects in the United States.[30] His abilities and energies may have been absorbed by construction ventures closer to home, his business acumen could have been in decline, or he may not have enjoyed good health, as he died within a few years. Regardless of the cause, both Story and Law lacked prior experience in managing a challenging construction project in a distant tropical country. Panama's climatic and geographical environment was vastly different from anything the two entrepreneurs had dealt with previously.

Law's attention may also have been deflected during the second half of 1852 by a political crisis that he had provoked. The Cuban authorities refused to allow one of his steamers to berth in Havana in September because of anti-Spanish revolutionary propaganda allegedly circulated on the island by the ship's purser. Law's belligerent response, which appealed to the more chauvinistic elements of the American public and press, was to defiantly threaten to sail his ship into Havana harbor and open fire if the Spanish authorities denied it entrance. This threat came close to provoking a war between Spain and the United States in the closing months of 1852. Law, however, failed to get the backing he expected from the White House. President Millard Fillmore made it clear that he would not allow the United States to be dragged into war with Spain over this issue and refused to support the shipping magnate. Law eventually backed down and the crisis evaporated.[31]

In July 1852, following the appointment of the Story-Law consortium, the executive and finance committee approved major changes to its management structure on the Isthmus. Totten's salary had been drastically cut from $12,000 to $5,000 per annum in December 1851, probably because of his failure to meet construction deadlines and the consequent decision to bring in an outside contractor.[32] Alexander Center, while retaining his position as the company's vice president, was appointed to the newly created post of resident superintendent on the Isthmus in July, 1852, at a salary of $5,000 per annum, equal to Totten's.[33] Center's new role may have overlapped that of the chief engineer.[34]

Totten became unhappy with this management restructuring and the division of responsibilities it entailed and tendered his resignation. Unspecified circumstances, possibly work commitments or health issues, prevented his immediate return to the United States. By the time of his eventual arrival in New York in October 1852, he had withdrawn his resignation, arguing instead for an increase in salary with additional payment for work performed over the preceding year.[35] While the outcome of these negotiations was not reported, Totten's continuation as chief engineer for the remainder of the project and long afterward would suggest that an amicable settlement was reached. Center, however, retained his dual role as resident superintendent of the railroad and vice president of the company.

The death of the company's energetic and experienced president, John L. Stephens, in October caused another upheaval in the company's upper echelons. Stephens, who had earlier been "in such a delicate condition of health as to induce the most serious apprehensions," died at the early age of forty-eight in New York City on October 12.[36] The cause of death was malaria, contracted in Panama, where he had been involved since 1848 in planning and overseeing an enterprise to which he had devoted all his formidable energies. As well as being a powerful and influential advocate for the Panama railroad, Stephens was also a noted explorer, author, and man of business. His travels in the Yucatan and his writings about the lost cities of the Mayas, some of which he had discovered, had made him a household name. "He was among the most popular of American writers. . . . He was a man of ability, energy, and enterprise."[37]

Stephens's death was a severe blow to the railroad because he was the only senior member of the company, with the exception of the chief engineer, to have extensive firsthand knowledge of conditions in Panama and the problems of railroad construction there. His loss deprived the company of the expertise necessary for the oversight of the recently appointed contractor. William Clarke Young (1799–1894), a former president of the Hudson River Railroad, who had acted earlier as a consultant engineer for Minor C. Story, replaced Stephens as president.[38]

The new contractor got off to a slow start. A month after the agreement had been signed, there was no sign of construction beginning, and no decision had been made on the recruitment of local or foreign workers.[39] Story may have been awaiting the outcome of an earlier instruction to General Paredes, the railroad's labor agent in Cartagena, to procure five thousand workmen there.[40] The general failed to recruit anything like this number for reasons that were not disclosed, and henceforth Story had to rely on the arrival of smaller contingents of workers from New Granada supplemented by white laborers from the United States. A start was made in July, leading the chief engineer to comment: "Mr Story's force progresses well."[41] The wet season had begun some months earlier, making operations more difficult. The pace of work soon slowed, and the contractor confronted a number of major problems, some of which he should have foreseen and others that were unexpected. These difficulties, cumulatively, had serious repercussions for the progress of construction.

The timing of the erection of the bridge over the turbulent Chagres was ill chosen, though this was not Story's fault. The river was three hundred feet at the crossing point, but the nature of the terrain on both banks required the bridge to extend over six hundred. In February 1852, the executive and finance committee approved a contract with D. C. McCallum, an American bridge builder, to construct a modified version of his patented timber bridge, adapted for the passage of trains. The work was to be finished by July 1.[42] The company paid almost $16,000 for this structure, which was assembled in Georgia by a team of twenty workmen at the end of May 1852.[43] It was then dismantled and shipped to Panama the following month. Two of its sections were each over two hundred feet in length, a span, it was believed, longer than that of any bridge in the United States.[44]

By the time the bridge's component parts arrived, the rainy season was well underway, resulting in high water levels in the Chagres throughout the latter half of 1852. Story's men had to await the start of the dry season before laying the foundations in the riverbed. However, the rains instead of ceasing in December continued throughout January 1853, further delaying the bridge's erection.[45] Native boatmen trying to damage the bridge's timbers, probably by arson, in October 1852, did not help matters. This was likely a futile attempt to preserve their jobs. The extension of the railroad across the Chagres threatened the livelihood of between fifty and one hundred boatmen who depended on the river to make a living. "Want and malignity made them desperate," and they vented their hostility on the railroad.[46] The miscreants were disturbed before much damage was done.

Story's failure to hire sufficient workers proved to be a critical factor in delaying progress. The contractor, unfamiliar with the debilitating effects of Panama's climate on laborers, seriously underestimated the manpower resources required to complete a challenging construction project in just over a year. Constrained by his contract price, Story was initially reluctant to sufficiently expand his workforce. His failure to recruit enough men also arose from competition for railroad workers in the American labor market at a time when rapid expansion in the rail network was taking place. The demand for railroad laborers in the United States remained high in 1852 and 1853. Other contractors were prepared to pay wages equal to, and in some cases greater than those offered by Story, for work that did not involve the discomforts of a sea voyage and the hazards of life in a distant tropical country.[47]

A writer to a New York paper in July 1853 claimed that contractors had great difficulty in procuring railroad laborers in midwestern states even though they offered workers from $1 to $1.25 per day.[48] The Illinois Central Railroad, forced by a shortage of workers, increased its daily wage rate to $1.50. "This is the highest figure ever paid for such work in the Western States."[49] The *Nation* warned Irish laborers in the United States against going to Panama, telling them that they could get better wages and better food in the midwestern states, where thousands were wanted on the railroads, with little risk to life.[50]

Adverse newspaper reports about living and working conditions on the Isthmus also hindered recruitment. Critical accounts by returning California migrants and by some former railroad employees meant that Story found it increasingly difficult to hire sufficient men. Some of this adverse publicity emanated from, or was propagated by, enterprises linked to or owned by Cornelius Vanderbilt, who backed the rival Nicaragua route to America's Pacific coast. Throughout the early 1850s, the Commodore mounted a thinly veiled propaganda war against his main competitors "emphasizing the dangers of the Panama route."[51] According to Captain Chappell of the Royal Mail Steam Packet Company, "The Panama Railway . . . has been grossly misrepresented by parties at Grey Town [San Juan del Norte, Nicaragua], Chagres and Panama even, possessing interests at those places which they fear will be seriously compromised by the success of the railway."[52] A Panamanian paper warned that false or exaggerated reports of murders, robberies, and deadly diseases on the Isthmus were being circulated by shipping lines serving Nicaragua in order to induce passengers to avoid Panama.[53]

Negative publicity of this kind adversely affected the railroad's image in the parts of America that had previously been major sources of recruitment for workers. At the same time, Panama's own labor market was never in a position to make a major contribution to the railroad's workforce because of the availability of more lucrative casual work servicing the transport and accommodation needs of migrants. A local newspaper commented on the difficulty experienced by local employers in finding laborers in 1852. "For the past four days it has been found almost impossible to procure laborers at any price, either in Panama [City] or Taboga.... In Panama the *hombres* are refusing to work by the day at any price, and it is now difficult to procure them unless by the hour; so that when they feel at all lazy they can stop working."[54]

Between one thousand and sixteen hundred men had been employed on the railroad prior to the start of Story's contract. By the end of 1852, however, the number working for the contractor had declined to between eight hundred and a thousand, far below what the project required.[55] Totten estimated that Story needed to have a labor force of six thousand at his disposal if he wanted to keep to his timetable and cope with an illness and incapacity rate of one-third of the total workforce at any one time. "It does not appear to me that Mr. Story has an adequate idea of the amount of work before him. He should have a force of 4,000 daily laborers [underlined] which will require a force of 6,000 men on the work, and recruits by every steamer to keep up the supply."[56]

Story's failure to maintain an adequate level of recruitment led Totten to complain in February 1853: "I am greatly disappointed in the progress which has been made as well as in the prospects for the future." Only forty to fifty workers were disembarking from the New York weekly steamers, a number barely sufficient to counterbalance the leakage in the labor force occasioned by the departure of men who had completed their contracts, as well as by those no longer available for work because of sickness, repatriation, or death.[57] Totten later concluded that the contractor's labor force did not exceed nine hundred employees on average.[58] Allowing for a one-third sickness rate, this meant that the number of men available for work at any one time was about six hundred, far too few to ensure the rapid advance of the rails.

Despite a chronic undersupply of workers, a series of press statements throughout the latter half of 1852 gave the misleading impression that the line was progressing rapidly and would reach Panama City the following year. The *Times* and other papers reported that construction would be finished ahead of schedule. "It was confidently asserted by the chief engineer of the Panama

Figure 4.2. Men on Hand Car Powered by Two Panamanian Workers Crossing the Isthmus of Panama, 1859. Shutterstock Stock Illustration.

Railway that on the 1st of March 1853, the line will be opened to the Pacific."[59] Some months later, a New Orleans paper announced that construction was moving ahead rapidly and that Panama City would be reached by May 1853.[60] Large-scale labor reinforcements were expected to arrive on British and

American steamers. "The intention is to have eight thousand laborers on the ground by spring."[61]

These optimistic announcements were presumably designed to reassure shareholders and potential investors. A visiting journalist was greatly impressed: "The immense difficulties and apparent impossibilities that have by ingenuity and perseverance been overcome surpass all that I have ever seen in any part of the world." Totten was singled out for his perseverance, courage and exertions, but no mention was made of the men who had spent months wading through the swamps and hacking through the jungle to carry out this grueling and exhausting work.[62]

Despite favorable press publicity, some of the earlier optimism started to evaporate by late October 1852. Rumors circulated that Story would be unable to complete his contract by the agreed date of August 1853 and might require an extension of three months or longer. Nevertheless, the contractor or the company, or possibly both, ensured that positive reports continued to appear in the press. According to a New York paper, Story expected to have seven thousand laborers at work within three months. "The most knowing ones seem to have sanguine expectations that the contractors will not be compelled to ask more than three months extension beyond their present contract, to finish in August, 1853."

A week later, however, the paper contradicted its earlier report, declaring that the work would be finished within the specified period. "The railroad was rapidly progressing towards completion. It is estimated that it will be entirely finished in eight months." The claim that "some two thousand hands are pushing the remainder of the road to a speedy completion" grossly exaggerated the actual number of men employed at that time.[63] The *New York Weekly Herald* predicted at Christmas that there was every prospect of the railroad being finished in 1853. "Workmen are to be put on it as thick as ever they can be, and the company intend [sic] to spare no expense or energy to complete the road next year."[64] Possibly as a result of these optimistic predictions, the company's share price remained high throughout the second half of 1852.[65]

Not only did Story fail to recruit sufficient men, he also had difficulty in retaining those he had hired. Men deserted because of harsh working and living conditions, and ill-treatment—in part because of the budgetary constraints imposed by the contractor's unrealistic tender bid. "A large number of Mr. Story's men have deserted—both white men and natives. The number of laborers now on that work is very small . . . the [dry] season has now arrived when that line should be covered with laborers. Not less than 6,000 men should be upon it in the month of January, when there will not be 1,000."[66]

Housing for Story's workers was often poorly constructed and maintained, and some buildings became uninhabitable during the long wet season. Force was allegedly used to discipline local workers but does not appear to have been applied generally to white employees. The *Panama Star* criticized Story's handling of his men and defended the right of Cartagena laborers to decent and humane treatment.

> As to the present contractors of the railroad, we have more than once said . . . that they mismanage their business most terribly . . . in some cases, we are told on high authority, the lash has been applied by the overseers. . . . The natives of Cartagena . . . are *free men* [italics], even if they are not exactly white in color. They have not been accustomed to be driven with a whip; nor to be kicked and hauled and cursed about from pillar to post . . . complaints [are] brought against the contractors, not only by natives, but by foreign workmen, some of which latter have come to this city and . . . have claimed the protection of their consul![67]

The *New York Herald*, however, claimed that Story handsomely reimbursed his white workers, paying them more than they would receive at home. "I am informed the contractor pays the men employed on the road with a liberality proportionate to the profits it will yield when completed."[68] The paper's portrayal of the contractor was not one that would have been readily recognized by those of his former employees, who subsequently filed through New York's courts seeking redress for breach of their employment contracts.

Some instances of Story's heartless treatment of his workers made their way into the local press. The *Panama Star* recounted that an Irish employee needing medical attention dragged himself as far as the capital, where he spent the night lying in the street in a helpless condition. California-bound migrants raised a small subscription to pay porters to carry him to the Foreign Hospital. Unfortunately, medical assistance came too late. "The poor fellow survived but a few hours arrival. He was buried yesterday afternoon."[69] The *Panama Star* reported that on previous occasions sick laborers had made their way across the Isthmus to the capital's Foreign Hospital, suggesting that the medical attention provided under Story's aegis was deficient or inadequate.[70]

Estrella de Panama, the *Star*'s Spanish-language supplement, complained about the contractor's practice of withholding a portion of the men's wages.[71]

In this regard, however, Story merely followed a precedent set by the railroad company. The *Panama Herald*, on the other hand, supported the practice of withholding a portion of the workers' wages to ensure that employees complied with the terms of their contracts.[72] The *Panama Weekly Star* contrasted the railroad company's employment practices with those of the contractor. "They [railroad supervisors] had suitable accommodations and food for their employees, and always maintained an efficient and capable medical corps—so that the great mass of their laborers were [*sic*] always satisfied with their employment and treatment."[73] The same newspaper had previously drawn attention to substandard working conditions under Story: "There has been notoriously, so much carelessness, recklessness of human life and comfort, stupidity and ignorance displayed in pushing forward the work . . . as warrants the strongest kind of condemnation."[74]

The *Panama Weekly Star* reprinted an article highly critical of the contractor taken from the *New York National Democrat*. According to the article, passengers arriving from Panama

> complain very bitterly of the management of this road, and the treatment of the laborers engaged upon it. . . . Laborers are . . . worked hard, have but scanty provision, and when they become sick, which happens with most of them in a short time, they are called, paid by the clerk just what *he* pleases, and packed off. If they can manage to get to the [river] landing and secure a place in the hospital, or crawl on board a steamer, they are deemed lucky. . . . Others who were wasting away with fever, were compelled to lie out-doors, or beneath old sheds, and without a particle of food for twenty-four hours . . . *home* was out of the question. A few weeks, or even days, perhaps would find them needing nothing more in this world.
>
> If these things be so . . . it is a thousand times worse than Cuban slavery. It can scarcely be believed that such horrid inhumanity can exist among a civilized people, and more particularly among those who are citizens of the United States . . . so few of the men ever live to get back again, that there is small chance of disclosure being made.[75]

An epidemic of cholera on the Isthmus during the second half of 1852, in addition to the ever-present threat posed by miasmatic fevers, or malaria, hindered Story's attempts to recruit men from the United States. The baneful effects of the epidemic on those he managed to hire also militated his being able to complete the contract on time. The local English-language press published scant details of the cholera outbreak and its effects on the population. The capital's physicians and its principal merchants were equally reticent and reluctantly admitted months later that there had been sporadic cases of the disease, though they denied that there was an epidemic.[76]

The outbreak, which began on the Caribbean coast in June, lasted for four months. The deaths of passengers on a ship from Aspinwall bound for New Orleans indicated the beginnings of the disease.[77] Cholera spread swiftly from Panama's Caribbean coast along the route of the railroad until it reached the capital. The inhabitants of the river port of Cruces were panic-stricken, according to an English engineer who visited it on June 24, 1852.[78] A New York newspaper reported that "the advices from the Isthmus are sad. The cholera had broken out at various points, and carried off quite a number."[79]

A letter from Chagres, dated July 2, reported that six deaths from cholera had occurred in Cruces and thirty at Miller's Station (Ahorca Lagarto) on the railroad. The disease carried away fifteen victims at the Navy Bay terminus in one day. Passengers on the steamer El Dorado, which lost fourteen passengers and crew to cholera en route to New Orleans, reported that there was much sickness on the Isthmus and that nonacclimatized persons were dying daily. On July 17, 1852, The Nation reported that passengers on ships plying between Panama City and San Francisco were dying of dysentery and ship fever, but cholera was likely to have been the real cause. The situation had not improved by early August. "The accounts from Navy Bay . . . are of a most distressing nature. Cholera, fever and ague, etc., were raging to a fearful extent, but more particularly in the interior. Numerous deaths are announced."[80] The British consul confirmed that there had been many fatalities in the capital and along the transit route from Navy Bay and Chagres to the city.[81]

The disease inevitably infected the railroad workers, whether they were employed by the contractor or by the company. According to one report, "There was not a white man at work on the whole line."[82] Center, the company's vice president, acknowledged later that there had been "a severe visitation of the cholera."[83] Totten reported that local laborers, fearful of catching the disease, were ready to abandon work at one station. Armed with machetes and knives, they confronted him and demanded their arrears. Totten refused to be intimidated, informing them that their back pay would be handed over only at the end of their contract. After a stoppage of one day, the men capitulated and went back to work. Totten admitted that "if they had been paid up, there is no doubt but that the majority of them would have left the work."[84] He was unperturbed by the risk that these men might contract cholera. Two weeks later Totten again reported on the effects of the outbreak. "A large number of the natives left the work on the appearance of the cholera on the Isthmus, and returned to Cartagena.... The force which was at Monkey Hill with the gravel train, vanished almost entirely."[85]

The cholera outbreak led Totten to make a macabre reference to deaths among his employees. Coffins supplied by local undertakers proved too small to accommodate the longer American and European corpses. This necessitated the removal of one end of the casket to allow the deceased's feet to protrude, a spectacle that upset the chief engineer and presumably his employees also. Writing in mid-July, Totten ordered a consignment of coffins in a variety of sizes. "In our present straights [sic] I have thought that a lot of readymade coffins—assorted sizes—would be advisable . . . another undertaker would find constant employment. Let it be understood, however, that the feet shall not stick out. [underlined] It's a doleful subject to write about, but one that must be looked to in these pestilential swamps. The dirt train has frequent return loads of late, which makes death palpable to our feelings—blunted as they are by its frequent occurrence."[86]

The train referred to carried earth, gravel, and rocks from the excavations at Monkey Hill and elsewhere to the low-lying Manzanillo Island and other marshy areas where infilling was required. All too often this train returned to Monkey Hill, later renamed Mount Hope Cemetery, with the bodies of dead workers for burial. This cemetery was later described as "one of the saddest graveyards in the world, acres of little white crosses falling over and rotting under the jungle of tropical growth."[87]

At the start of August, Totten claimed that the cholera outbreak had not been particularly devastating along most of the railroad route. The exception was Aspinwall, where "there have been numerous deaths, sometimes three or four daily.... Scarcely a day passes, however, without one or two deaths."[88] The *New York Herald* reported on August 15, that sixty of the men employed on the railroad had died from cholera within recent weeks. One historian has asserted that nearly all of the railroad's technical and professional staff, fifty-one engineers, surveyors, and draftsmen, perished from the disease.[89] This claim was repeated by Parker, who asserts that the worst year for deaths in the railway's history "was 1852, when a cholera epidemic killed unnumbered workers and all but two of the fifty American technicians then on site."[90] This allegation may have originated with a company surgeon's report that the epidemic had killed fifty white laborers and twenty-five native workers at Tabernilla. According to this account, work stopped there for one day during the outbreak, the only place where there was a complete standstill.[91]

Some members of a group of 160 workers who had completed their six-month term of engagement were unfortunate enough to contract the disease just before returning to the United States. Their sickness was blamed on an excessive consumption of *aguardiante*, the local rum. This proved to be another example of the Victorian tendency to link disease with moral culpability.[92] The annual report of the Foreign Hospital in Panama City revealed that while the scale of the outbreak in the capital had not been alarming, the victims' survival rate was poor: seventeen cholera patients had been admitted; fifteen had died.[93]

The fate of eight companies of the Fourth Regiment of U.S. Infantry, who had the misfortune of finding themselves in Panama at this time, may provide another indicator of the virulence of the outbreak. A detachment of about seven hundred officers, men, and family members had been ordered to cross the Isthmus on their way to California and Oregon. Captain Ulysses S. Grant was the regimental quartermaster.[94] What happened to these men and their dependents became a subject of controversy. The British consul and the *Panama Herald* alleged that the troops and their families had been abandoned by their officers. The army subsequently denied these allegations.[95] The cholera outbreak cost the lives of about one hundred men, women, and children of this regiment, about one-seventh of those who had left New York Harbor on July 5.[96] The impact of this cholera outbreak on railroad men may have been of a similar order of magnitude.

The cholera epidemic eventually burned itself out, leading the *New York Times* to report at the end of October: "The health of the Isthmus is good—very few cases of fever, and no cholera. . . . The Isthmus is quite healthy—no epidemic prevailing."[97] This outbreak undoubtedly played a part in sabotaging Story's prospects of completing his contract on time. However, as mentioned above, other factors, including an underpriced tender bid and the contractor's consequent inability or unwillingness to recruit and retain an adequate workforce, also played a part in holding up the railroad's progress.

FIVE

Hopes Dashed

EARLY IN 1853, THE RAILROAD'S WORKFORCE FACED ANOTHER LIFE-threatening crisis when yellow fever, the disease most dreaded by white inhabitants of the tropics, struck the Isthmus. "Yellow jack," whose characteristic symptom was "black vomit," was not endemic to Panama, but epidemics of this deadly illness periodically swept across the Isthmus causing panic whenever they appeared. "This illness held a particular fascination and horror for Europeans and North Americans. . . . It is an almost uniquely distressing, disgusting and terrifying disease. There is still no cure . . . a strong adult would have only about an even chance of surviving an attack. . . . If you do survive, you are then subsequently immune."[1] Confronted by this dreaded disease, the medical fraternity was helpless and could offer no remedy apart from keeping the unfortunate victim as comfortable as possible and hoping for the best.

On this occasion, yellow fever was reportedly introduced into Panama by passengers on a steamer that had touched at the Danish West Indian island of St. Thomas in December 1852. Most of the passengers died on board or shortly after reaching the Isthmus. According to Frank Marryat, an English visitor, the outbreak spread over the Isthmus with great rapidity. "The people being panic-struck, a great rush was made for the Californian boats, of which there happened, at this time, to be very few."[2] Travelers arriving from New York contracted the disease. About thirty of these succumbed, most of them in a former military barracks in the capital, which had been converted into an emergency fever hospital by the province's governor.[3] An American physician recounted that "a considerable number of cases made their appearance in the city of Panama, and of a very malignant and fatal character."[4] The British consul reported the deaths of several British subjects, and a number of the inhabitants of the Isthmus also perished.[5]

Yellow fever spread to passengers on ships leaving the capital for California with a high death toll in early 1853.[6] Marryat claimed, possibly with exaggeration, that his ship lost fifty of its passengers while en route to San Francisco. He recounted hearing "the splash of the bodies as they were tossed overboard with very little ceremony."[7] Press reports either gave no cause of death or suggested that the fatalities were due to dysentery and fever. The real cause was almost certainly yellow fever. Totten reported from the capital in January that yellow fever was "quite prevalent in this city, although it is kept very quiet." A lady in his party had reached the point of death from the disease.[8] The *Panama Herald* discreetly referred to "the appearance in our city of one of those malignant diseases to which all tropical climates are liable," though it did not name the malady. A public subscription to tackle the outbreak had been opened, and the paper published a list of contributors.[9]

The Vanderbilt line disseminated news of the outbreak quickly. Advertisements for its Nicaragua steamers in February 1853 boldly declared that there was "no Cholera or Yellow Fever by this route," adding that travel via Panama was notoriously unhealthy. A purser on the Vanderbilt steamer *Sierra Nevada* provided a frightening account of the epidemic to a California newspaper—though the paper's editor added a rider that these claims were "somewhat fanciful." According to the purser, "Panama and vicinity have been the scene of the greatest devastation from the ravages of the yellow fever—black vomit of the most malignant type. Whole ships crews were dying from it.... The residents of the city meet each other with suspicious inquiring looks, and the nights are spent in small silent processions of friends hurrying to the tomb with the remains of those that but a few hours since had been with them in the vigor of life."[10]

Aspinwall's Pacific Mail Steamship Company retaliated by drawing attention to letters that had appeared in the San Francisco press from disgruntled travelers on the Nicaragua route.

The railroad's documentation does not disclose the proportion of the workforce affected by the epidemic, but the scant evidence available would suggest that its impact was not as deadly as the cholera epidemic the previous year. While Totten announced at the end of January 1853 that "about one half of our present force is constantly on the sick list," most of his men presumably suffered from the usual variety of illnesses prevalent on the Isthmus. He added that yellow fever was abating and there was no fear of it becoming a prolonged epidemic.[11] According to the local press, the outbreak was of relatively short duration, with the *Panama Herald* optimistically reporting in February, "It is with pleasure we are enabled to announce that sickness has been on the decline in our city during the last four days; and there is every hope that the temporary [fever] hospital will soon cease to be required." A week later the paper again repeated that the outbreak was coming to an end. However, the British consul continued to report the deaths of British subjects from yellow fever up to July.[12]

The virulence of the outbreak can be discerned from the fact that out of twenty-two cases admitted to the capital's Foreign Hospital, nineteen proved fatal.[13] Accounts of this and previous disease outbreaks in the North American press reinforced Panama's reputation as an unhealthy destination and added to Story's difficulties in recruiting fresh workers. A report in a Virginia newspaper exemplified this negative publicity. "The great mortality among the laborers during the past year, has greatly retarded the work, and renders it difficult to procure men even at high prices."[14]

As early as December 1852, Totten had begun expressing his dissatisfaction with Story's progress.[15] In the six months following the commencement of the contract, the railroad had been extended by only three miles.[16] The bridge over the Chagres was also still not in operation, its completion being delayed by the rains of the wet season. Trains from Aspinwall continued to terminate at Barbacoas. The journey to that riverside hamlet across swamps and through dense jungle in December 1852—in open cars and on tracks laid on shaky trestle bridges for much of the way—made some travelers apprehensive.[17]

Story's lack of progress caused disquiet at a meeting of the executive and finance committee in December 1852. The members feared that unless the pace of construction improved, they might have to consider an alternative strategy for completing the railroad. In February 1853 the board of directors was informed that Story was behind schedule and alarm bells began to sound at the railroad's New York offices.[18] The company secretary reported, "It is of course evident that that part of our contract with Mr. Story providing for the road being ready for the engine to run to Gorgona by the 1st February will not be complied with."[19] Gorgona was only six miles beyond Barbacoas.[20] The railroad agreed to pay the contractor $73,600 for work done in January even though he had failed to keep to the timetable specified in his contract.[21]

Several more months passed without any discernible improvement in the contractor's rate of progress, and by April the company began to lose patience. When Story failed to attend a meeting of the executive and finance committee, its members instructed George Law, who had stood surety for Story's compliance with the contract, to impress on him the urgent need to finish the bridge over the Chagres and to extend the railroad to the Obispo station, which lay some miles beyond Gorgona.[22] Totten's criticisms now became sharper. "The bridge progresses slowly. . . . An unusual degree of sickness among the masons has retarded the work."[23] A local newspaper confirmed the effects of illness on the pace of construction. "Owing to sickness among the laborers the work is considerably retarded at present."[24] Moreover, only one-third of the preparatory work on the next stage of the line, from Barbacoas to Gorgona, on the far bank of the Chagres, had been carried out. Totten announced, "I am greatly disappointed in the progress which has been made as well as in the prospects for the future." He estimated that with the number of men currently at work, Gorgona could not be reached before July, and the railroad would not be completed before 1855.[25]

The early months of 1853 saw Story belatedly attempting to recruit large numbers of additional workers, and for the first time, he advertised for men in the American press followed by Panamanian newspapers. Until then, Story, like the railroad company, had relied on the services of labor contractors for the supply of unskilled and semiskilled men. Advertisements seeking three thousand laborers appeared in the *Boston Herald* in late January and early February.[26] Failure to secure a sufficient response led to a series of similar notices appearing in the *New York Herald* between March and June.[27] These appeared to be the only advertisements seeking a large number of laborers on the Panama railroad to run in the American press during the entire construction period.

On March 8, the *New York Herald* carried the following notice:

> 3,000 Laborers Wanted—Laboring men who wish to go to the Isthmus of Panama, to work on the Panama Railroad, can find employment by applying at the office of the undersigned . . . where written contracts will be made with such men as are employed. One dollar per day and found will be paid to men who understand railroad work. Good bridge carpenters and stone masons will be paid two dollars and a half per day and found. M. C. Story, contractor. Office, No. 92 Warren Street. P.S. Steamers sail from New York to the work, on the 5th, 12th, 20th and 27th of each month.

A subsequent advertisement offered slightly increased wages, probably in reaction to a lack of response to previous appeals. This advertisement also announced, "Board and lodging free. Passage free to the work."[28] A further variant of this advertisement appeared at the end of May, when the daily rate of pay for laborers increased again, probably an indication of Story's desperation to recruit more workers. "To good laboring men who understand railroad work $1.25 per day and board and lodging will be paid. Passage free."[29] These advertisements failed to attract the thousands of recruits required. Only a small number of white laborers signed up in April, as Totten noted in a letter to the company president.[30] By the time that Story withdrew from Panama in September, he had less than a hundred white men in his employment.[31] A Kentucky newspaper summed up the situation: "Laborers for the Panama Railroad are difficult to procure, and the work necessarily makes slow progress."[32]

In June 1853, Story, having failed to secure sufficient recruits in the United States, placed advertisements in an English-language Panamanian newspaper. These notices were aimed at a small, mainly white, expatriate community, as most local laboring men were unlikely to read English—apart from Jamaicans, whose presence in the capital, though growing, was still relatively small. Similar advertisements appeared in later issues of the paper.[33] "Wanted immediately for the Panama Railroad, Panama Station. A number of laborers for the purpose of clearing the track. Apply at the station on Monday and through the week. John Hume, agent, Panama, June 12, 1853." The number of laborers available for work in Panama City at this time was too small to make any appreciable difference to the size of the contractor's labor force.

Many of the men in Story's white workforce were Irish immigrant laborers living in the United States.[34] Nevertheless, most of the generally accepted accounts relating to the Irishmen recruited by Story should be considered erroneous. Schott, for example, claimed that the contractor chartered a vessel to bring workers from Cork in 1852 and that they arrived during the cholera epidemic that swept over the Isthmus that year. "An entire shipload of Irish laborers from Cork, arriving a few weeks before had caught the disease within a week and most of them had died." Schott implied that a second boatload of laborers from Cork arrived at the start of 1853 and that they worked on building the Barbacoas Bridge. "Poorly housed and looked after, they suffered many casualties to fever and heat stroke."[35]

Schott may have derived this information from an inaccurate report by Minter. "Story imported a shipload of Irishmen from County Cork, and soon had the bridge almost complete."[36] Minter, in turn, probably relied on Tomes's 1855 account: "From Ireland came crowds of her laborious peasantry.... Ships arrived from Cork crowded with Irish emigrants."[37] Tomes confounded a single shipload of laborers that arrived from Cork early in 1854 with other contingents of Irish workers hired by Story, who came to Panama, not from Ireland, but from their new homes in the United States. The fact only one vessel left

Cork with workers for Panama, arriving at the start of 1854—six weeks after the Barbacoas Bridge had been completed and eighteen months after the cholera epidemic—calls into question the assertions of Tomes, Minter, and Schott.[38]

Like Story, Totten was also short of men, but unlike the contractor, he was more successful in remedying this deficiency. The chief engineer continued recruiting relatively small numbers of mostly skilled employees during Story's period as contractor. Early in 1853 Totten requested thirty to forty quarrymen and twenty masons. They probably worked on strengthening embankments and bridges and carrying out improvements on previously constructed sections of track. He urged the railroad to offer increased wages to "induce the best men to come."[39]

In February Totten complained that he was still short of workers and asked for thirty to forty laborers to be sent as soon as possible. Two months later the engineer urgently requested five foremen to oversee quarrymen and masons and to supervise the engine shop. "We must have them at any price."[40] Totten again pressed for additional workers in May. "Our force of white laborers and trackmen is fast diminishing; please provide us with a force against this wet season." At the start of August, the chief engineer asked for tracklayers and laborers, as well as masons and quarrymen. He advised New York that more of the latter would be required as soon as the dry season began at the end of the year.[41]

The railroad regularly dispatched small contingents of mostly skilled workers to the Isthmus during the first half of 1853 in response to the chief engineer's requests.[42] To recruit these men, the company occasionally advertised in the New York press for skilled workers (mechanics) for the Isthmus. Advertisements appeared in both the *New York Herald* and the *New York Tribune* in January 1853. Both sought fifteen to twenty experienced quarrymen. In February, the company advertised for two machine blacksmiths.[43] The railroad also sought twenty to thirty able-bodied bridge builders and ships carpenters in May. Applicants were asked to report to the company's office at 78 Broadway. "Liberal wages will be given to such as bring good recommendations."[44]

Throughout the course of construction, the chief engineer had to contend with workers leaving his employment. In most cases, illness, the completion of contracts, or desertion were the reasons. During the latter part of 1852 and much of 1853, however, Totten had to deal with attempts by Story to poach his men. An early example occurred not long after the contractor had started work. Totten lost William L. Miller, one of his best foremen, when the latter accepted

Figure 5.1. Gatún Station, Nineteenth Century. F. N. Otis, *Illustrated History of the Panama Railroad* (London: Sampson Low, 1862). Courtesy of the British Library Board.

the position of Story's project manager in Panama. Despite this move, Totten and Miller remained on good terms.

Relations between the company and Story worsened in 1853, probably because the contractor, having failed in his attempts to hire sufficient men in the United States, switched his recruitment efforts to the company's existing workforce on the Isthmus. Totten remonstrated that Story's agents in Panama stole some of his best men by offering them higher salaries, doubling the company's rate of pay in at least one instance.[45] Miller, in an apparent breach of confidentiality, informed Totten, his former boss, that Story had given him "*instructions* [underlined in original] to hire any of our officers or men that he finds efficient or that may be useful to the contractor." Totten commented that this policy would undermine the good relations that ought to exist between the company and Story.[46]

In addition to difficulties in recruiting and retaining workers, Totten also had to deal with the deterioration of the centuries-old trail that connected Cruces, at the navigable limits of the Chagres River, with Panama City. By mid-1852, travelers could reach Barbacoas from Aspinwall by train in a few hours. From there they transferred to canoes and small rivercraft, and after being rowed or poled upriver for four hours, they reached Cruces, an unattractive riverside village.[47] Then the most exhausting part of the journey began. Travelers either hired a mule or walked over the deteriorated trail to the capital.

The trail's surface had been worn away by tens of thousands of migrants heading to or coming from the Pacific territories of the United States. Freight agencies using packtrains of mules also relied on this route to transport goods and merchandise of all kinds, as well as mail and gold shipments. Lacking maintenance and repairs, the condition of the path got steadily worse. "Not a train of mules—treasure, mails, or any other—goes over it without a large number of them breaking down. The wonder is, that they make the trips as well as they do."[48] The journey from Cruces to Panama City took at least eight hours, usually more in the wet season, and made an unforgettable impression on those who undertook it.

Totten, aware that the trail would continue to be essential until the railroad bypassed Cruces, proposed in April 1853 that the worst stretches be replaced by a plank road—the cost of which would amount to $40,000 to $50,000. He suggested that if the two major American shipping lines serving the Isthmus joined with the railroad company and the provincial government in sharing the cost, all would benefit. Totten again raised the issue in July after a lack of action. "The Cruces road is horribly bad."[49] Eventually, in August, possibly using his own discretionary authority, Totten contracted Ran Runnells, an American cargo agent based in Panama City, to carry out temporary repairs to the trail at a cost of $10,500.[50] His initiative spurred the U.S. Mail and the Pacific Mail Steamship Companies to collaborate with the railroad and provide up to $60,000 between them for this purpose.[51] New Granada's national and provincial governments subsequently pledged to contribute $15,000 and $10,000 respectively toward the costs of improving the Cruces trail.[52] The extension of the railroad made this trail largely obsolete within a few years.

On the morning of April 7, 1853, the level of the Chagres River rose dramatically as a result of heavy rains that marked the start of the wet season.[53] The river, although shallow for much of the year, could increase in height by thirty to forty feet or more in a single night during the rainy season when torrents of water would sweep down from the hills and mountains of the central Isthmus.[54] On this occasion a powerful surge of water swept away part of the almost-finished main span of the bridge, destroying any possibility that Story could complete his contract on time. "This will be a sad drawback to the completion of the work" was the verdict of a local paper.[55] The completion of the bridge, already well behind schedule, was now further delayed. In the immediate aftermath of this disaster, a dispute arose over who was responsible for the reconstruction costs, the railroad or the contractor. Rather than waste time arguing over liability, Totten instructed Miller to begin repairs, the cost to be borne initially by the railroad, "leaving the question of ultimate responsibility to be settled hereafter." Totten emphasized the urgency of rebuilding. "It is expected that this work will be pushed on with the utmost vigor, so that the bridge may be made passable in the shortest time possible."[56]

Story, however, lacked sufficient skilled men to repair and finish the bridge, just as he lacked workers in general. Totten reported in mid-May that Story's "carpenter force has dwindled to a very small number." The chief engineer announced that he would need thirty or forty good bridge builders or ships' carpenters should the company decide to assume responsibility for rebuilding the structure.[57] The directors, however, left reconstruction in Story's hands, but the latter failed to make much headway. "Mr Story's force of carpenters is too small to make the progress he ought to make in the Chagres River Bridge, as well as in other parts of his work. . . . One hundred carpenters are required for that work at the present time. Yesterday only five [underlined in original] were at work on the bridge." The following month Totten again complained. "It is important that Mr Story provides a large force of carpenters for the erection of the bridge."[58] Totten's criticism had little effect. By mid-July only thirteen or fourteen of the thirty carpenters assigned to the Chagres Bridge were actually at work. The situation deteriorated further the following month when Totten commented on the absurdly small force of workers that had been allocated to the bridge: five carpenters and five nailers.[59]

Following the disastrous collapse at Barbacoas, the chief engineer was instructed to inspect other bridges erected by Story. He found these to be little more than temporary structures, unsafe and in need of reinforcing to render them secure. "As now framed, I would not risk my own life over them, with a loaded train; I cannot, therefore, jeopardize the lives of others, and the property of the company by acceding to their adoption."[60] A Swiss engineer who had worked on the railroad was also apprehensive about the stability of these structures. "I feel frightened in contemplating these bridges, spun, like cobwebs, from one precipice to another, and resting on moving, rickety ground.

It is true the trains go [over them] very slowly at times, at the rate of hardly twelve miles."[61]

Totten returned to the standard of bridge construction in June. "Mr Story's bridges could have been made right as cheaply as they are made wrong."[62] Partly as a result of Totten's criticisms, the directors recommended that wooden bridges be replaced by iron structures, but this measure took several years to implement. In November 1855, one of these wooden bridges collapsed as a locomotive crossed it. Fortunately, no cars had been attached to the engine and no serious injuries were reported.[63]

The contractor's labor force, already deficient in numbers, continued to decline. In April 1853, the total number of men at Story's disposal, including those who were sick, was 1,085, leaving him with an operational labor force of only 811. By June, Story's effective labor force had shrunk even farther. "Mr Story's force is reduced to about 500 men, so says Mr Miller, Superintendent."[64] Recruits continued to arrive from New York, but only in small numbers, usually between three and fifteen men per steamer. Most of Story's remaining white laborers were due to leave in July, once their contracts expired, and the number available for work would then fall still farther.[65] The number of workers arriving from Cartagena was also relatively small, ranging from seventy to one hundred per shipment. About three hundred of these men had been brought over by British steamers. Some of them subsequently deserted.[66]

By September 1853, Story's total labor force amounted to only 594 men, and three-quarters of these were local workers from New Granada. According to Totten, some were deserters from the company's service, probably attracted by the higher rate of pay offered by the contractor.[67] Not only was Story's labor force too small, but the contractor had ordered a start to be made at the Pacific end of the line. Work on clearing the terrain at Playa Prieta, the railroad's Pacific terminus on the outskirts of the capital, began on June 20.[68] Totten had previously argued that Story should concentrate on finishing those sections of the line where construction was already underway, instead of dissipating his meagre forces still further.[69]

At the end of May, Totten, concerned at Story's failure to recruit sufficient laborers in the United States and New Granada, raised for the first time the possibility of employing Chinese workers. "From five to eight hundred natives [men from New Granada and neighboring countries] I believe to be as many as will ever be employed at one time on that work. White men, I presume, cannot be attained [sic]. Is there any alternative but to engage Chinese, who, I am assured, can be obtained in numbers? The contractor's attention should be turned to this subject in time."[70]

A week later Totten surmised that Story's inability to recruit white workers was due to the poor reputation the contractor had acquired among the American railroad fraternity. "I presume it is pretty well settled that white labor cannot be obtained for the completion of this road. The objection of these laborers appears to be the treatment of the contractor, more than to the company or the climate." The solution, repeated the chief engineer, lay in the recruitment of Chinese indentured laborers who were now available for $140 each.[71] Totten warned that unless large numbers of additional workers, including Chinese, were quickly recruited, "the road will not be completed to Panama [City] in less than two years from this time."[72] Coincidentally, the *Estrella de Panama* also suggested that the Chinese would make ideal laborers as they had acquired a reputation for hard work and modest wages in Cuba and in the Californian goldfields.[73]

By June 1853 Totten, convinced that the contract would not be completed on time, outlined four options for the company. It could prolong the existing agreement, but Totten opposed this. Secondly, the company could draw up a new contract with Story, but in this case, Totten specified that its terms should be precisely defined. Thirdly, the company could enter into an agreement with another contractor. Finally, the railroad could resume construction on its own account.[74] Acceptance of the last option could be regarded as an implicit admission by the chief engineer that his advice in 1852 to hire an outside contractor had been mistaken.

Relations between the railroad and the contractor plunged to a new low at a June meeting of the executive and finance committee. The directors noted "the very deficient and inefficient force now at work on the Isthmus," and Story and Law were warned "that unless they proceed immediately with more energy, and by a greatly increased force on the line of the road, that the company will find it necessary to take the work out of their hands, and assume the completion of it on their own account." To emphasize the gravity of the situation, the committee threatened to seek damages by reason of Story's failure to fulfill his contract.[75]

When Story failed to heed this warning, the game was over. On July 29 the board informed him that his contract would be terminated on August 1 "in consequence of your failure to prosecute and complete the work according to your contract."[76] The news of the termination was hardly earthshaking given that Story's contract was due to expire on that date in any case. As soon as he received confirmation from New York, Totten informed Story's supervisor at Aspinwall that the company would assume responsibility for finishing the railroad beginning August 17.[77] The railroad, disenchanted by its experience with Story, had no interest in transferring responsibility to another contractor. Totten, also, had recovered from his period of self-doubt and disillusionment in late-1852 and appeared eager to take up the reins of command once more.

Story's Panamanian staff ignored this directive, perhaps because of delays in receiving instructions from New York or because Story wanted to delay the handover so that he could negotiate better exit terms for failing to comply with his contract. Story's agents in Panama disregarded Totten's authority during the ensuing weeks, and the latter was powerless to resume charge of operations. The directors responded by instructing Totten to charge Story for the transportation of his personnel and materials on the railroad. Story retaliated by directing his subordinates "not to sell or lend anything whatever to the agents of the company."[78]

Weeks passed. Totten complained that he was unable to put his men to work on those sections of the railroad where Story's workers were deployed. "The state of things between the company and Mr Story is very detrimental to the progress of the work. . . . It is for the interest of both parties that this matter be arranged as promptly as possible." The following day the engineer advised the company secretary that "the Chagres Bridge must be pushed as hard as possible—as well as the small bridges beyond. We are delayed by Story holding on to the work."[79]

One span of the flood-damaged bridge, 201 feet long, had been rebuilt by September, but two further spans had yet to be put in place.[80] Totten, however, could not proceed because Story's superintendent refused to relinquish the timber required for construction. Totten hoped that a steamer from New York would soon "bring us the good news of a settlement with Mr Story."[81] His wish was granted when, late in September, word reached the Isthmus that Story, by the terms of an agreement dated September 5, had transferred all operations and materials under his control to the Panama railroad. On September 24, the chief engineer informed the company's president that construction was back in the hands of the railroad once more and the final phase of the project could begin.[82]

After resuming control of operations, Totten assessed the extent of the work carried out by the contractor up to September 5, 1853, when the latter's

Figure 5.2. View of the Village of Buena Vista on the Panama Railroad, Nineteenth Century. iStock Stock Illustration.

responsibility in Panama legally ceased. Totten also compiled an inventory of the contractor's stores and materials and provided receipts for these to Story's agents. His evaluation was distinctly unfavorable. The tracks had been extended by only three miles during the fifteen months that the contractor had been in charge. A further eight miles of the line on the opposite bank of the Chagres had been graded or prepared for the rails. Work on the damaged bridge over the Chagres River was far from complete.[83]

Four months later the board reached a financial settlement with Story. They agreed "to pay him the sum of $100,000 in full and final settlement of all claims or demands of every nature or kind."[84] A total of $816,347.34 was paid to the contractor between November 13, 1852 and March 20, 1854—a considerable amount for the disappointing results achieved.[85] The strain of his workload, together with the effects of the climate after several years' continual residence in Panama, took a toll on Totten. He announced in September he was planning a trip to New York to recuperate. "My health requires a change. Otherwise I would not leave here this season." Work commitments, however, made it impossible for him to take immediate leave; it was not until the end of the following month that he managed to board a steamer to New York.[86]

Why had the Story-Law consortium failed so abysmally to finish the railroad in the time allotted? Although other factors played a part, the contractor's lack of experience in undertaking railroad construction in a distant tropical zone, with a formidable topography, challenging climate, and disease-ridden environment, was largely to blame. Story underestimated the difficulties and obstacles confronting him. The result: his tender price was too low. In 1849, before work began, the company had estimated that construction would cost between $60,000 and $70,000 per mile, though it would have been aware by the time of the signing of the Story contract that this figure was no longer realistic.[87] Construction costs in Panama were much higher than in the United States because of the climate, the nature of the obstacles confronting the engineers, and the need to import virtually all materials, food and supplies, and much of the manpower over a distance of several thousand miles. This information was presumably not disclosed to Story. The cost per mile of the railroad, by the time the construction account finally closed in January 1859, amounted to just over $160,000.[88] The contractor's calculation that he could make a profit at $75,000 per mile was unrealistic.

Story's efforts to keep within budget led to the hiring of a smaller-than-required workforce, as well as the imposition of substandard working and living conditions for his employees. Resentment engendered by this parsimonious approach made it necessary to impose a harsh disciplinary system on his laborers. The negative publicity generated as a result militated against efforts to recruit sufficient additional personnel to complete the project on time.

Other factors also played a role in the failure to finish the railroad by August 1853. Competition for laborers from the rapidly expanding railroad network in the United States made it difficult to hire sufficient workers prepared to travel to a distant overseas location with a dangerous reputation for illness and disease. The 1852 wet season was unusually heavy and prolonged, adding to the existing impediments. The outbreak of two deadly diseases, cholera and yellow fever, in 1852 and 1853 reduced the size of the workforce and debilitated its survivors. News of these epidemics would have made the recruitment of additional employees more problematic. Story's final stroke of bad luck was the destruction of the partially erected Chagres Bridge by flooding.

The termination of Story's contract, for which George Law had acted as surety, inevitably affected the latter's relationship with the railroad. An early intimation of this was a dispute in June 1853 over property leased by Law on Manzanillo Island. Totten accused Law's agent in Aspinwall of encroaching on the railroad's property by erecting water tanks on company land. The antipathy between Law and the railroad became more evident when Law's agent refused to continue supporting the public hospital at Aspinwall, thereby threatening its existence. According to Totten, "This institution has so far been of great utility and is now destitute of funds. The payment of Mr Law's subscription, or the portion of it now due, would relieve us until other funds fall due, and the punctual payment on his part thereafter, with the other subscriptions, will carry us through the year."[89] The outcome of these disagreements was not reported.

Story's failure to comply with his contract had more significant repercussions the following year when George Law, his sleeping partner in this venture, ceased to be a member of the railroad's board. "His [Law's] failure to perform his contract to the company, which he took, to build the road by the first of August last, has led to his retirement from the direction."[90] The disappointing result of his involvement with the Panama railroad led Law to abandon any plans he might previously have harbored to establish a dominant position in the cutthroat transport business between America's east and west coasts. He sold all his shares in the railroad during the winter of 1853.[91] He also disposed of his interest in the U.S. Mail Steamship Company on March 18, 1854, and resigned from its board on April 4, 1854. At this point he preferred to concentrate on other aspects of his far-ranging business empire.[92] The repercussions of the contractor's failure were also felt at the apex of the railroad's management structure. William Clarke Young, president of the company since the death of Stephens in 1852, lost his position on October 31, 1853, because of his failure to ensure the project's completion and his close identification with the discredited partnership of Law and Story. David Hoadley replaced him as president.[93]

The termination of the contract between Story and the railroad inevitably affected the latter's stock exchange quotation. Panama railroad shares fell from $145 at the start of 1853 to $105 by August. The price continued to slide as shareholders, frightened by uncertainty of what was happening in Panama, became increasingly anxious about repeated postponements of the completion date. By October 1853, the share price had dropped to $88, slightly more than half what the stock had been worth nine months earlier.[94] Despite occasional volatile fluctuations in stock prices, the company maintained its tradition of paying generous dividends throughout the construction period in an attempt to bolster shareholder confidence and maintain credibility in capital markets. In 1852, shareholders received a 10 percent dividend—and in 1853, 8.5 percent.[95]

In retrospect, Totten and the railroad's board had been unduly pessimistic about the rate of progress in 1850 and 1851. While only seven miles of track had been laid by the end of 1851, the pace of construction picked up dramatically during the first half of 1852 once the Aspinwall terminus had become fully operational and tracklaying moved away from the low-lying Caribbean coastal swamps. Ironically, this spurt in construction coincided with negotiations to find an external contractor. By June 1852, when the project was transferred to Story, twenty miles of track were in operation, almost three times the mileage only six months before.

While the rationale for transferring responsibility to an outside contractor appeared to make sense in the closing months of 1851, this was no longer the case by mid-1852. But by then, the die had been cast. The consequences of this decision became apparent the following year. As the railroad's first historian noted, "Valuable time had been lost from the delay occasioned by the non-fulfilment of the late contract."[96] Lewis Middleton, coeditor of the *Panama Star*, believed that the decision to transfer the work to a contractor had been a serious mistake. "Had the company never had anything to do with Mr Storey [*sic*], I candidly believe the cars would be running to Panama before January next [1854]."[97]

SIX

The Final Push

AFTER OVER THREE YEARS OF WORK, THE LIMITED PROGRESS achieved by late 1853—only half the line in operation—threatened the future viability of the railroad. The rival Nicaragua route, financed and championed by Cornelius Vanderbilt, had been given valuable time to gain favor with the traveling public. It had become apparent to the Commodore by 1851 that his canal would cost a great deal more and take much longer to construct than originally envisaged, while his transit business offered immediate profits. This led Vanderbilt to subsequently abandon the canal project altogether.[1] A new Vanderbilt enterprise, the Accessory Transit Company, assumed control of the transportation of travelers and goods between America's east and west coasts via Nicaragua and proved to be financially successful.

By 1851 Vanderbilt's Transit Company had cut travel time dramatically by opening a route from Greytown (San Juan del Norte) on Nicaragua's Caribbean coast to San Juan del Sur on the Pacific side. This enabled travelers to cross the country in as little as three days in favorable circumstances using the company's integrated river, lake, and overland transport system. By providing his own steamship service to Nicaragua's Atlantic and Pacific ports and cutting fares, Vanderbilt offered a fast and economic passage to and from California, emerging as the Panama route's most serious competitor. His shipping line, on occasion, carried passengers between New York and San Francisco in twenty-five days, seven or eight days shorter than the average time via Panama.[2] By 1853, Nicaragua threatened to become the preferred route for travel to and from the U.S. west coast. That year, approximately twenty-seven thousand people crossed Panama in both directions, while about twenty thousand took the Nicaragua route.[3]

Growing competition from the Nicaragua transit aroused concern in the Panamanian press because of the threat it entailed for the local business community. An editorial in the *Panama Herald* in March 1853 criticized the railroad's lack of progress: "For all we can see, we are as far from having the railway completed as we were in the year of grace 1852, when Mr Storey [*sic*] undertook to make it, and Mr Law became his security thereof." The paper warned that unless progress was made quickly, alternative routes across Nicaragua or Mexico would prosper at the expense of Panama. In May, the paper reported, probably tongue-in-cheek, that a well-known resident was offering odds of three-to-one that the vastly longer transcontinental rail link across the United States, still in its incipient phase, would be completed before the Panama line.[4]

The *Weekly Panama Star* also worried about the progress. "Nicaragua . . . in a few months . . . has sprung up from a despicable nonentity to be a monster opposition. An opposition, which, at this moment, is shaking this route to its very foundation."[5] The paper estimated that the two thousand or so travelers crossing Panama each month contributed at least $70,000 to the local economy, excluding their passage money and railroad fare.[6] In November, the *Panama Herald* announced, "It is to be regretted that the Panama Railroad Company have been unable to push on their works towards completion with more vigor and success." Shortly afterward one of its editorials asked, "When will the Panama railroad be completed? If anyone knows, we hope they will inform us."[7]

Slow progress posed a further threat to the project's viability. With only half of the tracks laid after three years, directors worried that construction might not be completed within the six years specified in the company's agreement with New Granada's government.[8] They feared that having to seek an extension from Bogotá would damage the company's credibility in the financial markets and give a publicity boost to its Nicaraguan rival. Probably for these reasons, the company carefully projected an optimistic picture of progress despite the problems and delays it wrestled with.

The *Times-Picayune* reported on February 27 that "the Panama Railroad is progressing very rapidly." After a visit to its office by Totten and his staff, the *Panama Star* announced in March, "From these gentlemen we learn that the work on the railroad from Barbacoas this way [to the capital] is progressing satisfactorily." Some months later, a New York daily reported that "the work on the railroad is prosecuted with energy and rapidity." This was when construction was advancing at a snail's pace under Story. In July, the same newspaper announced that "the road is now in a very prosperous condition," before adding in August that "the Panama Railroad is progressing slowly, but surely. The contractors find a difficulty, I understand, in procuring labor, and that nothing but the want of hands prevents the work from being pushed on with vigor."[9]

Even before Story's contract had been formally abrogated, the company planned to make up for lost time by recruiting thousands of additional laborers to conquer the remaining miles to Panama City by sheer numbers. A local paper commented toward the end of 1853 that "as it is now, the company is making tremendous efforts to push the road through at the earliest possible day."[10] The financial constraints of the earlier phase of construction were loosened in an urgent attempt to get the job finished quickly. This might explain the chief engineer's willingness to resume responsibility for completing the project.

The company, however, now found it more difficult to hire sufficient men in the United States. The poor working conditions that prevailed under Story, as well as the debilitating effects of the climate, had become more widely known in the northern republic. Totten complained that the reports of workers' mortality in circulation were exaggerated. He claimed, without offering evidence, that many railroad projects in America's western states had higher rates of sickness than those prevailing in Panama.[11] Despite its best public relations efforts, the company's image as an employer of American labor had been damaged by the Story interlude, and this forced it to look further afield to maintain an increased supply of workers. The company secretary admitted early in 1853 that he was "finding it almost impossible to procure what men we want here [New York City]". He had accordingly authorized the recruitment of quarrymen, stonemasons, and carpenters farther west.[12] An Irish medical doctor claimed that his fellow countrymen living in the United States could not be induced to work for the railroad, even with the offer of high wages, because they knew of the dangers involved.[13]

While the fate of workmen on the Panama railroad had become widely known in the United States by 1853, the company's management presumed that this was not the case outside North America. This caused the railroad to seek men farther afield. On July 1, the directors discussed importing laborers directly from China and Ireland. They delegated the "power to make such arrangements as they may think advisable to accomplish that object" to the members of the executive and finance committee.[14] This committee then began preparations for the recruitment of Chinese workers. It also approved sending an agent to South America to procure laborers there, once instructions for this had been received from Totten. In any event, Totten never authorized the latter assignment.[15] The company was initially reported to be planning to recruit two thousand men from Ireland, but that number was later reduced to one thousand.[16]

Totten outlined his labor requirements on September 1, 1853, estimating that he would need thirty-eight hundred men by December 1853 or January 1854. Seven hundred of these could be transferred from Story's existing force, while a similar number had been ordered from China. The balance of twenty-four hundred men could be made up by fifteen hundred laborers from the interior provinces of New Granada and five hundred laborers from the Central American state of El Salvador. A labor agent called Gonzales had promised to deliver the El Salvadorian laborers at the end of 1853 or early 1854 at a contract price of twenty-five dollars each, though Totten admitted that he was "somewhat doubtful" these workers could be recruited.

Totten also hoped to hire two hundred men from Panama, as well as two hundred "coolies" from Jamaica. The latter were East Indian migrants whose contracts as indentured laborers on the island had expired. The possibility of recruiting almost four thousand workers from Central and South America, the Caribbean, and China led Totten to query the need for more Irishmen: "Under the prospect of attaining such large forces from this quarter, is it necessary to send to Ireland for more?"[17] The directors apparently felt that they were required and authorized a recruitment campaign in Ireland shortly afterward.

Totten asked to be supplied with timber and tools (shovels, pickaxes, and wheelbarrows) as quickly as possible for the expected arrival of a large number of workers. He also ordered a locomotive and twelve platform cars to be sent on the long voyage around Cape Horn to Panama City so that work could progress on the Pacific side of the line. Finally, he requested provisions for one thousand men for four months. "There is a prospect of increasing our force largely at once. Do not let us get short of anything, neither tools or [sic] provisions."[18] The following month Totten optimistically reported to New York, "The laboring and mechanical forces are increasing rapidly on the line of the road ... the prospects for obtaining a large native force continue favorable."[19]

By November 1853, the number of workers had increased to 1,590, greatly exceeding Story's average complement of 900 men.[20] Additional laborers landed every fortnight by steamer from Cartagena. By the year's end, Totten had 2,110 men under his command: 649 white men, 160 Jamaicans and East Indians, and 1,301 local workers. He expected a further 700 white men, including an Irish

Figure 6.1. View of San Pablo on the Panama Railroad (with Iron Bridge across the Chagres River), Nineteenth Century. iStock Stock Illustration.

contingent from Cork, to arrive in January 1854. He reported that he was short of masons, quarrymen, and bricklayers, as well as food supplies, wheelbarrows, cots, and mattresses. "Please see we are provided for them."21

In addition to seeking new sources of manpower outside its traditional areas of recruitment, the company also vigorously renewed efforts to engage men in the United States. It hoped to forward about 150 laborers and mechanics from the United States every month until the railroad was completed.22 Despite the disease-plagued reputation of the Isthmus and the negative publicity generated by working conditions during the period when the contractor was in charge, the railroad met with considerable success. Press reports showed a continuing flow of laborers, tracklayers, carpenters, machinists, and other craftsmen from New York. Men continued to arrive from Cartagena in British steamers, and black laborers, together with smaller contingents of East Indians, left Jamaica bound for Panama. Nevertheless, the target of 6,790 men, which Totten hoped to have under his control and which would allow him to complete the railroad by August, was not reached by early 1854.23

In October 1853, the first fatal accident involving passengers on the railroad occurred when a train traveling between Aspinwall and Barbacoas collided with a bull on a bridge spanning a stream. The engine, luggage wagons, and two passenger coaches fell into the ravine. "A native boy, and one passenger, an

Irishman, name unknown, were killed" and eight or ten passengers seriously injured. The cost of the accident to the company was estimated at $10,000.[24] Undeterred by this setback, construction continued. By the following month, eight locomotives, twelve first-class carriages, one hundred platform wagons, and one hundred dirt wagons for transporting excavated material were in operation on twenty-three miles of track.

A major turning point was reached when the first locomotive pulling five passenger cars steamed over the Chagres Bridge on November 24 and proceeded up the line for a distance of three miles.[25] A picnic dinner was held on the banks of the Chagres to mark this significant event. "After the ... uncorking of the champagne, a large number of sentiments were proposed and drunk with enthusiasm and warmth of feeling."[26] It had taken almost eighteen months to complete this impressive engineering feat, which totaled 625 feet in length, reportedly the longest wooden bridge in the world at the time.[27] Another formidable obstacle to the railroad's completion had finally been overcome.

In spite of the upheavals and setbacks experienced by the railroad during much of 1853, the year ended on a positive note. Story's ill-fated contract had terminated, and the company, with a more enthusiastic and optimistic Totten in charge, had again assumed responsibility for completing the project. The damaged bridge over the Chagres River had been repaired and completed. Trains from Aspinwall now traveled a few miles beyond Barbacoas. By the end of 1853, transit from ocean to ocean could be accomplished in approximately eight hours by a combination of train and mule.[28] The line of the road had been mapped out as far as the summit of the continental divide, approximately thirty-seven miles from the Atlantic terminus and eleven miles from the capital city. Less than twenty miles of rails now remained to be laid, and eight miles of this stretch had already been cleared of trees and vegetation. Track laying had also commenced at the Panama City end of the line. The railroad carried a total of 32,111 passengers in 1853 over the partially completed line, generating an income of $322,428.13. The company offered bonds to the value of $1,478,000 to finance the final stretch of the railroad.[29]

A traveler from Panama City who had trekked over the unfinished section of the railroad described the temporary terminus then located at Gorgona: "A large open space, covered with tired travelers and worn-out mules; a long train of carriages or cars extending along the single rail, partly filled with passengers; and a long wooden shed, the hotel, into which we are delighted to have the privilege of entering. The gratification we experienced on at last reaching an advanced post of civilization was intense."[30] By late January 1854, the tracks had moved farther on, as far as Obispo, seven miles beyond the bridge and thirty-one miles from Aspinwall. Passengers and freight arriving at Obispo transferred to mules for the final overland stretch to the capital.

Travel by boat on the Chagres River, "the most disagreeable as well as dangerous and expensive part of the route to travelers," had now become a thing of the past.[31] No longer would American ladies be forced to share the confined space of their canoes with the "naked, hungry looking natives," who manned these small craft. This, no doubt, would have come as a relief to one passenger who was outraged by the boatmen's scanty apparel, ignoring the fact they had to labor against the Chagres current in stifling temperatures. "I regard the blushless immodesty of the plebeians as an insult to civilization and an outrage to all decency."[32]

Skeptics began to believe that the rail link across the Isthmus, so long in the making, would actually be completed, thereby providing a much-improved means of communication with California and Oregon, the west coast of South America, as well as Asia and Australia. One major obstacle, the range of hills composing the continental divide, still confronted the engineers, however. To reduce the gradient of the track, the concluding section of the road would have to cut through this ridge, 275 feet above the tidal level of the Pacific. Totten and his colleagues had not fully taken into account that digging through the earth and rock of the summit ridge, with picks, shovels, and wheelbarrows would not be a quick, easy, and straightforward task.

A large labor force was dispatched to the Panama City end of the line, and these men, oblivious of the obstacle that lay ahead, pushed steadily across the plains, swamps, and hills. A local paper enthusiastically reported, "The Panama railroad is progressing more rapidly than ever before—the best employees of the company are outdoing themselves, and surpassing their own promises or expectation."[33] The renewed air of confidence that enveloped the project had beneficial financial repercussions also. The railroad experienced little difficulty in funding its greatly expanded construction program in 1854 despite a crisis in money markets that year.[34]

The company continued to pour workers into Panama throughout 1854 in an all-out effort to complete the project. This, the peak year for employment on the railroad, saw a steady stream of white laborers arriving on every steamer from New York. On January 8, the *Ben Nevis* docked at Aspinwall with 360 Irish laborers from Cork on board, the first and only group of Irishmen to be shipped directly from their native land to Panama. On March 31, the *Sea Witch*, a renowned clipper ship owned by William Aspinwall, the railroad's founder, arrived at Panama City with 705 Chinese laborers on board. A second shipment of 322 men arrived from Swatow, China, in a Spanish vessel, the *Bella Vascongada*, on May 28, bringing the total number of imported Chinese laborers to just over 1,000.[35] These workers were part of the first wave of Chinese migrants to reach Central America and the Caribbean in the mid-nineteenth century.[36]

The number of workers continued to swell as the months passed. Men leaving at the expiration of their contracts were immediately replaced by newcomers. The arrival of hundreds of Jamaicans and workers from New Granada augmented the Chinese force.[37] Between five thousand and seven thousand laborers were pressed into service during the closing months of 1854, the maximum number employed at any one time.[38]

Optimistic forecasts that construction would be completed in 1854 were not realized, and work continued in the final months of the year with thousands of laborers toiling on the slopes of both sides of the continental divide. As in previous years, heavy rains and the illnesses that accompanied the wet season impeded progress. "There had been a good deal of sickness on the Isthmus, but nothing serious."[39] To reduce the gradient of the track where it crossed the continental divide, a cutting, over thirteen hundred feet long and twenty-five feet deep in places, had to be dug manually out of rock and sticky clay that composed the summit ridge. This backbreaking task, requiring the excavation of thousands of cubic feet of earth, was made more difficult by frequent mud and rock slides that were the result of the torrential downpours that were a perennial feature of Panama's wet season. These landslides often undid in hours the work of days and weeks.

Decades later, the French and American canal builders found themselves confronted with the same problem, though on a much larger scale, when trying to dig a channel through the summit ridge for the passage of ships. Repeated landslides caused them endless headaches and delays, despite their use of powerful mechanized excavators and employment of a labor force many times larger than that available to the railroad. The railroad's workers had no mechanical equipment to assist them and had to rely on their own exertions, augmented by the use of mules and horses, to carve a way through the hilltops.[40]

In November, about one thousand men, under their supervisor, Mr. Gillett, finally completed the cut through the summit. It had taken these men two months to excavate the railbed through the rock and soil of the ridge when it

Figure 6.2. Railroad Bridge over the Chagres, 1863. Bedford Pim, *The Gate of the Pacific* (London: Lovell Reeve, 1863). Courtesy of the British Library Board.

was initially believed that two weeks would be sufficient. By the end of that month, a daily train service was in operation from the Caribbean terminus to a station on the top of the continental divide.[41] The pace of construction was now ratcheted up. The single daytime shift was abandoned, and men toiled around the clock in a relentless attempt to complete their assignment. According to a local newspaper, "Nothing is spared on the part of any of the officers or superintendents to push it forward as vigorously as possible."[42]

As a result of this intensified drive, enormous progress was made in the month of December. It was clear that the railroad would be finished very shortly. This led the *Panama Star and Herald* to predict that the completion of the line would be no common event: "It is one of the most important undertakings of the age, destined we believe to produce great results, and fraught with interest and importance to the whole world."[43] As in previous years, the transportation of passengers and freight over the incomplete line generated considerable revenues for the company. A total of 30,108 passengers were carried in the course of 1854, generating gross receipts of $453,572.04.[44]

Finally, at midnight on January 27, 1855, in darkness and driving rain, the final section of the rail link that traversed some of the most difficult and unhealthy terrain in the world was hammered into place. Totten, with characteristic lack of ceremony, drove in the spike that secured the final rail. Unfortunately for posterity, no journalist, writer, artist, or photographer happened to be present to record the momentous occasion.[45] After five years of epic struggle and hardship, the construction of the world's first interoceanic railway had been finished at a high cost in human lives and American dollars. An English newspaper announced that "a continent has been pierced, and two great oceans united."[46] A local paper highlighted the radical changes that the railroad's completion meant for travelers. "Mules and packsaddles are now and forever supplanted by the steam engine, and the mud of the Cruces road is exchanged for a comfortable seat in a railroad car."[47]

Three weeks later, a commemorative breakfast was held in Aspinwall, the first of several celebratory events used to mark the railroad's completion. The company shipped in a party of seventeen dignitaries, journalists, and major shareholders from New York to participate in the celebrations, and a formal dinner was held at 7:30 p.m. on February 17 in Panama City. Among the authorities and notables at this event were the American and Brazilian ambassadors to New Granada, the Bishop of Panama, the province's governor, the U.S. consul, and other dignitaries.[48] "Judging from what we saw, we feel safe in stating that never on this Isthmus did a pleasure party enjoy themselves better. The tables groaned beneath the weight of delicacies. . . . Several toasts were given on this occasion, which we would gladly publish did we remember them."[49]

Newspapers around the world attempted to sum up the significance of the railroad's completion. According to the *New York Times*, "It is the accomplishment of the grandest idea yet conceived by commercial enterprise, the union of the two great oceans. Though the road be scarce fifty miles long, and though there is but one track, yet it is the most wonderful railway in the world, not only because its termini are the Atlantic and Pacific but because of the difficulties met and overcome."[50] The *American Railroad Journal*, which had been lukewarm to the project at the start, now warmly welcomed its realization. "This important work has at last been completed, and the continent is now traversed by railroad from ocean to ocean! The value of such a work to the commerce of the world can hardly be over-estimated. The terrors of a voyage to the Pacific coast of the continent are almost entirely dissipated, and California is now brought to our very doors."[51] The verdict of a French newspaper was equally complimentary. "Nothing but the perseverance and the dauntless tenacity of Americans could surmount the unheard of difficulties which beset such an enterprise . . . one grave obstacle to the relations of humanity has been overcome."[52] A British naval commander was greatly impressed. "I have seen some of the greatest engineering works of the day . . . but I must confess . . . I have never been more struck than with the evidence, apparent on every side, of the wonderful skill, endurance, and perseverance, which must have been exercised in its construction."[53]

The directors awarded a bonus of $5,000 to the chief engineer, acknowledging him as the person mostly responsible for the successful completion of the project.[54] Totten, who had been present on the Isthmus from the inception of the undertaking, except for occasional brief periods of leave in the United States and who was its principal driving force for five years, was characteristically modest about his role. In a letter to one of the directors shortly before the railroad was completed, he explained, "Many exclamations are made at the difficulties overcome, which do not strike me. I am ashamed that so much has been expended in overcoming so little, and take no credit for any engineering science displayed on the work. The difficulties have been of another nature, and do not show themselves on the line."[55] Coping with the climate and the tropical diseases it engendered, as well as difficulties in obtaining and retaining sufficient workers and the logistical problems of transporting materials, equipment, and food from the distant United States, were doubtless among the obstacles Totten referred to.

There was no mention of extra payments or gratuities to the company's laborers, nor do they appear from press reports to have taken part in the celebrations that marked the railroad's official opening. In fact, the completion of the line resulted in many of these workmen being made redundant. The U.S. consul, commenting on the railroad's inauguration, referred to "the number of labors [sic] being suddenly thrown out of employment."[56] The men, whose energy, toil, and persistence had made the railroad possible, were now becoming superfluous, and the crucial role they had played in bringing the project to a successful conclusion was largely ignored or overlooked.

PART II

The Workers

SEVEN

The Men Who Built the Railroad

THOUSANDS OF MEN FROM FOUR CONTINENTS AND FROM AT LEAST a dozen countries carried out the building of the world's first transcontinental railway—probably the largest multinational labor force to be assembled in Central America in the mid-nineteenth century. During the five years that construction lasted, men were obtained from four main sources. There was a continuous supply of laborers from Cartagena and the adjoining regions of New Granada. These men were referred to as "natives" by the company.[1] The United States supplied most of the white workers. This category encompassed Americans and Irish, as well as much smaller numbers of British, French, Germans, Dutch, and Austrians. Most of these European-born employees were immigrants who had settled in the United States. The West Indies, principally Jamaica, was the source of several thousand black laborers. Jamaica was also the recruiting ground for hundreds of Indians and Malaysians, referred to at the time as "coolies."[2] These men, having previously migrated as indentured laborers from their Asian homelands to Jamaica, had completed their contracts there and were now free to accept paid employment on the Panama railroad as waged employees. Finally, China was the source of a sizable minority of railroad workers, who were also referred to at the time as "coolies" in company documentation. Unlike the rest of the men recruited by the railroad, the Chinese were contracted to work as indentured laborers.[3]

Before now, questions relating to the size and composition of the company's workforce have not been adequately answered. Information on this topic published at the time and subsequently was sparse, inconsistent, and often contradictory. The company's records contained scant information on the number of white men employed and were even more deficient on details of the nonwhite workforce. Newspaper reports gave the number of men at work at particular times, or referred to the size of groups of workers arriving at or departing from the Isthmus on specific dates. National origins were often omitted. Other sources, at the time or subsequently, provided varied and sometimes contradictory information on the number of men employed and their ethnicity.

There has never been agreement on the overall size of the labor force. According to a former company official, the total number employed did not exceed 6,000. Cohen claimed that between 6,000 and 7,000 men were contracted from 1850 to 1855. Kemble declared that "the total number of men employed by the railroad during construction is not available but it was not over 15,000."[4] Newton, on the other hand, estimated that an average of 5,000 workers were hired each year, which would amount to 25,000 over the entire construction period. Mack stated that "the maximum number of laborers employed at one time on railroad construction was probably about 7,000."[5] Based on a review of the limited statistical data available and on assumptions that I shall detail below, I have estimated that the total number of workers employed during the construction period was in the region of 17,500. I have also attempted to determine the ethnic composition of this labor force. While these are, to some extent, best-guess estimates, they are preferable to the welter of conflicting figures and untested assumptions relating to the size and makeup of the workforce that have hitherto appeared in the literature on the Panama railroad, often with little or no supporting evidence.

The meager and very uncertain historical evidence that survives makes it difficult to ascertain the ethnicity and national origins of the members of the railroad's workforce with any degree of precision. Company records, as a rule, did not refer to the nationality of men hired during construction. Workers were usually classified in general terms as "whites," "natives," "Negroes," or "coolies." The use of such terms reflected the racist attitudes prevalent in the nineteenth century.[6] However, these four categories were rarely subdivided into national groups, the main exceptions being references to Jamaican "Negroes," Chinese "coolies," and Irish white laborers. Nevertheless, sufficient fragmentary information has survived from which to deduce that the two largest categories of workers were the indigenous inhabitants of New Granada and white laborers, almost exclusively men imported from the United States. Jamaican and Asian workers occupied the third and fourth categories in numerical terms.

Totten and others initially used the term "native" to refer to men hailing from the Cartagena region of New Granada. It was subsequently extended to apply to workers coming from other provinces of New Granada, including Panama,

Estimated Ethnic Composition and Size of the Panama Railroad's Labor Force 1850–1855

Men from New Granada, including the Isthmus of Panama and other Central and South American countries	7,000
White workers, from Ireland, the United States, and some European countries	6,000
West Indians, mainly Jamaicans	3,000
Chinese, Indian, and Malay laborers	1,500
Total	**17,500**

as well as to migrant laborers from neighboring Central and South American states. The term "native" was therefore a broad one, encompassing mestizos and mulattoes, men with skin colors ranging from almost white to black. These men came from a number of countries in the region whose use of Spanish as a mother tongue was often their only common denominator.

Prior to coming to Panama, Totten and Trautwine had formed a favorable impression of the laborers of northern New Granada based on their experience of employing these men on their earlier project at the Canal del Dique. Men from the Cartagena area were a tough, hardy bunch. Many of them were descendants of the slaves of the Spanish colonial period, inured to laboring in tropical heat. Having been born and raised in a region where malaria was endemic and yellow fever a frequent visitor, they were largely immune to the latter and had acquired some resistance to the former.[7] As Cartagena was little more than a twenty-four-hour steamer trip from Panama, the transportation cost of these laborers was lower than that of workers recruited farther afield, increasing their attractiveness as a labor source.

Writing from Cartagena in 1849, Totten stressed "the necessity of using all the native laborers that can be obtained, in preference to foreigners, who I do not think can stand the climate." Four years later, Totten had not changed his opinion of these men, describing them as the most capable laborers in the railroad's employment. "The natives from the province of Carthagena [sic] are as accustomed to the pick, shovel and wheelbarrow, as are Irishmen. For the last nine years this portion of the laboring population of New Granada has been under my employment. Many of them have grown up from boys to the use of these implements. They are an elastic hardy race, and in all respects the most efficient common laborers than can be employed on your work. They are, also, excepting the Coolies, the most economical."[8]

Despite the potential danger to their health from the swamps and rain forest, large numbers of men from the Cartagena region sought employment on the

Panama railroad. The wages paid by the railroad, more than double those paid locally, were part of the reason. In addition, the chief engineer was well known and well regarded in that part of New Granada from his previous role as an employer on the Canal del Dique.[9] The principal drawback with the Cartagena workers was their tendency to abandon their work. The rush of gold-hungry migrants across the Isthmus created a wide range of employment opportunities and injected a large amount of additional cash into the local economy. This created a shortage of labor in Panama, and wage rates soared. Railroad officials found to their dismay that onerous manual work in often disagreeable conditions soon proved unattractive to many New Granadians, the men on whom they had pinned their hopes for a reliable supply of cheap manpower.

These laborers often deserted, preferring the casual and more remunerative work of transporting travelers and their baggage across the Isthmus and catering to their needs. Local laborers also lacked previous experience in building railroads, were unfamiliar with American construction techniques, and were unable to speak English, the language of the engineers and supervisors. Nevertheless, the chief engineer remained convinced that the merits of these workers outweighed their shortcomings and deficiencies, and they continued to form a key element of the labor force throughout the project's lifetime.

Company documentation does not disclose the number of local workers employed, in part a reflection of the low level of importance the railroad attached to nonwhite personnel. Also, apart from the first year or so of the project, most New Grenadians were not directly engaged by the railroad but were recruited by contractors or labor agents on its behalf. General Joaquín Posada Gutiérrez, one of these contractors, was paid $34,319 for procuring labor from Cartagena and other parts of New Granada between November 30, 1853, and March 31, 1855.[10] Totten reported in 1853 that the general could provide fifteen hundred men from New Grenada at a cost of $8 per head.[11]

Reliable information on the total number of men hired by Posada and other New Grenadian contractors has not come to light.[12] Bidwell reported in 1865 that he had been informed by an official involved in recruitment that eight thousand laborers had been hired from Cartagena and the surrounding region.[13] Totten estimated in 1853 that the maximum number of these laborers that could be hired at any one time, presumably on six-month contracts, was between five hundred and eight hundred, suggesting an approximate average annual number of thirteen hundred men.[14] This total would have been smaller in 1850 and 1851 and considerably larger in 1853 and 1854. Based on the incomplete figures provided by the company and by newspaper and other reports, I have estimated that the number of New Granada men, including those from the Isthmus of Panama, who worked on the railroad probably did not exceed six thousand.

In addition to the New Granada laborers, smaller numbers of workers, attracted by the possibility of earning a relatively good wage on the railroad, were likely to have migrated to Panama from neighboring Central and South American countries. In 1853 the company discussed the possibility of procuring laborers from unspecified South American states. Shortly afterward, the chief engineer raised the possibility of recruiting five hundred men from El Salvador.[15] There is no information to suggest that there was company-sponsored recruitment of workers from these sources, apart possibly from El Salvador. Nevertheless, considerations of geographical proximity, together with the attraction of remunerative employment, would suggest the likelihood of a small, spontaneous flow of men from neighboring countries to Panama, possibly amounting to a thousand or so workers over the five years of construction. These migrants, together with those estimated to have come from Cartagena and other provinces of New Granada, bring the total estimated number of Spanish-speaking workers to approximately seven thousand, making them the largest single category of employees. While this estimate must be tentative, it is hopefully more plausible than the speculations of some previous writers on the topic.

The second largest group of workers consisted of those in the white ethnic category. All white railroad employees in Panama were unaccompanied males, unlike some of their West Indian and New Granadian counterparts. This was likely due to the costs involved in transporting wives and families from the United States and to the short-term nature of the men's contracts.[16] Much of the documentation dealing with white workers concerned the relatively small number of supervisory and professionally qualified staff. Information on the laborers and mechanics who formed the bulk of the railroad's white workforce was rarely kept.

There were, however, some indicators of the total number of employees in the white ethnic category. Griswold, who was employed as a surgeon by the railroad, estimated that 2,019 white men had been hired during the first eighteen months of construction. By August 1853 the total number of white employees had grown to 3,352 according to the company secretary, indicating an annual average of 1,100 during the first three years of construction.[17] Following Story's dismissal as contractor, thousands of additional laborers, including many white men, were recruited in the latter half of 1853 and throughout the course of 1854.

Estimates of the total number of white laborers employed up to January 1855, when the line became fully operational, varied. The railroad's president declared in 1859, "I am unable to state the number of this [white] class of laborers employed on the work during that time [1850–1855], but it was not far from 5,000."[18] The railroad's accounts provide support for this figure, showing that the company paid for the passages of about five thousand men between the United States and the Isthmus from 1850 to 1855.[19]

These accounts, however, did not reveal the full picture, because the transport costs of some white workers would have been included in payments to labor contractors as well as to Story. The Washington correspondent for the *New York Times* reported in 1859 that 6,000 white men had been employed. The *Panama Star and Herald* had earlier announced that at least six thousand white men were connected with the work during the five-year construction period, though it subsequently increased its estimate to 7,000. The *New York Weekly Herald* referred to 7,090 white laborers. McCullough concluded that "there were at least 6,000 whites employed all told during the years of construction," and Kemble also opted for the figure of 6,000.[20] A consensus among commentators, both at the time and subsequently, indicated the number of white workers was somewhere between 5,000 and 7,000. While a categorical answer is not possible, a median figure of 6,000 seems plausible.

Evidence on the nationality of these white employees was not straightforward. The railroad's New York office would have been cognizant of the advantage of hiring men with a knowledge of English and preferably with previous experience in railroad, canal, or construction projects. Such men would be found among the white laboring population of the United States, a labor reservoir that was rapidly expanding as a result of a massive wave of immigration in the mid-nineteenth century, particularly from Ireland as well as German-speaking areas of Europe. With an abundant white workforce relatively close at hand, the company did not feel it necessary to directly import white workers from mainland Europe, with the exception of Ireland, nor did it consider employing free black workers from the northern states of the Union. This suggests that all of the 6,000 or so white workers employed on the Panama railroad, except for 360 men shipped from Cork, were recruited in the United States.

Relatively little attention has been paid to the nationality of the railroad's white employees. They were assumed to be Americans, as nearly all were recruited in the United States. Company documents and the press occasionally reported the number of men disembarking from American steamers, first at Chagres and later at Aspinwall, as well as their occupations or work skills—tracklayers, carpenters, laborers, masons, and so forth. Their nationality was not usually mentioned. Just how many of these white employees were American born and how many were immigrants from Ireland and other European nations living in the United States was specified only now and then. The likelihood is that Irish immigrants in the United States, because of their skin coloring and general appearance and because they were largely English-speaking, were lumped together in newspaper reports and company documents with other white American-born workers. I shall discuss these American-Irish workers, who constituted an estimated 61 percent of the white workforce, in more detail in a later chapter.

The number of other Europeans laboring on the railroad was inconsequential, consisting of small groups, probably of a hundred men or less in most cases, sharing the same nationality. The *American Railway Times* referred in 1854 to "the gangs of men brought directly from Germany and Ireland," but this was the only reference to recruitment from Germany that I have seen.[21] Otis, writing shortly after the railroad's completion, noted that Irish, English, French, German, and Austrian workers had been employed, but he did not provide numbers. Totten also occasionally referred to Dutch and German workers in his correspondence, in addition to more frequent mentions of Irishmen. One American journal mentioned the presence of Canadians in the workforce.[22] Overall, however, information on the employment of Europeans (apart from the Irish) in the railroad's workforce is meager, and the details are uncertain. It appears unlikely, however, that the total number of workers born on the European mainland exceeded 450 or about 7–8 percent of the total number of white employees.

Black English-speaking laborers, mainly from Jamaica, but probably including a small number from Barbados and other Caribbean islands, comprised the third-largest category of workers. Like the Chinese, these men with a cultural, linguistic, and religious background differing from that of Panama's inhabitants, attracted attention in the printed media at the time. White residents in Panama, as well as journalists and travelers crossing the Isthmus, were occasionally perplexed and discomforted by the independent demeanor of these free black islanders and commented on them in their writings and newspapers. Consequently, some information relating to this category of workers survived in the literature of the period.

Nevertheless, there was no reliable figure for the number of West Indians employed on the railroad. An American periodical reported in 1858 that five thousand Jamaicans had been hired during the construction period.[23] This would appear to be the only contemporary source providing specific numerical information, and the figure of five thousand has been repeated in several recent publications.[24] According to another more recent source, ten thousand Afro-Antilleans labored on the construction of the railroad, which, if correct, would mean that they outnumbered all other ethnic groups combined.[25] One author went as far as to claim that "black workers from the English-speaking West Indies (mainly Jamaicans) formed almost the entire labor force."[26] By contrast, another study calculated that the number of islanders migrating to work on the railroad was relatively small: "Nearly 2,000 men had left [Jamaica for Panama] by May 1854."[27]

An examination of the company's documents provided some clarity on this issue. Totten referred to the recruitment of small numbers of Jamaicans in 1850 and 1851 but made no further reference to this group until late 1853. According to the company secretary, 127 Jamaicans had been employed up to July 1853.[28] Payments to the company's Jamaican agents for the recruitment of islanders during the early years of construction were modest. Most of the Jamaican workers hired by the railroad arrived from mid-1853 onward. The generally accepted figure of five thousand Jamaicans was almost certainly an overestimate; it is more likely that about three thousand islanders had been employed by the time the railroad became fully operational in January 1855.

The total size of the expatriate Jamaican community in Panama was considerably greater, however, as some workers had been joined by family members. Furthermore, considerable numbers of islanders continued to be hired to improve the railroad between its initial opening at the start of 1855 and the closing of the construction account in December 1858, reflecting a growing appreciation of their effectiveness as workers in Panama's climatic conditions. These later recruits have not been taken into account here, as their employment commenced after the railroad's inauguration in 1855.

Why, given the apparent availability of New Grenadian and white workers, did the railroad feel the need to hire Jamaican laborers and why were men from that island prepared to migrate to Panama? Racial stereotyping, health considerations, and economic factors go some way toward providing an explanation. Once construction began in the mangrove swamps of the Caribbean coast, the difficult working conditions there led the company to diversify the sources of its laborers. There was a widespread view at the time that members of the "African race" were more able than most other ethnic groups to withstand the rigors of labor in a tropical climate. The comments of U.S. Navy Commodore Paulding in 1857 encapsulated this way of thinking. "It seems to be conceded, from experience, that the African race can alone persistently labor in this [Panamanian] climate."[29] Medical science was as yet unaware that one reason for the greater resilience of black Caribbean workers in tropical conditions was related to their inherited and acquired resistance to diseases like yellow fever and malaria.

Jamaica, 550 miles to Panama's northeast, was a close source of potential manpower. The island had been undergoing an economic crisis from the late 1840s with trade paralyzed and sugar plantations abandoned—due, in part, to the final emancipation of slaves in the British Empire in 1838.[30] Many former slaves opted out of the plantation system, and the island's sugar plantations could no longer compete with the cheaper slave-grown products of Cuban and Brazilian plantations. As a consequence, Jamaica had a growing pool of unemployed and underemployed laborers. "In 1805, Jamaica was England's richest colony; half a century later, it was a backwater, cast away on the changing tides of commerce."[31] By the time construction of the Panama railroad had begun, Jamaica's "economy, laws and social practices were severely oppressive to Afro-Jamaicans." Many faced a life of poverty and destitution.[32]

The presence of a potential labor pool relatively close at hand did not go unnoticed by the railroad's management. Men from Jamaica also had the advantage of being English speakers. In September 1850, the company's president wrote to Mr. C. Armstrong, a Jamaica merchant and labor contractor, asking him to send twenty to thirty black workers to the Isthmus "that an early trial may be made of the value of their labor."[33] A month later, thirty men arrived from the island on a six-month contract. This first group impressed the company sufficiently to encourage it to continue the experiment.

During the final months of 1850 and the first half of 1851, small contingents of Jamaicans arrived in Panama; they were attracted by the possibility of earning higher wages than they could get at home. Totten, however, soon became disillusioned with the quality of the Jamaicans dispatched to him by the company's agents. Referring to a group of fifty-seven laborers who arrived in December

1850, Totten stated, "The majority are not of the class we require. I would not object to good laborers from the mere fact of their having been in prison—the offences may have been slight—but it will not do to allow the prisons to be emptied upon us, nor do we want a colony of vagrants."[34]

The chief engineer proposed sending Jamaicans home in late December 1850 on the grounds that some had never worked and others were lame or blind. Totten again criticized the Jamaican workforce in early 1851. "The Jamaica men as a body are a great nuisance . . . Messrs. Wright Armstrong & Co. have done the company great injustice in sending us the most worthless vagabonds they could pick up about Kingston, instead of selecting good laborers from the country."[35] Totten also expressed dissatisfaction with the caliber of workmen sent to him by labor contractors regardless of their nationality. "I certainly am ashamed of my agents, and really know not who to trust. It is very true . . . every one robs us—and for this reason, I suppose, he [an agent] sent us his gang of scoundrels."[36] The railroad's first historian described the Jamaican workers as "a restless, turbulent set, requiring a strong hand to keep them in subjection; being, however, hardy and athletic, they have been much employed as laborers on the road."[37]

The company's ledger recorded the modest payment of $3,756.06 to Wright, Armstrong and Co., the railroad's agents in Kingston, between October 9, 1850, and October 6, 1852, to cover the cost of recruitment and transport. Passages for laborers between Jamaica and Chagres cost about $10 each way. Allowing for the fact not all of these workers returned home after the end of their contracts, somewhere between 150 and 300 hundred men had likely been shipped between the island and Panama in this two-year period.[38]

Some of these workers were joined by families and dependents, judging from the reference to a Jamaican community in Aspinwall in 1853 by a New Orleans newspaper. The behavior of these free men scandalized Americans, particularly those from the southern states, who were accustomed to the deferential demeanor of black slaves. "The British Jamaica Negroes must be brought into subjection and taught good orderly behavior. They are becoming excessively insolent and are disliked by both native Spaniards and American citizens."[39]

The first phase of the employment of Jamaicans did not last beyond the middle of 1852. No mention of the employment of Jamaicans appeared in the company's documentation or in the Panamanian press from this time until late 1853. Totten, possibly disillusioned by the quality of the workers sent to him from the island and confident of an adequate supply of men from elsewhere, suspended recruitment from Jamaica during the course of 1852. Story, likewise, despite his shortage of laborers, failed to exploit the island's large labor pool when seeking workers.[40] The recruitment of Jamaicans was not resumed, to any great extent, until the closing months of 1853.

A marked change of attitude to the hiring of Jamaican workers occurred after the company resumed control of operations starting in September 1853. With Ireland and China having been identified as potential labor sources, the chief engineer turned his attention once more to Jamaica. The railroad appointed Hutchins & Co., a Kingston firm, as its new agent in 1853. The services of the company's former representatives on the island, Wright, Armstrong & Co., were dispensed with.[41] Petras suggested that the earlier Jamaican workers, who had proved unsuitable, had been recruited mainly in urban centers, principally Kingston. Those hired from 1853 onward were laborers from the countryside, more accustomed to hard, manual work.[42]

Over the next sixteen months, probably close to three thousand Jamaicans were recruited, which caused the Kingston Morning Journal to comment: "It is to be regretted that so many of our countrymen are obliged to quit their native country, owing to the scarcity of employment for them."[43] The trickle of Jamaicans heading for Panama had turned into a steady stream by mid-1854. "The tide of emigration from this island to the Isthmus of Panama still continues to flow with strength and vigor. Vessel after vessel leave the port of Kingston in rapid succession, each one freighted with its cargo of laborers for the Panama railway."

The island's planters appealed unsuccessfully to the governor to curtail the outflow of men, which, they claimed, was detrimental to Jamaica's economic interests.[44] "In July 1854, the governor informed the Colonial Office that two to three thousand adult males had left Kingston for Panama and by the end of the following year almost five thousand had made the journey."[45] Many of the migrants who were employed on the railroad did not remain in Panama after the termination of their contracts. Some preferred to return home with their hard-earned savings. In August 1854, for example, four hundred Jamaican laborers sailed back to their homeland after their term of service had expired. As the year drew to a close, they were followed by hundreds more who were waiting to board ships at Aspinwall.[46]

West Indian laborers, like the inhabitants of New Granada, were more or less resistant to yellow fever. Many had acquired immunity in childhood.[47] They were also less susceptible to suffer severely from malarial fevers. Nevertheless, even though the islanders tolerated the ravages of the climate better than many white workers, they were not immune to the dangers of an environment that differed considerably from their own. They frequently became sick and often died from illnesses contracted on the Isthmus. West Indian newspapers reported that nearly every returning ship brought back sick laborers who reported numerous deaths and a high incidence of illness among their fellow islanders on the Isthmus.[48] The refrain of a song sung by returnees from Panama included the following ominous lyrics:

> Fever and ague all day long
> At Panama, at Panama
> Wish you were dead before very long
> At Panama, at Panama.[49]

Jamaican labor contractors presumed that men going to the Isthmus were likely to fall ill, whatever their physical condition at the onset. For this reason, recruiting agents apparently dispensed with medical examinations for railroad laborers in the 1850s.[50] Despite these threats to their well-being, the West Indians "quickly acquired a reputation for being the best pick-and-shovel men and the hardiest of the imported workers."[51] Jamaican workers were held in higher regard with the passage of time, and by 1858, according to one source, they "were accounted as the very best laborers on the line."[52]

Although Jamaica formed part of the British Empire, the Foreign Office was anxious to avoid the expense of repatriating Jamaicans from the Isthmus to their island home. London made clear to its consular officials in Panama that they should be "very careful" before granting relief to distressed natives of Jamaica who had been employed, or who had sought employment, on the Panama railroad.[53] In 1854, the vice consul at Aspinwall informed his colleague in Panama City: "Since the contract with the Panama Rail Road Company came into effect I have steadily resisted all applications made by the natives of the Island of Jamaica to be returned as distressed British subjects . . . not a single native of the Island . . . has received an order for a free passage from this consulate." This official was commended by his superior in Panama City for his refusal to send home destitute islanders.[54]

Parker claims that one thousand Africans were shipped to Panama to work on the railroad in 1852, a claim repeated by Conniff.[55] Both are possibly confusing West Indians with men born in Africa, as there is no mention of the importation of the latter in the press or surviving company records. In any case, as already mentioned, few West Indians were hired by the railroad in 1852.

Curiously, however, a recently discovered Arabic document confirmed the presence of at least one African Muslim among the railroad's workforce. The author, an escaped slave from West Africa, arrived in Panama via Sierra Leone and the West Indian island of Dominica to labor on the railway. His six-page manuscript dealt exclusively with religious matters.[56]

Company personnel, reflecting the racist outlook of the era, referred to men from Asia, including the Indian subcontinent, the Malay Peninsula, and China, as "coolies." Prior to March 1854, this term described a relatively small number of former Indian and Malayan indentured workers who had completed their period of labor service in the West Indies and had migrated to Panama. The infrequent and usually brief references to these laborers in the documents and publications of the period would suggest that they were few in number. After the arrival of the first shipment of Chinese workers in March 1854, the term "coolie" also applied to the company's recruits from China, with the context sometimes indicating the nationality of those thus referred to.

Indian indentured laborers started to arrive in Jamaica and other British West Indian possessions, the "sugar bowl of Europe," from 1838 onward, to replace freed slaves after the abolition of slavery in the British Empire. Most of these migrants went to Trinidad and British Guiana, but close to five thousand settled in Jamaica.[57] By the early 1850s, the contracts of many of these men had expired, and they were free to seek other employment. The prospects of employment on the railroad attracted a few hundred Indians and probably some Malayans and other East Asians. These men moved to Panama, following the trail of black Jamaicans. Totten remarked in September 1853 that a number of recently arrived "coolies" from Jamaica, who had been working on the railroad, "are doing well." Their ethnicity was not specified, but Totten was almost certainly referring to migrants from India and the Malay Peninsula, as Chinese laborers had not yet been deployed on the railroad. As a result, he had sent an emissary to Messrs. Hutchings & Co. with instructions to hire a further 150 to 200 of these men for Panama.[58]

Totten formed a favorable opinion of these migrant workers. "The Coolies are at first feeble and inefficient, but being steady workmen, temperate, and but little affected by the climate, as they become accustomed to the tools, and acquire strength from regular and wholesome food, they make useful workmen."[59] As a result of Totten's initiative, one hundred Asian workers from Jamaica landed at Aspinwall on January 14, 1854.[60] His optimism about the adaptability and resilience of these migrants was not universally shared. After Bishop Kip's ship docked at Kingston at the end of 1853, the prelate, en route to California, pessimistically commented, "We have an accession of passengers. Fifty coolies, imported into Kingston from the East Indies, to work in place of the Negroes, are going to labor on the Panama Railroad. Poor fellows! They will probably soon find their graves."[61]

The number of non-Chinese Asians who worked on the railroad between 1853 and 1855 was small in comparison to other ethnic groups and probably did not amount to more than four or five hundred. Their womenfolk accompanied some of these migrants.[62] An American reporter in Aspinwall described seeing an occasional "turbaned Musselman [sic] a Cooley from the East Indies." Tomes also referred to the presence there of "sad, sedate, turbaned Hindoos, the poor exiled Coolies from the Ganges."[63] Reports in local newspapers contained little information on these Asian migrants and their subsequent fate. Thanks to the widespread use of the term "coolie" at the time, their identities tended to be subsumed into that of the numerically larger body of Chinese workers, who had arrived shortly after them.

The Chinese were the largest Asian ethnic group to be employed by the railroad. Stephens, who had been contacted in April 1852 about the importation of 300 "Chinamen," declined the offer, possibly because of the ready availability of other sources of labor or the cost of $200 per head for bringing them from China.[64] According to two Panamanian writers, 228 Chinese reached Panama in 1852, with a further 329 arriving in 1853, but there is no mention of these migrants in the company's documents.[65] The railroad's New York office dispatched a trickle of Chinese kitchen staff to Panama in the early 1850s, and these people appeared to have been the only Chinese employed by the company before 1854.

When it had become obvious that Story would be unable to complete the railroad on time, Totten resurrected the idea of recruiting indentured laborers from China. They could now be had for $140 each, for four years' service, plus their monthly pay of $4 per head and the cost of their food.[66] His suggestion was accepted, and in July 1853, the board appointed the shipping firm of Messrs. Howland and Aspinwall to act as their agents in China and to import laborers in their famous sailing clipper, *Sea Witch*.[67] The following month the company instructed the agents to extend the indentured workers' contract to eight years, if possible. The board clearly had optimistic expectations of the adaptability and resilience of these Asian workers in a Panamanian environment. The directors also proposed the recruitment of an additional one thousand Chinese, and

Figure 7.1. Painting of the Clipper *Sea Witch*. Oil on canvas by a Chinese artist, about 1850. Courtesy of Peabody Essex Museum, Salem, Mass.

they agreed to increase the wages of new recruits to $10 per month should this be necessary to secure the extra men.[68]

The ship carrying the first batch of laborers from Hong Kong in China's Guangdong province "got under way amid the firing of crackers and the uproar of gongs and drums as a token of the emigrants' satisfaction. When they reached Panama they were not so happy," as they had been informed they were going to California.[69] On March 31, 1854, the *Sea Witch* docked at Panama City with 705 Chinese laborers on board.[70] A second shipment of 322 men arrived in the *Bella Vascongada* from Swatow (now known as Shantou) in Guangdong province, almost two months later, on May 28, bringing the total number of imported Chinese laborers to slightly over one thousand.[71] The fate of these men has gripped the Panamanian imagination and attracted the attention of writers and historians. The Chinese were exotic newcomers who were immediately recognizable by their coloring, hairstyle, clothing, and language, and as a result, we have considerable information on their stay in Panama.

These indentured laborers were, in reality, little more than slaves, tied to the company for years before they could become free agents. Otis maintained that the railroad diligently promoted the health and comfort of these men. "Their hill-rice, their tea, and opium, in sufficient quantity to last for several months, had been imported with them—they were carefully housed and attended to— and it was expected that they would prove efficient and valuable men."[72] Within a few weeks, however, questions arose about the suitability of the new arrivals. The *New York Times* reported at the end of April that on the previous Sunday, a number of Chinese came into Panama City, where some got drunk, "while others were buying or piteously begging for opium at the bar-rooms and apothecaries' shops." This suggests that the company had either stopped supplying opium shortly after their arrival or else that the supply was insufficient to meet the addicts' needs. The paper predicted that the new arrivals were unlikely to survive for long on the Isthmus. "Digging ten or twelve hours a day under a burning sun and in deluging rains will soon use poor John China up, and the buzzards are even now congratulating themselves upon the nice morsels to be added to their bill of fare."[73]

Over the course of the following months, many of these men, unable to cope with the onerous physical demands made of them, either were sacked by the railroad or deserted, ending up as vagrants and beggars. According to the *New York Herald*, the "large body of Coolies ... do not [*sic*], I am told, meet the expectations of the company, but soon break down under the combined effects of the climate and hard work."[74] The *Estrella de Panama* complained in May that some Chinese deserters were begging on the capital's streets. It asked the company to take responsibility for these employees when they fell sick or became incapable of working and not to simply fire them.[75] At the end of June, the directors were notified that thirty former laborers from China were now destitute and that efforts were being made by Panamanian residents and local businesses to raise funds to send them to San Francisco. The board referred a decision on granting these former employees a reduced fare on the railroad to the president and secretary for resolution.[76] The outcome was not disclosed.

Reports of destitute Chinese featured in the local press throughout the second half of 1854. "We noticed lately a number of Chinese begging about the streets; this should not be, it is neither fair to the poor fellows themselves nor to the public. If they can work the Company should insist on their doing so, and if they are incapacitated from so doing labor either by sickness or any other cause, they should be taken care of and not be permitted to roam about."[77] On August 13, the police arrested a group of "wretched, sickly Chinese, who have now become such an intolerable nuisance in our streets" and escorted them to the railroad's recently established terminus at Playa Prieta, on the outskirts of the capital. The station superintendent refused to accept responsibility for these men and turned them away.

The *Panama Star and Herald*'s reaction was scathing: "The moral, as well as the legal duty, devolves on the Company of taking care of these men whom they have brought from their own country among strangers. If the men are capable of work, the Company should insist on their complying with their engagements. If they have injured their health in the Company's service they should be taken care of, but under no circumstances should they be permitted, as at present, to wander about our streets half starved, half naked, and covered with loathsome sores—a tax upon the charity and benevolence of our citizens."[78]

A letter to the paper the following day alleged that Chinese laborers were to be found lying half dead not only in Panama City but along the entire route of the railroad.[79] Shortly before the arrival of the *Sea Witch*, the railroad's directors had considered that "some arrangements might be made for taking care" of sick Chinese laborers on one of the four Panama Bay islands in which the company had purchased a half share the previous year.[80] No steps were taken to establish offshore convalescent facilities, though a hospital about six miles from the capital was opened for the Chinese. The board seems to have decided that repatriation was not a viable option.

Responding to press criticisms of the company's handling of its sick Chinese employees, a correspondent claimed that the railroad was doing all it could to keep these invalids out of Panama City and that they were largely to blame for their own fate. "The Chinese, however, are averse to medical treatment, and, although every care is taken of them, they avail themselves of every chance to break out of the hospital and come down to Panama [City] to beg.... In Panama [City], they meet with considerable sympathy from many of the natives, who assist them with food and money, and thus encourage them to remain in the city. This should be stopped.... We will thus get rid of being troubled with these disgusting looking wretches at every corner of the city."[81] Chinese beggars reportedly continued to be a nuisance in the capital's streets in September.[82]

Britain maintained, through its Colonial Land and Emigration Commission, an interest in the fate of Chinese and Indian indentured laborers it had encouraged to emigrate to its Caribbean colonies. Interviews carried out with Chinese workers in Panama, in September 1854, by an interpreter at the behest of this body gave a valuable insight into their situation. The interpreter, Wang-te-Chang, reported that many of the Chinese appeared sickly, with pale, thin

Figure 7.2. San Pablo Station. F. N. Otis, *Illustrated History of the Panama Railroad* (London: Sampson Low, 1862). Courtesy of the British Library Board.

faces; sore feet; and swollen legs.[83] They claimed they had been recruited under false pretenses, having been given the impression they were going to work in California's goldfields. Approximately half had died from disease less than six months after their arrival. Thirty or so had been fortunate enough to leave for California, possibly the group referred to earlier. Of the remaining 450 workers, two hundred were ill, and all were anxious to leave Panama for Jamaica or anywhere else that would accept them.

The men, whose arrival had coincided with the start of the wet season, protested that they were saturated by torrential downpours and burned by a hot tropical sun. They lacked fresh provisions and were fed on salt pork, beef, and rice. Occasional yams were their sole vegetable. Tea, their favorite drink, was provided only once a day. When the Cantonese-speaking workers fell sick, they could not explain their condition to their Chinese overseers, who hailed from another linguistic region, possibly a Mandarin-speaking area. Because of the breakdown in communications, the Chinese foremen flogged men who were unable to keep pace with the rest of their labor gang, unaware that these men were sometimes ill.

The Chinese hospital, described as dirty and foul-smelling when Wang visited it, housed about 150 ill workers. The patients complained of a shortage of food and fresh drinking water. They claimed they were rationed to one bottle of water per day. The company's treatment of their dead horrified the Chinese workers. Bodies were dragged to a burial site, with no funeral ceremony, and thrown, without a coffin and often naked, into a communal grave.[84] These conditions drove some patients to abandon the hospital and roam the countryside begging for food and shelter. Some of these indigents eventually succumbed to malnutrition and exposure. Wang had even come across the corpse of one of these unfortunates clad only in rags. A minority, exhausted, hungry, and unwell, had given themselves up to despair and committed suicide.

Allegations were subsequently published that hundreds of Chinese took their own lives, many in a bizarre fashion. Wang-te-Chang, however, made no reference to suicide on this scale. The allegation of mass Chinese suicides originated with Tomes. He suggested that one reason for these deaths was the company's decision to cut off the opium supply, which may have been motivated by the cost, about fifteen cents per person, per day.[85] Minter repeated Tomes's imaginative claims: "The coolies . . . strangled themselves with their queues, hanged themselves from trees along the river, threw themselves on their machetes, weighted their clothing and jumped into the Chagres, paid the Malaysians to shoot them."[86]

Schott went one step further and quantified the number of suicides. He wrote that Sean Donlan, an Irish construction foreman and "a hardened veteran of two years on the Isthmus," reported to Totten that 125 Chinese had hanged themselves from trees, a further 300 were lying dead on the ground, while an undisclosed number had drowned themselves, adding up to a total of well over 425 suicides.[87] According to an article by Chen, possibly based on Schott's account, almost 500 Chinese took their own lives.[88] Mass suicide on this scale, involving half of the entire Chinese workforce, would, if true, have featured prominently in the Chinese interpreter's account, as well as in the local and foreign press. In September 1854, however, Wang-te-Chang reported that there had been thirty to forty suicides among his countrymen. Otis, writing eight years later, gave credence to Chang's figures when he referred to scores, rather than hundreds, of Chinese suicides.[89]

By August 1854, it had become clear that the experiment of using Chinese labor had failed, and the board raised the question of the fate of the survivors.[90] Negotiations were initiated with interested parties in Jamaica with a view to exchanging these men for Jamaican workers. Referring to the Chinese, a local newspaper commented that "it is evident that this climate is not suited to their constitution, nor are they adapted to the work required from them on the railroad."[91] The company's president contacted a Havana firm to discuss selling the surviving Chinese to plantation owners in Cuba, but this initiative proved unsuccessful.[92]

The directors were informed on October 2 that a Mr. Wortley, on behalf of the government of Jamaica, had indicated that he would take the remaining Chinese and replace each with a Jamaican laborer for a period of four months; he would also pay the latter's transport costs. The board agreed that this offer should be accepted, unless better terms could be obtained elsewhere. Finally, in November 1854, the directors implemented a modified version of this arrangement. Totten reported that "he had disposed of 197 Chinese to Mr. Wortley at $17.77 each, the estimated average expense of landing Jamaican laborers." The purchaser had paid for the men's passage to Jamaica. About twenty of the surviving Chinese suffered from ulcerated legs and general debility. One died during the sea passage.[93]

On November 1, 1854, 197 Chinese arrived in Kingston Harbour. According to another source, 205 survivors sailed to Jamaica "at an expense to the colony of £6 a-head, from Panama," but many of these "did not long survive their removal."[94] These men, together with the thirty or so Chinese who had earlier managed to migrate to California, constituted the survivors of the original contingent of just over one thousand.[95] The fate of the surviving Chinese from the Panama railroad after their arrival in Jamaica was inauspicious. An undisclosed number deserted from the plantations where they had been hired and drifted into vagrancy.[96]

The importation of workers from China, at an average cost of $111.50 per head, proved a bitter disappointment to the company as it obtained little return, in terms of labor performed, in exchange for the cost of procuring their services. On April 29, 1854, Messrs. Howland and Aspinwall were paid $78,607.50 for the first shipment of men, receiving a further $35,903 for the second shipment on August 14, 1854.[97] The *New York Times* claimed that the railroad had no desire to continue recruiting Chinese workers after witnessing the fate of the victims it had hired.[98] This initiative, of course, had been catastrophic for the men who lost their lives, as well as for those whose health had been undermined.

In his report to the directors the following year, the chief engineer revised his earlier optimistic forecast of the utility of Chinese labor. In a terse and dispassionate assessment, he observed that "their services were found to be much less efficient in that climate than was anticipated."[99] The verdict of the *American Railway Times* was blunt and heartless. The Chinese "turned out utterly unprofitable, being unable to labor on the Isthmus, and melted away rapidly from disease and desertion. They seemed to have no stamina."[100]

How can the deaths of approximately 50 percent of the Chinese laborers at the end of five months and close to 78 percent after seven months be explained? The evidence suggests that a combination of causes and circumstances contributed to a disastrous death toll. The debilitating physical demands of toiling in Panama's monsoon-like tropical climate, harsh treatment by overseers, and a radical change of diet, would doubtless have led to a decline in the men's resilience, energy, and strength. Psychological problems arising from adaptation to a very different cultural, linguistic, and geographical setting would also have taken a toll. Deceived by false promises and traumatized by their transfer to an alien environment from which they had little prospect of escape, many appeared to have become depressed.

Nevertheless, these factors cannot be held solely responsible for such a tragic death toll. Most Chinese emigrants in the nineteenth century, including those destined for the Panama railroad, came from the southern province of Guangdong, which had a humid, subtropical climate.[101] Emigrants from this region of China to other parts of Central America and California in the 1850s quickly acquired a reputation as resilient and industrious workers in difficult conditions and did not suffer from a mortality rate anywhere near as devastating as that in Panama. A decade later, tens of thousands of Chinese proved to be outstanding workers during the construction of the Central Pacific line in the United States.[102] They experienced a heavy death rate but nowhere near as catastrophic as that of their compatriots on the Panama railroad. Chinese indentured workers building railroads in Cuba in the 1860s reportedly suffered from a much lower annual mortality rate of 8 percent during their initial acclimatization period.[103]

Senior speculates that the Chinese recruited to work on the Panama railroad may have been town and city dwellers, unused to hard physical labor, differing in this respect from most of their compatriots who migrated to North and Central America in the mid-1800s.[104] If this hypothesis is correct, the urban and occupational background of this group of men would have made them particularly ill suited to the demands placed on them by the Panama railroad. It is unlikely, however, that we will ever find sufficiently detailed information on their origins to confirm this supposition.

The railroad's failure, in the case of the Chinese workers, to follow its usual practice of repatriating sick employees clearly contributed to the high death toll. When, within a few months of their arrival, many had fallen ill, and it had become obvious that they were unsuitable as laborers in Panama's challenging working conditions, the company did not ship them back to their distant homeland. The cost of a two-month voyage likely contributed to this decision. Furthermore, given the poor state of health of many by this stage, numerous shipboard deaths would likely have occurred. Unlike their fellow workers, sick Chinese were left stranded in Panama with questionable medical and convalescent care. The company was criminally negligent in not removing these laborers to Jamaica or elsewhere in the greater Caribbean area once it became clear that they were unsuited for working in a Panamanian environment.

A chronic addiction to opium among many of these men prior to their arrival in Panama might explain why their mortality rate was significantly higher than that of their compatriots, who successfully coped with hazardous and challenging work in other parts of Central America, the Caribbean, and the United States. Many Chinese male emigrants in the nineteenth century practiced opium smoking. Chinese workers on the Central Pacific line in the United States, for example, engaged in the practice, but only on Sundays, their day off, to help them relax. It did not affect their work performance.[105] Opium addiction, however, when carried to excess, had a debilitating effect on its devotees and was responsible for their physical degeneration and wasted looks.[106]

The Chinese laborers who arrived in Panama in 1854 came from Guangdong, where many inhabitants were reported to be addicts.[107] Some laborers from this region who migrated to Trinidad in the 1850s were described as chronic opium smokers, and their experience there was not dissimilar to that of their fellow countrymen in Panama. "They were deemed by many of the [Trinidadian] planters as 'utterly worthless' . . . they proved a source of continual annoyance to the estates that received them, and before six months had passed, they suffered so severely from dysentery and sores that the local government had to make the matter a subject of special enquiry."[108] An inordinate addiction

Figure 7.3. The Line at Ahorca Lagarto. Lucien N. B. Wyse, *Le Canal de Panama* (Paris: Hachette, 1886). Courtesy of the British Library Board.

to opium also prevailed among some, though by no means all, of the Chinese migrants to other parts of the British West Indies in the latter half of the nineteenth century.[109]

Otis maintained that the company imported a supply of the drug sufficient to last for several months. Tomes, on the other hand, claimed that the Chinese initially lacked their habitual opium and began to sicken soon after their arrival. The railroad then distributed the narcotic among them, invigorating them physically, before it was subsequently withdrawn, either for financial or public relations reasons. The Chinese, deprived of their usual stimulus, began to fall ill again.[110] Company documentation and newspapers did not mention the supply of the opiate or its alleged termination, probably because of the ambivalent attitude toward the use of this drug in nineteenth-century America.

The two shiploads of Chinese workers that arrived in Panama in 1854 may have contained men from urban backgrounds, unused to manual labor, who were more heavily addicted to opium than most of their rural émigré compatriots, and these factors could explain their tragic fate. The curtailment or withdrawal of the narcotic after their arrival, combined with the climatic and other hardships to which they were exposed, rendered them unfit for backbreaking labor. The railroad's failure to provide adequate medical attention and to repatriate sick workers or remove them to alternative healthier locations in the Caribbean, meant that death from disease, malnutrition, exposure, and neglect was the fate of the majority. While some of these hapless men took the desperate decision to end their own lives, the number of Chinese suicides has been greatly exaggerated.

EIGHT

Working Conditions

FOR FIVE YEARS, THE PANAMA RAILROAD ENGAGED IN A CONTINU-
ous drive to recruit, feed, house, and manage thousands of workers. Working
conditions throughout the construction period were challenging, especially
during the initial eighteen months. Before the first tracks could be laid, the
site of the Atlantic terminus at Manzanillo Island had to be cleared of its dense
mass of vegetation. This task began in May 1850, not long after the wet season
had commenced. As a result, "the working parties, in addition to being constantly drenched from above, were forced to wade in from two to four feet of
mud and water, over the mangrove stumps and tangled vines of the imperfect
openings cut by the natives, who, with their *machetas* [*sic*] preceded them to
clear the way."[1]

Once the island had been stripped of some of its vegetation, the company
began preparations for laying the tracks across miles of pestilential mangrove
swamps and dense jungle on the mainland. Draft animals were useless in the
mud. All materials had to be transported on men's shoulders or dragged by
them with ropes through the mire. No machines were available to help clear the
forest. Tropical hardwood trees, as well as a mass of tangled bushes and undergrowth had to be chopped down by men wielding axes or machetes. Some of
the trees in the rain forest were gigantic, with girths of thirty feet and heights
of over one hundred and thirty feet; they weighed several tons.[2]

Once the tracks had been laid across the coastal swamps, the worst was over,
but the laborers still faced daunting obstacles. Climatic conditions, according
to a long-term resident on the Isthmus, posed an almost insuperable challenge.
"The climate stood like a dragon in the way."[3] Densely packed trees interwoven
with creepers created an overhead forest canopy that kept out light and air;
this created a suffocating atmosphere. Heat and humidity sapped the laborers'

strength. Nightfall provided little respite, as mosquitoes tormented the men, leaving them tired and itchy in the morning and often incubating malaria. The refuse surrounding the workers' camps attracted reptiles, and the bites of some varieties, like the bushmaster and the coral snake, frequently proved fatal. McCullough graphically describes the torments faced by workers. "The punishing heat, the torrential Panama rains, the terrible fatigue of physical labor in such a climate, clothes that never get dry, scorpions in boots in the morning, the incessant mosquitoes, sand flies, ticks, the bad food—and nothing—not a blessed thing—to do but work and survive the jungle."[4]

Europeans and North Americans found it difficult to sustain bodily exertion for any length of time in a climate with year-round temperatures rarely falling much below 80 degrees Fahrenheit and an average humidity of about 85 percent. One hundred and fifty years before the coming of the railroad, the Scottish settlement of Darien in Panama failed partly because of the colonists' inability to endure the debilitating effects of laboring "under the fierce blaze of a vertical sun."[5] In 1855, a visiting author described being "dissolved in the perpetual warm-bath of the hot, moist climate . . . and feeling my energy oozing out from every pore . . . I felt almost too indolent to move."[6]

Fifty years later, an American journalist claimed that there was a "certain and unjustified cruelty" in making West Indian laborers work for eight to ten hours daily by digging the Panama Canal. "Until you have tried to do a good fifteen minutes' work with a pick and shovel during the rainy season . . . you can have no idea of the exhaustion that tropical heat brings even to the laborer who is used to it."[7] White laborers from temperate climates working in these equatorial surroundings must have also suffered unimaginably. Nevertheless, despite the wretched conditions they were frequently required to toil under, the railroad laborers were somehow capable of achieving an impressive daily output. According to one worker, each man shifted almost as much earth on average as laborers did in the United States.[8]

Railroad construction methods in Panama, as elsewhere at the time, were primitive and labor intensive. Most work had to be carried out by hand, using picks, shovels, and wheelbarrows supplemented, where conditions allowed, by the use of mules and horses. The only available mechanical devices were steam-operated pile drivers in the swamps, steam launches on the Chagres River, and railroad locomotives in places where tracks had already been laid.[9] Once the route for the railroad had been surveyed and marked out, gangs of

Figure 8.1. Virgin Forest, Panama. Lucien N. B. Wyse, *Le Canal de Panama* (Paris: Hachette, 1886). Courtesy of the British Library Board.

laborers using axes and machetes cleared a strip of ground from thirty to sixty feet wide of trees and vegetation. Timber that might prove useful was retained, and the remainder was removed or burned.[10] The ground was then graded to ensure that it was level and firm enough to support the track bed.

Tracks were not always laid in a continuous, linear fashion. Sometimes the difficulties of the terrain meant that short sections of track, separated from one another by patches of dense jungle or swamp, were laid. The gaps between these stretches of rail were gradually filled in, and the scattered strips of line were eventually united into one continuous track. The lower reaches of the Chagres River served as an important artery of communication during the early years because of the absence of roads on the Caribbean side of the Isthmus. Whenever practicable, boats transported labor crews, together with their equipment and materials. This was done either to break new ground or close the gap between completed stretches of rail.

Where the terrain was marshy, the clearance squads were followed by engineers who used pile drivers to sink wooden shafts of twenty-five, thirty, and even forty feet in length into the ground. Once the piles had been hammered into the mud, about six feet apart, a timber framework, known as "cribbing," was put in place around them. Vast quantities of stones and earth, some quarried from the nearby Monkey Hill, together with gravel dredged from the Chagres River, were poured into these wooden frames in a time-consuming operation to ensure the roadbed was firm enough to take the weight of a loaded train.[11] "It was almost as if the Isthmus were [sic] consciously resisting this human incursion as the swamps swallowed up the seemingly infinite amounts of earth dumped in them to try to establish a stable surface."[12]

Most of the first nine miles of track were laid on piles. Trestle viaducts, twenty feet high in places, initially lifted the line over particularly bad patches of swamp. Stronger earthen embankments gradually replaced these. Wooden bridges carried the tracks over more than a hundred rivers, streams, and ravines. Squads of laborers, carpenters, masons, and bricklayers were employed in these works. Once a firm roadbed had been laid down, tracklayers completed the operation by securing the rails to the crossties with metal spikes. Since early locomotives were not sufficiently powerful to tackle steep gradients, the tracks followed the contours of the landscape as far as possible.

Workers' remuneration was initially linked to their ethnicities, but differences in pay levels for men of different nationalities and colors quickly eroded because of the constant need to recruit labor, whatever its source. Unlike the division of workers into two categories based on color (silver roll and gold roll employees) that was established during the American construction of the Panama Canal, there was little difference in the pay levels of laborers from different ethnic groups hired by the railroad from 1851 onward. The Chinese indentured laborers hired in 1854 were the only exception, constituting the worst-paid section of the workforce for the brief period of their engagement.

Not long after construction had started, Totten admitted that it was difficult to find local men willing to work for modest wages.[13] At first laborers from New Granada were paid less than their white counterparts, but desertion and recruitment difficulties led the chief engineer to propose an increase in their wages from $0.40 to $0.60 per day, with food, in February 1851.[14] The company's president did not accede to this request, but the continuing scarcity of local laborers eventually led the railroad to increase their pay. A British engineer reported in 1852 that laborers from Cartagena had their passage paid to Panama and were given an advance of $4.00, together with a mat and blanket. They received $1.00 a day with food and board—or $1.50 per day if they fended for themselves.[15]

During the initial construction phase, Jamaican laborers earned $1.00 per day, half paid weekly and the remainder at the end of their contract. This was more than twice what they could earn at home.[16] According to another source, Jamaicans were paid $0.40 per day at first, but by the end of 1850, this rate had been doubled. Hutchins & Co., the railroad's agents in Jamaica, announced in the Kingston *Daily Advertiser*, on April 18, 1854, that the company paid its workers 3 shillings and 2 pence sterling per day—just under one $1.00—and wages were handed over every two weeks.[17]

While the railroad's route was being surveyed in early 1849, the company found it could hire California-bound gold seekers—stranded in Panama by a shortage of funds—as laborers. It paid these men a dollar a day, plus their board and keep, and provided them with steamer tickets to California when the survey was finished.[18] The company continued with an analogous arrangement during the early stages of construction. In exchange for their labor for a specified period (usually one hundred days), the railroad provided a free passage from the United States to Panama, and eventually on to San Francisco, at a cost of about $130 per worker.[19] Several hundred workers availed of these provisions for a free passage to California.[20] In May, 1851, for example, the railroad paid $6,600 to the Pacific Mail Steamship Company for the passage from Panama to California of "66 men who had worked out their 100 days."[21]

Workers hired under these terms sometimes received a small amount of cash, in addition to a free sea passage, on completion of their contracts. When recruiting laborers from Illinois under Colonel Baker in July 1850, the railroad agreed to pay each man twenty dollars after they had worked for one hundred days, as well as the fare to California.[22] The company also recruited men returning from the gold diggings after they had landed in Panama. These were impoverished adventurers who had failed to strike it rich in California and were now trying to make their way home. The returning forty-niners received tickets to New York or New Orleans as part of their payment. Totten found these men more useful than the average white laborer, probably because they had become accustomed to hardship and punishing working conditions during their gold-seeking days in the west.[23]

The company abandoned these ad hoc sources of labor in mid-1851 and concentrated henceforth on recruiting men for a six-month contract period. The wage rate of workers recruited in the United States depended on whether or not they had a trade, specialized skills, or prior railroad experience. White laborers were paid $1.00 per day, plus board and lodging, and their return passage from the United States. Workers who were classified as "mechanics" or skilled tradesmen, received higher wages. Carpenters, for example, earned $2.00 per day, while a foreman tracklayer was paid $2.50. A station superintendent received $4.50.[24] These wage levels remained relatively stable throughout the construction period.

The company adopted a flexible and pragmatic approach to promotion and pay increases. Men hired as laborers and found to be skilled were upgraded to foreman or mechanic status and received extra pay. Hugh Dougherty, probably Irish and an experienced wheelbarrow man, advanced to the rank of foreman in 1850 and was paid fifty dollars per month. James Halpin, who had been recruited as a laborer, was advanced to the post of cooper at a wage of forty dollars per month. Early in 1852, the ravages of sickness so depleted the ranks of engineers that Totten had no option but to promote some of his unqualified workers to that rank, but he did not specify whether their wages were increased as a result.[25]

Laborers who signed up for a second term sometimes received extra pay because of their previous experience and knowledge.[26] Not all former workers were welcomed back, and on occasion Totten warned the New York office against reemploying certain employees whose previous work record or state of health he deemed unsatisfactory. In 1853 he advised the company secretary not to send a certain employee back to Panama "as he has been *discharged*."[27] Later that year, Totten, referring to another worker who wanted to return, instructed the company secretary: "Do not send him." In July 1853, the chief engineer named four men he did not want back in Panama.[28]

Men were not generally paid their full wage at the end of each week. In an effort to reduce desertion, a major problem in the early years of construction, the company adopted the practice of retaining a proportion of employees' wages until they had completed their contract term. Workers resented this measure and preferred to be paid in full every week. This occasionally led to friction with the management. Although this provision was designed to inhibit desertion, it sometimes had the opposite effect. Some workers, angry at not receiving their full wages, simply walked off the job.[29]

How did a white laborer's wage of a dollar a day, all told, compare with that received by his counterparts in the United States and by those working for other employers on the Isthmus? Laborers' wages on American railroads during the early 1850s varied from $1.00 to $1.50 per day.[30] Men were frequently promised high wages, good food, and agreeable accommodation on distant railroad building projects. The reality was often different when they arrived, sometimes after traveling a long distance, and they found themselves working from dawn to dusk for about a dollar a day or less.

Wage rates in America's western territories were high in the early 1850s, reflecting a scarcity of labor in a newly settled and rapidly expanding frontier region, where much of the available manpower was engaged in prospecting and mining. In 1853 laborers could earn four dollars per day in California, while carpenters could command a daily rate of seven dollars.[31] Wage rates gradually fell, as the gold boom tapered off and the number of permanent settlers increased, but they still remained higher in California than in Panama or the Atlantic states of America. The higher wages obtainable along America's Pacific coast, as well as its healthier climate, acted as powerful incentives to desert for railroad workers slogging through the swamps and jungles of the Isthmus in the early years of construction.

In Panama City, wage inflation caused by the gold rush boom led to general laborers earning $1.50 daily in 1852, while "a good tradesman can earn five dollars a day."[32] Pay rates in Aspinwall in 1854 were higher than in the capital because of the Caribbean port's unenviable reputation for disease. Men laboring there received $2.00 to $3.00 per day, while carpenters and mechanics received $5.00 daily.[33] In summary, white laborers and mechanics employed by the Panama railroad earned about the same as their counterparts in most of the United States but less than workers in Panama City, Aspinwall, or in California. In addition to their wages, however, laborers and mechanics, in common with all other Panama railroad employees, were provided with free food and accommodation, medical attention, and free travel to and from Panama.

Remuneration at a senior level in the railroad was high in comparison to what the men hacking and digging their way through Panama's rain forest earned. Shortly after the formation of the company, the salaries of the president, vice president, and secretary were set at $5,000, $3,000, and $1,500 per annum, respectively. The president's remuneration was increased to $6,250 per annum in 1853.[34] Totten and Trautwine each received a salary of $7,500 when they were appointed to the posts of joint chief engineers in early 1850.[35] Following Trautwine's resignation at the end of 1850, Totten assumed sole charge of engineering operations. Shortly afterward the company increased his salary to $12,000 per annum, making him the highest paid functionary of the company. Totten defended his remuneration, arguing that his responsibilities were much greater than those of any railroad engineer in the United States.[36]

The company reduced Totten's salary to $5,000 following changes to the organization's structure in early 1852 and the subsequent hiring of Minor C. Story as an outside contractor. Totten was now expected to confine himself solely to his engineering duties. Totten, unhappy with this demotion, tendered his resignation, which he later withdrew, asking for a salary increase in return.[37] A settlement was reached, though we lack the details, and Totten remained at his post. Alexander J. Center was elected vice president of the company in early 1852 at a reduced salary of $1,500.[38] When he left New York to oversee the company's activities on the Isthmus as resident superintendent in July 1852, his salary was raised to $5,000 per annum. Two years later he received a further increase, bringing his annual remuneration to $6,000.[39]

In July 1852, John C. Campbell and James L. Baldwin were appointed assistant engineers. Campbell was paid $500 per month. The following year, Baldwin, now described as the principal assistant engineer, was awarded the same salary.[40] At the end of 1853, Charles H. Green was appointed company agent in Panama at an annual salary of $2,000.[41] Men like William Miller, employed as superintendents or midranking supervisors, were paid $1,800 per annum. Salaries of lower ranking officials were not mentioned in the company's documentation. However, the American consul reported that the railroad's clerical and administrative staff based in Aspinwall earned between $75 and $200 per month.[42]

These salaries highlighted the discrepancy in remuneration between a minority of well-paid executives and officials at the upper levels of the organization and the mass of lower-waged manual workers who hazarded their lives and health while battling their way through a hostile landscape under adverse conditions. Nevertheless, the generous salaries paid to senior Panama-based staff afforded them little protection against disease and sickness. Company executives who remained on the Isthmus for an extended period did so at the risk of their health and sometimes their lives. The most notorious example was that of John Lloyd Stephens, the railroad's president and a noted author and explorer. He died of malaria in 1852 in New York City, after contracting the disease in Panama. Dr. Franklin Gage, a senior physician; Mr. Putnam, the company's agent; and Dr. Hopper, the company's medical doctor at Aspinwall, were among other senior employees who succumbed to illnesses contracted during their employment in Panama. The deaths of the two physicians were a stark reminder that medical knowledge offered little defense against the diseases of the Isthmus.

The railroad's white employees were required to sign a contract before embarking for the Isthmus. Climatic and working conditions made it impractical to retain most members of the workforce for a prolonged period. Engagements, therefore, were limited to a maximum of six months for laborers, though some white-collar workers may have served for longer. Men were sometimes so enervated by the end of their contract that they required a period of rest and recovery outside Panama even if they wished to return. During the rainy season, when sickness was rife, one-third to a half of the workforce might be incapable of work on any given day. This placed an additional onus on the company when calculating its labor requirements.[43]

The railroad repatriated severely ill and incapable employees, rather than treating them on the Isthmus. As a result, a continual supply of fresh workers to fill the gaps arising from the departure of men completing their six-month contracts and losses occasioned by desertion, death, and repatriation following sickness was essential. Recruitment became more difficult as news of the unhealthy climate and difficult working conditions circulated in the United States.

Much of the available information about the terms of white laborers' contracts relates to the 1852–1853 period when Minor C. Story was in charge of construction. The contractor's shoddy treatment of his men led to several cases being taken against him in the New York courts. While Story's terms of employment were in many respects similar to, or identical with, those applied by the company, these provisions were frequently ignored in practice by the contractor's supervisors in Panama.

According to agreements made in late 1852, laborers hired by Story received one dollar per day, plus board and lodging, their return passage from New York to Panama, and a free passage home in case of sickness. In return, they agreed to work on the railroad for a period of six months and to "wholly abstain from the use of spirituous liquors upon said work." "He [laborer] will provide himself with such clothing, suitable to the climate, as he shall be advised." Men were to commence work on arrival on the Isthmus, unless prevented by sickness. Failure to start work immediately made them liable for the costs of their passage and any other expenses incurred on their behalf. The retention of wages by the employer, a practice initiated by the railroad company, was included in Story's contracts. "Sufficient of the wages, and not less at any time than forty dollars ... shall be in all cases retained to guarantee the faithful performance of this agreement."[44]

Bartley Monaghan, who was most likely Irish and hired in October 1852 by Story, was employed as carpenter at two dollars per day.[45] Monaghan's contract stated that he was to work for six months at his trade or at any other work he might be requested to do. The contract also contained a prejudicial clause that stated he could be discharged at any moment if his employer was dissatisfied with his performance. In case of dismissal, he would also forfeit his right to any arrears of wages that were due. After arriving in Panama, Monaghan was made foreman of a gang of workers at Barbacoas. During his first week there, these men staged a one-day strike, protesting at the standard of their accommodation and food. Following this, Monaghan, was sent back to Aspinwall, possibly because of his participation in the work stoppage. After some days Monaghan fell sick and was discharged.

Despite his illness, Monaghan was compelled to work his passage on a ship back to New York. Judge McCarthy of New York's Marine Court found that "he came home without having received from the defendant [Story] the care he was entitled to, shattered in health and enfeebled in body, with perhaps the seeds of a long, lingering sickness within him." The judge described the terms of Monaghan's contract as "one-sided, harsh and oppressive ... it endeavors to give all the powers, all the rights to one, viz.: the employer." The judge awarded the plaintiff $120 damages and $10 costs.[46]

John Murphy, another returned laborer, also brought a case against Story seeking to recover eighty-two dollars in wages, which he claimed were due to him. Both Murphy and Daniel Lyons, a witness who testified on his behalf, were illiterate and almost certainly Irish. Murphy was legally represented by Michael Doheny, a former Young Ireland leader who had fled to the United States after the failure of the 1848 rebellion against British rule.[47] In October 1852, Murphy and twenty-five others, including Lyons, signed an agreement at Story's office at 92 Warren Street, New York, to work on the railroad.

In November, heavy rainfall halted operations in Panama. Dalton, the overseer, whose name suggests that he was also Irish, told the two hundred men on his section that they would have to work in the rain if they wished to get paid because Story had complained that he was treating his workers too leniently.[48] Dalton announced that "he would be damned if he would give us a dollar a day, unless we worked for it . . . and he said then that he could get plenty of men in New York for fifty cents [per day]."[49] The men responded by striking for three and a half days during which they received no food from their employer. Five of the strikers were sent to prison in Panama City. Dalton was recalled to Navy Bay and was replaced by Mr. King as supervisor. The men then abandoned the strike and resumed their tasks.

Lyons testified that if the workers complained about their conditions, they were threatened and intimidated by an armed squad of local ruffians maintained by Miller, Story's superintendent. The laborers lived in shanties, slept on straw, "and if we asked for a bed, we would get a lick of a stick." The men had to eat their lunch in the open, regardless of the weather. They were afraid to complain in case Miller turned his armed henchmen on them. Murphy was admitted to hospital in March suffering from fever. During his two-week stay there, he claimed a doctor only saw him twice. According to Lyons's testimony, "The diet in the hospital was bad and sour." Murphy was then discharged from his employment on the grounds of sickness. The doctor failed to give him a written certificate to this effect, and Story used this technicality to justify his refusal to pay Murphy's arrears of wages.

Murphy had to pay two dollars a day for his accommodation and food while awaiting a ship at Aspinwall to take him back to New York. When he returned from Panama, Murphy became a charity inmate of a New York hospital and asked for his arrears of pay, "the price of his sweat, and blood, and health." Michael Doheny drew attention to the condition of his client, "standing before the Court today emaciated, sick, helpless, penniless and in rags." Doheny's eloquent pleading, as well as the facts of the case, led the judge to find for the plaintiff. The *Irish American* reported a similar judgement in a number of other cases but provided no details.[50]

In September, Michael Doheny was back in court, this time representing a plaintiff called Downing, another former Story employee. Downing sued the contractor on the grounds of illness allegedly caused by the deficient quantity and quality of food. This case was adjourned until September 27, but the New York papers remained silent on the outcome.[51] A few months later another case in New York threw more light on labor conditions during the Story period. Simpson Hamilton and nineteen other laborers signed an agreement to work for the contractor in November 1852. A dispute arose when Hamilton and his coworkers were told that they would not be paid on days when rain prevented them for working, a frequent occurrence during the wet season. The men protested and threatened the company's agents with violence. A storehouse was broken into and provisions stolen, probably because the men were not being fed while on strike. As a result Simpson Hamilton was sentenced to three months' imprisonment in Panama. He claimed that his incarceration by the company made it impossible for him to fulfill his contract, and he sought the wages due to him.

Not surprisingly, Hamilton lost his case. Justice Phillips ruled he had breached the terms of his contract. The judge, however, lambasted the workers' agreement with the contractor, describing it as "a harsh, inequitable, unjust and cruel paper, deserving but little, if any indulgence from any Court—a contract which places poor and ignorant laborers in a foreign and inhospitable clime, totally at the nod and mercy not only of the defendant [Story], but of any of his underlings who might be disposed to annoy or oppress them—a paper containing stipulations which any person of intelligence would indignantly reject, and at which humanity revolts."[52]

The engagement terms for technical personnel did not differ greatly from those of laborers, apart from the salary. The contract of an assistant engineer hired in April 1851, specified that the period of employment was six months with a salary of one hundred dollars per month, plus board, lodging, and medical attendance, together with a return passage by steamer. In the case of sickness, certified by the company's physician such as to require leaving the Isthmus, the employee would receive a free passage back to New York. One month's wages would be retained by the company as a guarantee for the faithful fulfillment of the contract, which would be forfeited if the employee left or deserted without the written permission of the chief engineer or the company's agent.[53]

Regulations for employees, circulated in 1856, provided insight into the railroad's ethos and the duties and obligations of its workers:

> Each officer and man shall devote himself exclusively to the Company's service, and he must serve *when* and *wherever* he is required, by day or by night, he being allowed for any extra work at his usual daily rate of compensation.
>
> Each person is *promptly* to *obey* all orders he may receive from the officers placed over him, and in whose pay-roll his name is entered.
>
> The Company shall have a right to *deduct* from the pay, such sums as may be fixed by the Chief Engineer, as fines for neglect of duty, and disobedience of regulations; and every man in the employ of the Company shall be considered as holding his situation subject to this *condition*.
>
> The use of intoxicating drink on the road, or on the Company's premises, is strictly forbidden, under penalty of *fine* or *dismissal*.
>
> No instance of *intoxication* on duty, or about the Company's premises, will ever be overlooked, and the offender will be *fined* or *dismissed*.
>
> Gambling on the Company's premises is *strictly* forbidden under penalty of *fine* or *dismissal*.
>
> No one will be employed or continue to be employed, who is known to be in the habit of drinking intoxicating liquor, or of gambling.
>
> Any one guilty of disobedience of orders, negligence or incompetency, will be *fined* or *dismissed*.
>
> Any one guilty of *incivility* or *rudeness*, or the use of *improper language* while on duty, will be *fined* or *dismissed*.
>
> Any one guilty of wantonly *destroying* or *injuring* the Company's property will be *fined* or *dismissed*.
>
> Any one who shall be dismissed before he has served three months in the Company's employ, shall refund the price of his passage from New-York to Aspinwall, which sum, together with such fine or fines as he may have subjected himself to, shall be deducted from any monies that may be due him.[54]

The company obviously considered that these stringent regulations were necessary to control and discipline a large all-male multinational labor force in a region largely devoid of the agencies of law and order.

As already noted, abandonment of their work by employees was a pressing issue for the railroad's management, particularly in the early phase of construction. Difficult working conditions, an unhealthy climate, and the facility with which easier, safer, and more remunerative employment might be obtained, either on the Isthmus or in California, led many workers to down tools and abscond. The California gold rush generated considerable wage inflation in Panama, making it difficult for the company to compete with better paid sources of employment. However, Totten's ability to respond, by offering higher wages, was constrained by the need to keep construction costs under control during the early years of the project when the company's financial situation was precarious.

The issue of desertion was acute in 1850 and 1851 when the gold rush was at its peak; the demand for services of all kinds by migrants crossing the Isthmus had soared. The company was understandably irked by the fact men it had hired and transported from a variety of locations, often at considerable cost, availed of their free passage to Panama to leave in search of better opportunities elsewhere. It has also been claimed that the "wily old predator, Cornelius Vanderbilt," sent agents to Chagres to entice workers to sign up with his enterprise in Nicaragua by offering higher wages, thereby depleting the labor force of his rival, Aspinwall.[55]

Inability to compete on the wage front, as well as desertion, led the chief engineer to adopt the tactic, previously mentioned, of retaining a proportion of the men's wages until they had completed their contracts. This measure was resorted to early on and was maintained throughout the construction period. The *Panama Herald* supported the policy of withholding part of the wages of laborers, particularly those from the region. "The plan of retaining a portion of the laborers' wages, as security for the due performance of their duties, is the only way to control them. It is scarcely necessary to tell those who know the character of the laboring classes in this country . . . that as soon as the native gets a few dollars in his pocket, he will do no work until it is spent, and no contract, however binding, can retain him, if caprice or the hope of bettering himself prompts him to break it."[56]

It has also been alleged that the railroad authorities resorted to more drastic methods to prevent desertion. Parker claimed that "as well as withholding wages, the Company authorized lashings by overseers and the use of stocks to keep men on the job."[57] The use of such brutal methods was, however, confined to Story's contract period when they were applied largely, though not exclusively, to the nonwhite workforce.

The railroad also tackled the problem of desertion by successfully persuading New Granada's civil authorities to punish men who abandoned their jobs before completing their period of engagement.[58] As a result, a number of railroad employees ended up in Panama's prisons because of desertion. Despite the sanctions of the civil authorities and the financial penalties imposed by the company, desertions continued, particularly while Story was in charge of construction.

Desertions became more infrequent following the contractor's departure in September 1853. In any case, the factors that had enticed workers to abandon their posts had lost much of their former potency by this stage. Working conditions for the company's employees improved after Story had left. Alternative employment opportunities declined as migrants now spent less time and money on the Isthmus thanks to the greater frequency and capacity of steamboat services to San Francisco and the growing monopolization of transportation across Panama by the railroad. The get rich quick lure of the California goldfields had also begun to fade by 1853. There was, however, a renewed though short-lived spike in desertions by Chinese indentured workers following their arrival in 1854.

Parker and Conniff maintained that a vigilante force organized by the railroad in 1853 and headed by an American merchant, Ran Runnels, suppressed desertion by workers, broke up a strike by employees, and publicly flogged the Panamanian official who had organized the stoppage. The source was an unsubstantiated account in Schott's history of the railway.[59] Schott, in turn, was probably influenced by Tomes, who maintained that New Granada's government delegated to the railroad the authority to control its large body of laborers and that it established a private police force for this purpose. This body "kept the thousands of unruly laborers in wholesome subjection."[60]

It is likely that Tomes confused an ad hoc group of armed locals, already referred to in the Murphy court case and known as Miller's men, with a separate paramilitary body under Runnels. Miller's armed gang intimidated workers during the 1852–1853 Story period, but this group had no connection with the later body organized by Runnels. This latter group, known as the Isthmian Guard, did not appear until the second half of 1854, when the railroad was close to completion.[61] The declared purpose of the Guard was to clear the Cruces trail of the bandits who plagued travelers and attacked the mule trains carrying gold and merchandise between the railhead and the capital. There is no record of a strike by railroad employees in 1853, and there were no reports of widespread unrest among the workforce in the latter part of 1854 or early 1855 that could have caused the company to use its private security force as strikebreakers. It is possible, of course, that labor disputes were not reported in the press and that the mere existence of the Isthmian Guard could have deterred potential strike organizers.

The short-term contracts under which men were employed may have led them to tolerate disagreeable working conditions while knowing that their stay on the Isthmus was transitory; this may explain the surprising lack of strikes reported. Long delays in paying wages, a common cause of strikes in railroad construction in the United States, did not appear to have been an issue in Panama.

As previously noted, the first strike occurred in the closing days of 1850 when laborers on Manzanillo Island refused to work until provided with better food. The strikers, some of whom were armed with revolvers and knives, threatened company officials. This stoppage ended quickly when the men were given mosquito nets and improved meals.[62] Some months later, a group of French laborers went on strike in May 1851, but again the stoppage was short-lived.[63] During the cholera outbreak of 1852, local workmen, fearing contagion, downed tools and assembling in front of a wages office, demanded their back pay with the intention of abandoning the work. Totten confronted the strikers and refused to concede to their demand.[64] The strike ended, and the men went back to work.

The main exception to this pattern of short and infrequent strikes occurred during the Story period when the number of stoppages by men infuriated by their working conditions increased. Some of these protests, as noted earlier, were provoked by the decision not to pay laborers on days when rain prevented them from working. This stipulation, which was not included in their contracts, generated resentment that was expressed in work stoppages lasting several days, a few of which turned violent. On other occasions, the men hired by Story called strikes to protest against insufficient food and its poor quality.[65]

In some instances those involved were imprisoned for alleged offences, while in other cases, Story's superintendents and foremen may have given way and acceded to demands. Rather than go on strike, some French employees opted to swear affidavits about their treatment in the presence of the French consul in the capital.[66] The number of labor stoppages declined after the company resumed control of construction in 1853.[67]

While labor relations during the construction period were characterized by occasional work stoppages, most of these passed off relatively peacefully. Only one strike was reported to have resulted in a fatality. A black worker from Cartagena was shot dead in a fight between engineers and laborers at the end of

1854. The event merited only a brief mention in the press, and no information on the cause and outcome of this fatality was provided.[68]

A decade later, the *New York Times* reporting on the suicide of James L. Baldwin, who had worked as assistant engineer on the Panama railroad from its inception, stated that he had been obliged to leave the Isthmus in the mid-1850s "to avoid punishment for causing the death of a Carthagena [*sic*] Negro, a laborer on the road."[69] Baldwin may have been responsible for the 1854 death, as he fled the Isthmus about that time. Following his return to Panama to resume work with the company some years later, he shot dead William Parker, a railroad superintendent in 1868, before fatally wounding himself.[70]

The relatively small number of protests and work stoppages was also a consequence of the absence of union activity among a multinational force, divided by race, language, religion, and culture. The location—thousands of miles from the nearest centers of labor organization in the United States, where, in any case, the labor movement was still in its infancy—also likely contributed. The enervating climate and the bouts of sickness it frequently engendered sapped the militancy of workers' leaders and would-be labor activists, making them more apathetic and compliant than might otherwise have been the case. Despite claims to the contrary, nothing suggested the absence of strikes was due to repressive policing of the workforce—the Story period being a possible exception.

The railroad company, as opposed to the contractor it temporarily engaged, maintained tolerably good labor relations with its workforce by mid-nineteenth-century standards. Most workers seemed satisfied with their conditions and pay, judging from a few statements by employees and from occasional press reports and comments by travelers. One newspaper explicitly linked the absence of strikes to good labor relations. "The general good treatment . . . has another excellent effect—it almost entirely prevents anything in the shape of 'strikes' individual or collective."[71]

The absence of reported legal actions by employees against the company also suggested that its industrial relations were more harmonious than those under Story.[72] Although an exacting taskmaster, Totten was aware of the benefits of treating his laborers with consideration and tact. Interpreters were attached to the squads of Spanish-speaking workers to ensure that their white foremen's instructions were clearly understood. The chief engineer explained that "I am very careful to visit them and to instruct the superintendents in the mode of treating and working them. As you say, the good man, who understands them,

Figure 8.2. Railroad Station at Aspinwall (Colón), Mid-nineteenth Century. Classic Image / Alamy Stock Illustration.

will do more with 8 or 10 of them than another man would with 50."[73] Trautwine subscribed to a similar solicitous labor relations approach. He maintained that migrant workers from the Cartagena region worked well if treated kindly and firmly, though he admitted that their attitude often changed when they became aware of their ability to earn more elsewhere.[74]

The working day lasted for a grueling twelve hours, closely matching the number of daylight hours that were constant throughout the year at Panama's latitude. Men rose before dawn and toiled from sunrise, shortly after 6:00 a.m., until the sun was close to setting, at 6:00 p.m., for six days per week. Sunday was their only day of rest. Given Panama's oppressive climatic conditions, and even allowing for one or more meal breaks, this represented a long and arduous shift for men working mainly with picks, shovels, axes, and wheelbarrows. While some of the Irish laborers resented being "rooted out of our beds at half past four in the morning," this early start was required so that men could breakfast and be at their appointed place of work by sunrise.[75]

A letter from a Jamaican laborer disclosed that he breakfasted at 6:00 a.m., had another light meal at 9:00 a.m., followed by dinner at 2:00 p.m., and supper at 6:00 p.m. It is not clear if this routine was enjoyed by all or only by the West Indians.[76] After their midday meal, the men resumed work until sunset. According to one press report, when the six o'clock evening bell sounded, operations ceased immediately. "Wheelbarrows were upset, shovels and picks gathered up, and the spot deserted, where a moment before all was activity and bustle."[77]

Laborers worked in gangs supervised by foremen. Conditions were frequently disagreeable and onerous, particularly in the rainy season, though the men may have enjoyed an occasional respite during particularly heavy downpours. In the course of the final months of construction, the dawn-to-dusk schedule was dispensed with, and men worked in shifts around the clock in a frenetic attempt to finish the line.

However, the railroad, reflecting the Protestant ethos of its founders and directors, was averse to Sunday working. The executive and finance committee, concerned by reports about "the profanation of the Sabbath by the Company's employees performing work," stressed "the importance of discontinuing Sabbath employments of every kind in connection with the business of the Company on the Isthmus."[78] The hard-pressed employees, whatever their religious persuasion, were doubtless relieved to have one day per week to recuperate from their backbreaking labors. Workers collected their pay on Saturday evening or Sunday morning.[79]

The Panamanian and the U.S. press, as well as travelers and writers visiting the Isthmus, generally viewed the company and the treatment it accorded its employees in a favorable light, though it was not clear how objective these judgements were. Most of the newspapers surveyed distinguished between the treatment accorded to the railroad's employees and that given to the contractor's men. They tended to be critical of Story's treatment of his workforce and contrasted this with what they claimed was the company's more benign management practices.

According to the *Panama Herald*, the company's employees were treated kindly and liberally and "universally express themselves satisfied."[80] The *Panama Star* agreed, claiming that "the great mass of their laborers were always satisfied with their employment and treatment."[81] During the early stages of construction, an American journal portrayed working conditions as almost idyllic. "The wages given are good, and every man is treated with attention and good feeling—no more work imposed upon him than is considered prudent.

The superintendents and engineers are perfect gentlemen of education and much travel—they are principally from New York."[82]

Another American publication painted the chief engineer as a benevolent father figure, a portrait that some of his employees might not readily recognize. Colonel Totten "sparing no energy, at his post, ever kind, attentive, and humane, to those under him, won the sympathy, good will and love of all."[83] According to the *Panama Star*, "The discipline [among workers], so far as I could hear and judge is excellent; and the men seem as contented and industrious as any body of men can be on such work."[84] The paper made no secret of its generally favorable disposition toward the railroad company.

> Our files will bear us out . . . that we have ever been the defenders of the railroad company against the animadversions of impatient or thoughtless assailants. We have never fawned upon nor played the flatterer to any individual connected with either its management or its construction; but we have always taken pleasure in commending their good works, and when opportunity presented itself, have done what we could to remove unjust prejudices and correct what we believed to be untrue statements in relation to it. For this we claim no credit, and seek no reward, other than the consciousness of having done what is right.[85]

The *Aspinwall Courier* also painted a flattering picture of the company as an employer. "One great secret of the success . . . of the Panama railroad is their treatment of the workmen along the line . . . we feel confident that the laborers on no public work in the world are better cared for than on this."[86] Some months later, the paper continued in the same obsequious vein. "There are no idle hands to do mischief: payments are regularly made, and with great care and exactness; the sick are constantly watched, and by a faithful, industrious and skillful corps of physicians, and the general duties of a prudent and vigilant supervision are daily discharged throughout the entire line of the road, by an emulous, energetic and experienced body of superintendents."[87]

The *Courier* was unlikely to criticize the city's largest employer, especially as the railroad had given it a small subsidy of $300 during its first year of publication.[88] Large-scale desertion by Chinese laborers in 1854 and the railroad's reluctance to ameliorate their subsequent state of destitution should raise doubts about the reliability of some of the above assertions and expose the ingenuousness of the local press's attitude toward the company.

These comments in local journals, which were often reprinted by American and other foreign newspapers, should be read with a degree of skepticism. The company was, after all, the most important business enterprise and the largest employer on the Isthmus, where it wielded considerable financial, commercial, and political influence. Local newspapers occasionally carried advertisements for the railroad. Their editors and owners, some of whom were Americans themselves, were probably loath to criticize an influential U.S. company that also happened to be an actual or potential revenue source.

Travel books and memoirs dealing with Panama in the early 1850s also tended to portray the company's treatment of its workers in an uncritical and flattering manner. A surgeon, formerly employed by the railroad, provided an example of the fulsome attitude adopted by many, though not all, writers: "The railroad company makes the most liberal provisions for their [laborers'] comfort."[89] The company, for its part, was adept in handling public relations. Its policy in this respect astutely foreshadowed that of twentieth-century corporations. Visiting American, British, and other foreign dignitaries, journalists and men of letters were entertained and hospitably treated by the railroad, which resulted in generally favorable reports in the printed media.[90]

One notable example was the invitation extended to guests, including American newspaper men, to attend the formal inauguration of the line in 1855. The company brought the group from New York on an all-expenses paid trip, lasting five weeks, during which they were liberally wined and dined. This resulted in favorable publicity for the company. One example was Robert Tomes's publication, *Panama in 1855*, a well-written and witty account of his trip containing an uncritical and unreliable history of the railroad's construction. It has, unfortunately, formed the basis for many later accounts.

In summary, conditions for the ordinary worker on the railroad varied according to the period under consideration. The situation was particularly grim during the early stages of construction but improved somewhat as the tracks moved away from the low-lying coastal swamps after 1851. Conditions deteriorated again during the period when Story was in charge of construction between 1852 and 1853 but got slowly better thereafter. Nevertheless, the climate, dense jungle, steep ravines, powerful mountain torrents, together with malarial fevers and tropical diseases, continued to make the laborer's life nasty, brutish, and sometimes short.

NINE

Workers' Amenities

INFORMATION ON THE AMENITIES AVAILABLE FOR THE COMPANY'S workers, as on many other mid-nineteenth-century railroad construction projects, is sparse. Details of the provisions made by the Panama railroad for the comfort and well-being of its thousands of employees during the course of construction are scarce, scattered, and often incomplete. Much of this information may never have been formally documented in the first place, reflecting the scanty importance attached to workers and their rights by employers during an era of unfettered capitalism. What the railroad attempted to provide by way of housing, food, and medical services for its small army of workers will be examined here to the extent permitted by surviving documentation.

Living quarters on the Caribbean coast were nonexistent at the start of construction in May 1850. There was nowhere to lodge the men employed in clearing the marshy Manzanillo Island of its covering of trees, bushes, and mangroves. Everyone involved—engineers, supervisors, technical staff, and laborers—was forced to sleep aboard an old two-hundred-ton schooner, which had brought construction materials from the United States and was now anchored in the bay. From May 1850 until the year's end, the annual rains deluged the landscape and conditions aboard the schooner got worse as more laborers arrived.

Otis supplied a graphic account of the discomforts to which all were subjected at this time.

> The whole party were forced to live on board the brig, which was crowded to its utmost capacity . . . below decks the vessel was alive with musquitoes [sic] and sand-flies, which were a source of such annoyance and suffering that almost all preferred to sleep upon the deck, exposed to the drenching rains, rather than endure their attacks. In addition to this, most of their number were kept [sic] nauseated by the ceaseless motion of the

Figure 9.1. The First Shanty. F. N. Otis, *Illustrated History of the Panama Railroad* (London: Sampson Low, 1862). Courtesy of the British Library Board.

vessel. Labor and malarious influences during the day, exposure and unrest at night, soon told upon their health . . . their sufferings were severe.[1]

A second vessel was later pressed into service for sleeping accommodation, and while it alleviated the pressure of numbers, conditions for those on board improved only slightly. James Baldwin, a senior engineer, attempted sleeping under canvas on the island, but he discontinued the experiment after he fell sick from fever within a week.[2]

Once a path for the railroad had been cleared through the mangroves on the mainland for a distance of several miles, it became too onerous and time consuming for the men to trudge between their work and their sleeping quarters on the old hulks out in the bay. Two prefabricated timber buildings, each twenty-five feet by one hundred feet, were sent from New York to provide sleeping accommodation as well as storage space for supplies, construction materials, and equipment.[3] Sickness among the carpenters—at one time only two out of twenty-eight men were able to work—together with desertion, delayed the erection of these buildings until the beginning of December.[4] Otis described the semiaquatic location of a shanty for the early accommodation of workers. "Here was erected the first dwelling-house, built of rude boards, high upon the stumps of trees, to raise it above the waters of the swamp, and in the heart of this dank, howling wilderness our hardy pioneers took up their abode."[5]

Early in 1851, the chief engineer listed the buildings he needed: sleeping quarters, with each man to be allocated a space of seven feet by three feet; dining rooms; kitchens; supervisors' quarters; hospital accommodation; carpenters' and blacksmiths' shops; and so forth. "Sheds will also be required about one mile apart, where the men can dine and shelter themselves in case of rain—very probably some of these may be made of palm leaves."[6] Not long after, a wooden-frame house belonging to the company was dismantled and stolen by thieves. "Robbing is no crime in these parts," Totten commented cryptically.[7]

A glimpse of the company's housing arrangements in early 1851 at the riverside hamlet of Gatún was provided by a workman. Ten tents, sleeping a total of 120 men, were grouped around a cluster of more permanent buildings. These included a storehouse, carpenter's shop, blacksmith's shop, engineering store, cooking galleys, and a small hospital under the charge of Dr. Masters. By mid-1851, Gatún camp had increased in size to accommodate between two hundred and three hundred men.[8]

Totten asked for two thousand yards of secondhand canvas to erect temporary shelters in June 1851, an indication that timber for housing was not arriving fast enough to meet the requirements of a growing workforce. He specified that the canvas should be coated with tar to waterproof and preserve it from the mildew and rot engendered by Panama's humid climate.[9] Temporary canvas accommodation remained in use for the next few years. In 1854, the Chinese interpreter Wang-te-Chang described staying overnight in one of these structures. "This station house is very small, its wall is made of cloth and the top covered with reeds."[10] The noise from thousands of croaking frogs penetrated the canvas walls of Wang's quarters, disturbing his sleep.

More substantial structures slowly superseded canvas housing. Clusters of shacks or shanties were built, often on stilts or platforms to raise them above the waterlogged ground, in which workmen, of the same nationality, where possible, were grouped. By November 1851, according to Captain Chappell of the Royal Mail Steam Packet Company, workmen had been provided with housing along the line of the railroad as far as Barbacoas, though the type of accommodation was not specified.[11]

The railroad also rented rooms in the growing number of privately owned timber-built hotels and lodging houses as an interim measure to meet its accommodation needs. These buildings had been hurriedly erected by enterprising local and foreign entrepreneurs to house migrants crossing the Isthmus. The construction of a large boarding house for railroad employees at Aspinwall was authorized in late 1852, but it was not until several months later that the building was ready for occupation. "Our carpenters on the Island are now engaged [in] finishing a boarding house for the men, with the object of bringing all of them within our own quarters, and putting an end to their boarding among the hotels."[12]

A traveler provided a brief description of Aspinwall's early buildings. "The houses are all of wood and built on piles, the first floor being raised about three feet over the ground. All the building material has come from the States."[13] Some of Chagres's timber buildings were dismantled and reassembled at Aspinwall, as the abandoned port declined into obscurity. Bishop Kip recounted that a wooden tavern in Cruces reminded him of the improvised accommodation provided by the railroad for its Irish workers. "It has no glass in the windows, and is about as enticing in appearance as the long shanties erected for Irish laborers."[14] Some of the railroad's stations at this time were "merely small collections of shanties and leaf-roofed huts, forming depots for the *materiel*, and lodging houses for the personnel." The laborers at Gatún were more fortunate, having moved into substantial plank-built, two-storied lodgings by 1853.[15]

Housing conditions had greatly improved by early 1855 with laborers occupying "large and commodious frame boarding-houses built at stated intervals upon the line of the road." These buildings had been transported from the United States.[16] The standard of the workers' accommodation impressed Trollope, the eminent novelist, who visited Panama some years later. "At intervals of four and a half miles there are large wooden houses—pretty-looking houses they are, built with much taste,—in each of which a superintendent and a certain number of laborers resides. These men are supplied with provisions and all necessaries by the company."[17]

References to the quality, standard of comfort, and internal layout of the railroad's housing accommodation were sadly lacking. "It is not known whether all the quarters were alike, how they were furnished, and how comfortable the occupants could have been."[18] All categories of employees likely shared the same quarters at the start of construction, given the shortage of housing. Administrative and supervisory staff would have moved into separate accommodation once initial difficulties had been overcome.

Beds were also in short supply in the early phase of construction. Cots, consisting of a wooden frame with a canvas base, were initially pressed into service. A shortage of these cots caused trouble after the arrival of a contingent of 150 men in December 1850. Totten appealed to New York to send more. In May 1851, he announced that he was awaiting the delivery of a further five hundred cots.[19] By the following year, the shortage of beds had been overcome, and iron bedsteads were being shipped from New York to replace the cots.[20] However, during the period when Story was in charge of operations, some Irish laborers complained that they had to sleep on straw in their shanties.[21]

Having a bed to sleep in was no guarantee of a good night's rest however, as one traveler confirmed. "My coverless cot was beset with fleas from below, and mosquitoes from above; and about midnight a huge spider had found its way to my person, and was marching with his multitude of crawlers leisurely up my back. . . . The body of this animal was an inch and a quarter in length, and half an inch broad; and was covered with red hair, like that of the horse or cow!"[22]

Because of the limited variety and volume of Panama's agricultural production in the 1850s, virtually all the provisions consumed by the workers had to be imported, almost exclusively from the United States. The logistical achievement of providing three meals a day to hundreds and eventually thousands of workers over a five-year period was remarkable, given the distance from suppliers in the United States, the slowness of sea-based transportation, the nonexistence of refrigeration facilities, and the almost total lack of a road network on the Caribbean side of the Isthmus. Tons of fodder to feed mules and horses also had to be transported from the United States and distributed to isolated work camps deep in the rain forest.[23] According to one estimate, the railroad chartered 158 vessels during construction to bring supplies and materials to Aspinwall.[24] A provisioning accomplishment of this magnitude can be justly compared to the challenge of supplying a small army in the field thousands of miles from its headquarters.

The chief engineer's correspondence occasionally included lists of food items. Soon after construction had started, Totten requested twelve barrels of beef, together with ham, codfish, herrings, beans, peas, cornmeal, sugar, butter, and potatoes. Also included in the order were soap, quinine, and axe handles.[25] A few months later, he ordered pork, beef, rice, flour, potatoes, molasses, and four barrels of pickles. Some of the men suffered from scurvy, which might explain the request for pickles.[26] Orders for tea and tobacco were made in later requisitions.

Workers on Manzanillo Island were clearly unhappy with their provisions at the end of 1850 because they staged a strike on December 22. They went on to pass resolutions not to resume work until they were provided with better food. A letter written by a worried subordinate to the chief engineer, who was absent at the time, announced: "Dear Sir, I am sorry to inform you that most of the white men on the island have this morning refused to go to work on account of bad coffe [*sic*] and bad bread. I am sorry to say they act as no well-bred men would act under existing circumstances. Your presence is much needed here."[27] This protest produced the required result because a day later, Totten announced that the men had been provided with good food and mosquito nets, "which should put an end to their troubles." The rapidity of his response suggested that Totten had released stockpiled provisions or that he had purchased additional supplies locally.

Shortly afterward, the chief engineer said that he expected the arrival of another 250 men and that he lacked food, knives, forks, cups, and plates and would have to purchase these locally.[28] Fortunately, prior to their departure from New Orleans for Chagres, each worker had been provided with wool blankets, a tin plate, cup, knife, fork, and spoon, and they brought their own cooking stoves.[29] Totten might have been able to acquire additional provisions locally by the time of their arrival. The quality of the food provided in early 1851 remained poor. According to one account, provisions given to workers consisted of old musty hardtack or sea biscuits, bread made from inferior flour, bad corned beef and pork, half-cooked salty beef (referred to as "salt horse"), and coffee without milk or sugar. Roasted yams were the only vegetables.[30]

As the size of the workforce expanded, larger quantities of food had to be imported and steps were taken to stockpile several months' provisions at Manzanillo Island.[31] Substantial consignments, amounting at times to hundreds of barrels of beef and pork, were unloaded on the island. On March 30, 1853, for example, two hundred barrels of beef, pork, and rice were shipped to Aspinwall.[32] Large quantities of beef, pork, flour, beans, rice, bread, molasses, tea, coffee, sugar, vinegar, soap, and tobacco continued to arrive throughout 1853 and 1854.[33] Some of these foodstuffs were dispatched from New York in sailing vessels, a more economical, though slower, form of transportation than side-wheel steamers. The average passage time to cover the 1,961 miles from New York to Aspinwall by sailing ship was twenty days, about twice as long as by steamer.

The length of the voyage by sail and the high ambient temperatures of the Caribbean caused perishable food to go bad and butter to melt. Totten complained in 1853 that "the vegetables spoil when the passage is long. Some lots have arrived good for nothing." He repeated his dissatisfaction with the quality of imported food shortly afterward. "Vegetables sent by sailing vessels are almost entirely lost. It would be best to send them only by steamer. Butter sent to the men is not fit to eat. I think cheese would be better."[34] Some tropical produce, like yams and plantains, were shipped from Cartagena, less than three hundred miles away, most likely to feed local workers.[35]

Food was not the only necessity in short supply during the initial construction period. The water tanks on Manzanillo Island, which relied exclusively on rainfall, were empty by January 1851, not long after the start of the dry season. The company was obliged to send to the nearby town of Portobelo for deliveries of water in casks.[36] Periodic water shortages occurred throughout the construction period. Although the company imported no alcoholic beverages in keeping with its teetotal policy for employees, local traders were not slow to supply this deficiency whenever an opportunity arose. These vendors frequently defied the efforts of the company to suppress the sale of alcohol at stations along the railroad's route.

A network of kitchens was gradually established in the camps along the line of the railroad, where meals were prepared and then distributed to the workers. Chinese kitchen staff, recruited in New York, did some of the cooking. The executive and finance committee noted in August 1851 that six "Chinamen" had been sent as cooks to the Isthmus by the last steamer. Another two Chinese cooks left from New York on October 20, 1852, together with other workers.[37] From 1851 onward, the company established commissaries or company stores at Aspinwall and other locations. These sold food, provisions, and clothing to company employees.[38] An advertisement in a Kingston newspaper in 1854 promised Jamaican recruits "a full supply of food and wholesome beef, pork and bread, and a doctor when necessary." Judging from a letter from one of these men, the company lived up to its culinary promises. "At six in the morning, green tea and biscuits; at nine o'clock yams, biscuits, beef and pork; at two o'clock dinner—soup, beef, pork, yams, biscuits; at six o'clock in the night—corn flour pap [mash], coffee and biscuits."[39]

The comments of some Irish workers about their food were not so flattering, especially during the Story period. John Murphy claimed that "the board we got on the railroad was not fit for a hog; many a hog would not eat it; we got biscuit that was so rotten and moldy that we would have to pick the maggots out of it; at other times we would get reheated rice that would be three days old and not fit to eat; at other times rotten biscuit and hickory beef."[40]

Story's men were not allowed to return to their shanties at lunchtime, probably to avoid the loss of working time. Instead, they ate in the open wherever they were, regardless of weather conditions. "We were in the habit of being sent out to eat in the hot broiling sun in a place where the trees had been cut away, and a notice was put up that if we went to eat in the shanties, that we would be fined ten dollars; Mr Miller put up a notice to that effect, and no matter what the state of the weather was, we would have to remain and eat outside, whether it would be raining or otherwise, or how hot it would be."[41]

Murphy was not the only employee to complain about the quality of food while the contractor was in charge of operations. A worker called Downing alleged in a New York court that his food, which he claimed was both insufficient and of inferior quality, had made him ill.[42] Another Irish worker employed by Story claimed that the men lived on salt beef, pork, and hard biscuit. "This food of itself, is enough to create a distemper in so hot a climate. What must it be when the constitution is broken down by the malaria of the country?"[43] Alexander Center, the company's vice president, quickly responded to this complaint. "The company have [sic] at all times, and will continue, to supply abundant food of good quality, and all necessary accommodations." Center repeated his claim shortly afterward. "I can confidently assert that in no instance has the company been discredited . . . by the want of ample supplies of good provisions. In this respect their men have been supplied regardless of any cost."[44]

A petition to the British consul from Irish workers in 1854 complained, however, about the quality and quantity of the food provided by the railroad company rather than by the contractor. The petitioners invited the consul "if you would be kind enough to come and inspect our food which we are quite certain you would not consider good enough for a wild African negro . . . our breakfast is cold coffee and hard bread, salt beef and pork, all boiled overnight and [we] have to work on that until such time as they consider it proper, at 12 or 1 o'clock, to let us in and have another feed of the same combustible [sic], beside it would not matter much if we were allowed to eat enough."[45] On the other hand, another Irish laborer informed a journalist shortly afterward that "the eating is good" and that his only grounds for complaint related to the climate.[46] The Chinese laborers were fed with salt pork, beef, and rice but lacked fresh vegetables, except for occasional yams, which caused them to complain. They were given tea once a day.[47]

Local newspapers printed approving reports of the workers' diet. According to one account, the men were furnished with "plenty of good food . . . we know that their food, etc., is generally best adapted for their proper sustenance and gratification—for we have several times eaten meals along the line at the same table with the large majority of those laboring at the stations, at which we have happened to stop—and we have always found those meals excellent."[48] A journalist's description of a meal at Gatún station suggested, however, that his fellow diners were senior staff rather than laborers. He sat down to "a well spread repast prepared by French cooks, and served up by waiters evidently familiar with their duties. It was agreeable to find . . . luxuries that do not always grace the tables of the well fed at home."[49]

The complaints of disgruntled Irish and Chinese laborers should be considered in the context of the food available to the general public in Panama at the time. Judging from a small number of published accounts, meals served in the capital's restaurants were little better than those provided to the railroad workers. A local newspaper reported that "measled [worm-infested] pork, diseased beef, bread made of the very worst kind of damaged flour, rotten eggs and such like, constitute the class of food that is daily forced upon us, the only sustenance procurable in the city. The bread sold in Panama at the present moment is, without exaggeration, sufficient of itself to create sickness; the very smell of it makes one sick—and yet the bakers through the city are allowed to vend such filth to the public as good and wholesome food."[50]

Vendors were known to sell sea biscuits—a hard, saltless biscuit eaten by sailors aboard ship—that were moldy and worm infested. An American correspondent witnessed diners "partaking of every description of what I denominate 'slush cookery', viz. things swimming in horrid lard and rancid butter."[51] The food served to those who could afford to dine in restaurants and hotels, although costly, was not appreciably superior in quality to that available to the ordinary consumer. "Food was scarce and expensive. Although strips of dried jerked beef were a staple, workers and whites alike ate monkey, iguana or snake stew to survive. Often it was best not to ask what was put in front of you in the so-called 'hotels'. Water was also hard to come by."[52]

At first sight, the absence of fish from the workers' diet might seem striking, given that Panama's coastal waters and rivers teemed with marine life.[53] However, a lack of fish curing and smoking facilities, combined with high ambient temperatures and nonexistent refrigeration, apart from expensive imported ice, curtailed the consumption of fish away from immediate coastal and riparian areas. Tropical fruits were also remarkable by their absence from the laborers' diet. Here again, a lack of refrigeration and a widespread prejudice against the eating of fruit that was characteristic of the era played a part. Indulgence in fruit was believed to be responsible for some outbreaks of cholera and fever. One travel writer admonished his readers that "it is best to *avoid all fruits entirely* [author's italics]; but if indulged in, let it be in moderation, and early in the morning."[54] Despite the dietary shortfalls and the criticisms listed here, the railroad accomplished a remarkable feat in sourcing large quantities of provisions in the United States, transporting them two thousand miles by sea, and distributing them to hundreds and sometimes thousands of workers in Panama's forested interior between 1850 and 1855.

Cultural and recreational facilities for the railroad's builders were virtually nonexistent. The company saw little reason to make provision for its employees' leisure activities. Construction gangs labored in a hot and humid climate for close to twelve hours per day, six days a week, often in isolated locations, and so it was unlikely that the men would have time, energy, or opportunity for recreational activities, apart from what they might engage in on Sunday, their one day off. It was not until after the railroad had been completed that workers at Aspinwall were provided with a library of sorts, a billiard room, and a church where those of a Protestant persuasion could worship.[55] Panama City lacked theatres, art galleries, libraries, and concert halls, and there were few amusements to entertain the general populace, apart from cockfights and bullbaiting. A *New York Times* correspondent complained that "Panama is still excessively dull; and a cock-fight each Sunday afternoon is the sum total of our amusements."[56]

Bullbaiting provided an alternative and more energetic source of amusement for the capital's residents. Every Sunday and holiday, a bull was tied to a stake in a city square. The unfortunate animal was roused to fury by being gored by pointed sticks and darts before being let loose to career through the streets, where he was challenged by men brave or foolish enough to shake colored blankets at him. "This sport is kept up until the poor beast becomes so exhausted that he is frequently unable to leave the ground without the severest beating."[57]

There were countless saloons and taverns where both drinking and gambling took place, in the towns and settlements along the line of the railroad. Prostitution flourished in most nineteenth-century seaports and Panama City, Chagres, and Aspinwall likely boasted a number of brothels. The conventions of the mid-Victorian period were so strong, however, that contemporary references to houses of ill repute in Panama in the 1850s are lacking. However, a steamship agent hinted at the expatriate lifestyle: "Most persons at Chagres become dissipated in a few weeks; and between drinking too much, running after women, or gambling, exhaust all their energies, and when they get sick, have no vitality left in their systems to recover."[58]

A more recent writer has claimed, without providing a source, that there were over two hundred prostitutes at Chagres during the early gold rush days, and that a brothel, known as the House of All Nations, was staffed by an assortment of white, brown, and black women from Panama, New Orleans, and Paris.[59] Aspinwall apparently boasted a famous brothel, the Maison du Vieux Carre, which specialized in French girls, though no references to this or similar establishments appeared in the local press.[60] Bordellos like these would have catered to the needs of the local population as well as serving the throngs of unattached male migrants on their way to and from California and Oregon. They would also have attracted the patronage of railroad men bereft of female companionship. Referring to the recreational haunts favored by California migrants, one writer reported, "The most sordid kinds of doss-houses, brothels, saloons and gambling dens were improvised to extract what was left of their savings, and some were left destitute." Another commentator claimed that the railroad laborers "by most accounts spent their earnings in bars, brothels and gambling dens."[61]

The company opposed the sale of liquor to its workmen in saloons or bars located close to the line, not for moral reasons, but because of alcohol's detrimental effects on the workforce's behavior and performance. Totten reported in 1851 that "quite a number [of local workmen] deserted from Gatún under the plea that they could not work in the water—but really under the influence of the rum from the village."[62] On another occasion, the company took drastic action to stamp out drunkenness among its employees. According to the chief engineer, "The men on the station [near Gorgona], in consequence of their

Figure 9.2. Panamanian Women in Typical Costume, 1845. Engraved illustration, *Magasin Pittoresque*, 1845. Shutterstock Stock Illustration.

free access to liquor, had become disorderly and almost uncontrollable."[63] The company demolished the grog shop in question provoking a dispute with the *alcalde* or local mayor, who sided with the saloon owner.

In November 1853, the chief engineer summarized the railroad's policy on the consumption of alcohol. "Spirituous liquors are not allowed to be brought to the railroad stations; persons not connected with the work are not allowed to build there; and disorderly persons are ejected from there. Where two or three hundred men are collected together, these regulations are necessary in order to maintain good order and discipline."[64]

The consumption of "spirituous liquors" was forbidden in employees' contracts and intoxicated workers faced dismissal. This was not an empty threat as some inebriates found to their cost. Totten ordered one of his foremen to return to New York in 1852 for this reason. "I regret to say that Mr Bell's habits of intemperance, since he has been at Barbacoas, do not permit me to retain him in this service, and I have therefore requested him to retire." The following year Totten fired one of his engineers for repeated drunkenness. "The engineer last out, Comstock, is such a drunken fellow, I have been obliged to discharge him. I gave him three trials, and yesterday made a bargain with him that if I caught him drunk again I should throw him into the sea. This morning he was ripe for the drenching, but I let it pass and [now] turn him off for good."[65]

The company also frowned on gambling. Regulations governing the conduct of employees in 1856 forbade gambling on the company's premises under the penalty of a fine or dismissal. Persistent gamblers were threatened with the loss of their jobs, though Totten's correspondence did not disclose if this sanction was ever imposed.[66] Despite the company's strictures, alcohol and gambling were among the few outlets for relieving the loneliness, boredom, and home-sickness that afflicted many employees. Conditions were particularly trying for white laborers, most of whom lived in primitive conditions in isolated work camps, far from home, among a population whose language and customs they did not share. Even trying to read at night was an exasperating experience; lamps and candles attracted swarms of mosquitoes and other flying insects that aggressively attacked the reader.

The railroad, in addition to housing and feeding its workers, attempted to look after their medical needs. The recruitment and transportation of large numbers of men to Panama represented a considerable financial outlay for the company. The provision of basic health services in a region largely bereft of these facilities was essential if its employees were to effectively carry out their duties, particularly given the well-deserved reputation of the Isthmus as a breeding ground for fever and disease. The company would have been aware, from mid-1850 onward, that nearly every white person going to work on the Isthmus was attacked with fever, generally within a few months after arrival, though it did not disclose this information to potential employees for obvious reasons. The occupational hazards of accidents and injuries that were the inevitable consequence of building a railroad across difficult and often challenging terrain reinforced the need for medical services.

Not long after work had started on Manzanillo Island, Totten ordered a supply of quinine.[67] Workers clearing the island were provided with the drug in an effort to reduce sickness levels from malaria, though how many of them actually took the bitter-tasting medication on a regular basis is not clear. Robinson claimed that "sulphate of quinine became a prime necessity—almost an article of diet."[68] The unpleasant side effects of taking large doses did nothing to enhance quinine's appeal to workers.[69] According to one employee, the workers were given doses of quinine that they washed down with a swallow of brandy.[70] Early in 1851, Totten reported that many of his men were sick with fever, his stock of quinine was exhausted, and he had been obliged to purchase supplies locally. Although one hundred ounces of the drug had been ordered by Dr. Gage, the company physician, the consignment had not yet arrived from New York.[71] Quinine, as well as other drugs and medical supplies, continued to arrive from the United States throughout the remainder of the construction period.[72]

Workers clearing the mangrove swamps were provided with gauze masks to cover their faces by day and nets to sleep under at night. This helped prevent them from being bitten by swarms of mosquitoes and flies. By the end of 1850, all of the men on Manzanillo Island had been provided with mosquito nets.[73] The number of employees was small at this point, and the cost of providing nets to everyone would not have been great. Without anyone realizing it, these measures would have been partially effective in reducing the incidence of malaria. At the time, however, it was universally accepted that the disease was due to miasma or bad air emanating from rotting vegetation. The connection with mosquitoes remained unknown.

There are no further references to the supply of mosquito nets, which might suggest that this beneficial practice may not have been continued once the workforce had moved to the mainland. At night workers customarily slept with the windows and doors of their quarters left open because of the heat. Without nets, they had no protection from mosquitoes and other insects that thrived in the rain forest. These practices unwittingly contributed to the spread of malaria and other illnesses. Furthermore, hard physical work in high temperatures and energy-sapping humidity tempted newly arrived laborers to discard hats and some of their clothing. This resulted in some being badly burned by an equatorial sun or becoming prone to sunstroke.[74]

In September 1850, not long after work on clearing Manzanillo Island had begun, the directors authorized the recruitment of a head physician and an assistant at an annual salary of $1,800 and $1,000 respectively. Shortly afterward, Dr. Franklin Gage and Dr. Masters were appointed to these posts. By December, additional medical staff, including Dr. J. A. Totten, a brother of the chief engineer, were in post, though a decision on building a hospital at Navy Bay was temporarily deferred.[75] Trautwine recorded that the doctors struggled heroically to treat numerous malaria patients. "Drs. Gage and Totten, of the Medical

Corps, repeatedly left their own sick beds to administer to the necessities of the workmen, although conscious that their so doing must cause a relapse of their own fevers."[76] A supervisor pleaded with Totten in 1850 for better medical facilities. "Our sick are suffering very much for the proper conveniences of the sick bed, both bedding and diet and many other articles which I have instructed the doctor to enumerate to Dr. Gage. It seems to me to be greatly for the interests of the Company to furnish these little necessaries to protect the health of the men."[77]

At this stage, the capital housed Panama's only public hospital, the San Juan de Dios Hospital. The infirmary was located on the far side of the Isthmus, with no road links from the Caribbean coast. The outlook for those patients who entered it was decidedly ominous. "There is such a plentiful lack of medical and other attendance, that the poor patient may be considered as dead from the moment he enters its portals."[78] The railroad obviously needed its own infirmary on Manzanillo Island to serve a growing number of workers. The chief engineer's advocacy of a company hospital was based on pragmatic rather than humanitarian grounds. Totten believed that if hospital admission regulations were strictly enforced, there would be less malingering among the workmen: "The well would be more easily distinguished from the sick; there would be fewer imaginary ills among the laborers."[79]

By January 1851, a prefabricated hospital was under construction in the United States, but its erection in Aspinwall did not begin until July.[80] In the meantime, Dr. Gage, the physician-in-chief, fell ill and had to be invalided home at the end of 1850. His deputy, Dr. Masters, replaced him as chief medical officer.[81] More medical personnel arrived from New York throughout 1851. Most of these physicians and surgeons, like the company's other employees, were hired on short-term contracts, usually remaining on the Isthmus for about six months.[82]

Allegations have been made that the sale of the pickled bodies of the company's dead workers, shipped in barrels to foreign medical schools, funded its hospital in Aspinwall. This accusation appears to have originated with Minter, who claimed that a high death rate brought the railroad's hospitals "a neat profit, from shipping cadavers in wholesale lots to medical schools all over the world."[83] Schott repeated the claim, adding that this initiative originated with Dr. Totten and that the bodies of men who had been murdered on the Isthmus were also disposed of in this way.[84] According to McCullough, "For years the Panama Railroad Company was a steady supplier of such merchandise, and the proceeds were enough to pay for the company's own small hospital at Colón."[85] Grigore alleged that the company sold about one thousand cadavers to medical schools.[86]

None of these writers provided documentary evidence to support these allegations.[87] If true, the railroad most likely would have concealed its involvement in this trade, and the absence of references to it in company documents would not be surprising. However, the disposal of the remains of their dead colleagues in such a callous and mercenary manner would have distressed surviving members of the workforce. The probability that this information would eventually enter the public realm was high, and no such disclosures appeared to have been leaked to the press or to visiting travelers in the 1850s.

Once the tracks reached Monkey Hill, this became the site of the railroad's cemetery later known as Mount Hope. Totten's correspondence disclosed that dead workers were conveyed by rail for burial there in 1852.[88] According to Gorgas, "Here sleep most of the men who died during the construction of the Panama Railroad."[89] During the 1852 cholera epidemic, Totten complained that the company's coffins were too small for many of the bodies of dead workers; he made no reference to pickling these cadavers. Chinese laborers did not refer to the alleged sale of bodies, complaining instead that their dead were interred in mass graves without any funeral ceremony.[90] Minter appeared to contradict his earlier assertion of the sale of cadavers when he alleged that a full-time crew of carpenters and painters was employed at Mount Hope Cemetery in 1851 to make and paint the crosses marking the graves of dead workers.[91]

Even if some bodies had been sold prior to the cemetery's establishment, the relatively small size of the workforce up to mid-1851 would suggest that the proceeds were unlikely to have been substantial enough to fund the establishment and operation of the company's hospital. Furthermore, as noted below, the railroad voluntarily contributed to supporting a public hospital at Aspinwall from 1853, in addition to a hospital for its own employees. This would suggest an altruistic element in the company's provision of medical facilities. It was not governed, in this matter at least, by purely profit-and-loss considerations. Until more substantial evidence is forthcoming, the cadaver allegation must remain open to serious doubt.

The railroad's principal hospital at Aspinwall provided employees with "medical attendance, nursing and all necessary attention while sick."[92] Smaller ancillary hospitals were opened at different locations along the line, including Gatún, Frijoles, Barbacoas, and eventually Panama City. A visitor to the village of Tabernilla in 1852 lodged next door to a log house "where the sick men were sent when no longer able to work on the railroad." She was awakened in the night by the coughs of bedridden men.[93] A passenger who glimpsed some of the railroad's hospitals from a passing train in 1853 remarked that their "windows ... showed many fever-worn and saddened faces, among which I fancied I saw a few unmistakably Irish features and lineaments."[94]

Press reports on the company's medical provisions were almost invariably favorable, probably a result of the company's excellent public relations system. "Good physicians are in constant attendance all along the line—and notwithstanding the frequent incomings of laborers, after the idleness of a long sea voyage, their sudden transition to hard labor—their change of fare—and their frequent imprudences—a comparatively very small portion of their laborers ever die upon the road."[95] Some months later the same newspaper reported that "the sick are constantly watched, and by a faithful, industrious and skillful corps of physicians."[96]

Another local paper also lauded the treatment of sick workmen. "They [the company] ... always maintained an efficient and capable medical corps—so that the great mass of their laborers were always satisfied with their employment and treatment."[97] The fact that medical personnel, with possibly a few exceptions, did not speak Spanish and would have been unable to understand the complaints of Central and South American workers, who amounted to about 40 percent of the workforce, was not mentioned. This inability to communicate with patients would have applied with even more force to the company's one thousand Chinese workers in 1854.

In addition to providing hospital care for its own employees, the railroad pledged to make $5,000 available for a public hospital in 1852 "for the relief of destitute and other sick persons at Aspinwall, the expense when ascertained, to be borne equally by this Company and the United States Mail Steamship Company."[98] Prior to the opening of this facility, the outlook for sick travelers at the Caribbean port was grim. The sight of "saffron-visaged skeletons, stretched side by side on cots, in the heated rooms of hotels, on whom death had set its seal, with no loved one near to ease the aching limb or wet the parched tongue" shocked a visitor in 1852.[99]

Following representations by the railroad, a public hospital was opened at Aspinwall on June 1, 1853, to cater to travelers who fell ill at the port. Local citizens, the railroad, and the U.S. Mail and the Royal Mail Steamship Companies raised between $7,000 and $8,000 to enable the facility to begin operating. By July 1853 this hospital, designed for the relief of indigent sick foreigners, housed between twenty and thirty patients.[100] Those who could afford to pay were charged $3 per day. According to the American consul, "The nursing and other attendance [sic] are good."[101] The hospital facilities at Aspinwall were apparently well run. According to a visitor in 1858, the infirmary consisted of "a couple of large, airy buildings, surrounded by generous tiers of piazzas [galleries]. A general air of tidiness and comfort prevailed around that spoke well for their management."[102]

Although the railroad was under no obligation to subsidize the operations of this public hospital, it continued to do so for several years. Between May 1853 and June 1854, the railroad's contribution amounted to $4,123.50.[103] In April 1854, the directors agreed to an annual subsidy of $2,500 to the hospital—provided the two steamship companies subscribed the same amount between them. It subsequently withdrew this condition. In August 1855, the directors again confirmed their subsidy to the Aspinwall City Hospital.[104] This voluntary contribution revealed a degree of humanitarian concern that went some way toward ameliorating the railroad's more widespread image as an uncaring and profit-driven enterprise.

As the railroad drew closer to the Pacific coast, some sick employees started availing of the facilities at the capital's Foreign Hospital.[105] This institution had been set up in November 1851, like its later counterpart in Aspinwall, to cater for infirm migrants. It provided facilities that were superior to those of the long-established but underfunded San Juan de Dios Hospital. Voluntary contributions from foreign residents and business houses supplemented by donations from passengers passing through the port supported the Foreign Hospital.[106] At first the hospital catered exclusively to Americans, but citizens of other nations were subsequently admitted.[107] The resort to this hospital by railroad employees may have been simply a consequence of its proximity, as in the case of men who fell ill while working closer to the capital than to Aspinwall. It might also have reflected a lack of confidence in the railroad's own medical facilities.

At first, railroad employees were freely admitted to the Foreign Hospital, leading the *Panama Star* to propose that the company be asked to contribute to its support.[108] The hospital's governors, faced with the possibility of a growing influx of sick railroad men, later decided "that all persons who have been in the employment of the Railway Company ... shall be excluded from the benefits of the Hospital."[109] This decision spurred the railroad to establish its own hospital in 1854 under the direction of Dr. Halstead at Playa Prieta, close to the Panama City terminus of the railroad.[110]

The company also set up a separate hospital located about six miles from the capital to look after the growing number of infirm Chinese laborers who had arrived that year. This institution, which housed 150 patients in September 1854, was criticized by those unfortunate enough to have to avail of its services.[111] Once trains started running from ocean to ocean, the need for a large labor force declined, and the company began to prune back its medical services. The directors instructed the chief engineer in August 1855 "to abolish all intermediate hospitals at the earliest possible moment."[112]

While the Panama railroad provided medical services for sick and infirm workers, its attitude toward incapacitated employees was not one of compassionate benevolence. Only those seriously ill were considered for hospital admission. Even then sick workmen were retained as patients only if there was a prospect of their making a rapid recovery and being able to resume work. Men not classified as severely sick were treated as outdoor patients, and workers in this category exceeded the number of those admitted to hospital.[113] "Sickness," the chief engineer remarked in his report to the company's president and board in 1853, "is a serious item of expenditure."[114] The treatment of men seriously incapacitated by malaria and other fevers could be both lengthy and expensive.

The cost of maintaining a sick man in a hospital, possibly for an extended period and with no guarantee of a complete recovery, was around two to three dollars per day.[115] This led the company to adopt a two-pronged approach toward illness among its hospitalized workforce: patients considered to have prospects of a quick recovery were kept in hospital; those diagnosed as requiring prolonged treatment were discharged and shipped home. Local workers and West Indians in the latter category were dispatched to Cartagena or Kingston, while white men were sent back to New Orleans or New York.

Men dismissed on the grounds of illness were given written certificates by the medical staff. These entitled them to arrears of wages and free transport to the port they had enlisted in. The experience of John Murphy, an Irish worker hired during the Story period, indicated that the system did not always operate as planned. Admitted to hospital in March 1853 suffering from fever, a doctor saw Murphy only twice during his two-week stay before he was discharged and dismissed from his employment. Daniel Lyons, a fellow Irishman, alleged that "the doctor had a written list the last time, and called out 'John Murphy', and told him to get ready and gather his things and go off to New York, that he was not fit to work anymore." In this instance the doctor failed to give Murphy a certificate that he had been discharged on the grounds of sickness.[116]

The company, under its terms of contract, was liable for the return transport cost of its employees. In these circumstances it made economic if not humanitarian sense for the railroad to disclaim responsibility for treating those of its incapacitated employees who were unlikely to make a speedy return to work and send them to their port of origin in steerage class.[117] Once there, they would have to fend for themselves, at no further expense to the company. Shipping invalids home had the added advantage of reducing the mortality rate, as sick workers died in many instances only after they had left the railroad's employ. According to a company physician, "Our patients were sent out of the country as fast as they became unfit for further service, always provided they were not too sick. How many or what proportion of them died on the voyage to their homes is to me unknown."[118]

Men battling with illness and disease would have found conditions in steerage on their return voyage particularly trying. "In those days steerage meant dirt, crowded berths, foul air, food unfit for human beings, and many other horrors . . . the food was certainly very bad—spoiled, even worm-infested, beef and bread, quite out of the question as food."[119] According to the historian Hubert Howe Bancroft, "The steerage passengers were treated more like beasts than human beings."[120] Totten was aware that conditions in steerage were sometimes dire, and it would be wrong to infer from his frequent resort to repatriation that he lacked compassion for those sent back as invalids. Writing to the company's president, he admitted "that the sick suffer on board the steamers I do not doubt. It grieves me to see men leave here in such feeble condition. Unused to the sea, confined to the steerage, and with debilitated constitutions, they must suffer inconceivably."[121]

Men sent home with an invalid ticket had their passage paid for, but many were unlikely to have accumulated much in the way of savings and would have found themselves stranded at their port of disembarkation. On one occasion Totten asked for permission to advance invalided workers fifteen or twenty dollars each to enable them to complete their journey home from the port of New Orleans. "Some such arrangement would have a good effect on them."[122] Sick employees returning to the United States sometimes had drugs and medication dispensed to them during the voyage, and small payments to ships doctors for this purpose were authorized on several occasions.[123]

Despite Totten's qualms about the suffering experienced by sick men in cramped steerage quarters, he continued to rid himself of several thousand of them by this means. Totten announced in January 1851, "This month I send home all those persons who the surgeons declare to be useless. This includes some good men." In August, he explained that a large number of workers had recently gone home as invalids. On another occasion he chartered a ship for $1,200 to take about forty invalided men back to New Orleans. Two died and five were discharged from the hospital before the vessel's departure, "which makes the price of passage high, but considering that we are relieved from their care and attendance for two or three weeks, it is probably after all the most economical arrangement we could make."[124]

Masters of vessels returning to the United States were not always happy with their cargoes of sick and diseased men, as they put an extra burden on the crew. There was also the worrying possibility that some might be carriers of contagious and possibly fatal diseases. Totten warned the company president in 1851 that "unless some positive instructions be [sic] given to the captains of the steamers, we shall have trouble in getting them to take home our invalids. They begin to complain about turning their ships into hospitals."[125] Stephens appeared to have resolved this matter as Totten did not raise the issue again. In 1853, the *New York Freeman's Journal* criticized the continual arrival of sick workers from Panama. "Will Mr Spies [company secretary] deny, dare he deny, that every steamer from Panama brings to the hospitals of this city an average of eight to twelve of their railroad men dying, or broken down, with the Panama fever? . . . We know a good deal more about the hospitals, and the stories they tell, than Mr Spies chooses to know."[126]

Not all sick workers were promptly shipped home. An Irish carpenter alleged that he had been left ill in Panama for thirty weeks without proper medical attention or food. The carpenter also claimed he had to pay his own fare to New York, although his contract stated that his employer was liable for this.[127] This was during Story's period as a contractor. The Chinese were the exception to the policy of repatriating sick workers. After falling ill, they remained in Panama, almost certainly because of the expense involved in returning them to their distant homeland. This partly explained their shockingly high mortality rate.

Totten, a hard driver of men, was not prepared to tolerate work-shy employ-ees. In September 1850 he announced that men who failed to report for work because of sickness or any other reason would be charged for their board and keep. He admitted privately that this measure was "more to prevent feigned sickness than for any real intention of charging board for those who actually fall ill upon the work. I perceive already a good effect from it."[128] The following year he threatened that workers would not be paid while they were sick. "There is no doubt a great deal of old soldgering [sic] throughout the work."[129] This announcement, designed to discourage malingering and false claims of sick-ness, like his earlier one, contained more bluster than substance. It would not appear to have been implemented. According to the *Panama Star,* workers put on the sick list by the company's doctors continued to be paid.[130]

At the same time, Totten warned the company against sending him unfit and unhealthy men, specifying in particular those suffering from lung complaints, diseased livers and spleens, and syphilis. Recruits infected with the latter had to be treated by physicians at considerable expense, and most sufferers either died or had to be sent home. On an earlier occasion, Totten complained that he had been obliged to send back to Jamaica a number of workers who were blind or lame. He also repatriated, probably to Cartagena, fifty or sixty workmen whom he considered unfit to labor—"old, feeble and diseased"—in August 1851.[131]

Disease and illnesses of one kind or another were the major cause of put-ting members of the workforce out of action. In contrast, there were few refer-ences to injuries or deaths arising from accidents. No doubt many work-related mishaps were never reported in the press or were deemed by Totten to be of little significance, an acceptable if unfortunate corollary of railroad construc-tion. Among the few recorded incidents was that of a foreman who had his leg crushed while felling a tree in July 1851. It soon became necessary to amputate the limb. The unfortunate amputee developed tetanus soon afterward.[132] In April 1852, a laborer fell from a moving wagon and was fatally injured. The *Panama Herald* believed that this was "the first death which has resulted from accident since the opening of the rail road."[133] In 1853, a workman fell from one of the railroad cars and sustained injuries. He was taken to the company's hos-pital, where his wounds were found to be less serious than at first thought.[134]

In summary, the provisions made by the railroad, as distinct from those implemented by its contractor, for the care and welfare of its thousands of employees in a difficult and hostile environment were in many respects ad-equate, judged by contemporary standards. The company's record in the administrative, logistical, and medical spheres compare favorably, for example, with the shortcomings and mismanagement of the British Army's leadership in these areas during the contemporaneous Crimean War (1853–1856.)[135]

The railroad's policy of repatriating seriously ill men (the Chinese excepted) was understandable from a purely financial perspective, given the limited medical facilities then available in Panama, and the likelihood that many sick employees would not recover quickly enough to resume their duties before their contracts expired. Leaving them to fend for themselves on their return home, however, displayed a callous lack of concern for men who had sacrificed their health, in some cases permanently, for the progress of the railroad.

The railroad's failure to put in place a satisfactory policy for dealing with its Chinese laborers, once it became aware that they were not suitable, was heartless and mercenary, and has damaged its reputation subsequently. The company was also guilty of a lapse of trust and responsibility by failing to inform prospective employees of the inherent dangers of spending six months on the disease-ridden Isthmus. The Panama railroad, in these and other matters, was an exemplar of unfettered nineteenth-century American free enterprise, where the lives and welfare of ordinary workers were not matters of paramount concern.

TEN

Mortality

THE HEALTH AND LIVES OF THE MANY THOUSANDS OF WORKERS who went to labor on the Panama railroad in the mid-nineteenth century were significantly influenced by the geoclimatic conditions of the Isthmus and the diseases to which they were exposed. Panama forms part of the Greater Caribbean area, a region that had been a dangerous abode, if not a death trap, for Europeans from the sixteenth century onward. The fate of British and French military adventures and of European colonization schemes in this region showed that most newcomers born and raised in more temperate zones did not remain healthy for very long, especially in the rainy season. Within a few months of arrival, many outsiders succumbed to the tropical diseases endemic to the region.[1]

During the Spanish colonial period, the Isthmus of Panama, and particularly its Caribbean coastal zone, acquired a notorious reputation as a fever-infested land. Heavy rains for two-thirds of the year created countless pools of stagnant water. Assisted by the high ambient temperature, millions of disease-carrying mosquitoes would breed there. These blood-feeding insects had been present in Central America before the arrival of Columbus, but the importation of slaves from West Africa from the sixteenth century onward led to the introduction of disease-carrying parasites in the mosquito population. Some varieties of mosquitoes then became the vectors for the spread of two deadly diseases, yellow fever and malaria.

Yellow fever was the disease most feared by whites throughout the Caribbean area from 1650 to the early 1900s. It was often referred to as "yellow jack" or the "black vomit" because of the effects it produced on those infected. About one in every two diseased victims died, but those lucky enough to survive were immune to further attacks. Outbreaks of yellow fever appeared to be random and unpredictable. Its irregular and episodic pattern, combined with its high mortality rate, made it the Caribbean's most feared disease. The disease was mainly found in urban populations, whereas malaria had a largely rural character.[2] That yellow fever is spread by the female *Aedes aegypti* mosquito became known only toward the end of the nineteenth century.

In Panama, malaria was endemic, but the incidence of the disease increased with the onset of the annual rainy season, which brought a surge in the mosquito population. Malaria in Panama was spread by the *Anopheles albimanus* mosquito. The disease would typically manifest itself in one of two forms: vivax malaria, a milder form of the disease, killed about 1 percent of its victims; and falciparum malaria, the more deadly form, killed about 10 percent of those infected.[3] Falciparum malaria suppressed the immune system so that victims already weakened by other infections, who would otherwise survive, succumbed. Many unfortunates probably suffered from both malaria and yellow fever at the same time. Survivors of an attack of malaria did not obtain immunity, unlike those who cheated death from yellow fever. They did, however, build up resistance by undergoing repeated bouts of the disease. Quinine, made from the powdered bark of the cinchona tree, was used from the seventeenth century as a prophylactic and sometimes as a treatment for malaria. However, its bitter taste and nauseating effects discouraged many people from taking it.

The susceptibility of the railroad's employees to these two diseases depended to a large extent on where they had been born and raised. The population in the Greater Caribbean tropical zone, of which Panama forms part, suffered high childhood mortality from malaria and a somewhat lower death rate from yellow fever. Those who survived childhood usually enjoyed immunity to yellow fever and had acquired some resistance to malaria. By the time they became adults, they were less likely to fall ill or die from these diseases.[4] As a result men hired by the railroad from New Granada (including Panama) and Jamaica, together with those from the tropics of the East Indies, enjoyed stronger resistance to infection than their American or European-born counterparts. White railroad workers and gold rush migrants arriving in Panama from temperate climate zones entered an alien microbial environment with unprepared immune systems. As newcomers they were much more susceptible to endemic malaria and sporadic outbursts of yellow fever than workers born and raised in the Caribbean and other tropical areas.

One of the most controversial and perplexing problems in writing about the Panama railroad concerns the size of the death toll during construction. There

is no definitive and unambiguous agreement on the number of men who perished, and a categorical answer has not yet appeared possible. Estimates of the
number of workers' deaths vary enormously, from the company's declared toll
of 293 white men to the twenty thousand fatalities announced by one writer.[5]
Reports of a frightening mortality rate began to surface in newspapers from
April 1853 onward, as Story's period as a contractor was coming to an end. The
death rate had undoubtedly been high during the first year of construction,
and it rose again between June 1852 and August 1853 as a result of epidemics
of cholera and yellow fever and because of the contractor's negligent management of his workforce. Once rumors of a high level of mortality during these
particular phases of construction started circulating in 1853, an assumption
took hold in many sections of the press—and subsequently in American and
European public opinion—that a devastating death rate was a characteristic
feature of the entire period of construction.

The *Irish American* newspaper was one of the first into the controversy with
a doctor's warning to his fellow countrymen against volunteering for Panama
in 1853.

> I . . . wish to enlist your sympathies in [sic] behalf of humanity and Irishmen, to prevent
> the fearful sacrifice of life which must ensure by using Irish labor on the Isthmus. Not
> one laborer in twelve who goes there will ever return alive; and of those who die, the
> average term of life will be but three months. Those who have been upon the Isthmus,
> and have seen the crowds of mounds a little aside of the railroad track, can testify, that,
> to the Irish laborer, Panama is another word for death . . . If the railroad must be built,
> let it be with native labor . . . and not at the expense of the lives of some thousands of our
> countrymen. I am, with respect, Thomas Antisell, M.D.[6]

The doctor provided no source for his alarming statistics on Irish mortality
in Panama.

A few months later, the London *Standard* claimed that twelve thousand men
had died by mid-1853.[7] Grim mortality statistics, provided by a "respectable
physician," were quoted in an editorial of the *New York Freeman's Journal* on August 7, 1853.[8] The following day's *New York Herald* reprinted extracts from the
Journal's editorial: "We are credibly informed that at the end of three months,
the average mortality is fifty per cent, and that at the close of the fourth month
the deaths range as high as eighty out of every hundred."[9]

Spies, the company secretary, quickly denied the veracity of these hair-
raising figures, claiming in a letter to the *Herald*'s editor that only 214 white
men had died.[10] The figure for nonwhite workers was apparently not deemed

worthy of note. The *Panama Herald* entered the fray, declaring that it was impossible to provide precise mortality figures in the absence of an official register of deaths. The paper was on less solid ground when it proclaimed that "we have no hesitation in asserting, in the most positive manner, that the mortality here is not greater here than in New York or Nantucket."[11]

A medical doctor, writing to the *Cork Constitution*, claimed to have seen "immense numbers" of New Granadian workers dead and dying in the streets of Aspinwall.[12] An article in the *Shipping Gazette* published about the same time was of a similar opinion, stating that "the number of the slain in making the road can already be counted by thousands."[13] According to reports in several newspapers, six thousand Irishmen, aside from laborers of other nationalities, perished during the construction of the railroad.[14] An Australian newspaper quoted from an article describing a rail journey from Gorgona to Aspinwall in 1854: "It is said that the number of laborers, principally Irish, who have perished in making this part of the road, is so great, that the cars might, like that of the Juggernaut, pass the whole distance over their bodies. . . . The Panama Railway is a great undertaking . . . although thousands of lives have already been sacrificed to it."[15]

The *Daily Alta California* claimed that Mount Hope cemetery contained the graves of six thousand victims of "Panama disease," who died while the railroad was being built.[16] An Edinburgh journal reported that "the short railway across the isthmus of Panama . . . cost the lives of five thousand men."[17] Bidwell, writing in 1865, referred to "the immense amount of human life which was lost in that undertaking." He claimed that "the road was strewed with dead laborers—victims of fever, exhaustion, suicide—like a battlefield."[18] Robinson, who had worked for the railroad, intimated in his memoirs that twenty-four hundred men, "not more than forty per cent [of a total of 6,000] died in the service" during the course of construction.[19]

The wife of an U.S. army medical officer, whose husband had crossed the Isthmus in 1852 with Ulysses S. Grant, recalled that "shiploads of laborers for the railway died as fast as they came—or, as the saying was 'An Irishman for every tie.'"[20] An engraving entitled "Irish residences, Panama Cemetery" in a book published in 1891 appeared to give credence to claims of a very high Irish death rate.[21] These were not Irish graves, however. The caption was an ironic reference to tombs where bodies had been disinterred for nonpayment of rent to the cemetery authorities at a time when evictions of tenant farmers in Ireland had gained worldwide notoriety.

According to Abbott, writing in 1913, "About 6,000 men in all died during the construction period."[22] Minter claimed later that "the railroad's official estimate of deaths during construction was 6,000. The actual figure, based on an average of calculations by several impartial authorities, was about twice that."[23] Howarth asserted in 1966 that "it is certainly true . . . that the death rate was very high," but he gave no figures, though he believed that there were many thousands of fatalities. The author of a recent global survey of railroads suggested that if the figure of six thousand deaths, corresponding to approximately 120 per mile of track, is correct, this would represent "a rate worse than for any railway project before or since." Grigore estimated that between six thousand and seven thousand died during construction.[24] Schott maintained that between six thousand and twelve thousand workers died, an estimate repeated by a number of more recent writers and historians.[25]

Conniff opted for the higher end of this range: "Perhaps twelve thousand employees died." A recent reference book on Panama claimed that "the project took an estimated 5,000 to 10,000 lives." Small believed that possibly as many as five thousand out of a total workforce of seventy-five hundred died during the five-year construction period. Greenfield believed that estimates of five thousand to ten thousand deaths may be too low. Senior referred to an estimated mortality rate of 35 to 45 percent of an annual average workforce of six thousand. Alfaro estimated that over ten thousand workers died, while Espino doubled the number to twenty thousand. This would put the death toll on a par with what had taken place during the French attempt to build the Panama Canal even though the French employed almost five times as many workers as the railroad.[26]

Workers' mortality during the construction period is a topic particularly prone to wildly different speculations and ill-supported fantasies. Some of the more outlandish mortality figures mentioned above were used by earlier generations of commentators and authors to heighten the dramatic effect of their accounts. They failed to provide firm evidence to support their assertions and fell victim to the temptations of overstatement and hyperbole when dealing with death and disease on the Isthmus. More recent historians have accepted these extravagant estimates in good faith, thereby perpetuating a distorted picture of mortality on the railroad. Panama has been aptly described as "a land as feverish to the imagination as to the body."[27] Trautwine warned in 1851 of the tendency of visitors to the Isthmus to get "carried away by the novelty of the scenes by which they are surrounded." Captivated by their experience on the exotic Isthmus, they tended to "lose sight of all plain, matter of fact, business views of things."[28]

Panama's malign reputation as a place of pestilence, acquired over the preceding centuries, encouraged writers and travelers to exaggerate the death toll and made the public receptive to these reports. There had historically been a particular dread of the Isthmus. The general perception of Panama in the United States and Europe during the nineteenth century was that of one of the most pestilential regions on earth, a "sweltering miasma of death and disease."[29] Numerous travelers, writers, and artists who crossed Panama during the gold rush era helped to propagate an image of the Isthmus as a diseased and hostile place. Beneath the appealing surface of a paradise-like natural landscape of lush vegetation and brightly colored flowers, there lurked the threat of danger and doom for temperate zone dwellers rash enough to venture there.[30] Perceptions of this kind, based on ill-informed and damaging preconceptions and prejudices about Panama, made Americans and Europeans receptive to the unrealistic overstatements that pervaded much of the literature dealing with mortality on the railroad.

A minority of sources asserted, at the time and subsequently, that the climate was not as malignant and the mortality rate was nowhere near as high as generally portrayed. A senior member of the railroad staff who spent most of the second half of the nineteenth century living in Panama asserted, "It is not the deadly halfway station between Hope and Hades, Life and Death, that it has been painted." He maintained that the railroad's death rate "was comparatively low."[31] The *New Orleans Delta* claimed that only 450 laborers had died during the first three years of the railroad's construction.[32] The *New York Weekly Herald* estimated in 1856 that the mortality rate among white workers during construction was less than 1.5 percent.[33] Wyse claimed that Totten had informed him that fatalities amounted to only 835: 295 white men, 140 black laborers, and 400 Chinese.[34] Kemble believed that "the illness and mortality among the laborers has been grossly exaggerated," and he referred to "the rather fantastic estimates of 50-per cent and 80-per cent mortality." According to Haskin, "The loss of life in the construction of this road, serious as it was, has been monumentally exaggerated."[35]

Mack also believed that rumors of an appalling death rate during construction were unfounded. DuVal maintained that "loss of life among construction laborers was not large, except in the case of the Chinese."[36] The *American Railway Times* also believed that the mortality of workers had been grossly

Figure 10.1. Railroad through the Panama Jungle. Shutterstock Stock Photo.

overestimated. "Probably of the whole force employed not over 1,200 deaths occurred on the Isthmus, independent of the China importation."[37] These proponents of a more moderate mortality rate, like the advocates of improbably high figures, were unable to provide documentary evidence in support of their claims.

A propaganda war, waged in the early 1850s between advocates of the Panama route and proponents of the rival Nicaragua route, added to the uncertainty about the number who perished during the construction period. The former painted a rose-colored picture of health conditions on the Isthmus, while the latter aimed to blacken Panama's reputation by exaggerating the dangers of traveling there by spreading rumors of a fearful death rate among the railroad's employees. This propaganda war may have been initiated by George Law and his fellow directors of the U.S. Mail Steamship Company. It has been suggested that Law and his partners, worried by the cutthroat competition from ships plying the Nicaragua route, had "resorted to a whispering campaign, spreading accounts of the poisonous [Nicaraguan] climate and long delays encountered on Vanderbilt's line."[38]

The Commodore was accused of using similar smear techniques against the Panama route. Throughout the early 1850s, Vanderbilt allegedly ran a publicity campaign warning travelers and railroad workers of the perils they faced in Panama. He "circulated stories in New York of the hardships, disease, and delays awaiting Isthmian travelers and the insurmountable difficulties Aspinwall was encountering with his new railroad."[39] Several newspapers, including one in Ireland, cautioned their readers about the veracity of a high mortality rate among the railroad's builders.

> Much misrepresentation has been industriously circulated in the United States respecting the first of the above routes [via Panama]. The opponents of the line from Chagres to Panama [City] have put forth a statement . . . that the climate of Panama was found to be so deadly to foreigners, especially those from a northern climate, that few, compared with the number that died, lived more than a few weeks when employed in the construction of the railroad; and parties interested in the rival [Nicaragua] route are striving their utmost to deter working men from going to Central America to complete the line in question.[40]

The railroad, aided by Panama's English-language newspapers, countered the propaganda of the Nicaraguan camp by alleging that the Isthmus was no sicklier than other tropical countries. Dubious claims were even made that Panama did not differ greatly from southern and western regions of the United States in terms of health and well-being. The company played down the dangers involved in building the railroad and was not transparent about the levels of illness and death among its employees. The railroad likely deliberately suppressed information on these matters, aware of the danger that full disclosure would have on its ability to recruit a steady supply of new laborers.[41]

The fact the Isthmian authorities did not register deaths, and that official cemetery and burial records date from Panama's emergence as an independent state at the start of the twentieth century almost fifty years after the railroad's completion, compounded the difficulty of arriving at a reliable estimate of railroad employee mortality. Burial registers for the 1850s, if they ever existed, have perished, been lost, or destroyed.[42]

There is evidence, however, which would appear to cast doubt on a horrifically high death toll. In the first place, the continued recruitment of men from the United States almost certainly would have become unsustainable in circumstances where a decision to go to Panama would not have been far short of suicidal. However, press reports and company documentation confirm the arrival of substantial numbers of white workers from the United States throughout the construction period. Secondly, if the mortality level was as deadly as claimed, one might expect that higher wages would be needed to maintain a continuous supply of labor from the United States and elsewhere. In fact, wages for laborers on the Panama railroad remained relatively stable from 1851 onward and were broadly in line with those offered on some American railroad projects at this period.

Furthermore, the willingness of some workers to return to the Isthmus after completing their initial contract would suggest that the death rate was not as horrendous as many commentators have depicted. Employees would be unlikely to reenlist if they felt they had been lucky enough to survive an almost certain death sentence during their first contract. However, men who had previously worked on the railroad signed up again as laborers for a second or even third term. These workers were often promoted on returning to the Isthmus because of their previous experience and knowledge. Isaac Patterson, a track-layer, was one of those who wished to return in 1852, and Totten commented that "we should be glad to have him here."[43]

Totten's occasional warnings to the New York office not to reemploy certain men underlined the fact some workers were prepared to return to the Isthmus. The chief engineer complained in 1852 that among the laborers who had recently arrived in Panama were some who had gone home as invalids the previous month "and are not proper persons to return here so soon." The following year he reported that a group of departing laborers who were leaving for New York were "good men and can come back if they desire it." He warned the secretary however, that one individual had been discharged and was not to return.[44]

The company's vice president reported in 1853 that "many [workers] have to my knowledge served through a second and third engagement of the usual period of six months each."[45] Finally, if the mortality rate was as catastrophic as some commentators claimed, the number of workers who survived their contract period and returned to their places of residence would have been small; this was contradicted by newspaper reports of sizable contingents of former railroad employees disembarking from Panama steamers at New York, New Orleans, Kingston, and Cartagena.[46]

Given the absence of trustworthy mortality data for railroad employees, an alternative, oblique approach to arrive at a more reliable estimate of railroad deaths between 1850 and 1855 was called for. The solution I have adopted was to examine two sets of Panamanian death statistics relating to the 1880s and early 1890s. Having ascertained that health conditions on the Isthmus in this period did not differ greatly from those applying thirty or so years earlier during the period of railroad construction, I concluded that mortality data from the 1880s would also have been germane in the early 1850s. This motivated me to retrospectively apply a mortality rate derived from the 1880s data to the railroad's labor force of the early 1850s. Fortunately, some information on the death rate among the capital city's residents and among the French canal company's employees during the last two decades of the nineteenth century was available. This was thanks to the efforts of a renowned American specialist in tropical diseases, Colonel William Gorgas. Gorgas, chief sanitary officer of Havana at the close of the Spanish-American War, was entrusted in 1904 with implementing a gigantic public health program in Panama during the American canal building project.[47]

Not long after his assignment to Panama, Gorgas set about collecting data on the causes of mortality during the ill-fated French attempt to excavate a waterway during the 1880s and 1890s. Willing to learn from the past, he was determined to improve Panama's public health environment now that the United States had committed itself to completing the canal abandoned by the French. In 1906 Gorgas published two sets of data relating to mortality rates in Panama. One dealt with deaths from various diseases among the inhabitants of Panama's capital city between 1884 and 1905. The other was a compilation of disease-related deaths among employees of the French Canal companies between 1881 and 1904.[48] While not comprehensive, these appear to be the earliest detailed mortality statistics available for Panama. They provided a viable statistical basis for inferring the mortality rate among railroad workers thirty years previously.

Using information taken from the Gorgas data sets, I concluded that the average annual death rate of Panama City's inhabitants from 1884 to 1893 was approximately 11 percent, and the death rate of workers building the Panama Canal under French auspices between 1881 and 1889 was slightly over twice as high, at 24 percent. These are tentative estimates based on the limited statistical data available. A detailed explanation of how these figures have been arrived at can be found in appendix 4. Assuming, therefore, that the workforce of the French canal company in Panama in the 1880s was exposed to an average 24 percent death rate, how applicable was this finding to employees of the Panama railroad in the 1850s?

Few differences between the factors affecting workers' mortality during the first half of the 1850s, when the railroad was under construction, and those pertaining three decades later were apparent. Both projects relied on a multinational workforce composed of men from a variety of ethnic backgrounds. The intervening period had seen no major improvement in Panama's sanitary and public health environment or in tropical disease control and treatment in general.[49] "Little had changed on the Isthmus itself in the quarter-century since the construction of the railroad," according to Petras. "Workers on the French canal confronted the same geoclimatic and health conditions under which men had suffered in the building of the railroad."[50]

Both sets of workers confronted epidemics of dangerous diseases, while malaria continued to be an ever-present threat. As previously mentioned, there was a serious outbreak of cholera on the Isthmus in 1852, which claimed numerous victims. Yellow fever made its unwelcome appearance in 1853, though the number of those who succumbed was not clear. The canal workers faced a harrowing epidemic of yellow fever between 1885 and 1887, which killed several thousand, though in a workforce that was close to five times larger than that employed on the railroad.

I have concluded, therefore, that the estimated workers' death rate of 24 percent derived from the French canal period was also valid for railroad employees between 1850 and 1855. It is clear, however, that this mortality rate would not have applied uniformly to all ethnic groups composing the railroad's workforce. The Panama railroad relied on a broad multiethnic mix of employees. White men composed just over 34 percent of the total. The death rate among these men, all of whom came from northern, more temperate latitudes, would have been higher than average, probably amounting to an estimated 28 percent. This figure would broadly align with Gorgas's belief that the mortality rate among white employees of the French canal company ranged from 20 to 33 percent, depending on the period under consideration.[51] There would have been some variation in the mortality rate within the category of white railroad workers, depending on where individuals had previously lived and worked. Some of those from the southern and midwestern regions of the United States, for example, might have had a higher degree of resistance to malaria than those from the north.

Most white employees, however, had unprepared immune systems and had not developed a level of resistance to the endemic diseases and fevers of the Isthmus. Not only that, a majority of those hired as manual workers would not have been accustomed to hard physical labor in a tropical climate. Some recruits were probably malnourished and in poor physical shape when they signed up for Panama, and the voyage to Chagres or Aspinwall in the cramped steerage quarters of a steamship would have done little to improve their health and fitness levels. For these reasons the mortality rate of a small minority of white workers, including those who were recruited in Cork, may have reached as high as 33 percent, a similar rate to that of some of the laborers from France, who came to dig the canal in the 1880s.[52]

While the death rate of individuals composing the white group was related to their geographical background, it was largely independent of their occupational position while working for the railroad. Laborers and mechanics who formed the great bulk of the white workforce were more likely to suffer work-related injuries and accidents and may not have enjoyed the same standard of accommodation, food, and health care as their administrative, supervisory, and professional counterparts. However, tropical fevers, dysentery, and cholera were the main cause of illness and death in all categories of white workers. The mosquitoes and contaminated water carrying these diseases did not respect the social and occupational status of their victims. The differences in the death rate among the various occupational categories of white workers was likely minimal.

Comparative mortality statistics for white men from the northern hemisphere in nineteenth-century Central and South America are sparse. Spanish troops sent to the West Indies in the colonial period generally lost about a quarter of their men to disease within a few months.[53] Most of the 417 men who sailed to Portobelo with the adventurer Gregor MacGregor in 1818 to participate in the South American wars of independence were soon taken prisoner in Panama. Out of 340 captives, only 121 survived seventeen months later, an annual mortality rate of about 45 percent.[54] The death rate among white mercenaries who accompanied William Walker in his filibustering invasion of Nicaragua in the mid-1850s was also high. Thirty percent of his initial small invasion force was dead by August 1856, a little over a year from their arrival. However, an undisclosed number of these deaths was the result of military engagements.[55]

White indentured workers from the Canary Islands hired to build railroads in Cuba in the 1860s had a much lower average annual mortality rate of 5 percent over their five years of service.[56] However, these islanders were used to working in semitropical conditions in their homeland. When the Spanish army attempted to put down guerrilla insurgency in Cuba between 1895 and 1897, it lost almost 25 percent of its men to yellow fever and other diseases.[57]

The 227-mile-long Madeira-Mamore line in Brazil's Amazon region was probably the closest South American counterpart to the Panama railroad in terms of climate, terrain, disease, and deaths. A U.S. corporation started building this railroad in the 1870s to exploit the international rubber boom. Climatic difficulties, tropical diseases, and attacks by tribespeople led to great loss of human life, possibly amounting to between 28 percent and 33 percent of the labor force, before the project was completed in 1912.[58]

From the limited information available in the Panamanian case, it would appear that an overall average death rate of approximately 24 percent for all employees—rising to 28 percent, and sometimes higher, among the railroad's white workers—was plausible. Health conditions on the Isthmus in the 1850s were poor, mainly because of a lack of scientific knowledge about the causes of tropical diseases and low standards of hygiene and sanitation. Nevertheless, the terrors of living and working in Panama for a period of six months were generally exaggerated in contemporary writings and newspapers and did not hold true except in times of epidemics. With a death toll of about one in four, Panama clearly was not a healthy location for men coming to work on the railroad, but neither was a stay on the Isthmus equivalent to an automatic death sentence.

According to the railroad company's secretary, 214 white men had died out of a total of 3,352 employed between July 1850 and July 1853, a mortality rate of approximately 6.4 percent.[59] By the time trains started running between the Atlantic and the Pacific eighteen months later, the publicly disclosed death toll among white workers had risen to 293, an average of 4.9 percent, assuming a total white workforce of 6,000.[60] The company's mortality figure of 293 was almost certainly a fabrication. The number of deaths of white workers was grossly understated because this figure was totally at variance with the fatality rate incurred by the French canal company, the *Compagnie Universelle du Canal Interoceanique*, when it attempted to excavate the Panama Canal three decades later. The canal followed much the same route as the railroad. Furthermore, despite major improvements in sanitation and medical advances in the early twentieth century, including the elimination of yellow fever on the Isthmus after 1906, the death rate of workers during the American construction of the Panama Canal still approached a disquieting 10 percent.[61]

The railroad claimed that a list of 293 deceased white workers was available for inspection at its New York office. This document does not form part of the company's surviving papers and may no longer exist. In July 1851, Totten informed the company secretary that he was keeping a record of white fatalities. "I will have a list of the deaths which have occurred here made out and forwarded to you; but let me premise [sic] on no account to have them published—nor let any editor get hold of them." He returned to this theme shortly afterward in a letter to the company president. "Dr. Masters makes you a return of the names of those who have died on this work, with dates, diseases, etc., which I promised to Mr Spies for the purpose of answering the enquiries of their friends. Let me renew my caution to Mr S.—not to let any editor have a sight of it. Although it is not an alarming document, it would not look well in print."[62] Totten, aware of the negative publicity that would result if the number of deceased workers leaked out, was insistent that the real death toll should be kept secret. However, his choice of phrase that the death list was not "an alarming document" would suggest that the toll, at least up to that point, while high, was not as catastrophic as some later writers have alleged.

How the company arrived at the total of 293 white deaths was not clear. In May 1851, the secretary asked for instructions "concerning the settling of deceased men's accounts." The executive and finance committee responded that payments could be made only to the legally authorized representatives of dead workers. In cases where small amounts were due to the widows of deceased men, the secretary was authorized to use his own discretion.[63] This response confirmed that the company recorded the details of its white workers and their next of kin, including employees it had hired itself and those recruited on its behalf by labor agents. Based on these records, the company likely kept two registers of fatalities: a comprehensive, confidential list for its own internal records, referred to by Totten, and a smaller list for public disclosure. The publicly available register of 293 fatalities probably included only those men who had failed to return from the Isthmus and whose families, dependents, or friends had already contacted the railroad's office for information or wages due to them. These were men whose demise could not be concealed.

As will be made clear later, a majority of the company's white manual workers were most likely Irish born, and nearly all of these were recruited from the
large labor pool of Irish immigrants in the United States.[64] Many of these men,
particularly those who were single, formed a floating population of casual laborers, migrating from place to place in search of jobs after their arrival in the
United States. A good number would have had no close familial ties in New
York City where the railroad's office was located. Close to half of Irish laborers
at this period were illiterate, and a sizable minority spoke Gaelic with a limited
grasp of English.[65] In these circumstances it would have been relatively easy for
the railroad to keep quiet about fatalities among men of this class. Their deaths
in distant Panama were unlikely to provoke inquiries or investigations. The
company would also have been aware that the veracity of its list could not be
challenged, as the civil authorities on the Isthmus collected no data of this type.

Some deaths were likely to have gone unnoticed and unrecorded by the railroad in any case. Fatalities occurring in 1850 and early 1851, before the company
had established hospitals and ancillary medical facilities, were unlikely to have
been certified by the small number of physicians and surgeons then in post.
Even after hospitals had been established, many men would have succumbed
to illness and disease in isolated work camps and died before they could avail
of whatever medical assistance was available. The company would not always
be aware of their demise. Nor would the railroad have a record of the deaths of
sick and invalided ex-employees, which took place on board ships during their
return voyage or after these men had reached their destinations in the United
States. There was also a considerable level of desertion among white workers,
particularly during the project's early years. The company would not have been
aware of the fate of men who abandoned its employment in search of better
prospects elsewhere on the Isthmus or in California.

While the company would not have known the full extent of white fatalities,
there were obvious reasons why it would wish to conceal the extent of those it
was aware of. A full disclosure would generate unwelcome publicity for the railroad and for the Panama route generally. Statistics of this kind would frighten
the public and strengthen the widely held belief that disease and death were
real possibilities for anyone opting to cross the Isthmus. Potential travelers
might well take fright and decide to switch to the "healthier" Nicaragua route
instead. Furthermore, public disclosure of the risks involved in working on the
railroad would make it more difficult to recruit the constant stream of laborers

Figure 10.2. Aspinwall (Colón): Departure for Panama City. F. N. Otis, *Illustrated History of the Panama Railroad* (London: Sampson Low, 1862). Courtesy of the British Library Board.

and mechanics that was essential to complete the project. Wages might have to be increased to compensate these men for the acknowledged risks involved. This, in turn, would have implications for the cost of a project that had already overrun its original budget. Finally, publicizing the true death figure would do little to inspire public confidence in the undertaking, thereby weakening the company's share price and making its bond issues less attractive to potential investors.

If the six thousand or so white workers employed during the five years of the railroad's construction suffered from an estimated 28 percent mortality rate, then approximately seventeen hundred of these men perished—almost six times the total the company admitted to. It would be difficult to reconcile the discrepancy between the railroad's declared white death toll and the figure proposed here, even allowing for the possible extenuating factors listed above. Nevertheless, while a mortality rate of somewhat over one in four white men was appallingly high, it was nowhere near as devastating as that claimed in some of the alarming accounts published at the time and subsequently.

Difficulties also arose in attempting to estimate the number of fatalities among nonwhite workers, as the railroad kept no record of this kind. Most of these workers were recruited by labor contractors in their places of origin, far from New York. The names and details of those who died were unlikely to have been notified to the company's office or, if listed there, were soon discarded. The railroad would have felt no compulsion to keep a tally of these deaths because it was unlikely that relatives and dependents of deceased men hailing from New Granada, the West Indies, other Central and South America countries, or Asia would ever turn up at its New York office seeking information or unpaid wages.

The Panama railroad was not alone in neglecting to keep a comprehensive register of fatalities among its workforce. Railroads throughout the world at this period rarely recorded the number of men killed or injured during construction. Newspapers and journals of the period, as well as contemporary travelers, also displayed an indifference to, and lack of interest in, the welfare of the company's nonwhite workforce, reflecting a disregard, commonplace at that time, of these men. The fate of these laborers in a distant land did not greatly concern entrepreneurs and investors—or most of the press-reading public in North America and Europe.

The calculations presented here postulate a mortality rate of 24 percent for the entire cohort of workers employed by the railroad. The death rate clearly would have varied among the different ethnic groups, being lower among the New Granadian and other workers of the region, as well as among the Jamaican, Indian, and Malay laborers. This is not to imply that nonwhite workers would have found it easy to cope with Panama's heat and humidity or that they escaped the ravages of malaria or other fevers and diseases. However, malarial infections and relapses among these men would have caused less severe reactions than those experienced by North Americans and Europeans, and there was less likelihood of a fatal outcome.

Indian and East Indian migrants to the Caribbean area would have acquired some resistance to malaria prior to leaving their homeland.[66] Those who had suffered from dengue before arriving in the Caribbean might also have acquired resistance, and possibly immunity, to yellow fever.[67] Offsetting this was the probability that they did not receive the same level of medical attention from company personnel as white workers. Based on considerations of this kind, a tentative estimate suggests that the mortality rate among nonwhite workers, excluding the Chinese, was probably about two-thirds of that of the entire workforce. While this proportion cannot be proved, it is probably not too far from the truth. At approximately 16 percent, the estimated nonwhite death rate exceeded the 11 percent rate calculated for the inhabitants of Panama City, who enjoyed greater inherited or acquired resistance to the Isthmus's diseases, but it was also considerably below the 28 percent of their white counterparts. Even so, a lower mortality rate among nonwhite laborers should not blind us to the reality of the suffering and deaths experienced by this category of workers.

The horrendous death toll among the unfortunate Chinese workers, approaching 80 percent, far outstripped that of all other ethnic groups. The exceptional circumstances affecting this group of workers have already been discussed. A combination of opium addiction, with its ensuing mental and physical consequences, together with an inability to cope with the severe laboring demands made of them, caused many of these men to fall ill. Others deserted and became homeless. As chronically malnourished vagrants, they were highly susceptible to illness and disease. However, the policies adopted by the railroad to deal with its Chinese workforce, including the provision of second-rate medical care, and especially the absence of arrangements for the removal or repatriation of sick workers from Panama, were crucial causal factors in the appallingly high death rate of this group,

The death rate of railroad workers varied during the course of the five years of construction. It was higher for all ethnic groups during the first year while the line was being built over the low-lying marshes extending inland from the Caribbean coastline. These mangrove-covered swamps were ideal breeding grounds for *Anopheles albimanus*, the main malaria carrier in the region. Anecdotal accounts suggested that mortality was also higher than usual during the period when Story acted as the main contractor. His period of management, characterized by a deterioration of working conditions, coincided with the outbreak of epidemics of cholera and yellow fever.

The death rate may have fallen slightly from mid-1853 onward when construction was taken out of the hands of the contractor and the labor gangs had moved out of the unhealthy Caribbean lowlands and the Chagres basin to work on higher ground. The company, benefitting from its early experience of treating sick employees on the Isthmus, might also have improved the standard of hospital and medical care for its workers in the course of the final years of the project.

Recent investigations by climate scientists suggest a possible link between the occurrence of the El Niño weather phenomenon in the Pacific Ocean in the nineteenth century and spikes in diseases such as malaria and yellow fever in adjacent tropical regions.[68] Research has shown that in Colombia, formerly New Granada, the incidence of both vivax and falciparum malaria increased during the year of an El Niño occurrence and the following year.[69] Some climate investigators expressed high confidence that events of this kind took place in 1850 and 1854. There may also have been another El Niño event in 1851–1852.[70] If correct, these findings would go some way in explaining reports of high mortality among railroad workers that were probably due to falciparum malaria in 1850, 1851, 1852, and 1854 and to yellow fever in early 1853.

With a likely mortality rate of 24 percent, close to 4,200 men out of the Panama railroad's total workforce of 17,500 perished in the early 1850s, either on the Isthmus or shortly after leaving it. These deaths occurred at a time when the loss of workingmen's lives was considered a price worth paying for the advance of technology, progress and civilization. The value put on these lives was too often outweighed by the prospects of shareholders' profits. Consideration for the lives of ordinary workers was sadly lacking, particularly if these were not white. This was "an era when the life of a laborer counted very little if profits were in sight."[71] All too often, more attention was paid to safeguarding the rights of property and capital than to preserving human life. "Labor is exposed to dangers, difficulties, and even semi-starvation. Money is surrounded by safeguards."[72]

In this period of aggressive and relatively unconstrained American capitalism, investors, financiers, and entrepreneurs were not unduly concerned about the fate of workers in a distant country. In the words of a contemporary American journal, the railroad company was "undeterred by pestilence and death," and the cost of completing the rail link, in terms of human suffering and death, was of secondary consideration. "The undertaking was essentially a mercantile speculation, in which a profit on the capital advanced was the end of the project."[73]

White workers—Americans, Irish, and other Europeans—suffered the heaviest numerical death toll, with approximately 1,700 estimated fatalities. Laborers from New Granada and the Central American region, who formed

Estimated Death Toll of Workers on the Panama Railroad, 1850–1855

Ethnicity/Nationality	Number Employed	Mortality Rate (%)	Number of Deaths
New Granadians and Central Americans	7,000	16.00	1,120
Whites	6,000	28.30	1,698
West Indians	3,000	16.00	480
Chinese	1,027	77.9	800
Indians and Malays	473	16.00	76
Total	**17,500**	**23.85**	**4,174**

the largest ethnic category, rank next in the casualty list with an estimated 1,120 deaths. They were followed closely by the Chinese, who suffered proportionately the heaviest casualties, losing 800 men in less than a year. The remaining deaths, amounting to over 550, were distributed among the West Indian, Indian, and Malay workers, who were subject to an estimated lower mortality rate of approximately 16 percent.

To maintain that one in every four workers died during the five years of the railroad's construction or shortly after completing their contracts cannot be proved, but this estimate is probably not too far from the truth. Given the unreliability and lacunae in the company's records, and the absence of mortality statistics for Panama in the nineteenth century, the figures presented here can be no more than approximations. They are based, however, on an analysis of the limited statistical data currently available, rather than findings derived from historically dubious or inaccurate sources—or the products of fertile imaginations. Nevertheless, dry statistics and dispassionate estimates of mortality cannot come close to describing the everyday reality of illness and death that confronted the workers on the Panama railroad.

PART III

The Irish

ELEVEN

The American Irish

THE ESTIMATED NUMBER OF WORKERS EMPLOYED ON THE RAIL-road during the five years of construction was 17,500, made up of men from different ethnic groups. White employees, numbering about 6,000, formed the second largest of these groups, composed of an estimated 5,640 men hired in the United States and 360 in Cork. Most workers in the white category were laborers, with a sizable sprinkling of mechanics or tradesmen. Only a small number, probably in the region of 5 to 10 percent, could be classified as white-collar employees: engineers, draftsmen, administrators, supervisors, survey-ors, bookkeepers, clerks, and medical personnel. Nearly all employees in these positions were American born.

The question of what nationalities were represented among the thousands of white manual workers who toiled across the Isthmus has not been properly ad-dressed hitherto. There was a general assumption in the press and among most commentators at the time that because white laborers had been recruited in the United States, they could be classified as Americans. Workers arriving in Pan-ama from the United States were usually assumed to be natives of the northern republic. In this matter, however, appearance and language could be deceptive. Many of these Americans were likely to have been Irish-born men living and working in the United States. To the casual non-American observer, these Irishmen were virtually indistinguishable from their U.S.-born colleagues and were frequently subsumed into the general category of Americans.

The Irish were the largest English-speaking immigrant group in the United States at midcentury. They were identical in color, appearance, and dress to white, working-class Americans. Their manners and customs were not too dissimilar either. Irishmen constituted a majority of the laboring class of many northeastern American towns and cities in the 1850s, and they predominated in railroad construction. A sizable proportion of these immigrants, thanks to the efforts of the Democratic Party and Tammany Hall, would have obtained American citizenship during residency in their adopted homeland. Weaving themselves into the fabric of life in their new country, they were in the process of becoming Americanized. Many would have proudly self-identified as Americans. It is not surprising, therefore, that most of those leaving U.S. ports to work as laborers on the Panama railroad were mistakenly described as Americans or assumed to be Americans. A more accurate description would be American Irish.[1] The story of this category of white manual workers remains untold, in contrast to the considerable attention devoted to their Jamaican and Chinese counterparts by writers and academics.

Numerous references were made in company documents, newspapers, and travel accounts to Irish personnel among the railroad's employees, some of which have been mentioned previously. Between fifty and one hundred Irish workers, and possibly more, were brought from New Orleans to Manzanillo Island in 1850. Early the following year, Totten instructed Miller, one of his foremen, to go to the United States and recruit "young, hearty Irishmen," though Germans were also included in the engineer's hiring list. Miller returned to Panama in March 1851 with 153 men. A good proportion of these would have likely been Irish.[2]

When it came to hiring men for laboring work, the chief engineer was averse to engaging Americans. Totten complained in 1850 that American laborers were work-shy, wanting to do the minimum possible to ensure their passage to California. Some months later, he warned the company against hiring his own countrymen for manual work. "Americans are not fit for that work."[3] It would not be surprising, then, to find that a considerable proportion of the white labor force was not American born.

In June 1851, the steamer *Falcon* landed 180 Irish laborers from New York at Chagres. "Some difficulty occurred upon their landing, by the desertion of a number of them, who were subsequently secured and placed in irons."[4] The remainder of the group was dispatched to Gatún, about eight miles inland, to complete the stretch of track that linked it to the terminus at Navy Bay.

Totten's correspondence contained periodic references to Irish personnel among the workforce. In August 1851, he commented, "Miller has the natives working at this end of his work, in the swamp, and the Irishmen above," that is on a section of the mainland between Navy Bay and Gatún.[5] Evidence in a

New York court case suggested a considerable Irish presence on the railroad during its early years. Robert Fuller, a native of Killarney, appeared as a witness in a case relating to the recruitment of mercenaries for William Walker's disastrous filibustering expedition to Nicaragua in the mid-1850s. Fuller had worked on the railroad for a year, and in the course of his cross-examination, he stated that about five hundred Irishmen went to Panama at the commencement of the railroad.[6]

From time to time, the press reported the deaths of railroad men who were identified as Irish or who had Irish-sounding names. On February 18, 1851, Patrick Carroll, of New York, aged fifty and employed as a laborer on the Panama railroad, died of fever on board the *Cherokee* en route to New York. Not long afterward, on May 3, Christopher Mooney fell from the upper deck of the *Crescent City* at Kingston, Jamaica, and drowned. The ship was en route to New York from Chagres. Nicholas Synott, aged about forty, from Wexford, Ireland, died in Panama on October 22 but might not have been employed by the railroad. The death of another Irishman on his way back to New York from Aspinwall was noted in 1853: "September 9, Hugh Young, aged 37 years, a laborer from the Panama Railroad, died of chronic diarrhea, on board the *Illinois* and was buried at sea."[7]

Some of these press reports concerned alcohol-related deaths. The *Panama Herald* reported on April 21, 1851, that "the body of a man supposed to be an Irishman who had been employed on the Rail Road, was found floating in the Chagres River, a few days ago, since which we learn that two men have been arrested and charged with the murder. It is stated that the three had been on a 'spree', got intoxicated, and in all probability had a fight, the result of which was the death of one of them." A passenger traveling from New York to Aspinwall, in 1853, stated that two Irish laborers going to work on the railroad drank too freely of the bad liquor they had brought aboard. One died and was buried at sea, leaving a wife and child in New York.[8]

In another incident, "an Irishman, by the name of James Casey, a laborer on the Panama Railroad, was found dead yesterday morning, near the house of John B. Donalicio [probably Donnelly]. This is the effect of continued drunkenness, and if a number of his friends were to take warning in time, they might be saved from a similar fate."[9] These and similar newspaper reports neglected to mention that laboring long hours at backbreaking work in stifling temperatures in a far-off country tempted lonely and homesick men, devoid of other recreational opportunities, to drink their troubles away.

Workers with Irish-sounding surnames cropped up periodically in the company's records. The executive and finance committee resolved in June 1851 that a number of men, including a J. Ryan, who had completed their contracts, and who had been charged thirty dollars each for their return passage to New York, should have this money refunded to them.[10] A worker called James Halpin, who had initially signed on as a laborer, was subsequently employed as a cooper at forty dollars per month. Totten employed a man called Cavenagh as his steward, and the engineer recommended that his son, Peter, be hired as a waiter should he present himself at the New York office.[11] On December 13, 1851, James Whelan was listed among workers arriving at Panama on the brig *Rogelin*. An employee named John Burke petitioned the company for financial assistance in February 1853. He was awarded one hundred dollars, but no details of his appeal were disclosed. About the same time, Totten asked the company secretary, "Can you find another good masonry foreman to replace Dougherty?" A few months later, the chief engineer instructed New York that "Charles McManus is not to return."[12]

Commentators agreed, both at the time and subsequently, that many, if not most white laborers hired by Story for Panama, were Irish. Story, a prominent figure in the American construction world, would have had longstanding links with labor agents in the immigrant ghettoes of American cities.[13] These links could ensure a ready supply of Irish pick-and-shovel men. Referring to the 1852–1853 period in Panama, Otis wrote, "At times there was a force of several hundred men employed; but they were mostly Irish." His claim was echoed by the novelist Anthony Trollope: "The high rate of wages enticed many Irishmen here." Schott recounted that Story's labor force was "mostly Irish" and unused to the tropical climate. Howarth follows a similar line. "The contractor brought in a force of several hundred Irishmen, the 'navvies' who had done the spadework of the railways and canals of England."[14] The Irish and Anglo-Irish surnames mentioned in legal actions against Story in New York's courts for breach of contract, as well as the evidence presented, would suggest that most of these plaintiffs and witnesses were Irish born rather than American.[15]

A small number of Irish employees came to public attention because of allegations of criminal behavior. In February 1853, several Irishmen were charged with breaking into a company storehouse at Barbacoas. They were sent to the Panama City prison to await trial. The detainees applied to the British consul for release, alleging that they had been imprisoned because of their refusal to work. When the consul was informed of the reason for their arrest, he refused to interpose on their behalf. The prisoners, not lacking in ingenuity, then contacted the U.S. consul claiming that they were American citizens, having emigrated from Ireland to the United States. The American consul contacted the province's governor, who replied that the authorities were compiling statements from witnesses to the robbery and that justice would have to take its course. A local paper concluded that any sympathy for the Irishmen was mistaken.[16] The following month convicts working for the municipality as street cleaners recovered the body of an unnamed Irishman from the Playa de las Monjas near the capital. Nothing indicated how the victim had died.[17]

Another serious incident involving an Irish employee occurred in March 1853. A carpenter called John McHugo (probably McHugh), having refused to carry out his foreman's instructions, was put in the stocks by a supervisor called Young. This penalty revealed the harshness of the workers' treatment during the Story era. McHugo managed to escape from his degrading punishment and swore vengeance on Young. Armed with a sharp chisel, he mistook a superintendent called Stephenson for Young and fatally stabbed him. The expiring victim's cries led to the apprehension of McHugo. The accused was handed over to the authorities in Aspinwall, where he was almost lynched by the citizenry.[18]

McHugo faced almost certain execution for his crime but died before sentence was pronounced. According to one report, he "committed suicide last week in the gaol at Aspinwall, by taking poison." Another newspaper stated that the Irishman died from fever, "refusing to take the prescribed remedies for the cure."[19] A year later, two Irishmen, who may have been railroad employees, were arrested when they attempted to sell stolen items of jewelry at a price that excited suspicion. The Irishmen likely found items that had been discarded by the original thief while being pursued and decided to sell them rather than hand them over to the authorities.[20]

Irish laborers continued to be employed following Story's departure. The Episcopalian Bishop of California observed Irishmen at work while crossing the Isthmus in early 1854. "Occasionally, too, we saw groups of the Irish, who were employed as workmen on the railroad. They looked pale and miserable, and reminded me of the wretched peasantry seen in the vicinity of the Pontine Marshes in Italy. It is almost certain death to them to be employed here, and we were told that every foot of the road, so far as it has been finished, has cost the life of a laborer, and yet they are coming out by hundreds to complete it."[21] Widespread contemporary references to the myth that a laborer died for every foot of the railroad or for every tie laid was evidence of the persistence of Panama's grim reputation for disease and death—and, by implication, the railroad's image as a heartless employer.

Occasional press reports attested to the continued presence of Irish workers throughout the period of construction. In July 1853, a letter from Rory O'Moore, "the well-known and humorous Irish Consul in this city," possibly a pseudonym of John Power, editor of the *Panama Herald*, suggested that a significant part of the railroad's workforce was Irish at the time. The writer stated, "I . . . hope that Col. Totten and the *Irish Brigade* [my italics] under his command will push along the railroad to its completion with all speed."[22] Another reference to an Irish laborer came from a Dublin woman seeking to amend her marriage settlement. Her husband, William Moore, immigrated to America in 1852, where he signed up with the railroad. He contracted fever in Panama and, like many other sick employees, was repatriated to Ward's Island Hospital, New York, where he died in July 1854 of fever and ague.[23]

In 1855, the British consul sought the assistance of George Totten in tracing the whereabouts of John Fitzgerald, an Irishman who had arrived from Texas in 1851 to work on the railroad, bringing his wife and child along. The consul believed that "the poor man is probably dead," given that no communication had been received from him in recent years. The consular records contained no further reference to this matter. Fitzgerald's fate remains unknown.[24] We get a brief glimpse of another Irish worker in 1855 in Tomes's account of a visit to the railroad's hospital. While being shown around by the physician in charge, he encountered a patient suffering from fever, probably malaria. "Opposite, a brawny Irish laborer, with glaring eyes, a face glowing red like a furnace, his mouth gasping, his hot, steaming tongue protruding, and his great chest heaving, was tossing heavily about his bed, and throwing his great arms restlessly from one side to another. The Doctor rubbed his hands here, and whispered the remark, 'Good constitution, excellent stamina, will get well.'"[25]

An anecdote, possibly apocryphal, told of an Irish stationmaster employed by the railroad in 1855 who refused to accept dismissal unless he was defeated in a fair fight by his replacement. Numerous candidates proved to be no match for the incumbent until an American after a long and bloody boxing match finally beat him. However, the new American stationmaster, exercising his right to hire, then reemployed the Irishman as his assistant.[26] Two historians have also referred to an Irish presence among the company's employees. McGuinness recounted that recent Irish immigrants to America were recruited for Panama, but he did not supply any figures or percentages. Conniff wrote, "A fairly large number of Irish arrived also," but did not specify what he meant by "fairly large."[27]

The only country, apart from the United States, where the railroad hired white manual workers, was Ireland. The company was unlikely to embark on an expensive recruitment drive there if its prior experience of employing laborers from that country had not been reasonably satisfactory. Totten expressed his opinion of Irish laborers at the end of 1853 after over three years' experience in managing them. "Irish laborers are not so efficient on the Isthmus as in cooler and healthier climates, yet, for a period from four to six months, which is the term of their engagement, they perform a fair amount of work."[28] He was sufficiently satisfied with their previous performance to continue their recruitment.

These references to Irish workers, as well as others mentioned throughout this work, confirm the existence of a substantial, though unquantified, Irish presence among the railroad's white workforce. The problem of determining more precisely what proportion of the almost six thousand men who were estimated to have come to Panama from the United States were Irish born could not be answered readily.[29] However, a look at the demographic and occupational structure of the labor market in those regions of the United States where the railroad recruited men yielded clues to the likely national origin of white laborers.

The cities of New York, Boston, and New Orleans—and their surrounding areas—were the principal reservoirs of manpower from which the railroad drew the bulk of its white, unskilled workforce. Shipping reports and advertisements in the U.S. and Panamanian press suggested that approximately two out of every three American passenger-carrying steamers docking at Panama's Caribbean ports between 1850 and 1855 had sailed from New York, with the remainder coming from New Orleans.[30] These were the only two cities on America's Atlantic coast with regular scheduled sailings to the Isthmus.

The port of New York, the nation's busiest by the 1850s, was the main departure point on the east coast for steamer services to Panama. Throughout the early 1850s, ships of the U.S. Mail Steamship Company, in conjunction with those from competing lines, provided a weekly service to the Isthmus from piers not far from the railroad's head office. A fortnightly steamer service from New Orleans to Chagres began operation in 1850. At first this service was indirect, with ships stopping at Havana, where passengers changed to vessels for Chagres, and later Aspinwall. Sailing ships provided a slower direct service.

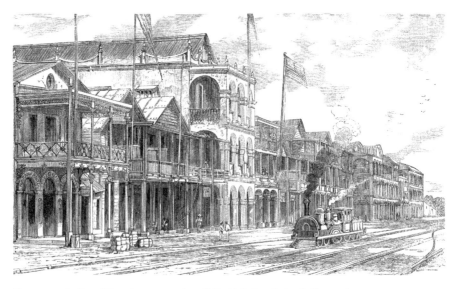

Figure 11.1. Railroad Terminus at Aspinwall (Colón). iStock Stock Illustration.

Weekly direct steamer sailings from New Orleans to Navy Bay commenced in March 1852.[31] Probably two-thirds or so of the railroad's white employees who were hired in the United States likely left from New York because of the greater frequency of sailings to Panama from this port. Most of these men would have been domiciled in the Northeast, particularly in the metropolitan areas of New York and Boston. The remaining third of the railroad's U.S.-based white workers most likely hailed from the South and Midwest. These would have embarked in New Orleans.[32]

The Panama railroad had its administrative headquarters at lower Broadway, in the heart of New York City. Labor contractors in city, many of them Irish or German, hired the men needed throughout the country for railroad construction.[33] The company's recruitment of manual workers was delegated to agents like these with the railroad assuming responsibility for hiring skilled, technical personnel. Recruits sent to Panama by labor agents were not always satisfactory. Totten complained in 1853 that some men, described as carpenters, had never worked as such. "One was a quack doctor." Others were ill and "were not in a fit state of health to come to this country," and a few had died.[34] Some Irish immigrants were apparently hired by labor contractors while their ships were still in quarantine in New York port. Once cleared by public health officials, these men transferred to Panama-bound steamers, attracted by the pay and the prospect of immediate employment.[35]

The railroad's labor agents in the North likely opted, on the grounds of convenience, logistics, and cost, to concentrate most of their recruitment drive on the working-class ghettoes of New York, Boston, and other urban centers of the northeastern region. A New York newspaper reported that "Irish regiments were recruited at the North and shipped to Aspinwall, and the Herculean labor began."[36] The fact that advertisements seeking three thousand laborers for the railroad in 1853 appeared only in newspapers circulating in New York and Boston bolstered the view that the northeastern states were the principal targets for the recruitment of white manual workers.[37]

A letter from an Irish doctor in New York to the *Irish American*, the newspaper boasting the largest circulation among the Irish community of the metropolis, confirmed that these advertisements were aimed at the sizable Irish laboring class in these two conurbations. The writer's warning to his fellow countrymen appeared under the ominous heading "Correspondence. Irish Graves in Panama." "Seeing the frequent advertisement of 3,000 laborers required upon the Panama railroad . . . I call your attention to it, and wish to enlist your sympathies in [sic] behalf of humanity and Irishmen, to prevent the fearful sacrifice of life which must ensue by using Irish labor on the Isthmus." The paper's editor added an admonitory postscript to the letter. "We recommend it to the careful consideration of Irish laborers."[38]

Demographic and occupational data from American censuses in the 1850s strengthened the likelihood that thousands of laborers hired by the railroad in the United States were Irish born. From the early decades of the nineteenth century, there was an increasing outflow of Irish emigrants to the United States—to the cities of New York, Boston, and New Orleans in particular. During the thirty years prior to 1845, between eight hundred thousand and one million Irish emigrants sailed to North America.[39] This migration was due to deteriorating economic circumstances in Ireland and an explosion of employment opportunities in the United States.

The stream of emigrants turned into a torrent as a result of the Great Famine of 1845–1849, as people desperately sought to escape from the hunger, deprivation, and despair of an Ireland that appeared to be doomed to many of its inhabitants. Numerous Irish immigrants, particularly those of the poorer class, were almost destitute on arrival. They settled in, or close to, the port cities where they had first landed.[40] During the years when the Panama railroad was recruiting laborers, almost six hundred thousand Irish stepped ashore in New York seeking employment and tens of thousands more landed in Boston and New Orleans.[41]

The timing of these new immigrants' arrival was fortunate. A transformation of the American economy was taking place in the half century after 1815 as northern and eastern states underwent an industrial revolution that created considerable employment opportunities for the Irish newcomers. "Impoverished peasants in Ireland, they became in America a mobile army of cheap, unskilled labor for the industrial revolution."[42] Irish immigrants "found rough manual labor awaiting them, their brawn being needed for the internal improvements and the industrial growth of the nation. Irish peasants who would dig were a godsend to the urban contractors."[43]

Many Irish male immigrants in the 1840s and 1850s entered at the bottom rung of the American workforce with pick and shovel. "Wherever there was hard, dirty work, there you would find the Irish."[44] Large numbers of these men gravitated toward canal, railroad, and other construction projects and led nomadic lives. Others settled in disease-ridden ghettoes of American cities where they "were disproportionately concentrated in the lowest-paid, least skilled, and most dangerous and insecure employment."[45] Irish immigrants and manual labor were so closely intertwined in the public's mind that the renowned poet Ralph Waldo Emerson was inspired to comment: "The poor Irishman, the wheelbarrow is his country."[46]

During the years in which the Panama railroad was being built, between 26 and 28 percent of New York City's population was Irish born.[47] A huge pool of Irish immigrants lived in the city, which served as the main recruitment center for workers heading for the Isthmus. Even more relevant was the overwhelming Irish preponderance among the city's laboring class. The 1855 New York State census revealed that Irish laborers numbered 17,426 out of a foreign-born laborer population of 19,783 and a total native and foreign-born laboring population of 20,238, although the latter tally may be understated.[48] "In New York [City] nine out of ten laborers were Irishmen."[49] White New Yorkers tended to avoid manual labor, as did other European newcomers. "In 1855 only about five percent of the gainfully employed Germans, Scandinavians, and Italians respectively, were laborers." The percentage of laborers among English, Scottish, and Welsh immigrants living in New York was even lower, at 3 percent.[50]

Not all Irishmen in New York fell into the unskilled worker category. Many Irish-born males were to be found in semiskilled jobs and trades connected with building. "The sons of Erin contributed more than three fourths of the foreign-born masons, plasterers, and bricklayers, nearly half the carpenters, and a third of the painters and glaziers."[51] As a result, they dominated the construction unions in New York City.[52] In summary, during the 1850s Irish-born persons constituted over a quarter of the total population of New York City. More significantly, Irishmen made up almost 90 percent of the metropolis's laboring population and were also strongly represented in the semiskilled and skilled trades, particularly those connected with building and construction.

From the 1830s onward, as America's rail network expanded, an increasing number of Irish male immigrants acquired experience and rudimentary technical skills in what was then a revolutionary new form of transportation. From the 1840s to the 1870s, Irishmen became almost synonymous with railroad construction, and during those decades many, if not most, railroad laborers in the United States were Irish immigrants.[53] Described as "rough, hard-drinking, and often violent and short-lived men," they were frequently "abused and cheated in a way to disgrace human nature" by American railroad contractors.[54] The Panama railroad's management and its labor contractors would have been aware of the conspicuous role of Irishmen in building the country's railroads and would have regarded them as ideal potential recruits for the labor-hungry project on the Isthmus.

Not all those embarking for Panama out of New York port would have been residents of the city. Many would come from the urban centers of the surrounding states, where Irishmen also predominated in the laboring and semiskilled workforce. Boston, like New York, was home to a large Irish laboring population. Approximately one in every four Bostonians in 1850 had been born in Ireland, and the occupational profile of the Boston Irish mirrored that of their compatriots in New York.[55] Most, lacking training and capital, were forced into the ranks of the city's low-paid proletariat.

According to the 1850 federal census, 82 percent of Boston's unskilled male labor force was Irish. This figure remained largely unchanged throughout the decade. "No other nationality depended so heavily upon unskilled work." In contrast, no more than 5 percent of native-born Americans and only 10 percent of blacks and Germans living in Boston were described as laborers in this census.[56] Irish laborers from Boston worked not only in the city, but also on construction projects all over North America. Advertisements in Boston's Irish newspapers showed that contractors throughout America saw the city as an important reservoir of cheap manpower.[57]

Thus, a very considerable proportion—possibly two-thirds, if not more—of the railroad's estimated workforce of 3,760 hired from the New York–Boston region were likely to have been Irish born. These men were mainly laborers, with a smaller number employed as foremen or mechanics. If this assumption is correct, approximately 2,500 of the white workforce recruited in the Northeast were Irish. The remainder consisted of native-born Americans, as well as immigrants from the European mainland.

There were occasional references to European workers in the press and company reports, though the numbers involved in each instance appeared quite small. As previously noted, census data revealed that very few European male immigrants in the Northeast, apart from the Irish, earned their living as laborers at this period. Mainland Europeans constituted a small proportion (probably about 7 percent) of the Panama railroad's total white workforce. These men were almost certainly hired in the United States as there was no evidence of the recruitment of manual workers in Europe, apart from Ireland. [58]

New Orleans was the other major embarkation point for men leaving the United States to work on the railroad. Transport links between the Crescent City, as New Orleans was then known, and the Isthmus were good. A scheduled steamship service operated via Havana from 1850 onward, with a direct service to Aspinwall beginning in 1852. Tens of thousands of Irish entered the United States through New Orleans in the years following 1830. As a result, they became a significant presence in the southern city in the antebellum period. Thousands of Irishmen helped build the New Basin Canal, linking New Orleans with Lake Pontchartrain between 1832 and 1838. Digging their way through fever-infested swamps, at least three thousand—and probably more—died.[59] The total Irish-born population in the South by 1850 was 54,551, of whom 24,266 lived in Louisiana, according to that year's federal census. By the mid-1850s, the number of post-Famine immigrants pouring into the city threatened to overwhelm its authorities.[60]

Many of these Irish immigrants were destitute on arrival, like their compatriots who settled in the Northeast. They were disproportionately represented among the laboring class and were condemned to perform the roughest and heaviest kind of labor. The supply of unskilled workers in New Orleans often exceeded the demand for their services. Consequently, Irish laborers took work wherever they could find it in Louisiana and other parts of the South. Irish-men were cheap and expendable. For this reason they were frequently used as substitutes for slaves. "Their undesirable presence was only suffered because they worked for low wages and proved to be more affordably replaced than African-descended slaves."[61] Hiring the Irish at a daily rate of one dollar or less and replacing them with others if they got sick or died proved to be more economical than to use more costly slaves.[62]

The southern states, and Louisiana in particular, were not healthy locations for immigrants from temperate zones. A local newspaper went as far as to as-sert that New Orleans's climate was more deadly to white incomers than that of Panama's Caribbean coast.[63] The terrible mortality during the yellow fever epidemic of 1853 confirmed the dangers of living in this southern city.[64] Irish workers from New Orleans hired for Panama had the advantage of being ac-climatized to toiling in semitropical conditions.[65] Press advertising did not play a major role in recruiting men from the South, and most Panama-bound work-ers embarking at New Orleans were hired by labor contractors based there or elsewhere in the South and Midwest. Only one advertisement seeking workers for the Panama railroad appeared in the New Orleans *Times-Picayune* during the construction period.[66]

The ready availability of local laborers, together with considerations of re-cruitment costs and logistics, would suggest that possibly half of the estimated 1,880 men who sailed for Panama from New Orleans were hired either in the city itself or in its environs, with the corresponding likelihood that a high proportion was Irish. The remainder of the laborers leaving from the southern port would have come from the Midwest, which was linked to New Orleans by river steamers and an expanding road and rail network. The proportion of Irish immigrants in the Midwest at this time was much lower than in New Orleans, or in the urban centers of the Atlantic seaboard. This reflected the pattern of Irish immigrant settlement in midcentury America. Only a minority of men recruited in the Midwest for work on the Panama railroad were likely to have been Irish born, reflecting their scattered presence in the region's population at this time. In the light of these settlement and occupational patterns, it is likely that somewhere in the region of 800 of the estimated 1,880 workers who departed for Panama from New Orleans were Irish, while 900 were Americans, with the remainder having been born on the European mainland.

Why would Irish laborers and mechanics living in New York, Boston, and New Orleans, or in the regions surrounding these conurbations, want to risk their health and possibly their lives by going to work in the fever-ridden rain forest of the Isthmus of Panama? In fact, there were not too many alternatives for unskilled or semiskilled Irish immigrants struggling to survive in an economy characterized by cycles of boom and bust. Marginalized and living on the fringes of American life, Irish laborers were often hired and paid on a day-to-day basis.

Living costs were high; employment was erratic, particularly in the winter months; and wage rates were depressed by the constant influx of new arrivals from Europe, including Ireland. Most laborers were lucky to get two hundred days' work per year.[67] Employers took advantage of the labor surplus to depress wage levels and to condone poor working conditions. Poverty was an ever-present threat, particularly to the less skilled. In these circumstances many Irishmen would have been susceptible to the allure of a contract offering six months' guaranteed employment at wage rates comparable to those in the United States—with the added incentive of free travel, board, lodging, and medical care.

In summary, Irish immigrants were disproportionately represented among the laboring class in those regions of the United States from which the railroad recruited most of its manual employees. In addition, Irish laborers had an established tradition as workers on construction and infrastructural projects in America and had become almost synonymous with building the country's railroads. This analysis credibly suggests that somewhere in the region of 3,660 Irishmen, or 61 percent of the total white labor force of 6,000 men, helped build the world's first interoceanic railroad.[68] The Irish proportion of the railroad's total workforce of 17,500 was much smaller, at about 21 percent. Even so, an Irish presence of this size would explain recurrent references to Irish workers in the documentation and literature of the period.

How did the thousands of men employed on the Panama railroad, with different skin colors, from widely dissimilar backgrounds and national origins, speaking various languages, and professing different religions, interact with one another at a time when racist attitudes were almost universally subscribed to and openly expressed? Schott reported that racial relations were not always amicable, singling out the Irish, in particular, for blame. "No other nationality displayed so much animosity toward people of darker skin and foreign ways as the Irish. Their attitude became so hostile that Totten moved the Chinese camp as far from them as possible." Schott's allegations about the racism of Irish workers have influenced subsequent writers who have accepted his account as historically reliable.[69]

Schott maintained that the Orientals worked harder and were more productive than their white counterparts and this "infuriated the sensitive Irish even further." He also claimed that the Irish were critical of the Chinese workers' nightly practice of bathing, anointing themselves with scented water, and changing their clothing before dining. Their habit of opium smoking also shocked the Irishmen. Schott added that the Malays were "also despised by the Irish, but greatly feared" because they "were murderous adversaries" armed with rifles and knives.[70]

Schott provided no documentary proof to support these allegations. Totten's correspondence was not available for 1854 when the railroad briefly experimented with the use of Chinese labor. No references to racial clashes between Irish and nonwhite workers in other company documents, in the local or American press, or in the reports of contemporary travelers were found either. The interpreter hired by the Colonial Land and Emigration Commission does not mention discrimination or harassment by Irish workers in his list of the grievances of Chinese laborers.[71] Schott's information came from unknown sources, and his allegation that Totten was forced to segregate the Chinese from the Irish remains unproven.

Schott's assertion that the Irish were infuriated by the superior work performance of the Chinese was contradicted by press reports of the latter's inability to withstand the heavy physical demands made of them and the rapid decline in the number of Chinese laborers available for work. The railroad's decision not to continue with the recruitment of Chinese laborers was evidence that their performance failed to meet expectations. The claims of nightly bathing, anointing themselves with scented water, and donning clean clothes before their evening meals also seem far-fetched, as facilities for personal hygiene and the daily laundering of clothes in the railroad's isolated and humid jungle camps were primitive or nonexistent.

Totten was also unlikely to have permitted one particular ethnic group, the Malays, to carry firearms, given the potential danger this posed in a multinational workforce where company-enforced discipline and control were essential. Most of the Irish laborers hired by the railroad had experience of living and working in large American urban centers and would have been aware of the predilection of some Chinese male immigrants for opium smoking. While they probably disapproved of this habit, it was unlikely to have shocked most of them when they came in contact with it in Panama.

Schott also alleged that Irish antagonism toward the Chinese was indirectly responsible for many of the latter becoming severely depressed and committing suicide. He claimed that one of the railroad's Irish workers, "distinguished among his fellows by his ability to read and write," contacted a New York priest who accused the company of trafficking in drugs because of its practice of providing the Chinese with opium. This letter was allegedly published in the *New York Herald*. The likelihood of further unfavorable publicity in the American press, together with the continuing cost of supplying opium to the Chinese, was reportedly responsible for the company's decision to stop importing the drug into Panama. The abrupt withdrawal of their habitual opiate allegedly then led many Chinese to take their own lives.[72]

Schott's allegations of Irish hostility to the Chinese might be based on a reference by Totten to Irish antipathy toward Jamaicans. Throughout the course of his extant correspondence, the chief engineer referred only once to possible Irish racial prejudice. While awaiting the arrival of Jamaican laborers on Manzanillo Island in September 1850, Totten wrote that the black islanders would have to be "put on a different part of the work from the other laborers . . . if placed among the Irishmen, I should fear an occasional row."[73] At this time, the only Irishmen on the island were recent arrivals from New Orleans, where they were likely to have imbibed southern attitudes of antipathy, if not overt animosity, toward black workers. However, Totten's use of the phrase "an occasional row" suggested that he did not anticipate serious hostility between the Irishmen and the Jamaicans.[74]

Schott may also have been influenced by documented incidents of Irish racial hostility to Chinese workers during the building of the U.S. transcontinental railroad more than a decade after the completion of the Panama rail link.[75] Irish immigrants on America's west coast in the 1860s and 1870s feared labor competition from Chinese workers and were instrumental in securing a federal prohibition on the immigration of Chinese laborers to the United States in 1882.[76]

Schott, and those later writers who have repeated his claims, likely assumed that this racial antagonism had its roots in Panama in 1854, when Irish railroad laborers came into contact with their Chinese counterparts. Behavior by the Irish of the kind alleged by Schott had the potential to provoke and inflame the workforce's nonwhite majority, paving the way for destabilizing ethnic conflict and endangering the collaboration and teamwork necessary for the project's completion. The railroad was unlikely to have continued employing Irish work-ers throughout the construction period if they had acquired a reputation for aggressive racial hostility. The Irish were not immune to the racist attitudes that prevailed in their new American homeland; however, they were probably no better or worse than their American-born colleagues.

The railroad's workers appeared to have been separated on the basis of eth-nicity, but this segregation might not have been solely due to racial hostility on the part of the Irish or other nationalities. It probably made sense, from an organizational perspective, to group together laborers who shared a common language and culture. In the early stages of the project, separation might also have been designed to conceal disparities in remuneration and working condi-tions. The chief engineer made it clear in 1850 that he did not want the West Indians placed among workers from Cartagena because of the discontent that would arise should the different wage rates paid to each group become common knowledge.[77] From the company's perspective, the segregation of workers on the basis of ethnicity had the advantage of restricting their potential to band together to demand better conditions or higher pay.

Overt racism was endemic throughout the nineteenth century and was un-doubtedly present on the Isthmus during the railroad's construction. Most Irish workers arriving at Panama had been exposed to the racially charged atmosphere of 1850s America, where they struggled to win acceptance as part of the white community.[78] Living and working in a country where black slavery was legal in some states would have affected their attitudes to the nonwhites they encountered in Panama. Most Irishmen would inevitably adopt the racial pecking order of their new country and subscribe to the widely accepted at-titude of white racial superiority over "inferior" people of color. According to Ignatiev, "They [the Irish] came to a society in which color was important in de-termining social position. It was not a pattern they were familiar with and they bore no responsibility for it; nevertheless they adapted to it in short order."[79]

Some Irish workers likely engaged in racist behavior at the individual or small-group level. Attitudes of racial antipathy held by Irish railroad employ-ees in Panama never spilled over into overt large-scale physical aggression, however. Their stance toward men of different ethnic origin was not any more discriminatory than that displayed by their American-born fellow employees.

Despite the prevalence of racist attitudes on the Isthmus, relations between the various nationalities composing the railroad's workforce appeared to have been reasonably harmonious by the standards of the time. No serious incidents of ethnic conflict, including attacks on white workers from members of other ethnic groups, were reported among a large multinational workforce during the five years that construction lasted. The record of the Panama railroad in maintaining relative racial harmony compared favorably with that of later French and American initiatives to excavate a canal across the Isthmus. Whatever racial animosities might have existed between the Irish and the Jamaicans, and possibly the Chinese, during the early 1850s could not compare, in scale or intensity, with the more explicit and violent interaction between ethnically different sections of the workforce that erupted several decades later during the construction of the Panama Canal.[80]

The fate of most of the estimated 3,660 Irish-born workers on the Panama railroad was broadly similar to that of other white workers. Applying a mortality rate of 28 percent to these men would suggest that over 1,000 of them died in Panama or shortly after leaving it as a result of their employment on the railroad. However, as previously mentioned, the estimated mortality rate for white workers varied, depending on a number of factors, including the time period under consideration and the men's background, experience, and state of health prior to their arrival in Panama. Irishmen, like their coworkers, would undoubtedly have suffered during the cholera outbreak of 1852, which was no respecter of national origins. However, allegations that the Irish workers were almost wiped out by the disease were exaggerated.

The 3,300 or so Irishmen who had been living and working in the United States were marginally more likely to adapt to conditions in Panama than the much smaller number of their compatriots who arrived directly from Ireland in 1854. The American Irish, familiar with the routines and discipline enforced by U.S. employers, came to the Isthmus with skills and experience acquired during their period of residence in the northern republic. Some would have previously worked on railroad or canal construction. They were also acclimatized to laboring in more extreme climatic conditions than those experienced in Ireland and may have acquired greater resistance to some diseases by virtue of their residence in the United States. This would have been particularly the case with the estimated 800 men who had been recruited in New Orleans and the surrounding states, a number of whom might have acquired immunity to yellow fever and some resistance to malaria. The fate of the small group of 360 men hired in Cork—many of them undernourished and all totally unused to laboring in a tropical climate—was less salutary, with an estimated one-third of them perishing within a few months of their arrival on the Isthmus.

Figure 11.2. View of Panama City, 1882. Created by De Bar. Shutterstock Stock Illustration.

Most of the deaths of Irish railroad workers occurred in Panama as a result of illnesses, diseases, and injuries contracted there. Some invalided Irish workers, carrying within them the seeds of disease, survived long enough to escape from the Isthmus but succumbed en route, lacking the resilience and medical attention to cope with the rigors of the voyage back to their American homes. Others completed their return journey to New York, Boston, New Orleans, or other American cities and towns, where, broken in health, they cheated death for weeks or months, before expiring from illnesses and diseases contracted on the Isthmus. Concentration on the unfortunate fate of those who died should not blind us to the fact the majority of the men from Ireland and other countries who built the railroad survived the experience, though the health of many would have been undermined to a greater or lesser extent by their stay in Panama.

The fate of many fellow Irish immigrants who chose to remain in the United States was not always appreciably better than that of their compatriots who volunteered for Panama. Because of the wretched conditions in which many Irish male immigrants lived and worked in the United States during the middle decades of the nineteenth century, their average life expectancy was short. Housing conditions for many were deplorable. In the 1850s, thirty thousand

Irish immigrants lived in dank and often flooded cellars and basements in New York City. Many fell prey to disease.[81] As late as 1872–1873, the annual death rate in a notorious tenement building in a predominantly Irish area of the city was 9.2 percent.[82]

According to one estimate, Irishmen, on average, survived for only six years after landing in the United States, though another study gave them a somewhat longer life expectancy: "So many died soon after arrival that it was said the Irish lived an average of only fourteen years after reaching Boston."[83] While the gamble taken by some Irish immigrants to improve their economic situation by enlisting in Panama posed a considerable risk to their lives and health, the alternative facing many of these men was not all that more salubrious.

The Panama railroad, one of the great engineering projects of the mid-nineteenth century, required the employment of large numbers of workers, the majority of them involved in occupations requiring hard physical labor. Approximately 17,500 men worked at one time or another on the project, and about 6,000 of these were white. The largest national group among the white cohort was the Irish, estimated to number just over 60 percent of the total, most of whom were recruited in New York, Boston, or New Orleans and the regions adjoining these cities. Their predominance reflected their domicile as immigrants in states adjoining the two U.S. Atlantic ports that had scheduled shipping services to Panama, as well as their overwhelming numerical superiority among the manual laborers of those urban centers where they had settled. It is also reflected their preeminent position in the American railroad laboring fraternity at midcentury.

Just over one thousand of these men, slightly more than a quarter of the total, likely died as a result of their employment on the Isthmus. The great majority had settled in the United States prior to coming to Panama. As poor white immigrants in the northern republic at a time of increasing tension over the future of slavery, they shared many of the racist attitudes of native-born white Americans. Nevertheless, little evidence has come to light to support the oft-repeated claim that Irish laborers in Panama in the 1850s were noticeably more racially aggressive than other white workers, especially in their dealings with their Chinese coworkers.

TWELVE

The Men from Cork

WHEN IT BECAME CLEAR THAT MINOR STORY WOULD BE UNABLE TO finish the railroad by August 1853, the directors discussed the recruitment of laborers from new sources. Gripped by a sense of urgency, they aimed to complete construction before the public and investors lost faith in their enterprise and before the rival Nicaragua route had the opportunity to dominate the transit trade between east and west. They decided on two new labor sources: Ireland and China. The company also discussed El Salvador and unspecified countries in South America, but no decisive action was taken with these. For the previous three years, the railroad had been relying on Irishmen living in the United States for much of its white labor force. It now decided to recruit Irish workers directly from a homeland recovering from a catastrophic famine. It assumed that the Irish public would be unaware of the dangers and risks involved in working on the Isthmus.

On July 8, 1853, the executive and finance committee voted to send the company secretary, Francis Spies, to Great Britain "for the purpose of sending out a force of laborers to the Isthmus."[1] The directors added that Spies, based in the New York office, should be accompanied by someone with personal experience of working conditions on the Isthmus. At this stage, the company considered hiring two thousand men in Ireland and shipping them directly to Aspinwall.[2] On September 3, for reasons that may have been related to Spies's lack of personal experience of Panama or his heavy workload, Alexander Jenkins Center (1808–1879), the company's vice president, assumed responsibility for the Irish recruitment drive.[3] Center, a graduate of West Point, had served in the U.S. Army until 1837, when he resigned and took up the profession of civil engineer before joining the railroad.[4] Center had firsthand knowledge of conditions in

Panama, where he had acted as the railroad's resident superintendent for over a year. The company now decided to scale back its recruitment campaign in Ireland to one thousand laborers and mechanics, probably because of its belief that a sufficient supply of men from other sources was guaranteed.[5]

By late September Center was in London, where he visited the offices of Cavan Brothers, the company's financial agents in the United Kingdom.[6] Cavan Brothers appointed the firm of N. & J. Cummins in Cork, Ireland's second city, to act as their Irish representatives.[7] Cummins, in turn, delegated some of the responsibility for hiring men to local labor contractors. This attempt by an American-based railroad to recruit men in Ireland was unusual and possibly unprecedented. It generated considerable press coverage.[8]

The company began its recruitment drive by contacting the boards of guardians of Irish workhouses for the purpose of hiring able-bodied inmates but failed to receive the cooperation it expected. "Circulars, we understand, have been sent by the promoters of the Panama Railway to the Irish boards of guardians, requesting to be furnished with list of names of such able-bodied paupers as they wished to be relieved from the burden of supporting. In one instance, at least, we know that the vigilance and intelligence of one of the guardians defeated the project, and in all probability saved the lives of many poor Irishmen."[9] The Cork Union was the only workhouse to respond to the company's request, and Center henceforth confined his recruitment activities to that city and county.

A network of workhouses had been established in Ireland under the provisions of the Poor Law (Ireland) Act of 1838 to provide relief for the destitute. A board of guardians who were responsible to a central body in Dublin, the Poor Law Commissioners, administered each workhouse. Within each workhouse district, or union, a poor law rate or property tax was levied to support paupers in its area. The guardians, most of whom represented local property and business interests, were anxious to keep the poor law rate low. This meant misery and discomfort for the unfortunate inmates who frequently suffered privation and humiliation. Their diet was not much above subsistence level; they slept in overcrowded dormitories; and they were often deprived of proper clothing, footwear, and washing facilities.[10] The strict regime imposed on inmates, and the deaths and suffering that occurred in these buildings during the famine years and in the decades that followed, gave the Irish workhouse a notorious reputation.

In late 1853, the three thousand or so inmates of the Cork Union workhouse came from a variety of backgrounds and occupations. Bad luck, poor health, and temporary or permanent poverty were their only common denominators. Prospective employers would contact these "warehouses of the poor" seeking potential employees. Rear Admiral Sir William Carroll, commander of the Queenstown naval base near Cork, sought boys for the Royal Navy among the Cork Union's orphans in September 1853. The guardians were happy to accede to his proposal.[11] The company also enthusiastically received a request from a Manchester mill for orphan children. The board accepted "with pleasure the proposal . . . to have some of the orphan children of this house employed in the cotton spinning in Manchester."[12]

By early October, Center was in Cork, where he was probably informed by the workhouse guardians that the number of able-bodied adult male inmates was unlikely to exceed four hundred in October or November.[13] Realizing that there was no prospect of recruiting all the men he required from among the workhouse inmates, Center widened his search by placing the following advertisement in the *Cork Examiner* and *Cork Constitution* for one thousand laborers, masons, and quarrymen.

> Good able bodied men, without families. The term of engagement to be for six months, from the commencement of work.
>
> A free passage, including food, will be furnished from Cork direct to the work, and also on the expiration of the term of engagement, from Aspinwall, the Atlantic terminus, per steamer either to New York or New Orleans, as may be selected by the men.
>
> Lodging with good and abundant food and medical attendance, will also be furnished free on the work.
>
> Very liberal wages will be given.
>
> As expenses of passage are paid, food found during the entire period, and as money earned cannot readily be expended on the Isthmus, the men will probably land in the United States with considerable means.[14]

This advertisement sparked off a vigorous debate in the local press, most likely to the vice president's surprise, as he would not have expected the city's inhabitants to have any knowledge of conditions on the distant Isthmus of Panama. Less than a week after the publication of the first advertisement, Robert Francis O'Callaghan wrote to the *Cork Constitution*. His claims about the grim conditions faced by workmen during the period when Story had been the contractor would have done little to encourage recruitment. "The longest period I have known any man to have his health there was five or six weeks, and after that he is of no use to them or himself . . . I was erecting a bridge across the river which flows from Chagres to Gorgona, at Granwang Station.[15] The poor fellows were dying at the rate of fifteen or twenty a day."[16]

The following day, the *Cork Examiner* published another damaging letter from O'Callaghan. "I feel myself bound to caution any who may be induced to go there, for so sure as they go, so sure will they leave their bones there. There were 200 went out to where I was employed at Barbacoa [Barbacoas] and I am the only survivor now, though the station where I was, was considered the most healthy on the line. At Granwandy [Juan Grande] station the poor fellows were falling at the rate of twenty per day."[17]

A few days later, N. & J. Cummins denied being involved in "an undertaking imperiling human life" and claimed that the alarm excited by O'Callaghan was "without reasonable foundation . . . we can state, with truth, from inquiries made by us some time since, that the climate of the Isthmus of Panama, where the railroad is being constructed, is not more unhealthy than any of our West India Islands, and less so than New Orleans, and other ports to which emigrants are constantly proceeding."[18]

The controversy in Cork over labor conditions in Panama now caught the attention of the Dublin press. *Saunders's News-Letter and Daily Advertiser* carried a notable article on October 24, which was reprinted by the *Cork Constitution* the following day. The Dublin newspaper asserted that apologists for the Nicaragua scheme were involved in a propaganda campaign, which was supported by the *Times* of London, to discourage men from working for the Panama railroad. The public were advised to be wary of the alleged perils of Panama made by advocates of the Nicaragua route who were "striving their utmost to deter working men from going to Central America to complete the line in question." *Saunders's News-Letter* repeated the claim of the company secretary that workers' deaths up until July 1, 1853, amounted to only 214 out of a total of 3,352 employees from the United States.[19]

The *Cork Constitution's* continued preoccupation with Panama caused it to reprint two alarming articles, from British and American newspapers, dealing with mortality rates on the Isthmus. According to a London journal, "The number of the slain in making the road can already be counted by thousands . . . it would be an act of humanity if you would obtain the insertion of a word of caution, in some paper or papers that would be likely to meet the eye of those who may be exposed to so great a danger."[20] The *Constitution* also published a report from the *New Orleans Delta* on September 25 entitled "Panama Fever."

Figure 12.1. Shandon on the Lee, Cork, Ireland. Victorian engraving, 1840. iStock Stock Illustration.

"Four hundred and fifty laborers have died on the Panama railroad during the effort to build it. Nearly every white person going there to work is attacked with the fever, generally within a few weeks after arrival."[21] The *Constitution* asked the railroad to "set anxiety at rest by some authentic and satisfactory statement" in response to these worrying allegations.

At an event held on October 25 to mark the recent appointment of Admiral Carroll as the naval commander of Queenstown port, Mr. Cummins observed it was in the railroad's interest to look after workers brought out from Ireland because their recruitment and transport costs were high.[22] On the following day, at the weekly meeting of the workhouse's board of guardians, the first reference to sending inmates to Panama was made. "The Clerk said he had to announce to the board the very gratifying intelligence that 20 male paupers had been selected for emigration tickets for Panama." The chairman declared that he felt obliged to warn these men of the dangers of working in a tropical climate.[23] The guardians approved a proposal "that the sum of one pound [$5] each, be given to provide clothing for the paupers of this house, who are about to emigrate to Panama."[24] On entering the workhouse, inmates surrendered their clothes, which often amounted to little more than rags, and were issued a uniform that would remain the property of the guardians. The apparel was not appropriate for the tropics in any case.

The controversy in the Cork newspapers over working conditions in Panama intensified following the reply of Alexander Center to O'Callaghan's original letter and the publication of a letter from a medical doctor signing himself "Patriot," which supported O'Callaghan's claims. The company's vice president rejected O'Callaghan's "false and exaggerated statements" and said that he was not aware of a single death during the erection of the bridge at Barbacoas. "His assertion that all out of a party of 200 (himself alone excepted) had died, is a grossly false assertion, and bears upon its face its own refutation ... I have every reason to believe, that with due precaution on the part of the men, they can perform their work, and I would be reluctant to engage them, did I not think so."[25]

The second letter may have come from a surgeon on one of the steam packets that plied between Britain, the West Indies, and Panama.

> Sir ... I have been frequently on the Isthmus of Panama, and have had an opportunity of seeing something of the awful mortality which occurred amongst the Irish laborers who constructed the part of the line already finished, and which has obliged the directors to come all the way to Ireland to find Irishmen who are unacquainted with it, for the Irishmen of the States know too well the danger of working on the Isthmus to accept even the highest wages for doing so ... I am a medical man and am acquainted with the diseases of the Isthmus ... I am sure not 100 men out of the 1,000 will survive the six months, and even those that are fortunate as to live till pay day, will remain for the rest of their lives wretched invalids. I hope, Sir, you will assist me in my endeavor to point out the danger of emigration under such circumstances, by giving this letter a place in your columns.[26]

Then Robert Francis O'Callaghan returned to the fray with a second letter to the *Cork Examiner*, which cited the deaths in Panama of two sons of a local resident, Mr. Herbert, of the Cork Porter Brewery, to highlight the dangers of working for the railroad. O'Callaghan finished with an appeal to his fellow countrymen not to encourage men to sign up for Panama. "Let no Irishman lend himself to forward the interests of a cause so fatal to his fellow creatures."[27]

Some days later, the *Cork Examiner* reprinted two letters that had first appeared in the *Cork Constitution*. In the first, N & J Cummins declared that allegations about the dangers of the climate and the high mortality rate in Panama were exaggerated. The agents believed that it was up to the men themselves to decide whether the financial inducements offered would compensate them for the risks involved in laboring in a tropical climate. In the second letter, Center admitted that the company had sent him to Ireland in the belief that a substantial number of laborers could be recruited there. He repeated the company secretary's assertion that only 214 men out of a total of 3,352 white workers had died in three years. He argued that it would not make financial sense for the company to transport men to the Isthmus and pay for their onward passage to the United States if it was not confident that they would be useful while in Panama.[28]

On the same day as it published these two letters, the *Cork Examiner* carried a short report from an American correspondent of the *Nation* warning "Irish laborers against the Panama railroad . . . they can get better wages and better food in the western states of America, where thousands are wanted on the roads, without any risk of life. They are treated he says like slaves on that railroad, and if they attempt to leave are sent manacled to the pestilent dungeons of the Panama, like common felons."[29]

Just over a week later, the *Waterford News* carried a warning to prospective Irish recruits, taken from the *New York Freeman's Journal* of August 7, 1853, "that this is a contract for their almost certain death."[30] The Cork press did not report this admonition. On November 16, the *Cork Examiner* printed a report that may have quelled unease among prospective volunteers for the railroad. According to this news item, there was no sickness on the Isthmus except for "an occasional slight attack of fever." The hospitals were almost empty, and the physicians of Panama City were "entirely out of employment."[31]

On November 17, the *Ben Nevis*, a sailing ship of 1,163 tons register and 3,000 tons burden, equipped to carry up to 650 passengers, arrived in Cork to take on board workers for Panama, with Captain Herron in command. This vessel, 180 feet long, was part of the White Star Line and was originally designed for the emigrant trade to Australia.[32] The *Cork Constitution* claimed that the demand for passages exceeded the ship's capacity, but this was clearly a ploy to encourage tardy emigrants. The newspaper also carried an embarkation notice: "The men engaged for the Panama Railway are requested to assemble at Cork on Tuesday next, to embark on Wednesday morning [November 23], the vessel being now at Queenstown." The ship was due to sail on Saturday, November 26.[33]

The departure did not to go ahead as planned because on November 21, seven sailors were brought before Queenstown's resident magistrate for refusing to rejoin the *Ben Nevis*. The seamen gave no reason for their decision. The ringleader was sentenced to three months' imprisonment and the rest to two months—in all cases with hard labor. On hearing this, the sailors pleaded with the bench to be allowed back on board. However, Captain Herron said he could not depend on their promises. The refractory seamen were hauled off to the county jail.[34]

The captain needed time to replace his imprisoned crew members, and this contributed to delaying the departure of the *Ben Nevis* for another two weeks. However, the slow response to the advertisements for workmen, as well as the bureaucratic procedures of the poor law system, also added to the holdup. The local board of guardians had to await authorization from Dublin's Poor Law Commissioners for permission to assist late applicants wishing to go to Panama and claiming the £1 clothing allowance due in such cases.

The press announced on November 24 that twenty-four more workhouse men had volunteered for Panama, and the minutes of the board of guardians confirmed that a further nineteen inmates had applied to leave on the *Ben Nevis*.[35] This represented a substantial increase from the initial group of twenty men, who had offered to go a month earlier. Despite the authorities' warning on laboring in a tropical climate, the number of workhouse applicants continued to grow. The prospect of six months' paid employment, followed by a free passage to the United States, also appealed to a number of married men who were not workhouse inmates. Two women complained to the police court on November 25 that their husbands had deserted them and were aboard the *Ben Nevis*. The bench advised them to make an application to the courts for their husbands' restoration.[36]

A few days later, three more women complained that their husbands had abandoned them and joined the Panama expedition. The mayor issued a warrant to have the husbands brought ashore from the *Ben Nevis*. "There are a very large number of similar cases; and the Mayor has issued directions to have proceedings immediately taken against the offenders."[37] Two noted thieves also took advantage of the impending departure of the Panama-bound ship to secure their freedom. After being sentenced to three months' jail, with hard labor, the bench accepted the prisoners' proposal that if pardoned, they would leave Ireland on the *Ben Nevis*.[38]

Passengers began boarding the *Ben Nevis* on November 24 and continued until Friday, December 2, by which stage there were between 350 and 360 emigrants on board, of whom 133 were workhouse inmates.[39] The ship lay anchored about sixty or eighty yards from the quay at Queenstown. Boats leaving the ship were watched to prevent the emigrants from escaping. A few of the more reckless among them got over the difficulty by jumping overboard and swimming ashore. The mayor and magistrates issued arrest warrants for fourteen or fifteen men as a result of applications from abandoned wives. The errant husbands were removed from the ship and sentenced to one week's imprisonment

Figure 12.2. *Ben Nevis* Sailing Ship, 1852. *Illustrated London News*, September 4, 1852. Courtesy of the British Library Board.

on the charge of abandonment.[40] In view of the fate that was to befall some of their fellow passengers on the *Ben Nevis*, a short spell in a Cork prison may well have been a stroke of good luck for the men concerned, although they were unlikely to think so at the time. Finally, at about 3:00 a.m. on Saturday morning, December 3, the *Ben Nevis* raised anchor. Dense fog prevented her from leaving Queenstown harbor, and she had to be towed out to sea by a tug ten hours later with "the passengers cheering loudly and enthusiastically for the land that probably very few amongst them will ever return to."[41]

A list of the names and details of the 133 individuals accepted by the Poor Law Commissioners for emigration assistance to Panama proved impossible to locate. In an attempt to discover who these men were, I compiled a register of all adult males aged from fourteen to sixty, admitted into the Cork Union workhouse in the fifteen months prior to November 26, 1853, and discharged between November 20 and December 2, 1853, and who had remained as inmates for more than one night.[42]

This list contains the names of 144 individuals who were potential passengers on the *Ben Nevis*. Six of these suffered from physical or mental conditions. Dependents accompanied a further six, who, for this reason, appeared to be less likely candidates for emigration. That left 132 individuals, which almost matched the 133 inmates helped by the Poor Law Commissioners to emigrate. I have included the names and details of all 144 individuals as they appear in the relief registers in Appendix 3. This list provides the only specific information currently available on individual Irish laborers who went to work on the Panama railroad.

A majority of these men hailed from Cork city and county with the remainder coming from adjoining counties. A small number came from more distant parts of the island. Only ten were recorded as Protestants, the rest being Roman Catholics, reflecting the denominational distribution of the population of southern Ireland and the somewhat higher socioeconomic status of many Irish Protestants. Single men, with fewer family ties or commitments, numbered 121, as opposed to only six married men and ten widowers. The remaining seven were described as orphans or deserted juveniles.

The age breakdown of these Panama laborers was also revealing. Almost two-thirds (ninety-one) were between fourteen and twenty years old, while a further thirty-one were aged from twenty-one to thirty. Only twenty-two men were over thirty-one years.[43] A closer inspection of the fourteen- to twenty-year-old group showed that youths in their early to midteens formed a majority. A workhouse inmate of fifteen and above was regarded as an adult, and most of the fifteen-year-old boys in the Cork workhouse in 1853 were classified as able-bodied laborers. The occupations of the 144 discharged paupers varied considerably with laborers (fifty-eight) forming the largest single category. Mendicants or beggars constituted the next biggest group (thirty-three), their number illustrating the parlous state of the Irish economy at the time. The remaining fifty-three men had been engaged in a variety of occupations. Seven fourteen-year-olds, who were officially juveniles and therefore too young to have an occupation, were listed as orphans or deserted.

The reasons why 133 men and boys from the workhouse chose to abandon their native country and hazard their future in a distant tropical land can only be surmised. Most were likely desperate to escape from a harsh and oppressive environment where their future outlook was bleak. A visitor to the Cork workhouse in 1852 described it in harrowing terms. "Never did I visit any dungeon, any abode of crime or misery, in any country, which left the same crushing sense of sorrow, indignation and compassion—almost despair."[44] Conditions in the Cork workhouse in the first part of 1853 were grim with deaths averaging forty per week, twice the normal rate. According to the *Cork Southern Reporter* in May 1853, the workhouse was "one vast infection place and charnel house, for the poor. The destitute seem to be received into it only that they may sicken and die."[45] An inspection of the infirmary wards that summer disclosed great overcrowding—three sick adults to a bed in some cases.[46]

It was not only the harsh physical aspects of life in the workhouse that led some inmates to consider risking their health, and possibly their lives, in the distant rain forests of Panama. "The sheer monotony of workhouse life with its predictable routines, lack of stimulation, overcrowded and impersonal wards, and a repetitive diet of plain and unimaginative food must have had a depressing effect on many inmates."[47] In these circumstances the prospect of starting a new life elsewhere would have had a psychological appeal for many. A free passage, first to Panama and then to the United States, would not only liberate them physically from the joyless confines of the workhouse but would also provide them with the opportunity to make a fresh start in new and very different surroundings. Finally, the idea of working in Panama, a far-off exotic land, with its attendant risks and dangers, would doubtless have appealed to the sense of adventure that was characteristic of many boys and young men.

With winter approaching, perhaps the Isthmus, despite its reputed dangers and diseases, had become an attractive alternative to remaining in a workhouse crowded with over three thousand paupers and with little prospect of finding employment locally before spring or summer. Furthermore, the remuneration offered by the railroad to laborers of $1.00 per day, all found, greatly exceeded the pay in Ireland for similar work. In October, able-bodied laborers in the Cork workhouse had been offered employment for $0.37 per day.[48] Skilled workers in the south of Ireland earned the equivalent of approximately $4.00 per week in 1854, less than a laborer's pay on the Panama railroad, without taking into account the latter's free board and lodging.[49]

When the Ben Nevis finally raised anchor in December 1853, the 360 or so passengers on board were far short of the thousand workers the railroad had sought, despite the existence of a sizable pool of unemployed men in Cork and the surrounding areas.[50] Several hundred able-bodied males remained within the grim confines of the Cork Union workhouse. Some of these were recent arrivals, whose admission had come too late for them to be considered for a passage to Panama. Others had remained immune to Alexander Center's blandishments and were unwilling to embark on a voyage into the unknown. Men from the laboring population of the city and county failed to volunteer in sufficient numbers to compensate for the shortfall in workhouse applicants.

Figure 12.3. Queenstown, County Cork, Ireland. Victorian engraving, 1840. iStock Stock Illustration.

Unfavorable press coverage and the controversy over conditions on the Isthmus must be held largely responsible for the failure to recruit the expected one thousand men.

We know nothing about most of those who sailed out of Queenstown harbor on a foggy December morning, apart from the workhouse contingent and two criminals who had narrowly avoided prison by volunteering to depart on the ship. According to a local press report, the *Ben Nevis* emigrants consisted of four distinct groups: the workhouse inmates of Cork Union; unemployed or underemployed men including porters, runners, and coachmen whose livelihood had been adversely affected, if not destroyed, by the recent advent of the railroad; a sizable criminal element from the city's underworld anxious to escape justice; and a band of former volunteers who had served in the last Brazilian war and professed to know a great deal about South America.[51] The type of emigrants the railroad had presumably hoped to entice, namely agricultural laborers, experienced railroad and canal workers, and skilled craftsmen, were largely notable by their absence.

Both the city's main newspapers expressed themselves happy with the ship's departure. The *Cork Constitution* reported that "those that left to work at the railway were for the greater part a happy riddance for the city, the only decent looking men amongst them being those from the Cork Union workhouse."[52] The *Cork Examiner* expressed its satisfaction that part of the city's criminal population was leaving Erin's shores for good and claimed that the ship's departure had done more for "promoting the protection of public and private property in this city, than the action of the police authorities might have effected for some time."[53]

Ten days after the *Ben Nevis* had sailed, Dublin's Poor Law Commissioners informed the Cork Union that workhouse inmates wishing to emigrate to Panama in future were unlikely to receive financial assistance. The commissioners had been instructed by the Home Office in London "that it is desirable to discourage persons wishing to emigrate to Panama on account of the unhealthiness of the climate."[54] The warning reached Cork too late for those on the *Ben Nevis*, who were now about one-third of their way across the Atlantic—on a journey to a very different country from the one they had left behind.

Just over five weeks after leaving Cork, the *Ben Nevis* docked at Aspinwall on January 8, 1854. All 360 laborers on board arrived in good health, with only a few minor cases of sickness having occurred during the voyage.[55] According to the *Panama Herald*, "The majority are [*sic*] able bodied young men, apparently not much more than twenty years of age, and evidently accustomed to hard labor."[56] The *Aspinwall Courier*, in an article entitled "The Irishmen Have Come," commented that "the men, on their arrival here, looked robust and ready for hard work. They are chiefly young men. We think there is a fair prospect of their doing much service, and retaining their good health—for though they are to be distributed along the line of the road, they are pretty much all to go into the healthy mountain region—they are commencing their residence in most beautiful weather, and their youth will enable them to acclimate much faster than many of those who have come here from the United States."[57]

The acting British consul in Panama City noted that the men, estimated to number between 366 and 370, were not given long to acclimatize themselves and were put to work on January 14.[58] About 120 were stationed at the Pacific end of the line near Panama City. The company sent others to excavate the cutting through the hills of the continental divide, about ten miles from the capital. It distributed the remainder along the rest of the railroad. Health conditions at the time of the men's arrival were good, with a local paper announcing that "there exists now no sickness of any kind on the Isthmus."[59] The incidence of malaria usually declined once the dry or summer season began in December and increased again when the rains commenced in April or May, when the mosquito population expanded.

The *Panama Herald* provided a glimpse of the recently arrived Irish laborers about two weeks after they had started work.

> Following up the track, which is here temporarily laid, we come to the first cutting, where about fifty lusty Irishmen were busy with pick and shovel in an excavation about four feet deep, and who for the few days they have been at work, have made wonderful progress. . . . Lazy-looking natives were seated around, watching with all the astonishment they had energy to express, the rapidity with which the workmen labored;—dark-eyed senoritas muttered a *Jesus*! or an *Ave Maria*! as they saw the huge cars moved by a single man, or the heavy rails handled as if they were so much wood . . .
>
> It is pleasing to learn that among the workmen lately arrived from Ireland there has not been, nor is there at present a case of sickness, and that the men generally express themselves highly satisfied with the treatment they receive from the company.
>
> On the other hand we learn that though the new arrivals are not generally of the class of men accustomed to such work, or to handle the pick and shovel, they are rapidly learning its use, and are likely to prove a valuable force to the Railroad Company.[60]

A petition, dated February 1 and presented to Donald MacDonald, the acting British consul, contradicts reports in the local press of the Irishmen's excellent state of health, as well as their alleged satisfaction with their employment.[61] This document presented a somber view of the conditions faced by some of the men brought out from Cork.[62]

The petition was not signed, and it is impossible to know how representative it was of the views of the men from the *Ben Nevis*. The allegation that men fell ill after just over three weeks in the country and that some had died was alarming. Their appeal for a priest lent credence to this claim, as did the acting consul's confirmation that four men were deceased. The consular records did not contain any further information relating to this petition. MacDonald might not have wished to get involved in a dispute between workers and their American employer. He could have taken the view that the Irish petitioners, like their Jamaican counterparts, whom the consulate also refused to help, had voluntarily signed a contract to work in Panama and that their onward passage to the United States was guaranteed at the end of six months—or earlier if they were discharged as invalids.

The fact that William Perry, the consul, was on leave of absence throughout 1854 might also explain the consulate's failure to follow up on the Irish workers' complaint. Perry, who held an official post in Dublin in the 1830s, had dealt sympathetically with a small number of destitute Irishmen on the Isthmus in the early 1850s.[63] MacDonald might not have taken the same interest in Irish complaints.

An account by a visiting American journalist confirmed that the fate of many of the men from Cork was not auspicious. He reported the following exchange, which took place probably in April 1854.

> An Irish laborer came in [to the train] at one of the stations. He looked very pale; very thin; very woe-begone. "Had he the fever?" "Had the same," says he. "Very bad with it?" "Mighty bad entirely," says he. "Bad climate?" "Couldn't be worse". "Long out from Ireland?" "Not long; little better than three months; wished I had never come." "Why so?" "The climate," says he, "who the devil can stand it, but the monkeys and wild beasts." "Anything else bad but the climate?" "Nothing else we've a right to complain about. The eating is good; and so is the lodging, and the wages, and the doctors, and everything else: but the climate, no one can stand it." "Deaths numerous?" "Mighty numerous," says he, "Out of the three hundred and twenty that sailed two months and a half ago from the Cove of Cork, you can't count fifty among them now."[64]

This Irishman, unlike the petitioners of February, had no complaints about his food, accommodation, or treatment by the company. His explanation for the heavy Irish casualties consisted of having to labor long hours in blistering heat and high humidity. The timing of the arrival of the Cork workers had not gone to plan. Initially supposed to commence work in early December so that their contract period would largely coincide with the dry season, delays in the recruitment process postponed their arrival for over a month. This exposed them to hot, though relatively dry, weather for the first few months of their stay. Once the wet season started in late March, their working conditions would have become more oppressive.

The Cork workers were probably more vulnerable to disease and illnesses than their fellow workers, having come directly from a temperate North European climate and with unprepared immune systems. Many had never worked with a pick and shovel, and unlike their fellow countrymen who had spent months, if not years, laboring in the United States, they had little opportunity to adjust to hard physical work in debilitating temperatures. Even so, it was unlikely that as many as 270 men had perished within a few months of their arrival, though it was possible that only a minority remained fit enough to work, with many of the remainder being incapacitated as a result of illness.

Two accounts published not long after the arrival of the Irish immigrants suggested that their fate was inauspicious. According to Tomes's book, written a year after they had landed, "A cargo of Irish laborers from Cork reached Aspinwall and so rapidly did they yield to the malignant effects of the climate, that not a good day's labor was obtained from a single one; and so great was the mortality that it was found necessary to ship the survivors to New York, where most died from the fever of the Isthmus which was fermenting in their blood."[65]

Tomes was prone to hyperbole and had the entire contingent fallen ill immediately after arrival as he claimed, this setback would have been mentioned in the company's documentation and in the local press, as occurred in the case of the unfortunate Chinese. No references to casualties on this scale appeared. In fact, the *Panama Herald* commented nine weeks after their arrival that "we are glad to learn that the Irish workmen lately brought out from Cork, enjoy generally excellent health, and are becoming daily more useful to the company from whom they receive every attention."[66]

Otis, the author of the railroad's first history, published eight years after the arrival of the *Ben Nevis*, might have taken some of his information about the fate of these Cork workers from Tomes's account. "The freshly-imported Irishmen . . . also suffered severely, and there was found no other resource but to reship them as soon as possible." Otis suggested that many of these men were not hardy, able-bodied laborers. He hinted that their previous habits and modes of life had made them ill-suited to the demands of manual work in a tropical climate and that this was the reason for their high sickness rate.[67] Two Cork and Panama newspapers were in agreement and reported that many of the *Ben Nevis* men were not accustomed to the use of the pick and shovel.[68]

The railroad's records contained little information on the fate of the Cork immigrants who formed a tiny percentage of the total work force of about five thousand men in April and May of 1854.[69] Brief references in the board minutes suggested that the optimistic picture of the "lusty Irishmen" propagated by the Panamanian press was no longer entirely valid. The company's practice of shipping sick white employees to the United States now led to an unforeseen complication.

On arrival in New York in March 1854, some of the discharged Cork workers, suffering from malaria and other fevers, were admitted to the Quarantine Hospital on Ward's Island in the East River.[70] These were men "who had been employed on the Panama Railroad and had returned affected with fevers, some of a very malignant character."[71] The railroad had overlooked the fact that the laborers who had arrived on the *Ben Nevis*, unlike other returning sick workers, had not been admitted previously to the United States as immigrants and had not paid the immigrant tax of $1.50, a form of temporary health insurance entitling newcomers to hospital treatment if ill on arrival or if falling sick within a year.[72] The U.S. Steamship Company, which had transported the sick workers to New York, was fined for failing to comply with the entry regulations for infirm aliens. When the steamship company disputed these payments, the matter was referred to an arbitration committee that confirmed the shipping company was at fault. It imposed a fine of $35 for each man admitted to the Quarantine Hospital.

Not surprisingly, the shipping company sought to recover this money from the railroad. The latter's board referred the matter to a committee, but unfortunately the records made no mention of the outcome.[73] The fact remained that an undisclosed number of the Cork laborers became too ill to continue work within a few months of their arrival and had to be removed from the Isthmus. A considerable number, probably suffering from falciparum malaria or other fevers or infections, likely succumbed to their illnesses. The *New York Herald* reported the deaths of two returning railroad laborers in May but did not specify if they formed part of the Cork contingent.[74] Not all laborers arriving in New York at this time disembarked as invalids. On August 11, fifty workmen from the railroad arrived on board the *Empire City*.[75] No reference was made to their state of health, implying that there were no cases of serious illness among them. Some or all of these men might have been part of the Cork contingent, whose six-month contract with the railroad had recently expired.

At least three of the Cork workers managed to return to their native city in September 1854, ten months after their departure. One of these men, "a wretched looking creature, with a sallow burnt up complexion, and attenuated pinched features, who gave his name as John Brien, appeared before the magistrates seeking workhouse relief. He stated that he was one of those who had gone out as laborers to Panama and that he had returned about a fortnight earlier, with two others." He informed the magistrates that he had suffered from fever and ague in Panama. Asked how many in this group had died, Brien said, "I could not account for that. I suppose most of them all died [*sic*]." He claimed that the railroad company had sent him home and that he had spent whatever he had earned in Panama since returning to Cork. "The Bench desired the applicant to be put by until an order for his admission to the workhouse could be procured."[76]

Brien's evidence was puzzling. That the railroad would have paid his fare back to Ireland, and possibly that of his two companions—when it had contracted to be responsible only for the passage from Panama to New Orleans or New York—was curious. On the other hand, it might have been cheaper for the company to pay for their passage to Cork, thereby avoiding liability for hospital charges in New York for infirm aliens who had not been admitted to the United States as immigrants. What became of Brien and his two coworkers after their return home is not known.

In 1858, the *Cork Examiner*, provoked by an article published in an American magazine some years previously, and which had just come to its notice, criticized the Cork Board of Guardians for sending paupers to Panama. The article in question, a condensed version of Tomes's book, *Panama in 1855*, repeated the claim that the Irish laborers from Cork fell ill on arrival and were unable to work. The article further claimed that the survivors had been shipped to New York, where most of them allegedly died.[77] The *Cork Examiner* was angered by what had supposedly happened to these emigrants. "Our own locality, it will be seen, contributed its quota to the holocaust; the 'guardians of the poor' having, against the remonstrances of the press and public, relieved the rates by shipping a number of able-bodied paupers to this charnel house." The following year the paper renewed its attack on the board of guardians when it referred, inaccurately, to "the loss of nearly 300 paupers shipped in 1853 from the Cork Poor-house to the Panama railway."[78]

The fate of the 360 men who sailed from Cork to Aspinwall in December 1853 remains uncertain. These laborers were likely more susceptible to the diseases and hardship of Panama's climate than their fellow countrymen who had spent some time in the United States and who had become partly acclimatized as a result. Many of the men from Cork had not previously worked as laborers. Those who had been inmates in the workhouse were most likely undernourished and in poor physical shape. After five weeks in the cramped quarters of a sailing ship, all were faced with the need to adjust from the cold and damp of an Irish winter to the oppressive heat of a Panamanian summer. None would have had prior experience of the debilitating effects of manual labor in high temperatures and energy-sapping humidity. As a result, many would have become unfit for work sooner than other white laborers.

No record of how many of the *Ben Nevis* emigrants died either in Panama, or after their arrival in New York or New Orleans, from diseases or illnesses contracted on the Isthmus could be found. Claims that practically the entire contingent had been wiped out within a short time of the men's arrival in Panama were almost certainly exaggerated. However, the fatality rate among the Cork contingent was more devastating than the estimated 28 percent applying to white workers in general; the mortality rate of these men could have been as high as one in three. Those *Ben Nevis* emigrants fortunate enough to serve out their six-month contract would have left Panama for the United States in July or August 1854. There they embarked on a new life in a country that many had only dreamed of going to. Once ashore, they disappeared into the vastness of America and history does not record their fate.

PART IV

Epilogue

THIRTEEN

Railroad-Government Relations

RELATIONS BETWEEN THE PANAMA RAILROAD COMPANY AND NEW Granada's public officials and elected representatives during the early and mid-1850s fluctuated considerably. The relationship with the railroad was frequently cordial and accommodating at the upper echelons of government but occasionally became hostile and antagonistic at the provincial and municipal levels. The company had committed itself to building a major infrastructural project, an initiative that governments had been waiting for in Bogotá for decades—and which, it was hoped, would stimulate international trade, generate additional revenue, and bring about an era of progress and prosperity. The government's grant of close to three hundred thousand acres of land to the company in its 1850 charter, together with a right-of-way for the rails through public property on the Isthmus indicated its willingness to cooperate fully with the Americans. Consequently, the company usually counted on the sympathetic support of members of the political class in Bogotá, as well as that of Panama's governors, to secure legislation and administrative decisions that operated to its benefit.[1]

In November 1853, the railroad's board expressed its satisfaction with the cooperation shown by the country's authorities after almost four years of operations. "The Board take much pleasure in stating that the government of New Granada . . . have manifested every disposition to second the Board in their efforts to promote the objects they have in view." The directors referred to "the spirit of liberality and the courteous deportment, which have characterized the government in all their intercourse with the officers of the company."[2] The railroad's relationship with lower-ranking local and provincial officials and elected representatives, such as judges, prefects, police officers, and *alcaldes* (mayors), drawn from Panamanian people of mixed race, the *gente de color*, proved more problematic.

During the early stages of the project, the desertion by workers, both local and foreign, whose recruitment and transport costs had been paid for by the company became a major concern. The railroad successfully sought the assistance of the authorities to curb this outflow. Following representations from the railroad, Governor Bermúdez issued a proclamation early in 1851 that "all persons coming here to work on the [rail] road, under contract, and deserting after their arrival, will be arrested and put in jail."[3] Totten reported that desertions had stopped following this edict and that some absconders had voluntarily returned to their work. He declared that the railroad was indebted to the authorities "for the disposition and determination which they exhibit to assist the company."[4]

The authorities firmly enforced the antidesertion decree. Shortly after it had been issued, twenty-five laborers who had abandoned their work were arrested and imprisoned. Seventeen were penitent and were marched back to work again, while an obstinate minority remained in prison.[5] This step prompted the railroad to warn deserters of their likely fate. "The contractors of the Panama Railroad give notice to all persons coming to the Isthmus on contract to work on the road, that, if they desert the work, they will be put in prison."[6] The prospect of incarceration in a Panamanian prison was distinctly unpleasant. Irish-born Archibald Boyd, the acting U.S. consul in 1854, described the prison conditions of an American citizen awaiting trial. "The place where the man is confined is a most loathsome cell, exceedingly unhealthy, and filled with the lowest class of negro culprits."[7]

The company also secured military and police cooperation in apprehending miscreants involved in damaging its property. Growing unemployment and increasing impoverishment among sections of the local population caused by the decline of river-borne traffic, and by an easing off of the migrant rush for California, had repercussions for the security of the railroad and its passengers. It sought and obtained government protection after attempts were made to vandalize the bridge over the Chagres River at Barbacoas in 1852 and 1854. Those involved were most likely local boatmen and others connected with the once lucrative trade of transporting migrants. They rightly feared that the railroad was squeezing them out of business. Following the first unsuccessful attempt to damage the materials for the projected bridge in October 1852, Alexander Center requested protection for its property at Aspinwall and Barbacoas. Governor Herrara responded by dispatching twenty-five soldiers who were provisioned and quartered at the railroad's expense. General Jiménez subsequently rounded up thirty of those allegedly involved in attacks on migrants crossing the Isthmus and brought them to Panama City for trial, while General Páez authorized a military detachment to protect travelers and suppress murders and robberies.[8]

The company again sought and received military assistance after arsonists made another attempt on the recently completed wooden bridge two years later. Fortunately for the company, the damage was not significant. Troops captured twenty alleged offenders on this occasion and committed them to trial; seven others drowned in the river while trying to escape.[9] In 1851, the chief engineer feared that the disturbed political situation in New Granada might lead to the conscription of local men, thereby adversely affecting the railroad's recruitment of New Granadian workers. He might have used his influence with military and political leaders to protect his supply of potential local laborers. When civil war broke out again in New Granada in 1854, Totten intervened with the authorities and prevented the company's local workers from being drafted into the government's military forces.[10]

There were, however, some policy arenas that brought the company into conflict with Panama's authorities. These points of disagreement concerned the jurisdiction of local government officials over the railroad's property and the company's treatment of Panamanians. The latter half of 1853 witnessed several clashes over these issues, leading Totten to complain that local officials were interfering in the concerns of the company when they had no right to do so. It was no coincidence that these confrontations began not long after New Granada's 1853 constitution had come into operation. This radical charter granted the vote to all adult males and opened the doors to political office, initially at the local and provincial level, to men of mixed race, regardless of their property-owning status.

The chief engineer fought hard to successfully establish the company's right to overrule the authority of these local functionaries when it saw fit. The first of these conflicts occurred in September 1853 when the superintendent of the Gatún station ejected a Panamanian, alleged to be drunken and disorderly, from the company's property. The man was beaten when he resisted. The local alcalde then arrested the superintendent and put him in the stocks. Totten immediately hastened to Gatún with the district judge and obtained the superintendent's release.[11]

A further clash of authority occurred when the company detailed laborers to work under Gillett, the local station superintendent at Cruces, to repair the mule track to the capital. This ancient trail continued to be heavily used by tens of thousands of migrants crossing the Isthmus while the railroad was under construction and its condition had now deteriorated further. The laborers assigned to this project were paid $0.80 per day instead of the promised $1.20 but were told that they would receive the retained portion of their pay on resumption of their usual railroad tasks. The company argued that local workmen sometimes abandoned their work as soon as they had accumulated a little money, greatly inconveniencing the progress of the railroad. "The object of this arrangement [retention of wages] was to keep the men under control, and to ensure their return to the railroad work." The unhappy workers complained to the local judge, who asked Gillett to pay the men the full daily rate. When the superintendent refused, he was imprisoned and put in irons. Following an appeal from the company, the judge's superiors subsequently ordered Gillett's release.[12] The *Aspinwall Courier*, outraged at this treatment of an American citizen, called for the stationing of U.S. men-of-war at both ends of the transit route over the Isthmus.[13]

Another confrontation occurred when local residents at Matachín station, hoping to profit from the earnings of railroad workers based in the locality, erected huts or shanties where gambling took place and alcohol was sold. The result was predictable. "The men on the station, in consequence of their free access to liquor, had become disorderly and almost uncontrollable." From the beginning the railroad had banned the sale of alcoholic drinks on its property. The company did not want its workers to consume alcohol, seeking to ensure that its employees carried out their work effectively and to guarantee its control over a large male workforce. The station superintendent at Matachín opposed the erection of these shacks because of the company's antialcohol policy, and when his orders were ignored, he had the shanties torn down.[14]

The alcalde of the nearby town of Gorgona, who had granted authorization for these saloons, responded by informing the railroad superintendent that anyone had the right to build at the company's stations and sell liquor there. He also declared his intention of charging rent on the company's buildings at Matachín. Only the forceful intervention of Totten saved the superintendent from punishment. One of the demolished shanties predated the arrival of the railroad, and Totten was unsure if the company was legally within its rights in knocking it down. "The act of pulling down the house (a mere shed) . . . was illegal, inasmuch as it existed there before the establishment of the railroad station, but it was also, in a strong sense, justifiable, as an act of self-defense. The owner and occupant of the house persisted in selling liquor to our men against every remonstrance."[15]

In the closing days of 1853, Totten cited what he regarded as another example of interference by local officials in the company's concerns. This incident again involved the assertive alcalde of Gorgona, who claimed that the railroad was a public highway and local citizens had his permission to drive their cattle over it. On December 29, the alcalde turned up with an entourage of armed men to enforce this right of public access but was resisted by company officials under Baldwin, one of Totten's assistant engineers, causing Totten to comment, "Can you suppose a more dangerous abuse of authority than that of insisting to drive a herd of cattle over a railroad, in the midst of a gang of tracklayers and other workmen, and to the peril of the locomotives, trains, and passengers, as well as to the cattle themselves?"[16] While the outcome of this incident was not reported, Totten and the company prevailed and the tracks remained the private property of the railroad.

As a consequence of these events, Totten proclaimed the primacy of the company in its relationship with local officials, and he insisted on the railroad's right to overrule the authority of these Panamanian authorities when it saw fit.

> I wish to establish a precedent, that the petty officers of the country have no authority or right to interfere with the regulations of the company and that our power comes from a higher source, to which only we are responsible.
>
> You will observe that this does not prevent the *alcaldes* or other officers taking cognizance of misdemeanors committed by the servants of the company personally; on the contrary I only wish they would be more active in such cases.
>
> But with the rules and regulations of the company, or for the execution of an order given by the authorities against the company, especially in everything relating to its management, I hold that the petty officials, *alcaldes*, etc., have no such jurisdiction as they have exercised.[17]

Totten announced that he intended to raise this matter in person with the provincial governor and was optimistic about the outcome. "I do expect much assistance from him."[18] As the author of a recent study of Panamanian politics in the 1850s has pointed out, "The building of the railroad had produced places on the isthmus in which the railroad's officers effectively ruled, with little oversight by local political officials and sometimes in direct contravention of their orders."[19]

The creation and expansion of the new port city of Aspinwall on the Caribbean coast provided another example of the growing power and assertiveness of an American-owned railroad operating within New Granada. Planned and built to serve as the railroad's Atlantic terminus, Aspinwall's administration appeared to have been largely in the company's hands. Local government officials played a minimal role.[20] Even the name of the new city, Aspinwall to the Americans, Colón (Columbus) to the citizens of New Granada, reflected opposing views of the extent of the company's power and authority.

Not long after the founding of the new settlement, Totten proposed calling it Mansanilla City after the island on which it was built.[21] But New Granada's Congress officially named the railroad's terminus Colón in October 1850, the title to come into effect as soon as there was a sufficient population to sustain public offices in the new settlement. The railroad was either unaware of this decision or chose to ignore it when it named the new town Aspinwall eighteen months later.[22] The company's decision to arrogate to itself the right to name the new settlement was indicative of the control it felt it was rightfully entitled to exercise in a foreign country.[23]

The naming of the settlement took place at a ceremony to lay the cornerstone of the company's administrative building, the island's first brick-built structure, in February 1852. Victoriano de Diego Paredes, New Granada's ambassador to the United States, was present along with other distinguished guests, including George Law and Minor C. Story.[24] The diplomat proposed, at Stephens's suggestion, that the new town be called Aspinwall, a title that was quickly repudiated by his own government.[25] William Perry, the British consul, claimed that the railroad exceeded its authority by calling the terminus Aspinwall when its official name was Colón. He asked the chargé d'affaires in Bogotá to "take such steps as you may deem proper to put a stop to this apparent usurpation of authority by the North Americans." Perry feared that the American company's initiative might establish an unwelcome precedent and enable it to appoint future provincial governors and municipal authorities "without regard to the sovereign rights of this republic [New Granada]."[26] The consul's attitude reflected the underlying British view that the building of a railroad across Panama by an American-controlled enterprise posed a threat to New Granada's sovereignty and challenged the United Kingdom's power and prestige in the region.

For almost the next forty years, confusion surrounded the title of the new settlement. New Granada and the United Kingdom refused to accept the American name and persisted in calling the port city Colón, after Columbus, whose ships had reportedly touched at Manzanillo Island during his voyages of discovery centuries before. An American historian regretted that the name

Figure 13.1. U.S. Mail Steamship Premises, Aspinwall (Colon), 1855. *Illustrated London News.* Antiqua Print Gallery / Alamy Stock Illustration.

and glory of Columbus had been rejected in favor of that of a New York magnate.[27] The railroad, which had created this town out of a mangrove-covered swamp and oversaw its expansion and growth until it became the second city of the Isthmus, felt that it, rather than the government authorities, had earned the right to name and administer the new settlement.

For decades after its foundation, this new urban center was run virtually as a company town. Panama's local government officials exercised only nominal authority. A British naval officer referred to the town's semiautonomous status in 1863. "Although Aspinwall is in the territory of New Granada, it has a separate municipal government vested in American residents, for the most part connected with the railway company."[28] Another British writer noted that while the laws of New Granada nominally governed Aspinwall, in reality it was run by the railroad. The "Americans and particularly the railroad people almost look upon the place as a colony of their own."[29]

The settlement may have served as a prototype for later American-controlled economic zones located outside the United States. As McGuinness points out, Aspinwall, "a virtual mini-state," became "arguably the first instance of a U.S.-dominated commercial enclave in Latin American history—a place that remained formally within the bounds of Nueva Granada but was effectively ruled by a foreign-owned company."[30] However, the railroad was eventually forced to give way on the nomenclature issue and accept Colón as the city's name in 1890 after the Colombian postal authorities refused to continue delivering letters addressed to Aspinwall.

Another arena of confrontation emerged when the railroad joined with American shipping companies in challenging the right of Panama's provincial government to levy a tax on ships and passengers docking at the ports of Panama City and Aspinwall. The opposition of the American corporations to these taxes brought the province close to bankruptcy. The origins of this issue date to the late 1840s, when New Granada's legislature abolished taxes on international trade crossing the Isthmus in an attempt to stimulate commerce, satisfy the aspirations of Panama's commercial elite, and put into effect the ruling Liberal Party's ideological commitment to free trade. This move, however, deprived Panama's provincial and municipal authorities of an important revenue source on which they had hitherto relied for the provision of public services. The provincial assembly had little alternative but to increase the tax burden on merchants, shopkeepers, and others in the local population.

When popular opposition made it difficult to collect these local taxes, the province's legislators attempted to compensate for the revenue shortfall by levying controversial taxes on shipping and on travelers crossing the Isthmus. On January 1, 1854, masters or owners of vessels became liable for a head tax for every passenger landed at, or carried from, the Isthmus. They had also become liable for a tonnage tax on shipping capable of generating a potential annual income of $50,000.[31] An American newspaper blamed Don Justo Arosemena, a prominent politician and political thinker, known as "the father of Panamanian nationality," for this tax legislation. The paper disagreed with Arosemena's stance that tax revenues from the transit trade should be used to finance public expenditure, thereby reducing the fiscal burden pressing on the province's inhabitants.[32]

The railroad supported the shipping companies in their refusal to pay these charges, claiming that they contravened the Mallarino-Bidlack treaty of 1846 between the United States and New Granada. Furthermore, New Granada's 1850 contract with the railroad had granted tax-free status to the ports at either end of the line. Taxation of passengers and goods would add to operating costs and would probably lead to an increase in fares and charges, which, in turn, would cause migrants and freight to switch to a less expensive interoceanic route.

The American consuls in Panama City and Aspinwall, and eventually the American government, supported the stance of the shipping companies and the railroad. The commander of the U.S. corvette *Cyane*, anchored in Navy Bay, declared his intention of protecting his countrymen if any violent means were taken to enforce the collection of the passenger tax.[33] The U.S. chargé d'affaires in Bogotá bluntly expressed his opposition to the taxation of American shipping in a letter to the consul in Panama City. "I must confess I see no end to these repeated harassments but in punishing those scoundrels, who neither respect the obligations of law or honor. . . . The robber once successful, rarely stops short of the gallows." The diplomat referred to the New Granada authorities as "vagabonds" and to New Granada as "so contemptible a state."[34]

New Granada's treasury failed to come to the assistance of the cash-strapped provincial administration in Panama, preferring to retain most of the modest annual payment it received from the railroad for pressing central government expenditure.[35] The Panamanian authorities, on the other hand, lacked the power to enforce the payment of their taxes on shipping and passengers. The resulting revenue shortfall brought the provincial government and the *cabildos*, town councils, close to bankruptcy.[36] Policing was underfunded and undermanned at a time when growing unemployment and increasing poverty led to a rise in crime.

Ironically, the shipping companies' failure to fulfill their tax obligations and the consequent near collapse of law and order caused the Pacific Mail Steamship Co., in conjunction with the railroad, to establish and finance a private security force, the Isthmian Guard, in 1854 and 1855. This cost both companies considerably. The controversial taxation issue was temporarily resolved when the republic's executive announced in 1855 that legislative initiatives of this kind were the exclusive prerogative of the central government and that the Panamanian assembly lacked the constitutional right to enact these taxes.[37]

Attempts by the railroad to protect its employees, passengers, and freight in an insecure and frequently dangerous country was another issue that brought it into conflict with state authorities. Ensuring the protection of its infrastructure, equipment, and stores concerned the company's management throughout the early 1850s, but this issue did not become particularly pressing until 1854 and 1855. The company's initiative in establishing and operating its own private police force in those years, and in apprehending and punishing those it deemed to be criminals, infringed on New Granada's right to control public security and maintain the integrity of its judicial and penal systems.

The Isthmus suffered from a generalized lack of security during the 1850s as a result of insufficient funding for policing and the influx of huge numbers of migrants on their way to or from California. Many of these migrants had scant respect for the law. Perry, the British consul, informed his superior in 1850, "At present there is no security for life and property; there are no funds to support either a police or military force, and the militia when called out refuse to attend." He blamed the railroad and the American presence in Panama for this situation. "The Americans command but do not govern and they express dissatisfaction at the weakness of the governing powers, when the privileges accorded to the railway and those assumed by themselves are the causes of the bankruptcy and extreme impotency of the state."[38] The following year, Perry referred again to "the frightful state of disorder" and anarchy in the province due to the absence of a strong police force and an adequate military garrison.[39]

U.S. consuls echoed the claims of their British counterpart about the prevailing disorder in Panama but failed to accept any American responsibility for the situation. They repeatedly requested the presence of American men-of-war, with marines on board, to guarantee the safety of their citizens and property. "For under the weak and almost powerless government which exists here, no security is felt."[40] Henry Tracy, the U.S. Mail Steamship agent in Panama, informed his New York office in August 1850 that "there are from 50 to 100 as precious villains on the Isthmus as ever went unhung." He then asked for a consignment of arms to be sent down to protect the company's gold shipments.[41] A migrant who crossed Panama in 1853 advised visitors to carry a gun. "A revolver is generally esteemed a valuable auxiliary." The local press warned travelers to band together for protection and carry weapons. "The road is infested with most dangerous characters. . . . We repeat that it is not only advisable but actually necessary that strangers crossing the isthmus, should not undertake the journey alone, nor without being well armed."[42]

Until the end of 1853, the railroad, as noted earlier, dealt with security issues by appealing, with considerable success, to the province's governors and other public officials for the protection of its property. The threat to the lives of its passengers and workers had not been particularly worrying up to that point. However, the security situation worsened during the course of 1854 to the extent that the company felt obliged to act unilaterally to protect migrants crossing the Isthmus. Another civil war had broken out in Nueva Granada. The Bogotá government withdrew locally based troops to confront rebels in other parts of the national territory leaving the Isthmus even more unprotected from lawless elements. Furthermore, the railroad's advance had thrown many of those previously engaged in transporting and looking after migrants out of work, which deprived porters, muleteers, boatmen, and others of their previous sources of income. Criminal and other disaffected elements took advantage of the security vacuum, and a wave of assaults, robberies, and murders ensued.

José María Urrutia Aniño, the province's governor, faced a growing crime wave on the one hand and insufficient resources to finance the necessary security response on the other. As a result, "Life in Panama was positively dreadful." This view was reiterated by Thomas Ward, the Dublin-born U.S. consul in the capital, in a report to the secretary of state in 1854. "Robberies and murders on this Isthmus have become so frequent and common that they are not noticed by the authorities. There is no police in the city of Panama, none on the Isthmus, none in Aspinwall, and all the [tax] money collected goes into the pockets of a parcel of greedy officials, who continue to cry for more, more tax upon the foreigners and withal there is no protection given to the lives and property of those who are so onerously taxed."[43]

Ward's consular counterpart in Aspinwall complained of "the abandonment of this city to anarchy and disorder." He believed that the provincial authorities were punishing it because of the U.S. Mail Steamship Company's refusal to pay the passenger tax.[44] A journalist who subsequently became president of Colombia later claimed that the government could furnish only "a few dozen sickly soldiers, badly dressed, without discipline, sometimes starving and always discontented" to protect the transit route across the Isthmus when, in his view, a force of two thousand men was required for this purpose.[45]

The deteriorating security situation led foreign merchants and residents in Aspinwall, supported by the railroad, to form a vigilance committee on March 20, 1854, following a precedent established in San Francisco some years earlier. The declared purpose of this self-appointed group of vigilantes, composed of "sober, intelligent and enterprising American citizens" was "to detect, judge, and punish criminals to the fullest extent necessary."[46] The committee's advice to the city's foreign merchants to cease paying taxes in response to the administration's failure to safeguard their businesses brought it into conflict with the governor.

The activities of the vigilance committee were largely circumscribed to Aspinwall and its surrounding region.[47] Meantime, travelers on the mule road between Panama City and Obispo, where the railhead was then located, were subjected to continual outrages. On July 17, Ran Runnels, an American businessman operating a transport agency, found John McGlynn, a native of the north of Ireland, lying badly wounded near the summit of the continental divide. McGlynn was returning to San Francisco from New York when he was stabbed and robbed of his steamer ticket and twenty-five dollars. While his ultimate fate was not reported, the nature of his injuries would suggest that he was unlikely to have survived.[48] This attack, following others of a similar nature, acted as a catalyst for the establishment of a private security force by the railroad.

In view of the governor's declaration that he had neither the men nor the money to protect travelers, the *Panama Star and Herald* proposed the formation of an armed private police force. This, the paper suggested, should consist of about twenty mounted men headed by Runnels, mistakenly described by later writers as a former Texas Ranger. The force's objective would be to clear the mule trail between Obispo and the capital of the gangs of murderers and robbers with which it was infected.[49] The newspaper suggested that steamship companies serving Panama should levy a passenger tax to defray the expenses of this paramilitary force.[50] The paper's plea coincided with an almost identical request from Totten to the governor to authorize the formation of a special security force to be financed by the railroad, local business, and commercial enterprises.

The timing and content of these initiatives would suggest that discussions about the formation of this force among Panama's expatriate business community had already taken place. The governor, finding himself in a difficult situation, acquiesced, possibly reluctantly, and in a decree dated July 21, 1854, transferred powers to Totten and others to form and arm a paramilitary unit.[51] Acting swiftly, the chief engineer arranged with Runnels to raise a force of men at the railroad's expense. Four days later, Runnels and twenty men, all locals and fully armed, left Panama City to begin their mission.[52]

This paramilitary force, whose membership fluctuated between twenty and forty or so men, became known as the "Isthmian Guard," or the "Armed Guard on the Isthmus." Having been invested with authority by the civil power to reestablish law and order, its subsequent actions had a strong claim on legitimacy.[53] This unit was not authorized to decide on the punishment of captives, but its disregard of this stipulation soon brought opprobrium on the governor's head from Panamanians upset at the appropriation of judicial authority by foreigners. Carlos Zachrisson, a prominent Swedish businessman, and Gabriel Neira, a local merchant, assisted Runnels in organizing and operating the Guard.[54] Less than a week after leaving the capital, Runnels returned with a prisoner named Edward O'Leary, possibly Irish born, who was suspected of being one of the principal bandits on the mule trail. Some months previously the public had been warned that O'Leary, recently imprisoned for robbery and swindling, had escaped from jail.[55]

Foreign rather than local criminals were believed to pose the greatest threat to peace and security at this period. According to one historian, "Of all robbers and swindlers on the Isthmus white men were the worst, and compared to them the natives were humane, faithful and honest."[56] Many of these outlaws were probably unsuccessful forty-niners, failed prospectors trying to make their way home from the Californian goldfields, who found themselves stranded penniless in Panama. An English traveler provided a graphic picture of these desperados. "Stamped with vice and intemperance, without baggage or money, they were fit for robbery and murder to any extent; many of them I doubt not were used to it." He continued, "Long gaunt fellows, armed to the teeth, line the streets [of Panama City] on either side, or lounge about the drinking bars and gambling saloons; and among these there is quarrelling and stabbing, and probably murder, before the night is out."[57] In the following days, Runnels arrested more prisoners. Five were transported to a convict settlement near Buenaventura at the railroad's expense and with the permission of the authorities. The *Panama Star and Herald* refuted the rumor that the Guard had hung five men. Even so, these developments led to a stampede of criminal elements out of the capital.[58]

The railroad's directors approved Totten's decision to establish an armed, privately run police force to protect life and property on the Isthmus the following month.[59] This paramilitary group initially received a monthly subsidy of at least $2,000, and possibly more, from the railroad. When the board attempted to reduce its contribution to $1,000 per month from November 1, Totten retorted that the Guard could not be maintained as an effective force for less than $2,000 monthly. The board accepted his plea, and he was authorized to expend that amount for November and December.[60] The Pacific Mail Steamship Company also made at least one payment of $3,386 toward the cost of maintaining this private force. The U.S. Mail Steamship Company, on the other hand, failed to contribute to its running costs.[61] Operating on the margins of the penal code and dispensing with courts and judiciary, Runnels gradually reestablished order and security. Suspected criminals were rounded up and imprisoned, and others were forced into exile.

By the end of its first month in operation, the Isthmian Guard had dealt with forty-seven men suspected of involvement in criminal activities. Sixteen white men had been deported to New York, San Francisco, and Valparaiso; a number of New Grenadians had been lodged in Panama City's prison or shipped to Cartagena and the country's penal colony at Quindío. Some Jamaicans had been sentenced to forced labor on the railroad. Two men were acquitted for want of evidence against them. No mention was made of any hangings.[62] However, the governor's decision to transfer police powers to Runnels proved unpopular with many Panamanians, and in mid-September he rescinded the decree given two months earlier to the Isthmian Guard "apparently over questions raised about its legality and its possible infringement on individual rights."[63]

The railroad and the Guard turned a blind eye to the governor's decision. The paramilitary force continued to implement its law-and-order mission. In October, the railroad informed the governor that it would continue to finance the Guard for the protection of life and property on the Isthmus. This decision was put to a vote at a meeting in Panama City and unanimously carried.[64] That same month a public subscription for Runnels, Zachrisson, and Neira, the founders of the Isthmian Guard, raised $950. The money was used to buy them presentation gifts.[65] Urrutia Aniño, on the other hand, became a target for public hostility and ridicule, and his life was threatened. In November 1854, under the pretext of an unofficial visit to the interior, he retired to his family estate, effectively abandoning his role as governor.[66]

Ran Runnels and the exploits of the Isthmian Guard have entered the realm of Panamanian mythology. Accounts of this period of the history of the Isthmus referred to the mass execution of criminals supposedly carried out by Runnels and his private security force. These claims are spurious, and much that has been written on the topic is untrue. A recent scholarly study demolished the myths surrounding the Guard and Runnels. It found that there was no documentary evidence to confirm these alleged hangings, which, it added, "can be traced ultimately to flawed or fictitious sources."[67]

The myth of Ran Runnels, allegedly a Texas Ranger, a terror to criminals and the doer of many deeds of daring, originated with Tomes's 1855 book. This author reported that the Isthmian Guard was formed to control the unruly workforce and to clear the Isthmus of robbers, but he did not mention any mass hangings.[68] There were no references in press reports at the time or in the railroad's documents to the use of the Isthmian Guard to police the railroad laborers. Otis, in his history of the railroad, first published in 1861, made no reference to Runnels or the Isthmian Guard. Bancroft, in his 1887 *History of Central America*, was apparently the first to refer to the executions of wrongdoers. He alleged that Runnels captured, hanged, and buried a number of criminals "without scandal or noise . . . and out of sight and without witnesses, other than his own men."[69] Bancroft cited a Panamanian jurist, Simón Maldonado, author of *Asuntos Políticos Panameños*, as his source. Maldonado, however, failed to provide any evidence for his claim.[70] Robinson hinted in his 1907 memoirs that Runnels might have carried out some extrajudiciary executions. "His services had been valuable at a time when nerve to hang an outlaw to the nearest tree, without judge or jury, was regarded a virtue."[71]

The number and manner of these executions has been sensationalized by subsequent writers. Horace Bell, in his memoir, *On the Old West Coast*, embellished Bancroft's earlier assertion.[72] Minter, in turn, elaborated on Tomes's and Bell's account in his 1948 book, *The Chagres*. He wrongly claimed that Urrutia Aniño transferred police powers to the railroad in September 1851 and that Ran Runnels secretly formed his Isthmus Guard in the closing months of that year.[73] According to Minter, Runnels hung thirty-seven men on the ramparts of Panama City in January 1852 and a forty-one more in April. He described these bandits as "Derienni," a term taken from a fictional account of a band of robbers on the Isthmus published in 1853.[74]

During the following three years, Runnels was reportedly responsible for the deaths of more than a hundred highwaymen who "were left hanging from trees along the banks of the Chagres."[75] Bell's and Minter's fictitious accounts were given additional credence and embellishment in Schott's imaginative and partly fabricated narrative of the railroad's construction and became part of the accepted history of nineteenth-century Panama. Conniff, for example, referred to Runnels as "the hangman of Panama" because of his alleged mass executions of criminals, citing Schott as his source.[76]

Although a New York newspaper announced that the Isthmian Guard would be disbanded once the railroad was completed, it continued to operate throughout 1855, though by June its strength had been reduced to twelve men, reflecting a considerable improvement in the security situation.[77] With the railroad now fully in operation, the number of travelers using the Cruces Road, the favorite haunt of bandits, declined dramatically. Furthermore, many of the criminal elements that had previously terrorized the Isthmus had fled, been imprisoned, or were banished from the province. Not all of the region's miscreants had been dealt with by the Isthmian Guard, however, because an attempt was made to shoot Runnels a little before midnight in April 1855, in the capital's Cathedral Plaza. "The ball struck the wall immediately over Mr Runnels' head and knocked down some of the plaster almost on him." The assailant escaped, but suspicion rested on a noted scoundrel and a warrant for his arrest was issued.[78]

The railroad's decision to provide its own security force cost it $25,535.31 between October 30, 1854, and December 31, 1855. An additional monthly sum of $2,000 and possibly more was spent on the Guard from its formation in late July 1854 to the end of October.[79] A total expenditure of over $30,000 was presumably a price that the company's directors felt was worth paying in the absence of a properly state-funded police service. Runnels's role in heading the Isthmian Guard led him to a career in the American public service. A sinecure was created for him: the special inspectorship of U.S. Customs on the Isthmus of Panama, with a salary of $5,000 per annum.[80] A few years later, Runnels was promoted to the post of American consul in San Juan del Sur in Nicaragua.[81] Urrutia Aniño, on the other hand, was subsequently dismissed as governor, partly because of his unpopular decision to delegate authority to the Isthmian Guard.

These developments in the early and mid-1850s throw light on the unequal and sometimes antagonistic relationship between an influential and increasingly assertive American company and the authorities of a politically unstable and financially weak state endeavoring to protect its sovereignty and the rights of its people. The railroad represented probably the largest capital outlay by a U.S. corporation in Central America in the 1850s, and this would have reinforced the sense of importance and self-confidence felt by company officials in dealing with their Panamanian counterparts.

An attitude of superiority toward Panamanians and Central Americans in general was characteristic of many North Americans and Europeans, a product of the endemic racist attitudes of the period.[82] The doctrine of Manifest Destiny, the belief that the United States had been chosen by God to dominate the entire American continent, gave added credence to these attitudes. According to this doctrine, widely subscribed to in the United States from 1845 until the end of the century, American expansion in the region would be a blessing for all concerned, bringing with it a continent-wide empire of order, liberty, and progress.[83]

Figure 13.2. Panama Railroad, 1880s. Hand-colored woodcut. North Wind Picture Archives / Alamy Stock Illustration.

The company's sometimes abrasive attitude in its dealings with New Granada's public authorities was also based on its economic leverage in Panama and its political influence in Washington. Bogotá's capacity to constrain the American company in the 1850s was impaired by sporadic political unrest and a perennial shortage of revenues to fund its public administration. The contest between the railroad and the civil authorities was essentially an uneven one, where the company's monopoly of Isthmian transport and its commercial influence in Panama, together with its confidence that it could rely on Washington's backing in a crisis, usually gave it the upper hand.[84] The history of the Panama railroad in the 1850s appears to reinforce the maxim that "whoever controlled the routes and the technology of transnational trade held power."[85]

A disproportionate share of the benefits accruing from the relationship between the railroad and New Grenada's civil authorities went to the more powerful partner in this partnership. In 1855, Bogotá got the modern transportation link across the Isthmus that it had yearned for since the 1820s, but the economic benefits it expected would result from the railroad failed to materialize. Instead, Panama stagnated economically, and the province was faced with a combative American company determined to assert its autonomy and freedom of action and ready to challenge the state's authorities. Panama in the 1850s was one of the first arenas in Latin America in which a contest for power and influence between a U.S.-based corporation and government authorities played out, often beneath the surface of day-to-day politics. Scenarios like this, involving similar protagonists, and with somewhat analogous outcomes, were to be enacted over the course of the succeeding century and a half in many other Central and South American countries.

FOURTEEN

The Aftermath

ALTHOUGH TRAINS RAN FROM OCEAN TO OCEAN AT THE END OF January 1855, construction was by no means completed. Heavy rains damaged the tracks, and shortly after the railroad had come fully into operation, floods weakened the ill-starred bridge across the Chagres River once again. This time the damage was quickly rectified, and traffic was interrupted only for a few days.[1] Much of the construction work carried out up to then was of a temporary character. The railroad had been rushed through to satisfy the aspirations of anxious shareholders and to meet the insistent demands of migrants for speedy transportation across the Isthmus. The building of this line exemplifies the tactics of early American railroad promoters. Competition for capital at this period was intense, and railroad entrepreneurs were usually short of investment funding for their projects.

The response of the early railroad builders was simple: first, get the tracks laid quickly and start running trains to generate income. As traffic increased, revenue growth would create additional capital to carry out improvements.[2] The railroad company had this strategy in mind in 1850 when it planned to build the Pacific sector of the line first. Once completed, revenues from this section would help finance the second phase to the Atlantic. Circumstances caused this plan to be abandoned, but as soon as the railroad began to carry passengers over part of the route from 1852 onward, this self-financing approach was again embraced. There was a pressing requirement therefore to carry out a considerable program of improvement once the urgent need to complete the line had been met.

The company invested between $2 million and $3 million of additional capital in upgrading the railroad from 1855 to 1858. A reduced but still sizable workforce was retained to improve the infrastructure, though the numbers employed declined as time went on. There was no longer a need to import white laborers from the United States, and henceforth the manual workforce consisted mainly of local men and West Indians. In March 1855, three thousand laborers were still employed, earning $0.80 per day, plus a $0.30 daily living allowance. A smaller number of mechanics and foremen, mostly from the United States, assisted them and received between $2.00 and $3.00 daily.[3] Some of these men were deployed to improve and expand the terminus at Panama City, constructed on thirty-four acres of land purchased by the company.[4] A wooden jetty, 450 feet long and adjoining the station, was built out into the bay. Because of the large rise and fall of Pacific tides, this pier served only small vessels under three hundred tons' burden. These were able to ground on the mud at low water. Small steamboats transported passengers and freight between this jetty and ships anchored several miles offshore.[5]

Men were also engaged in laying a telegraph line alongside the tracks between Aspinwall and Panama City.[6] Preliminary discussions about a telegraphic link had taken place in 1852, but nothing came of these.[7] Three years later the railroad completed this project, and the first messages by telegraph between the Atlantic and the Pacific were exchanged on August 12, 1855.[8] The telegraph provided the company's officials on the Isthmus with a vital communication tool, keeping them informed of the arrival and departure times of trains at both ends of the line and of the number of passengers arriving by sea.

By 1856, the railroad's workforce had been considerably reduced. "The company keep [sic] about 1,300 men constantly employed on the line, which every day is improving."[9] According to a New Orleans newspaper: "Great improvements are in progress on the Panama railroad. 1,500 natives are constantly employed quarrying stone and improving the route. Iron bridges, with stone abutments, are to take the place of the wooden ones."[10] Between 1857 and 1858, the average number of men working for the railroad declined further to about 1,100.[11] New Granada and Jamaica supplied most of the laborers, while the mechanics and officials were mainly American.[12] Renovations and improvements continued to be made until the end of 1858, when the construction account finally closed. The railroad, in addition to reducing the number of men it employed after 1855, also cut the salaries of most of its employees by between 10 and 25 percent, despite making substantial profits from its monopoly of transisthmian travel—a decision that was criticized by the *New York Times*.[13]

The line was divided into sections approximately four miles long for main-tenance purposes. Stations where locomotives could take on wood to fuel their boilers were built at intervals along the track. Each station house was the residence of a trackmaster who was assisted by a gang of ten laborers who earned sixty cents a day in the 1860s. Sidings were built at Gatún, Barbacoas, Matachín, and the summit to allow trains to pass one another on the single track. Original wooden crossties, which soon rotted in Panama's tropical cli-mate, needed constant replacement with more durable ones made from black guayacán (*lignum vitae*), a hardwood timber imported from Barranquilla and Cartagena. Climbing grades were reduced, and curves and bends in the line were straightened out. The maximum grade on the Atlantic side was 1 in 90; on the Pacific descent, it was 1 in 88.[14]

In 1857, a more robust iron structure replaced the wooden bridge over the Chagres River at Barbacoas. Costing over $200,000, it was said "to be one of the largest and finest iron bridges in the world."[15] Stronger and more perma-nent iron structures also replaced other wooden bridges. Embankments and viaducts were reinforced, and the track was shored up where it crossed swamps. Rolling stock amounted to twenty-two passenger cars with a capacity of sixty passengers each, as well as fifty-one boxcars and seventy-two flatcars.[16]

Warehouses for storing freight, as well as buildings for the temporary ac-commodation of passengers, were built at both terminals, including a huge stone-built depot at Aspinwall, three hundred feet long by eighty-five feet wide, adjacent to the wharves.[17] By 1859, four wharves had been constructed at the Caribbean port, where the largest vessels of the period could berth. Trains ran along the dockside allowing the transfer of passengers and freight from ship to shore, or vice versa, with the minimum of delay and disruption. Thanks to this program of improvements, transit time across the Isthmus was eventually reduced from about four and a half hours to just over three hours.

An American journalist was pleasantly surprised at the standard of work-manship he encountered in 1856. By the end of 1857, the railroad was considered "equal to many of the best roads in the Atlantic States."[18]

> I had been led to suppose that it had been hastily built, and that it was an unpleasant and unsafe public way. Instead of this, I found a well-constructed and smooth road that will compare favorably with the best roads in the United States. The bridges that have been first put in of wood, are now being replaced with iron ones, and this work . . . will make the road a most complete and permanent structure.[19]

While these improvements were being implemented, a serious accident occurred. When a train rounded a curve near Gatún, just over a year after the railroad's opening, the outer rail became displaced. Eight coaches derailed and toppled down an embankment into the marsh below. Forty-four passengers were killed and over sixty injured, including a number of Irish.[20] This disaster did not appear to greatly affect the railroad's business, probably because fatal train crashes were relatively common in that epoch and also because travelers had no alternative means of crossing Panama, apart from river and mule transport, which was slow, onerous, and potentially more hazardous to life and health than traveling by train.[21]

During this period, the railroad company made a modest foray into shipping on the Atlantic and the Pacific oceans. It established its own line of ten sailing vessels, the Brig Line, to carry freight between New York and Aspinwall. These boats left the metropolis for the Isthmus with cargo destined for Central America and the Pacific coast of the United States. On their return trip, they brought back minerals and raw materials from Peru, Ecuador, and the Central American republics. The round trip lasted about thirty days.[22] The Panama railroad also established the Central American Steamship Company, whose ships plied coastal routes in the Pacific between Panama City and Central American ports from 1856.[23]

These small fleets boosted business for the railroad during its golden decade, from 1859 to 1869, a period when the company enjoyed a near monopoly of transoceanic transport. However, the placement of the Pacific terminus at Panama City was not advantageous from a shipping perspective. The location inhibited the growth of the railroad's freight traffic. Because the capital lacked a deepwater port, the Bay of Panama was used as an open roadstead, with vessels anchoring offshore. Barges were required to transship cargo between ship and shore, increasing costs and transport time.

Aspinwall, founded in 1850 as the railroad's Caribbean terminus, quickly developed into Panama's principal Atlantic port. From late 1851 it became the entry point for the railroad's workforce and migrants heading to California. The growth and expansion of Aspinwall mirrored the success of the railroad to which it owed its existence. Despite its unfavorable location in the Caribbean swamplands, climatic drawbacks, and a fearsome reputation for disease, the town survived and grew. Low-lying areas were gradually filled in with excavated earth and rocks, and streets were laid down.

By the middle of 1853, the town's population included about 250 Americans, and almost one hundred houses had been erected during the previous year. Rents from plots on the island yielded an annual income of $15,000 for the company.[24] Three years after the first vegetation had been cleared, what had previously been an uninhabited island covered in mangrove swamps barely above sea-level, now boasted three hundred substantial houses, five hotels (one of which could accommodate five hundred guests), two hospitals, three wharves, and a variety of workshops, as well as a large freight depot for the railroad. An American journal described Aspinwall in 1854 as "a town raised as by enchantment from the sea, in defiance of every natural obstacle."[25] By 1855 the population was estimated to number between two thousand and three thousand inhabitants.[26]

The town's continued expansion caused it to eventually encompass the entire island of Manzanillo and become Panama's second city. Its port grew in commercial importance. During the course of 1855, 128 vessels with an aggregate tonnage of 82,263 tons docked there.[27] Sanitary conditions, however, remained poor, and the new port proved to be just as unhealthy as Chagres, its predecessor. The place repulsed novelist Anthony Trollope. "A rose by any other name would smell as sweet, and Colón or Aspinwall, will be equally vile whatever you may call it. It is a wretched, unhealthy, miserably-situated, but thriving little American town . . . I can say nothing in its favor."[28] An American visitor was even more acerbic. "Probably there was not in all the world where man dwells a more loathsome spot than this town of Aspinwall, with its hybrid population and streets of intersecting stagnant pools."[29] Robert Tomes painted a vivid, though exaggerated, description of the inhabitants' state of health in 1855. "I do not believe there is a wholesome person in all Aspinwall."[30]

The estimated cost of the railroad at the initial planning stage was between $3 million and $3.5 million. This was subsequently increased to $5 million. However, expenditure to January 1855, when trains began running from coast to coast, amounted to between $5 million and $6 million. The company then poured in another $2 million to $3 million to improve the line between 1855 and 1858 so that by the time the construction account closed on December 31, 1858, total expenditure had escalated to just over $8 million, over twice the original estimate.[31] This made the Panama railroad, at approximately $165,000 per mile, one of the most expensive in the world to build, mile per mile, up to that time.[32] The railroad was also the highest-priced in the world to travel on, on a mile-per-mile basis, with a one-way ticket costing $25 for a journey of just over forty-seven miles. Even so, this was a considerable saving on the $50 to $100 that travelers had paid to cross the Isthmus in the prerailroad era.[33]

Migrants probably considered the exorbitant fare to be money well spent, as facilities for getting to or from the American west coast had been immeasurably improved by the rail link. After disembarking from a ship on one ocean in the morning, travelers could be aboard another on the opposite ocean by nightfall. Their speedy transit across the Isthmus protected them to a considerable extent from the country's fevers as well as from the bandits and human vultures who had preyed on their predecessors in earlier times. As a result, migrants no longer needed to be armed. Until then "two-thirds of our California travelers deemed it necessary to carry arms for self-protection while crossing the Isthmus . . . the opening of the Panama Railroad has pretty much dispensed with six-shooters among passengers by that line."[34]

The railroad's completion also drastically reduced the time needed to transport freight between the Pacific and the Atlantic states of the United States. It was now possible, for example, to deliver a cargo of ice, a luxury on the tropical Isthmus, from Boston to Panama City in thirty days, less than one-quarter of the time previously required to ship it around Cape Horn.[35] By 1860, the average traveling time between New York and San Francisco via the railroad was twenty-three days, while 138 days or more were required by clipper ship around the Horn. Freight from Asia or the west coast of South America landed at Panama City could reach England in less than thirty days, while delivery would take four months if sent around South America.[36]

Although costly to build, the railroad had generated a growing stream of revenue from transporting passengers and their baggage, as well as mail and other freight, along the stretch of line that gradually advanced across the Isthmus. Annual reports for 1852–1856 revealed the railroad's ability to self-finance a substantial proportion of its construction costs from passenger and freight receipts. Between 1852 and 1855, while construction was taking place, the railroad took in over $2 million in gross receipts from transporting over 121,820 passengers, gold shipments valued at $171,157,421.25, and silver worth $29,403,793.49.[37] Schott claimed that, on paper at least, the railroad had paid for itself within four years of its formal opening, with expenditure of slightly over $8 million being covered by gross earnings of the same amount.[38]

From 1855 until the completion of the U.S. transcontinental railroad in 1869, business on Panama's short stretch of tracks boomed. In the course of one

Gross Receipts of the Panama Railroad (US$), 1852–1856

1852	1853	1854	1855	1856
250,161.81	322,428.13	453,572.04	1,099,069.33	1,350,740.30

Source: Annual Reports Panama Railroad Company, 1852–1951.

unusually busy day in November 1859, trains carried twenty-three hundred passengers and generated an income of $57,500.[39] Total annual receipts in 1868, the peak year for earnings, amounted to $3,558,195.49.[40] Minter described the railroad in the 1850s and 1860s as "Midas on Wheels" because of its generous dividends and rising share price. He calculated that each dollar invested by shareholders in the early stages of the project had generated a return of $100 by 1869.[41] As one writer noted with the benefit of hindsight, "It is very doubtful if many of the men who rushed across the Isthmus to the California gold fields did as well by themselves as if they had stayed at home and invested their passage money in Panama railroad stock."[42] An Australian newspaper commented that "though a costly line, it is about the best paying railroad in the world."[43]

The company, with an initial capitalization of $1 million in 1849, was valued at over one hundred times that amount by 1867, and shares that in 1852 had sold for only a few cents reached an all-time high of $369 in 1868, twice the price of the next highest stock quoted on the New York Stock Exchange.[44] Because of high freight and passenger charges linked to its monopolistic position, the Panama railroad "was considered the safest investment on Wall Street and by far the most successful enterprise ever attempted outside of the continental limits of the United States."[45]

Share ownership in the company was largely in American hands at first, but by the late 1850s British investors reportedly owned a sizable proportion of the enterprise. According to a letter to the company's president in 1859, "It is well known that a very large amount of the stock of your company is held by capitalists in England."[46] The election of Edward Cunard of the eponymous steamship line to the railroad's board in 1858 reflected British ownership of one-third of the bonds and shares in the enterprise, and by 1865 over half the shares were said to be British owned.[47] Paradoxically, the company did not attract local investors, either from the Isthmus or the rest of New Granada, at least in its early years. "It is a curious fact that not a single share of the Panama Railroad stock is held by a native of the Isthmus, and, we believe, not by a citizen of any part of the Republic [New Granada], as far as we can learn."[48]

Statistics on the railroad's performance in the years after its completion are impressive. Over the following decade, this single track carried nearly four hundred thousand passengers. Annual receipts were in excess of $1 million during half of these years. The discovery of silver in Nevada in 1859 generated a new mining boom that benefited the railroad. Between 1856 and 1866, more than $500 million in gold was transported, over $147 million in silver, $5 million in jewelry, and $19 million in paper money, with the company collecting a percentage fee of the value of all precious cargo. A huge volume and variety of freight was also hauled over the line, including over 614,500 tons of mail, baggage, and assorted merchandise.[49] The railroad's ability to transport coal from the Atlantic to the Pacific led to a fall in its price on the west coast, where it was in demand to fuel the increasing number of steamships operating in the Pacific from the 1850s onward.[50]

While business on the Panama railroad boomed after 1855, traffic on the rival Nicaragua route declined drastically. The first blow came in 1852 when Vanderbilt, who had invested heavily in promoting this alternative transport link between East and West, failed to secure the Pacific mail contract from the U.S. Congress.[51] Boardroom battles over the control of his company further weakened the competitiveness of the Nicaraguan transit. The completion of the Panama railroad dramatically undercut the appeal of this alternative route to the west coast of America. A period of civil war and political upheaval in Nicaragua then destroyed Vanderbilt's dream. This began with the invasion of a small expeditionary force in 1855, led by the filibuster William Walker, an archetypal mid-nineteenth-century American soldier of fortune and would-be empire builder.[52] He succeeded in seizing and maintaining control of Nicaragua until early 1857, hoping that the United States would come to his aid by annexing it, but Washington failed to respond.

Walker's invasion and the civil war that followed caused a great deal of destruction in the Central American country. Walker antagonized Vanderbilt by seizing his transit company's property in Nicaragua and transferring ownership to the Commodore's rivals, who had been waging a boardroom battle for control of the enterprise. Walker paid a heavy price for this decision. The angry multimillionaire delivered a mortal blow to the filibusters by providing much-needed funds and arms to an anti-Walker coalition of Central American forces.

Numerous foreigners, including Irish residents of New York's slums, attached themselves to Walker's mercenary force, enticed by promises of land, livestock, and good wages.[53] They were sadly deceived. Many discovered, far too late, that their wages amounted to "nothing a month, and six feet of earth."[54] A considerable proportion of these men, most likely including some redundant ex-railroad employees, perished, some in battle, others from disease, and some after falling into the hands of the enemy.[55] In March 1857, 126 deserters from Walker's forces crossed Panama *en route* back to the United States. They denounced their former leader and urged his remaining men to abandon him.[56]

Even though Walker was driven out of Nicaragua in 1857, his activities had aroused fear and distrust of Americans among the country's ruling class and in much of the population. This delayed attempts to resurrect the transit route. Nicaraguan politicians and the wider public feared a restored transport link might become a latter-day Trojan horse for filibusters to again infiltrate their country.[57] By the late 1850s, the previously busy passenger route through Nicaragua was largely abandoned. Transit across Nicaragua was restored in 1862 and survived for another decade, but the numbers using it remained small.[58] Vanderbilt's Nicaraguan venture, "the single most original enterprise of his long career," had slipped out of his grasp, and the Panama railroad had weathered a significant threat to its viability.[59] The Commodore's numerous other business ventures thrived however, and by the time of his death years later, he was worth many times more than the combined wealth of Aspinwall and Law, his old rivals.

Walker was not the only filibuster active in Central America at this period whose activities were interlinked with the progress of the Panama railroad. Henry L. Kinney, another American adventurer, laid claim to part of Britain's Mosquito Coast protectorate bordering the Caribbean coast of Nicaragua and Honduras. Some Panama railroad workers who had been made redundant once trains started running from Atlantic to Pacific in 1855 signed up as mercenaries in his private army. A Panamanian newspaper reported: "We learn that quite a number of unemployed foreigners will leave Aspinwall in a few days to join the Kinney expedition in Nicaragua. We hope they will be more successful than they have been on this Isthmus."[60] Kinney led a small invasion force into Mosquito Coast territory but, like Walker, was forced to abandon his claim in 1857.[61]

Much of the railroad's early success was due to its monopolistic position once the Nicaragua route ceased to pose a serious threat. An exorbitant charge of over fifty cents per mile to cross the Isthmus had been arbitrarily decided on in 1852 to discourage passenger traffic until the line was completed.[62] The company found to its surprise that passengers were willing to pay this expensive fare, so it remained in effect. Some complained, however. In 1855, petitions signed by several hundred citizens were presented to the New York legislature, which had granted the company its charter in 1849, claiming that the railroad was a monopoly and its charges were based on the "extravagance or rapacity of the parties engaged in the enterprise." However, a legislative motion calling for a reduction in the passenger fare was lost.[63] In 1858 a letter writer to a New York paper complained that the railroad was making an enormous profit. "The Panama Railroad . . . is . . . a gigantic monopoly, because it is now the only open road of commerce across the continent. . . . The Panama Railroad charges $25 a head for every passenger traversing its 49½ miles [sic] of iron rail, and has the power to charge as much more as it may see fit."[64]

Between 1849, when the California gold rush assumed huge proportions, and the completion of the railway in 1855, the Isthmus enjoyed an income estimated at $125,000 to $150,000 a month from the transportation of passengers, baggage, freight, bullion, and specie (money in the form of coin).[65] This revenue was widely distributed among many sectors of the population. During these years, in addition to thousands of migrants, an enormous amount of California gold flowed across the Isthmus. This gold was bound for banks on the east coast of the United States and for Europe. Local freight agencies employed hundreds of muleteers, warehouse men, and guards to handle much of the lucrative trans-shipments of the precious metal going east as well as U.S. coinage heading west.[66]

Panama City's economy boomed during the first half of the 1850s. By 1853 there were eighty-five foreign-run mercantile firms in the capital; three English and three Spanish-language newspapers; nine hotels capable of accommodating two thousand guests; a half dozen good restaurants; and direct steamship communication with several Pacific ports.[67] Thirteen countries had consular representation in Panama City in 1854, underlining the importance of the Isthmus as an international transit hub.[68] Aspinwall, on the Atlantic coast, had mushroomed in size within a few years, with a growing number of passenger and freight vessels from America's east coast and Europe docking at its port.

Much to the surprise of Panama's business class and press, the completion of the railroad failed to bring about an expected economic bonanza. In fact, the opposite occurred. The pre-1855 level of economic activity declined sharply as the Isthmus found itself reduced to the status of a rail corridor through which passengers and freight were quickly shuttled on their way to or from the east and west coasts of the United States. Once the railroad became fully operational, the flow of money into the local economy fell dramatically. Each traveler paid only twenty-five dollars to cross Panama, compared to fifty to one hundred dollars or more for transport and subsistence in the prerailroad era. Migrants, instead of spending days traversing the country, and often weeks at Panama City awaiting ships to take them to California, now spent only hours, or at most a day, on the Isthmus. They had little need or opportunity to spend money during their usually brief stay.

Furthermore, virtually all of this transit revenue was monopolized by the railroad company, which also supplied most of the food and accommodation needs of its employees. Almost everything required for the railroad's operations continued to be imported from the United States with little benefit to the Panamanian economy. A sizable section of the local population that had earned a considerable income for the previous six years from servicing the needs of migrants and freight companies now found that the demand for its services had almost totally disappeared. The end result was that impoverishment rapidly replaced prosperity for many inhabitants of the Isthmus.

In 1855, local businessmen awoke to the fact that they had lost control of the lucrative cross-Isthmian passenger, freight, and storage trade. The decision by one of the largest mule owners in Panama City to dispose of his entire stock of animals at a public auction in January 1855 was an early indicator of the crisis that was to follow. Out of seven major hotels, which at one time carried out a thriving business in Panama City, only two survived by September 1855, and with a much-lowered volume of business.[69] Newspapers, both foreign and local, were struck by the changes the completion of the railroad had brought. A *New York Times* correspondent remarked that "it is quite clear that the railroad has not materially benefited the Isthmus, but rather the reverse."[70] Local newspapers painted an equally gloomy picture of the economic consequences. "The year 1855 will also be long remembered for the rapid decline of business among the citizens of Panama, caused by their sources of profit being cut off by the opening of the railroad."[71]

Instead, then, of the prosperity that the completion of the railroad was expected to bring, numerous Panamanians experienced unemployment and impoverishment. Workers from New Granada, Jamaica, and farther afield were thrown out of employment and had to choose between returning home and remaining in Panama to eke out a subsistence existence. The Isthmus sank back into poverty. A local newspaper plaintively complained that the railroad should have foreseen this change "and they should have provided in some way to prevent the general ruin consequent thereon."[72] The Panamanian press and the local business community, which had generally been enthusiastic supporters of the railroad, had completely failed to anticipate the economic impact of its completion. In summary, the railroad contributed to ushering in a brief period of affluence in the local economy, but it also bore considerable responsibility for the lengthy depression that followed after 1855.

Resentment at Panama's economic recession soured the relationship between local inhabitants and the railroad. Rumors circulated that disgruntled Panamanians might strike at the company that had deprived them of their former modes of earning a living. In October 1855, the American consul reported that he had received information from his French counterpart "that the natives here in Panama have in contemplation the destruction of the railroad, by infuriating the black population."[73] Nothing happened on this occasion, but discontent continued to simmer beneath the surface until it exploded in the "Watermelon Incident" (referred to by Panamanians as *El Incidente de la Tajada de Sandía*) six months later.

The trouble allegedly started when a passenger called Jack Oliver, en route from New York to San Francisco, refused to pay a Panamanian vendor for a slice of watermelon while waiting in Panama City to embark on the ship that would take him and his fellow passengers to California.[74] In the violent disturbances that followed the altercation between Oliver and the native salesman on April 15, 1856, eighteen foreigners, mostly Americans, and one Panamanian were killed and at least fifty wounded. A great deal of damage was done to the railroad's Panama City terminus.[75] The *Times* New York correspondent claimed that resentment at the railroad was the principal factor behind the Watermelon Affray.[76]

The U.S. government appointed Amos Corwine, a former American consul in Panama (1849–1853), to inquire into the circumstances of these disturbances. Corwine reported that the railroad's completion and the consequent growth of unemployment was one of the reasons for the "considerable ill-feeling cherished by the colored natives of Panama towards citizens of the United States."[77] The verdict of President Mallarino of New Granada was somewhat different. Addressing Congress in Bogotá in February 1857, he blamed the railroad for the riots as it had imported a considerable number of migrant workers and then dispensed with their services once construction was complete. Many of these foreign workers remained in the country, forming an impoverished colony of marginalized residents. Their resentment fueled the riots.[78]

While Panama sank back into economic depression after 1855, the period from then until 1869 was a golden one for the railroad, which enjoyed a monopoly of transoceanic transport. Its runaway economic success was relatively short-lived, however. When the last spike to connect the rails of the Central Pacific and the Union Pacific was driven in near Promontory Point, Utah, on May 10, 1869, it marked the completion of the transcontinental railroad across the United States. This epochal achievement came more quickly than the directors of the Panama railroad had anticipated. The U.S. Congress had been discussing this gigantic project from the 1850s, but the divisive issue of slavery made it impossible to settle the route. The building of the western stages of this railroad only became possible after the withdrawal of the slave-owning states from the Union in 1861.[79] The inauguration of the railroad across America marked the end of the Panama's transoceanic rail monopoly and terminated the company's fourteen-year-long economic bonanza.

Other factors, including ineffectual management, poor planning, lack of enterprise, and insufficient investment in infrastructure and rolling stock from the late 1860s onward also contributed to the railroad's loss of its preeminent position.[80] The fact that David Hoadley continued as company president for eighteen years, from 1853 to 1871, and that Totten remained in control in Panama until 1875, indicated a degree of complacency and inertia at senior executive levels. Tracy Robinson, an ex-employee, believed that Totten was the wrong man to have remained in charge once construction was completed. Totten "was not a businessman. . . . The very virtues which recommended him as chief engineer of the Panama Railroad during its construction, particularly a tenacity of purpose amounting to obstinacy, were unfavorable to continued success."[81]

High freight tariffs also undermined the long-term profitability of the enterprise. A local newspaper remonstrated that the railroad's uncompetitive charges in 1855 made it prohibitively expensive to move bulk freight where delivery time was not a major consideration.[82] A decade later the *New York Times* complained, "Their [the company's] monopoly of the transit of the Isthmus had enabled them to force passenger and freight rates to a most exorbitant height."[83]

The railroad's failure to reach agreement on charges for passages and freight with the Pacific Steam Navigation Company lost it a valuable source of future revenue. Rather than incorporating the rail link over the Isthmus into its global shipping schedule, this major maritime concern opted instead for a direct steamship service from Britain to the west coast of South America via the Magellan Straits in 1868.[84] The opening of the Suez Canal in 1869 dealt a further blow to the railroad's freight revenues. The canal provided the shortest direct eastward sea route from Europe and America's Atlantic coast to China, Japan, India and Australia. Freight agencies, importers, and exporters now had competitive alternatives to the Panama railroad.

Although deprived of its once-dominant position after 1869, and with its fortunes ebbing, the rail link across Panama continued to be profitable. It retained popularity with the traveling public during the 1870s and 1880s because it was still cheaper, easier, and possibly more comfortable to travel from New York to San Francisco via the Isthmus than to go by train across America.[85] Although the American transcontinental train route was faster, there was no direct single-ticket coast-to-coast rail service in the late nineteenth century. Crossing the country by train could take as long as seven days.[86]

The 1850 contract between New Granada and the railroad company ran for a term of forty-nine years but gave the government the option to acquire ownership in 1875 for the relatively low price of $5 million. The railroad had somehow overlooked this flaw in its original agreement, an error that would now cost it dearly. Aware by the mid-1860s that the railroad had developed into a very profitable enterprise, and worried that Colombia, as the former state of New Granada was now known, might exercise its option to purchase, the railroad's directors hastened to negotiate a new contract with Bogotá, this time for ninety-nine years. While they successfully concluded an agreement on August 16, 1867, its terms were onerous for the company. The railroad undertook to make an immediate payment of $1 million to the Colombian government and annual payments of $250,000 thereafter. Once details of the terms reached Wall Street, the company's share price fell "from the rosy region of three hundred [dollars] to the gloomy depths of eighty in a single week."[87]

When Ferdinand de Lesseps announced his grandiose plan to excavate a sea-level ship canal through the Isthmus in 1880, a Wall Street financier, Trenor W. Park, realized the strategic importance of the railroad in the implementation of this gigantic enterprise. He quickly bought up most of the railroad stock and refused to sell to de Lesseps for anything less than $20 million. On June 11, 1881, de Lesseps reluctantly gave way, and the Panama railroad was purchased outright by the *Compagnie Universelle du Canal Interoceanique*, set up to execute the French entrepreneur's plan. After over thirty years in American hands, the Panama railroad had now passed into French ownership. The astute American financier was reputed to have made a profit of $7 million on the transaction.[88]

Figure 14.1. Panama City Railroad Terminus, November 3, 1906. Photo, author's possession.

Throughout the 1880s, the new owners used the railroad to shift vast quantities of excavated earth and rocks in a valiant but doomed effort to gouge out a sea-level canal similar to the one de Lesseps had earlier built at Suez. The French entrepreneur's attempt to dig his second canal failed disastrously. In 1894 the bankrupt *Compagnie Universelle* transferred ownership of the railroad to its successor, the *Compagnie Nouvelle du Canal du Panama*, which was little more than a holding corporation, prepared to sell its canal concession and a partially completed waterway, for the best price it could obtain.

A decade after de Lesseps's failure, independence-minded politicians on the Isthmus, aided and encouraged by the United States, declared Panama a sovereign nation in 1903 and no longer part of Colombia. Washington, eager to establish a short sea route between its powerful Atlantic and Pacific naval fleets following its war with Spain in 1898, was ready to embark on its own attempt to build a canal across Panama. The United States accordingly purchased the *Compagnie Nouvelle* from the French in 1904. Majority ownership of the Panama railroad, valued at $7 million, formed part of this deal.[89]

Figure 14.2. Railroad at Tabernilla, Early Twentieth Century. Photo, author's possession.

The railroad now became part of the U.S. government-owned Isthmian Canal Commission, a body that had the financial resources, technology, and administrative expertise necessary for success. The commission also benefitted from the recent eradication of yellow fever on the Isthmus, one of the diseases that had ravaged the workforce of its French predecessor.[90] "By then the line was in sad shape. Equipment was long out of date and in bad repair; the road itself needed to be completely overhauled from end to end and double-tracked."[91] A considerable stretch of rail had to be repositioned on higher ground because many miles of the original line ran over what was destined to become the canal bed. Much of the old 1850s railroad now lies submerged beneath the waters of

Figure 14.3. Train Leaving Panama City Terminus, June 9, 1930. Photo, author's possession.

Lake Gatún, a huge man-made body of water that feeds the locks of the Panama Canal.

The railroad went on to play a crucial role in the building of the Panama Canal by the United States, just as it had done during the failed French attempt twenty years earlier. The railroad served "as a vital dress rehearsal for the future canal."[92] In fact, the Canal could not have been successfully completed without the railroad's assistance. While construction was underway between 1904 and 1914, this short line became the world's busiest, with over two hundred trains in operation every day. In the course of one year (1909–1910) the railroad shifted three hundred million tons of earth and rock.[93] Once the canal opened in 1914, the railroad reverted to its original purpose of providing passenger and freight services between Panama's Atlantic and Pacific coasts. It continued in operation under American control for most of the twentieth century. Then in 1979, its ownership changed once again when, under the terms of the Carter-Torrijos Treaty between the United States and Panama, Washington transferred control of the rail link to Panama's government. The running stock, equipment, and infrastructure were by now in urgent need of upgrading, but little was done by the Panamanian government apart from essential maintenance.[94]

After almost twenty years in Panamanian ownership, the railroad was sold once more in 1998, this time back into American hands. The new owner, the Panama Canal Railway Company, was a joint venture between Kansas City Southern Railroad and Mi-Jack Products, a leading North American freight terminal operator. Awarded a fifty-year concession by the Panamanian authorities to operate the line, the new company embarked on the task of reconstructing and upgrading the rail link to the highest international standards. By 2001, after an investment of $80 million, ten times the cost of the original project, the refurbishment of the line was completed, and the rail link, now known as the Panama Canal Railroad, was able once more to resume coast-to-coast passenger and freight train services, just as its predecessor had started doing almost 150 years earlier.

Conclusion

WHEN WILLIAM ASPINWALL AND A SMALL GROUP OF NEW YORK–based financial and shipping magnates decided to build the world's first interoceanic railroad in the late 1840s, they underestimated both the scale of the difficulties facing them and the magnitude of the rewards they would ultimately reap. Thousands of laborers, rather than hundreds, had to be employed; five years were needed to finish construction instead of the two planned for; and the final cost was over double the initial estimate. Given the difficulties of climate, disease, and topography confronting the railroad's builders, it was remarkable that the project was completed by 1855. While good luck or fate played a role—particularly the fortuitous timing of large-scale migration across Panama following the discovery of gold in California in 1848—the initiative, tenacity, enterprise, courage, and unwavering determination of the men behind the project were decisive factors in bringing it to a successful conclusion. Yet without the back-breaking labor, sweat, pain, and dogged persistence of thousands of laborers of many nationalities and ethnicities, the iron rails would never have progressed much beyond their starting point in the mangrove swamps of Manzanillo Island.

During the five years it took to build the railroad, a multinational labor force of around 17,500 men was recruited and deployed. Most of these men came from outside the Isthmus of Panama itself. The contribution of these workers of many nationalities to the success of an infrastructural project that helped transform global trading patterns should not be overlooked. The largest contingent, about seven thousand, came from New Granada, as Colombia was then known, and from neighboring Central and South American countries. The second most important group, in numerical terms, was the six thousand or so white workers of various nationalities who were almost entirely recruited in the United States. The majority of these men were hired in the Northeast, with the remainder hailing from the Midwest and South.

I have estimated that just over 60 percent of these white employees, approximately 3,660 men, were Irish-born immigrants, many of whom had fled their native land to escape the ravages of a terrible famine. The railroad hired nearly all of these American-Irish workers after they had settled in the United States, though 360 men were recruited and shipped directly from Ireland. At least 3,000 West Indians, mostly from Jamaica, and 1,500 Asians, mainly Chinese, but including several hundred men from the Indian subcontinent, and a smaller number from the Malay Peninsula, made up the balance of this multinational workforce.

The completion of this short stretch of railroad was a significant infrastructural achievement because of the relatively recent advent of rail transport throughout most of the world. In 1855, Panama, with slightly less than forty-eight miles of railroad in operation, compared favorably with the entire South American continent, which had a total of sixty miles of track, and Africa with only twenty-five miles. Even in much of Europe, the railroad was a relatively recent arrival. Norway had forty-two miles of rail, Spain only sixty, and Sweden had seventy-five miles in use in 1855.[1] The Panama railroad was, then, an early participant in one of the great technological revolutions of the nineteenth century when a new invention, the steam-powered locomotive, effectively broke down the terrestrial barriers of geography and distance that had separated humanity for millennia.

The building of the Panama line, one of the earliest passenger and freight-carrying tropical railroads in the world, was also remarkable given the formidable array of difficulties confronting the chief engineer, his assistants, and his multinational army of workers. They had no reliable maps, no modern surveying equipment, no canned, powdered, or frozen food supplies, no understanding of the causes of the many diseases—some fatal—to which Panama was subject, and no modern medicines or effective insect repellents.[2] There were no roads on the Caribbean side of the Isthmus, where rivers provided the principal mode of transport. Surveying the railroad's route was immensely difficult and was carried out by a handful of men on the ground without the benefit of reliable maps, aerial photography, or modern topographical equipment. In the absence of telephones, radio, or the telegraph, communications between geographically dispersed sections of the workforce on the Isthmus, and between the chief engineer and the company's head office in New York, were slow and sometimes unreliable.

Construction methods were rudimentary, relying largely on human endeavor, muscle, and sweat—supplemented, where conditions allowed, by the use of mules and horses. The equipment employed was primitive for the most part, consisting of picks, shovels, wheelbarrows, axes, saws, and machetes. A few steam-powered pile drivers and a handful of river launches and railroad locomotives were the only mechanized aids at the builders' disposal. The bed for the tracks had to be laid across miles of glutinous swamps and hacked and cut by hand through a wilderness of dense undergrowth and tropical hardwood forest without the assistance of mechanized equipment such as trucks, bulldozers, or chainsaws to speed up progress.

Accommodation for officials and men was primitive by today's standards, with no running water, sewage facilities, electricity, or air-conditioning to ameliorate a humid climate and oppressively high temperatures. Almost all of the provisions needed to feed hundreds, and sometimes thousands of workers, had to be imported from the distant United States across almost two thousand miles of sea. These were subject to rapid deterioration in the absence of refrigeration. A journalist, writing not long after the completion of the project, compared the task of building this railroad, where almost everything—men, equipment, and food—had to be shipped in from thousands of miles away, with the logistics of supplying the British army before Sebastopol during the Crimean War.[3]

There were significant differences of opinion over the size of the death toll while rails were being laid across the narrow Isthmus of Panama. The number of those who perished has been greatly exaggerated by some writers with vivid imaginations who appear to have fallen under the spell of Panama's tropical luxuriance, making them prone to ill-supported fantasy. Furthermore, the grisly historical reputation of the Caribbean region as a graveyard for Europeans had become embedded in the minds of many writers and travelers.[4] A pervasive memory of the Central American and Caribbean region as a death trap for earlier generations of white men contributed to the tendency to overstate the railroad's mortality rate.

In addition, some writers and commentators at the time, and subsequently, did not adhere to the canons of evidence-based history. The information they provided was all too often incorrect, and this has misled later generations of historians. The railroad's failure to retain records of the size and composition of its workforce, and of the number of employees who died during construction, together with the absence of official statistical data on mortality in Panama in the 1850s, did little to curb a tendency to sensationalize the number of deaths.

These factors led me to embark on an alternative, more oblique approach to the controversial issue of mortality. This involved calculating the approximate death rate of workers building the Panama Canal in the 1880s and applying it to the men who had constructed the railroad over much the same terrain and in similar ecological conditions three decades earlier. Applying an overall mortality rate of 24 percent, derived from the canal construction period to the railroad's workforce, suggested that approximately 4,200 employees of all nationalities and skin colors likely died between 1850 and 1855. White employees coming from more temperate climes, unused to toiling in high temperatures and humidity and lacking resistance to Panama's endemic diseases, would have had a higher than average mortality rate, estimated at slightly over 28 percent. This suggests that about 1,700 white workers perished during their stay on the Isthmus or from diseases acquired there shortly after their return to the United States.

Out of the 3,660 Irishmen who I believe worked on the railroad, just over 1,000 were likely to have succumbed, including up to one-third of the shipment of workers who had arrived from Cork. Men from New Granada, the West Indies, the Indian subcontinent, and the Malay Peninsula, used to working in the tropics and with greater inherited and acquired resistance to malaria, and possible immunity to yellow fever, would have experienced a lower fatality rate, estimated at about 16 percent. Their deaths would have amounted to close to 1,700. The Chinese, with about 800 confirmed deaths and a catastrophic mortality rate of 78 percent, occupied a gruesome and unenviable category of their own, distinct from the remainder of the workforce.

These estimates of the number of fatalities, like the data on the number and origins of men who were recruited for the railroad, should be considered as tentative, based as they are on an analysis and interpretation of a limited amount of reliable information currently available on these topics. The figures presented here are hopefully closer to reality than the jumble of conflicting and often inaccurate and inconsistent data that have hitherto appeared on these topics.

Even before it was completed, the rail link across Panama had a significance that stretched far beyond the borders of the Isthmus. It helped to fuel the expanding American economy during the gold rush era. Most of the estimated

370 tons of gold, worth $16 billion in today's terms, extracted by miners in California between 1848 and 1853, was securely transported by the partially completed railroad before being shipped north.[5] Throughout the 1850s and 1860s, the railroad's role in continuing to securely transport gold, as well as silver from Nevada's mines, across the Isthmus contributed to the growing financial importance of the United States, enabling Wall Street to emerge as the undisputed nucleus of the nation's banking and investment activities, and one of the world's leading financial centers.

During the 1850s and 1860s, the new rail link served as a vital artery of communication between the big eastern cities of New York, Boston, Philadelphia, and Washington, DC, and the country's rapidly developing Pacific seaboard with San Francisco as its nucleus. Once the railroad had been completed in 1855, a through trip from east to west via Panama could be made in less than twenty-eight days. Ten years later the average time had been reduced to three weeks.[6] This short stretch of tracks across Panama facilitated a huge migration of people from east to west in the United States and helped to bind distant western territories closer to the nation's heartland.

For a brief fourteen-year period, between 1855 and 1869, the "iron necklace" across Panama, less than fifty miles long, was one of the most important communication and transportation links in the world, connecting Europe and the eastern United States with the Pacific coasts of North, Central, and South America and with the Far East. During these years, prior to the completion of the American transcontinental railroad and the opening of the Suez Canal, the Panama railroad benefited from a disproportionate share of the transportation of merchandise and passengers between Atlantic and Pacific nations.

This rail link proved invaluable to the Union government during the American Civil War, enabling it to move troops and materiel from its western territories to reinforce its armies in the East and South. More importantly perhaps, the safe transit across Panama of large quantities of gold and silver from the mines of California and Nevada deprived the Confederacy of a resource it desperately needed to bolster its foreign credit, while at the same time strengthening the solvency of the Union government.[7]

The Panama railroad ironically hastened the completion of its great rival, the transcontinental line across the United States. Equipment and materials urgently required for building the Central Pacific section of the tracks through California, Nevada, and Utah were shipped from America's industrial centers

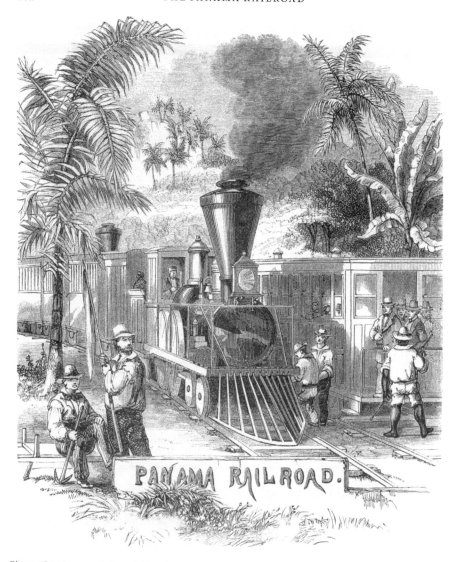

Figure C.1. Panama Railroad. Wood engraving, 1870 Shutterstock Stock Illustration.

and transported by rail across the Isthmus before being dispatched to San Francisco and eventually Sacramento.[8] The completion of this monumental trans-American undertaking in 1869, together with the opening of the Suez Canal later that year, fatally undermined the Panama railroad's dominant role in east–west transportation. For many years afterward, however, the railroad continued to make a significant contribution to trade between the United States and the Pacific coastal regions of Central and South America.

This pioneering engineering project can lay claim to distinction in a number of areas. In the opinion of one leading railroad historian, "The conditions for construction were more hostile than for any other railway project yet attempted and, indeed, probably for almost any thereafter, apart from some equally murderous schemes in equatorial Africa. It was the railway from hell." As a result, in terms of cost per mile, it was the most expensive railroad built up to that time.[9] From the early 1880s, when the French began their attempt to construct the Panama Canal until that project's completion by the United States in 1914, this railroad was one of the most intensively used stretches of track in the world, calculated at the amount of freight carried per kilometer of line.[10] The railroad proved to be extremely lucrative for investors during its early decades; its shares at one point were among the most expensive on New York's Stock Exchange. With an initial capitalization of $8 million, its total earnings from 1855 to 1898 amounted to $95 million, while operating expenses came to $57 million, yielding a profit of almost $38 million.[11]

Paradoxically, the railroad's economic impact on the region it traversed and served was far from positive. Although the surge of migrants triggered by the California gold rush, which had played a major role in boosting Panama's economy in the late 1840s and early 1850s, continued for several more decades, it contributed little to economic growth on the Isthmus once the railroad had been completed. The Panamanian economy went into a deep, decades-long slump after 1855 as the railroad monopolized transport across the Isthmus, displacing scores of businesses and hundreds, if not thousands, of small-scale providers who had previously met the transport and accommodation needs of travelers and provided the manpower for handling the carriage and storage of freight. By depriving many families of their former livelihoods, the completion of the railroad increased racial tensions between local inhabitants and American citizens and generated animosity toward the foreign-owned company considered to be largely responsible for the economic recession.

The economic benefits that had generally followed the introduction of the railroad in Europe and North America did not materialize in Panama. In part, this was because the Isthmian economy had not yet developed the capacity to produce a sufficient volume of valuable export commodities, while its domestic market was too small and impoverished to generate a significant flow of imports. Panama's experience showed that technological progress on its own did not invariably promote broader socioeconomic development.

On the positive side, the building of this rail link led to the introduction and assimilation of new ethnic groups into the isthmian population. Even though most of the thousands of railroad workers from the United States, Europe, Jamaica, and parts of Asia who built the rail link did not settle permanently in Panama, the descendants of the minority who remained after the railroad was completed affected the demography of the region. The offspring of these men have made useful and valuable contributions to Panama's economy, society, and political and intellectual life over the past century and a half.

The construction of this short stretch of line, despite its negative effects on Panamanians' economic well-being, helped lay some of the foundations of today's global trading economy. The railroad was among the first initiatives of its kind to demonstrate the usefulness of an international, mobile, low-cost labor force—the kind required by future large-scale construction schemes in vastly separate global regions. Its successful completion not only highlighted the utility of transnational migrant labor in major infrastructural projects but also established an early precedent for the profitable deployment of American investment capital outside the continental United States. By demonstrating that a combination of technological know-how, large-scale capital investment, logistical capability, and sheer determination could conquer what appeared to be insuperable natural barriers, the success of the Panama railroad contributed to the self-confidence and assurance that epitomized subsequent generations of American entrepreneurs, investors, builders, and engineers.

The railroad's successful completion was also an early indicator that the transformation of the tropics was possible. It provided reassurance that the battle with tropical nature could be won and that the hitherto hostile environment of the earth's tropical zones could be challenged and made subservient to the transportation and trading requirements of other regions of the globe, particularly North America and Europe. The Panama Canal, one of the modern world's great infrastructural achievements, could not have been built by the United States in the early twentieth century without the logistical support of the railroad and its capacity to speedily and economically shift the millions of tons of soil and rocks that had to be gouged out of the earth during the excavation of the Big Ditch. "The railroad was the key to the enterprise; without it, construction of a canal would have been impossible."[12]

The Panama railroad not only helped to reshape global trade patterns, it helped to tilt the balance of power and influence toward the United States and against Britain in the Central American region. The successful completion of this project contributed to the rise of American power in what was later labeled the "American Mediterranean." In the 1820s, Britain entertained realistic hopes of being able to exert great influence over the newly liberated republics of Central and South America. George Canning, British foreign secretary and later prime minister, wrote in 1824, "Spanish America is free, and if we do not mismanage our matters sadly, she is English." He also announced, "Behold the new world established, and if we do not throw it away, ours."[13]

Thirty years later, Britain's dream of controlling the destiny of Spain's former colonies began to dissolve. Although the Isthmus of Panama had been surveyed in the intervening decades by English and French engineers, and possible routes for a railroad and a carriage road were drawn up, no decisive action was taken. Britain failed to grasp the opportunity of building a modern communications system across Panama and left it to American entrepreneurs to begin the task. The United States, as a result, gained in influence, eventually becoming the "warden" of the Isthmus of Panama.[14]

In 1863, a royal navy commander, referring to the Panama railroad, declared, "Its political importance to the United States is immense; by means of it the real control of the Pacific commerce falls into the hands of our rivals." The United States, he continued, "possess an immense vantage-ground in the Panama Railway; and while it continues the only gate to the Pacific, of which they hold the keys, they must be the winners."[15] The railroad's completion marked a significant turning point in the changing balance of geopolitical power between Britain and the United States in Central America. As one American traveler remarked after crossing the Isthmus, "Let us assure the world ... that if the 'sun never sets' on England's boasted possessions, neither will it ever again rise upon her commercial or political supremacy."[16]

Despite the jingoistic appeal of the doctrine of Manifest Destiny to many Americans, and the strategic importance of the transisthmian railroad, the United States did not succumb to the temptation of formally annexing Panama during the latter half of the nineteenth century. Instead it chose to exercise a varying degree of control over the affairs of the Isthmus, including direct, though short-lived, military intervention on a number of occasions.[17] The origins of an informal U.S. empire in Latin America can be traced to the construction of the railroad across Panama. For decades after its foundation, this American-run enterprise administered its Caribbean terminus at Aspinwall, and its rail corridor across the Isthmus, almost as an autonomous state within New Granada. The thriving city of Aspinwall, with its busy port, was one of the first commercial enclaves to be established and largely controlled by an American company in Latin America.

Following the establishment of Panama as an independent state in 1903, the constitutional and political status of the Isthmus changed radically, together with American policy toward it. The Panama Canal was of far greater strategic and economic importance to the United States than the railroad had been. This led Washington to abandon its former policy of indirect control over the affairs of the Isthmus and establish what was essentially an American colony based in the ten-mile-wide zone surrounding the canal and the railroad. The newly independent state of Panama, having thrown off its status as a neglected backwater of Colombia, now became a quasi-dependency of the United States, a role it remained burdened with for most of the twentieth century.

Today, almost 170 years after the Panama railroad's inception, passenger trains run daily between Colón (previously known as Aspinwall) and Panama City, just as they first started to do in 1855. While the railroad itself is still very much in existence, a considerable portion of the original track now lies buried beneath the waters of Gatún Lake, which was created over a century ago to feed the Panama Canal's giant locks. A one-way adult passenger ticket costs twenty-five dollars in 2020, the same price that applied in 1855.

The railroad's real revenue earner today, however, is the transportation of containers between the two great oceans that lap Panama's shores. Numerous freight trains shuttle around the clock in both directions between Atlantic and Pacific. Every day thousands of containers are unloaded from giant cargo ships at one end of the Panama Canal, double-stacked on flat freight wagons, and made ready for stowing on container vessels at the other end of the waterway, almost fifty miles away, in a matter of hours. The railroad currently handles about five hundred thousand containers a year and has the potential to greatly expand this number. Panama is the only place in the world where it is possible to transship containers in a seamless, duty-free operation, from the Atlantic to the Pacific or vice versa in under four hours.[18]

This rapid and efficient freight service removes the need for many vessels to make the expensive and time-consuming transit of the Panama Canal. This is particularly the case with the enormous Super-Panamax container ships, which are too bulky to pass through the man-made waterway, despite the recent construction of an additional channel and greatly enlarged locks.[19] It is an impressive sight to see powerful diesel locomotives hauling long trains of double-decked containers alongside the glittering waters of the canal or powering their way through the luxuriant foliage of the rain forest, their loud klaxon horns reverberating far and wide. The vision of the railroad's instigators and promoters has been vindicated by over a century and a half of continuous operation.

The secretary of the Isthmian Canal Commission, the American government agency that assumed responsibility for excavating the Panama Canal in the early twentieth century, believed that the achievements of the railroad's constructors far outstripped the endeavors of the more widely publicized French and American canal builders. His assessment provides a fitting epitaph for those countless thousands of workers of many nationalities, and not just the Americans he singled out, who hacked a path across almost fifty miles of swamps, jungles, ravines, and forested hills to lay the tracks of the world's first interoceanic railway.

"The story of their struggle with the obstacles and perils of a tropical wilderness, with sickness and death as their constant companions, is a record of American pluck and indomitable persistence, rarely equaled and never surpassed in our annals. Nothing that those who followed them in canal work, under French and American direction, were called upon to endure was comparable to what they encountered and overcame."[20]

The glory for completing the railroad went to its founders and engineers. According to the railroad's first historian, "They were men whom personal perils and privations could not daunt, whose energy and determination toil and suffering could not vanquish."[21] Even before it had been fully completed, the railroad's profits, in the form of operating surpluses, dividends, and buoyant share prices, poured into investors' pockets and enriched the company's coffers. The laborers who built the line with their toil, suffering, and all too often their health and lives received little in the way of financial reward and were subsequently ignored and largely forgotten. Their story has never been fully told.

Most of these men, prior to their arrival in Panama, were unaware of the difficulties and perils of working in tropical rain forests and swamps. Their initial lack of preparedness was matched, in most cases, by their fortitude, endurance, and dogged persistence. By transforming the nineteenth century's interoceanic transport system, they collectively helped to physically alter the world in which they lived, although as individuals they would have been unaware of their contribution to global change. It is fitting, then, that we acknowledge the part that these men of many nationalities played in a lengthy, valiant, and ultimately successful battle against climate, topography, and disease.

It is regrettable that no stone or bronze monument stands to commemorate the achievement of the 17,500 workers who struggled for five weary years to finish this audacious undertaking. There is not even a simple plaque to remind the passerby of their labors. The recollection of what these nameless thousands of railroad workers endured and achieved induces feelings of pride and wonderment, mingled with sadness at the fate that befell many of them. The laborers of the Panama railroad fought a long and arduous fight against the forces of tropical nature, and their victory was won at a great cost in lives and physical well-being.

The continued operation of today's modern railroad is a fitting memorial to these workers who toiled through Panama's forbidding interior for five years in the heat and rain. Their participation in "one of the grandest and boldest enterprises ever attempted" has not been entirely erased by history. It is appropriate that the railroad that exacted such a heavy toll on their health and lives continues to serve an essential function. "Their only monument today is the Panama Railroad, the completion of which marked one of the greatest achievements of the age and will ever be a memorial to the dauntless courage of its brave builders and their story is one of the most gallant in the annals of commerce."[22]

Appendix 1

Panama Railroad Construction Account, 1850–1858

Period	Amount (US$)	Total Cost to Date
Aug. 31, 1850–Apr. 8, 1851	241,200.72	241,200.72
Apr. 8, 1851–Nov. 6, 1851	397,498.43	638,699.15
Nov. 6, 1851–Aug. 20, 1852	568,848.82	1,207,547.97
Aug. 20, 1852–Sep. 19, 1853	525,705.94	1,733,253.91
Sep. 19, 1853–Jun. 30, 1854	2,035,871.69[1]	3,769,125.60
Jun. 30, 1854–Mar. 31, 1855	1,278,808.92	5,047,934.52
Mar. 31, 1855–Feb. 29, 1856	936,996.78	5,984,931.30
Feb. 29, 1856–Jan. 19, 1857	663,720.21	6,648,651.51
Jan. 19, 1857–Oct. 31, 1857	1,022,617.74	7,671,269.25
Oct. 31, 1857–Dec. 20, 1858	339, 257.28	8,010,526.53

Source: *Panama Railroad Company Bank Ledger, 1849–1862*, 126–129, 226–231.

1. This includes Story's payment of $816,347.34.

Appendix 2

Panama Railroad Passage Account by Date of Ledger Entry, 1850–1855

Period	Cost of Passages (US$)
Nov. 8, 1850–Aug. 24, 1851	93,525.00[1]
Aug. 24, 1851–Apr. 9, 1852	37,612.70
Apr. 9, 1852–Feb. 17, 1853	38,298.30
Feb. 17, 1853–Dec. 22, 1853	41,048.00
Dec. 22, 1853–Aug. 24, 1854	63,202.69
Aug. 24, 1854–Jul. 24, 1855	24,457.50
Total	**298,144.19**

Source: *Panama Railroad Company Bank Ledger, 1849–1862*, 130–131, 160–163.

Early ledger entries include data on the number of individual passages and destinations. For example, fifty-six passages from Chagres to New York cost $1725 or $31 each; twenty-five passages to Jamaica cost $250 or $10 each. Twenty-four passages to California from Panama City cost $2475 or $103 each. Passenger fares on the Atlantic and Pacific were high in 1850, 1851, and 1852 but generally declined thereafter.

Some workers would have required one-way tickets only. This includes those who died on the Isthmus; those who had arrived on the Isthmus from California and required a passage to New York or New Orleans; and those who had arrived in Panama from the United States at their own expense and required a ticket to California. In addition, the transportation cost of many workers would have been included under other headings—payments to labor contractors, for example. I found no reference to passages to or from Cartagena. These were presumably paid by labor recruitment agents who subsequently recouped the cost from the railroad. A small number of passages to and from Jamaica were listed in 1851 but not in other years.

Most payments listed here related to travel between New York and Chagres/ Aspinwall and were, therefore, for white workers. Given that the total cost of passages was almost $300,000 and that the average cost of transporting a worker to Panama from the United States and then returning him home was about $60, the maximum number of such workers covered by this account would be approximately 5,000. Allowing for one-way fares and for workers whose passage was debited under other headings, a total estimated figure of 5,640 white workers from the United States is plausible.[2]

Appendix 3

Likely Cork Workhouse Emigrants to Panama, December 1853

Surname	Name	Age	Status[1]	Occupation	Health[2]	Condition[3]
Ahern	Denis	16	single	vagrant	AB	ragged
Ahern	Philip	30	single	discharged soldier	nearly blind	indifferent
Barrett	James	30	single	baker	AB	indifferent
Barry	Richard	32	single	carpenter	AB	
Barry	William	22	single	laborer	AB	indifferent
Bassett	Joseph	15	single	laborer	AB	—
Beale*	Abraham	25	single	laborer	AB	indifferent
Blair*	John	48	widower	discharged soldier	AB	indifferent
Bowler	John	15	single	mendicant	AB	indifferent, no shirt
Brien	Charles	14	orphan			indifferent
Browne	Daniel	18	single	laborer	AB	ragged
Buckley	John	15	single	mendicant	AB	indifferent
Buckley	John	38	widower	baker	AB	indifferent
Buckley	Maurice	17	single	laborer	AB	indifferent
Buckley	Timothy	36	single	laborer	AB	indifferent
Buckley	William	16	single	laborer	AB	indifferent
Burke	Michael	18	single	laborer	AB	indifferent
Burke*	Walter	16	single	laborer	AB	indifferent
Callaghan	John	14	orphan			indifferent
Callaghan	Timothy	30	single	lawyer	AB	ragged
Collins	Con	18	single	servant	AB	
Collins	John	21	single	mendicant	AB	indifferent
Connell	Michael	16	single	mendicant	AB	
Connell	Morgan	23	single	laborer	AB	
Connell	Timothy	26	single	laborer	AB	indifferent
Connolly	Michael	16	single	vagrant	AB	nearly naked
Connor	Alexander	20	single	laborer	AB	indifferent

Surname	Name	Age	Status[1]	Occupation	Health[2]	Condition[3]
Connor	Michael	16	single	mendicant	AB	indifferent
Connor	Thomas	14	deserted			indifferent
Corcoran	Timothy	15	single	mendicant	AB	indifferent, no shirt
Corkeran	Michael	22	single	laborer	AB	indifferent
Corkerry	Con	30	single	laborer	AB	indifferent
Cottrell*	John	44	widower	ship's carpenter	AB	
Crane	David	16	single	vagrant	AB	ragged
Creane	William	16	single	laborer	AB	nearly naked
Cronan	Daniel	18	single	laborer	AB	ragged
Cross*	Thomas	16	single	laborer	AB	indifferent
Crowley	James	17	single	shoemaker	AB	indifferent
Crowley	Timothy	27	single	laborer	Paralyzed	indifferent
Cummins	John	16	single	mendicant	AB	
Daly	Daniel	18	widower	mendicant	AB	indifferent
Daly	Edward	15	single	mendicant	AB	indifferent
Desmond	Michael	23	single	laborer	AB	
Dinan	Jerry	17	single	laborer	AB	indifferent
Donovan	John	16	single	laborer	AB	union clothing from jail
Driscoll	John	21	single	drover	?	indifferent
Driscoll	Tim	46	single	laborer	AB	
Fallen	John	19	single	clerk	AB	indifferent
Flynn	Denis	18	single	laborer	AB	ragged
Flynn	John	15	single	mendicant	AB	ragged
Foley	Mossy	17	single	laborer		
Foley	Timothy	28	single	smith	AB	indifferent
Gillespie	Edward	27	single	gardener	AB	indifferent
Good	Joseph	16	single	vagrant	AB	ragged
Horgan	Edward	18	single	mendicant	AB	ragged, no shirt
Houragan	Jerry	20	single	laborer	AB	indifferent
Hunter	John	26	single	barber	AB	tolerable
Hurley	Gerry	24	single	laborer	AB	indifferent
Hyde	William	48	married	pensioner	AB	indifferent
Johnston	William	19	single	laborer	AB	indifferent
Keeffe	Cor	17	single	vagrant	AB	
Keeffe	Daniel	53	widower	laborer	AB	ragged
Keeffe	David	17	single	laborer	AB	indifferent, no shirt
Keeffe*	Michael	29	married	clerk	AB	indifferent
Kelleher	Jeremiah	15	single	laborer	AB	ragged
Kelleher	Pat	18	single	laborer	AB	ragged
Kelly	John	16	single	laborer	AB	in rags
Kepple	James	22	single	laborer	AB	indifferent

Surname	Name	Age	Status[1]	Occupation	Health[2]	Condition[3]
Leary	John	18	single	mendicant	AB	
Leary	John	16	single	mendicant	AB	ragged
Leary	John	16	single	mendicant	AB	ragged[4]
Lehane	Michael	18	single	weaver	AB	ragged, no shirt
Leonard	Geoffrey	20	single	sweep	AB	ragged
Linehan	Denis	17	single	laborer	AB	indifferent
Looney	Norry	15	single	mendicant	AB	indifferent
Lowther	Thomas	15	single	laborer	AB	indifferent
McAuliffe	John	16	single	laborer	AB	ragged
McAuliffe	John	20	single	shoemaker	AB	indifferent
McCarthy	Charles	16	single	laborer	AB	ragged, no coat
McCarthy	Charles	29	single	laborer	hospital	ragged, no coat
McCarthy	Denis	18	single	mendicant	AB	ragged
McCarthy	Justin	16	single	servant	AB	indifferent
McCarthy	Michael	18	single	mendicant	AB	ragged
McCarthy	Owen	15	single	laborer	AB	union clothing
McDermott	Michael	47	widower	weaver	AB	ragged, no shirt
McLaughlin	James	18	single	laborer	AB	indifferent
McLaughlin	William	17	single	mendicant	AB	no clothes
McNamara	Gerry	15	single	laborer	AB	
Minahan	Michael	16	single	sailor	AB	ragged, no shirt
Morrissey	James	40	single	pensioner	AB	ragged
Morrissey	John	27	single	mendicant	AB	indifferent
Mulcahy	Jerry	23	single	laborer	AB	indifferent
Mullin	Michael	16	single	servant	AB	no shirt
Murphy	Daniel	28	single	lawyer	AB	ragged
Murphy	Denis	18	single	laborer	AB	in rags
Murphy	Denis	19	single	mendicant	AB	indifferent
Murphy	Gerry	26	single	laborer	AB	indifferent
Murphy	Gerry	43	single	laborer	AB	indifferent
Murphy	Harry	34	widower	paper stainer	AB	indifferent
Murphy	James	42	single	laborer	AB	indifferent
Murphy	John	20	single	laborer	AB	indifferent
Murphy	Michael	53	widower	smith	AB	in rags
Murphy	Patrick	34	married	chandler	hospital	indifferent
Nagle	Stephen	60	widower	baker	aged	indifferent
O'Keeffe	John	15	single	servant	AB	
Parker	William	22	single	sailor	hospital	indifferent, no coat
Power	John	36	married	laborer	AB	indifferent
Quigan	Pat	32	single	discharged soldier	AB	rags
Quinlan	John	25	single	laborer	disabled	
Rea	Peter	15	single	mendicant	AB	ragged
Regan	Denis	14	deserted			ragged, no shirt

Surname	Name	Age	Status[1]	Occupation	Health[2]	Condition[3]
Roche	James	18	single	mendicant	AB	
Rubie*	Richard	19	single	harness maker	hospital	indifferent
Russell*	John	15	single	mendicant	AB	nearly naked
Ryan	Denis	16	single	mendicant	AB	indifferent
Ryan	Michael	19	single	mendicant	AB	indifferent
Scannell	Michael	20	single	baker	AB	indifferent
Seymour	William	17	single	vagrant	AB	ragged, no shirt
Shea	Michael	16	single	laborer	hospital	ragged
Shea	William	29	single	clerk	AB	tolerable
Sheehan	David	16	single	mendicant	AB	ragged
Sheehan	Owen	18	single	shoemaker	AB	indifferent
Shine	John	17	single	mendicant	AB	indifferent
Smith	James	32	single	laborer	nearly blind	indifferent, no shirt
Sullivan	Daniel	14	orphan			indifferent
Sullivan	Denis	18	single	laborer	AB	indifferent
Sullivan	John	18	single	laborer	AB	indifferent
Sullivan	John	18	single	laborer	AB	ragged
Sullivan	John	21	single	laborer	hospital	in rags
Sullivan	John	57	widower	cooper	AB	indifferent
Sullivan	John	22	married	clerk	AB	indifferent
Sullivan	Joseph	20	single	mendicant	AB (idiotic)	ragged
Sullivan	Maurice	15	single	mendicant	AB	indifferent
Sullivan	Owen	18	single	laborer	AB	ragged
Sullivan	Pat	17	single	scavenger	AB	indifferent
Sullivan	Pat	40	single	laborer	AB	indifferent
Swiney	Con	17	single	mendicant	AB	indifferent
Tarrant	William	22	single	laborer	AB	indifferent
Twomey	John	46	single	mendicant	AB	
Walsh	Cor	14	deserted			
Walsh	Edward	15	single	mendicant	AB	indifferent
Walsh	John	15	single	mendicant	AB	ragged
Walsh*	Richard	23	single	hostler	AB	indifferent
Williamson*	William	14	deserted			ragged

Source: Cork Board of Guardians, Indoor Relief Registers, No. 7 (February 25, 1852–March 25, 1853); No. 8 (March 26, 1853–November 13, 1854). BG69/G

1. If adult, whether single, married, or widower. If child, whether orphan, deserted, or bastard. An inmate of fifteen years or older was defined as an adult.

2. AB: able-bodied. If disabled, the type of disability.

3. General appearance of pauper on admission.

4. I have treated the two John Learys listed here as different individuals because their departure dates from the workhouse differ.

This is an alphabetical register of 144 males aged fourteen through sixty admitted into the Cork Union Workhouse from September 1, 1852, to November 26, 1853, and discharged between November 20 and December 2, 1853. These inmates remained for more than one night. One hundred and thirty-three of those listed above received assistance to emigrate to Panama from the Poor Law Commissioners in Dublin. Males entering the workhouse after November 26, 1853, would not have been eligible for assistance from the commissioners. Men leaving the workhouse after December 2, 1853, would not have had time to embark on the *Ben Nevis*, which sailed on December 3.

Only males between the ages of fourteen and sixty are listed here, as it was unlikely that men outside this age group would have been accepted for work on the Panama railroad.

All inmates are Roman Catholics unless indicated by an * beside name, in which case the person was a Protestant.

Six of the inmates listed here were unlikely to have boarded the *Ben Nevis* because of their physical or mental condition (nearly blind, paralyzed, disabled, aged, idiotic). A further six men had been admitted to the workhouse hospital, but some of these may have recovered sufficiently to have been discharged prior to December 3. Six inmates were accompanied by dependents—wives, children, and younger siblings—and may have been less likely candidates for emigration than inmates who were already separated from immediate family connections: John Flynn; Michael Keeffe; John O'Keeffe; Peter Rea; Denis Regan; and John Sullivan.

Appendix 4

Estimates of Mortality of the Inhabitants of Panama City, 1884–1893, and among the Workers Constructing the Panama Canal, 1881–1889

Estimates of the death rate of Panama City's inhabitants and of employees of the French canal company have been arrived at from an analysis of statistical data published in 1906 by Colonel Gorgas.[1] I compiled an annual summary of Gorgas's monthly data of deaths from disease in Panama City between 1884 and 1893. I carried out a similar exercise based on Gorgas's report on employee mortality in the *Compagnie Universelle du Canal Interoceanique* between 1881 and 1889. The timeframes of 1884–1893 and 1881–1889 respectively were chosen because they were the closest available to the 1850s. They were also chosen because they overlap one another to a considerable extent and French efforts to build the canal virtually ceased after 1889. Gorgas provided no source for his statistical tables, but he likely relied exclusively on hospital records as comprehensive statistical registers were not compiled until after Panama achieved independence in 1903.

The total number of deaths in Panama City between 1884 and 1893 from hospital-recorded diseases was 15,574. Just under half of these deaths were caused by seven named diseases. Gorgas placed the remaining deaths under the heading of "other diseases." Among the named diseases, malaria was the biggest single killer of the capital's inhabitants. Deaths from malaria (3,504) were almost four times more numerous than those from yellow fever (916), proving that the former posed a deadlier risk to life than the more-feared "yellow jack." Deaths from yellow fever fluctuated considerably, revealing a pattern of periodic outbreaks alternating with periods of quiescence. Dysentery killed almost as many people as yellow fever in Panama City. Smallpox, typhoid, and beriberi between them carried away over five hundred residents. The annual death rate from all diseases in the capital fluctuated considerably, from a high of 121.44 per thousand in 1887 to a low of 38.67 in 1892, reflecting the ebb and flow of epidemics that periodically swept over the Isthmus. The average annual mortality rate over the ten-year period was 73.9 per thousand inhabitants.[2]

This figure does not reveal the full picture, however. Records examined by Gorgas exclude deaths from causes other than disease, as well as deaths that had occurred outside a medical institution. Nonhospital deaths are likely to have been numerous given the limited access to medical facilities available to the large poorer section of the capital's population at this time. For this reason the actual mortality rate would have been substantially higher than the one Gorgas recorded.[3] I estimate that if nonhospital deaths, as well as fatalities resulting from causes other than disease were included, the real annual death rate in Panama City was likely to have been at least 50 percent higher than the rate based on Gorgas's data—111 per one thousand or more.[4]

Gorgas also calculated the monthly death rate from disease per one thousand employees of the *Compagnie Universelle du Canal Interoceanique* between 1881 and 1889. These statistics, like his figures on mortality among the capital's inhabitants, appear to have been derived solely from an analysis of hospital records. During these years, a total of 5,618 employees died, an average annual death rate of 58.16 per thousand employees.[5] This figure does not provide a credible picture of canal workers' mortality at the time. It is difficult to believe that the average death rate of the mainly foreign and unacclimatized canal employees (58.16 per thousand) was substantially lower than that of the hospital-recorded deaths of the inhabitants of Panama City at roughly the same period (73.9 per thousand). Most capital city residents were Panamanians with an inherited or acquired degree of resistance to some of the diseases of the Isthmus. One would expect the mortality rate of non-Panamanians hired by the canal company, who lacked resistance to local illnesses and infections, to be substantially higher than that of the native inhabitants. A second element casting doubt on the veracity of the relatively low mortality rate of the *Compagnie's* employees concerns the total death toll. Historians of the Panama Canal estimate that between 20,000 and 23,000 workers died during this decade with several opting for the figure of 22,189.[6] These figures greatly exceed the 5,618 hospital deaths listed by Gorgas.

Gorgas concluded later that only one-third of the total number of deaths of canal workers occurred in hospitals and other medical centers maintained by the French on the Isthmus. The remaining fatalities were not recorded, and Gorgas acknowledged that hospital statistics compiled by French administrators did not include the bulk of the canal death toll.[7] Gorgas's data are based on disease and exclude deaths caused by injuries and accidents, whether in the workplace or outside it. Many laborers were fatally injured or killed outright while undertaking the hazardous excavation of the canal bed. Others would have died outside the workplace from a variety of causes including domestic and personal disputes.

Furthermore, a sizable proportion of the workers who fell ill in the 1880s did not enter the company's hospitals. The contractors who employed them were often reluctant to pay for the medical treatment of their employees, and parsimony on the employers' side often tended to outweigh any humanitarian responsibility they might have felt. In some instances, workers who reported ill were dismissed on the spot to avoid liability for medical costs by their contractors. In addition, some sick men refused to enter hospitals because of their well-deserved reputation for propagating disease. Hospital patients in Panama at that time were grouped together in unscreened wards on the basis of nationality and not according to the illnesses they were suffering from. This arrangement afforded ideal conditions for the spread of yellow fever, malaria, and other contagious ailments. It was common knowledge that many patients admitted to the hospital for minor injuries or illnesses contracted a fatal disease while there. With a high hospital mortality rate, admission to a ward became strongly and rightly linked in the workers' minds to a likely death sentence.[8] These factors explain the discrepancy between Gorgas's hospital-based toll of 5,618, and the widely accepted figure of 20,000 or more deaths.

If we accept the estimate of 22,189 deaths, the number of fatalities noted by Gorgas (5,618) needs to be multiplied by a factor of 3.95 to arrive at a realistic figure for the total number of deaths. If the actual number of deaths for canal workers was 3.95 times higher than the figure derived from hospital records, then Gorgas's death rate of 58.16 per one thousand employees clearly underestimates the real figure and needs to be increased by the same factor. This gives us a mortality rate of 22.97 percent. According to one authority, the French employed a total of 86,800 men on the construction of the Panama Canal.[9] If we assume that 22,189 of these died, this pushes up the mortality rate to 25.56 percent. I have adopted the mean of these two estimates (22.97 and 25.56), approximately 24 percent, as the likely death rate for employees in all ethnic categories during the French construction period. This mortality estimate for

French canal workers coincides with that quoted by McNeil on the basis of Gorgas's evidence.[10] A mortality rate of 24 percent does not greatly exceed the calculation of Bunau-Varilla, general manager of the French canal company in the mid-1880s, who reported that twenty out of every hundred employees were dead after six months on the Isthmus.[11]

The 24 percent mortality figure is over twice the rate that I have calculated for the inhabitants of Panama's largest city (11.1 percent). However, the discrepancy between the mortality rate of the capital's inhabitants and that of the men engaged on the construction of the Panama Canal in the 1880s is to be expected. The climate in Panama City was healthier than that in the rain forest interior or on the Caribbean coast, where most of the canal laborers were based. Not only were canal workers carrying out difficult and dangerous work in an inhospitable environment, most of them were not indigenous to the region and lacked resistance to the diseases of the Isthmus.

In summary, if my assumptions are correct, the inhabitants of Panama City were exposed to an annual mortality rate of approximately 11 percent during the decade of the 1880s, while workers building the French canal had an overall death rate of 24 percent. The latter mortality rate was subject to variation among the different ethnic categories of the workforce. These figures are, to some extent, conjectural, but they are based on an analysis of available statistical data and are supported by considerable anecdotal evidence. These estimates hopefully represent an improvement on the existing situation where the historical evidence is meager and uncertain.

Appendix 5

Petition of the Irish Laborers to the British Consul, Panama City, 1854

To the consul of the British in the District of Panama.

Sir,

We, the railroad laborers of this station, do petition you in the name of Her Majesty Queen Victoria as her subjects, as we have no other source to apply to for protection than you, that you will take it into consideration and see us satisfied according to our contract. The subject is, we were inveigled to this country with fair speeches and foul promises. We are now getting sick every day in numbers and dying also for the want of care and proper usage. We have applied frequently to clergymen of this city to come and give the dying the rites of the Church and they say that they cannot come without your authority. We therefore petition [you] to authorize one of them to come and attend when called for. We do not want to intrude too much upon your time and privacy but if you would be kind enough to come and inspect our food which we are quite certain you would not consider good enough for a wild African negro. We are rooted out of our beds at half past four in the morning and our breakfast is cold coffee and hard bread, salt beef and pork, all boiled overnight and [we] have to work on that until such time as they consider it proper, at 12 or 1 o'clock, to let us in and have another feed of the same combustible [*sic*], beside it would not matter much if we were allowed to eat enough. Our coffee which we get –no tea – is sweetened with molasses.

By taking this petition into consideration and seeing us satisfied,
We in duty bound shall ever pray
We are Sir with respect,
Your most humble petitioners,
The Panama Railroad Men at Panama Station.

The following comments were attached to the petition, presumably by the proconsul.

> 366–370 arrived at Colón on 9 January. Have been at work since 14 Jan and four men
> have since died.
> Joseph Kenny—City of Cork—Ben Nevis—Roman Catholic.
> John Toomey[1]   ditto   ditto   ditto
> Thomas Hannegan   ditto   ditto   ditto
> Panama Railroad Irish Laborers. 1st February 1854.[2]

It is likely that the above names were those of three of the deceased.

Notes

INTRODUCTION

1. In 1858, New Granada was retitled the Granadine Confederation. In 1863, it became known as the United States of Colombia, assuming its present name, the Republic of Colombia, in 1886. The term "Panama" can refer to the Isthmus of that name, to the province of Panama within New Granada, and to the capital city of that province. To avoid confusion, I refer to the latter as "Panama City." Since 1903, the term "Panama" has also referred to the independent state of the same name.

2. A comprehensive survey of the Irish in Latin America can be found in Murray, "Ireland and Latin America," who estimates that between sixty thousand and one hundred thousand went to the region, though many subsequently migrated elsewhere (84). See also Murray, *Irish in Latin America and Iberia: An Annotated Bibliography*.

3. The Panama railroad was not the first in the Caribbean region to employ Irish labor. Between three hundred and four hundred Irish workers helped build Cuba's first railroad in 1835–1836. Brehony, "Irish Railroad Workers in Cuba," 183–188.

4. Cohen, "The Chinese of the Panama Railroad"; Chen P., "De la China a Panamá"; Mon P., "Mecanismo de Adaptación Psicológica"; Tam. "Huellas Chinas en Panamá."

5. Barima, "Caribbean Migrants in Panama and Cuba, 1851–1927"; Frederick, *Colon Man a Come*; Lewis, *West Indian in Panama*; Newton, *Silver Men*; O'Reggio, *Between Alienation and Citizenship*; Petras, *Jamaican Labor Migration*; Senior, *Dying to Better Themselves*; Westerman, "Historical Notes on West Indians on the Isthmus of Panama."

6. Greene, *Canal Builders*; McCullough, *Path Between the Seas*; Parker, *Hell's Gorge*.

7. Tomes, *Panama in 1855*.

8. Before taking up journalism and writing as a career, Tomes (1817–1882) served as a surgeon on a vessel belonging to the Pacific Mail Steamship Company and made several voyages between Panama and San Francisco, possibly in the early 1850s. This would have enabled him to acquire additional information on Panama. *Memphis Daily Appeal*, September 7, 1882, http://newspapers.com/clip/34925345 /robert-tomes-md/.

9. October 6, 1855. My italics.

10. *Illustrated History of the Panama Railroad.* New York–born Otis (1825–1900) served as a ship's surgeon for the Pacific Mail Steamship Company from 1853 to 1859. In addition to writing the first history of the Panama railroad, he was a pioneer in the medical field of urology and became a professor in Columbia University's medical department. *British Medical Journal* 1, no. 2060 (June 23, 1900): 1566.

11. In April 1860, Otis asked the railroad for financial assistance to write its history. The directors agreed to purchase one thousand copies of his book at a cost not exceeding one dollar per copy. Minutes of the meetings of the board of directors of the Panama Railroad Company. April 5, 1860 (hereafter cited as Minutes, Board of Directors).

12. "History of Construction of the Panama Railroad."

13. Minter, *Chagres*, xiv, 391.

14. A manuscript collection of letters, diary, and memorabilia of Octavia Charity Marsden was one of Schott's sources for *Rails Across Panama*. Schott admitted in 2005 to the historian David C. Humphrey that these documents were spurious. "Myth of the Hangman," 17–18.

15. Haubert, review of *Rails across Panama*: 314–315, is critical of the author's lack of documentary evidence. McGuinness, *Path of Empire,* 211n1, expresses doubt about the reliability of much of Schott's information.

16. McGuinness, "Aquellos Tiempos," 145. Schott, a former FBI agent, died in 2018 at age ninety-seven.

17. *Panama Route,* 166–199.

18. *Path Between the Seas,* 35–38; "Steam Road to El Dorado."

19. Grigore, *Influence of the United States Navy upon the Beginnings of the Panama Railroad*; Grigore, *Presidents of the Panama Railroad Company*; Parker, *Hell's Gorge:* 25–35; McGuinness, *Path of Empire:* 54–83; Senior, *Dying to Better Themselves:* 21–60.

20. Bayor and Meagher, *New York Irish,* xx.

21. Haubert, review of *Rails across Panama*: 314.

22. Ward and Junkins, "Panamanian Historical Sources," 129. The publication of the multivolume *Historia General de Panamá,* edited by Alfredo Castillero Calvo (Panama City: Comisión Nacional del Centenario, 2004), marked a significant advance in our understanding of modern Panama.

1. THE GRAND DESIGN

1. When Gran Colombia disintegrated into present-day Ecuador, Colombia, and Venezuela in 1830, Panama remained linked to neighboring Colombia as part of a political entity known as New Granada, which was ruled from Bogotá.

2. Senior, *Dying to Better Themselves*, 355n30, citing Ernesto J. Castillero, *La isla que se transformó en cuidad: Historia de un siglo de la ciudad de Colón* (Panama: Imprenta Nacional, 1962), 48.

3. "Notes respecting the Isthmus of Panama. Communicated by J.A. Lloyd. 1831," 69; Lloyd, "Account of Levellings Carried across the Isthmus of Panama," 59, 65–66.

4. Sheldon, "History of Construction," 1–2. See Perez-Venero, *Before the Five Frontiers*, 51–62, for early nineteenth-century schemes to establish an interoceanic route across Panama.

5. A. Vigneti to Mariano Arosemena, José de Obaldía, and Blas Arosemena, January 8, 1835, in Manning, *Diplomatic Correspondence of the United States* 3, *Central America 1831–1850*, Document 781:115. The recipients were Panamanian deputies in New Granada's legislature.

6. Kemble, *Panama Route*, 178. Two directors were English. Grigore, *Influence of the United States Navy*, 26.

7. Grigore, *Influence of the United States Navy*, 34, 40.

8. Mack, *Land Divided*, 130. The agreement was formally canceled by the government in July 1849. Kemble, *Panama Route*, 178.

9. Their survey was probably connected to the fact that in 1846, this steamship company, operating between Britain and its Caribbean possessions, extended its service to Chagres on Panama's Atlantic coast.

10. Liot, *Panama, Nicaragua and Tehuantepec*, iii, 25; *Times*, August 16, 1849; *Times-Picayune*, September 12, 1849.

11. Stiles, *First Tycoon*, 172.

12. In the twelve months following December 1848, 762 vessels departed from North American ports for California. Ibid., 173.

13. *American Railroad Journal* 6, no. 44 (November 2, 1850): 688.

14. McCullough, *Path Between the Seas*, 33. The argonauts got their name from Jason's followers, who sailed in quest of the Golden Fleece in Greek mythology.

15. James Gadsden, an American diplomat, negotiated the purchase of thirty thousand square miles in present-day Arizona and New Mexico from the Mexican government for $10 million.

16. The Panama route proved to be the most popular one for travelers from east to west between 1848 and 1860, despite the popular misconception that the great migration westward exclusively consisted of pioneers heading over the plains and

mountains in their covered wagons. Roughly 218,546 people traveled via Panama, as opposed to 198,000 who went overland via the South Pass. McGuinness, *Path of Empire*, 7, table 1.

17. Howarth, *Golden Isthmus*, 164–5.

18. Richards, *California Gold Rush Merchant*, 7.

19. Stiles, *First Tycoon*, 174, 642n47.

20. Wiltsee, *Gold Rush Steamers*, 5–6.

21. Mail was to be carried between Panama and Oregon once a month for an annual government subsidy of $199,000. When the delivery was increased to twice monthly, the subsidy went up to $348,250. *Times-Picayune*, May 6, 1850; July 22, 1852.

22. The first three Pacific mail steamers each had cabin accommodation for only twenty-five persons, an indication of the expected limited demand for first-class passages from Panama to California and Oregon in 1848. Barker, *Memoirs of Elisha Oscar Crosby*, 7.

23. About two hundred foreign travelers crossed the Isthmus in 1845, increasing to 335 by 1848. Liot, *Panama, Nicaragua and Tehuantepec*, 58; Aguirre, *Mobility and Modernity*, 8.

24. Cuba built the first railroad in Latin America in 1837. Jamaica got its first line in 1845. Wolmar, *Blood, Iron and Gold*, 38, 196, 199.

25. Somerville, *Aspinwall Empire*, 25.

26. Stephens was best known for his *Incidents of Travel in Central America, Chiapas, and Yucatan*, published in 1841.

27. In Panama, the continental divide consists of a ridge of hills and mountains separating the watersheds of rivers flowing into the Atlantic and Pacific. It is an extension, greatly reduced in height, of the Rockies to the north and the Andes to the south.

28. Grigore, *Influence of the United States Navy*, 41, 44.

29. Thomas William Ludlow (1795–1878), one of the founders of this Trust Company and vice president of the National City Bank of New York, was a close associate of Aspinwall and later became the first president of the Panama Railroad Company.

30. Wolmar, *Great Railway Revolution*, 43–44.

31. *Memorial of Messrs. Aspinwall, Stephens & Chauncey, presented at the last session of Congress*, 23–24 (hereafter cited as *Memorial of PRC, 1849*).

32. Law hoped to receive government aid for a mail contract of his own across the Isthmus. Kemble, *Panama Route*, 180.

33. Grigore, *Influence of the United States Navy*, 20–24; Perez-Venero, *Five Frontiers*, 60–62; *Times*, February 6; March 21; and August 3, 1849.

34. *Memorial of PRC, 1849*, 7.

35. Ibid., 8. The proposed tunnel was about three thousand feet long. *Scientific American* 4, no. 37 (June 2, 1849): 290; 6, no. 20 (February 1, 1851): 153.

36. The company's contract stipulated that trains should cross the Isthmus in twelve hours or less, which was feasible using horse-drawn carriages on a route of just under fifty miles. Horses were occasionally used in the United States in the 1840s to pull trains up steep gradients. Wolmar, *Great Railway Revolution*, 55.

37. Minutes, Board of Directors, March 4, 1859. Nevertheless, passengers in 1852 allegedly had to alight whenever a steep ascent was encountered. Marryat, *Mountains and Molehills*, 361–362.

38. *Memorial of PRC, 1849*, 7. Actual journey time in 1855 was closer to four hours.

39. *Times*, August 3, 1849.

40. The recent advent of rail travel in the United States meant that a legal formula to register a railroad corporation had not yet been devised. Entrepreneurs had to obtain a charter from a state legislature. Wolmar, *Great Railway Revolution*, 37.

41. U.S. Interstate and Foreign Commerce Committee, *Report of Subcommittee of Committee on Interstate and Foreign Commerce on Investigation of Affairs of Panama Railroad Company* (hereafter cited as *U.S. Interstate Committee. Report of Subcommittee on PRC*), 62. For details of the 1849 charter, see 9–14.

42. Harding, *History of Panama*, 17. The government of Tomás Cipriano de Mosquera (1845–1849) signed this treaty fearing that Britain might extend its control over Central America from its Mosquito Coast colony as far as the Isthmus of Panama. The United States was regarded as the only ally of New Granada capable of containing the expansionist ambitions of Great Britain. Ardila, "Los Estados Unidos como aliado natural," 241–242.

43. *Times*, April 4, 1856.

44. Minutes, Board of Directors, June 28, 1849.

45. *Evening Post*, June 18, 1849. The company's capital stock was later increased to $5 million and then to $7 million. Bishop, *Panama Gateway*, 45.

46. *Memorial of PRC, 1849*, 10; Mack, *Land Divided*, 150. Kemble, on the other hand, citing the *New York Herald*, claimed that the entire amount of stock was subscribed by 3:00 p.m. *Panama Route*, 183.

47. Minutes, Board of Directors, July 2, 1849. Changes were made to the composition and powers of these bodies in the course of time.

48. *Memorial of PRC, 1849*, 8. This was the amount calculated by the Congressional Committee on Naval Affairs earlier in the year.

49. Ibid., 12–13, 18–19.

50. This clause proved to be a serious drawback, forcing the railroad to renegotiate its contract in 1867 at a very considerable cost.

51. This condition had already been complied with.

52. A *fanegada* equaled 1.73 acres.

53. *Contract between the Republic of New Granada and the Panama Rail-Road Company, 1850.*

54. Stiles, *First Tycoon*, 372–373. According to the *Nation*, March 6, 1852, Law was estimated to be worth between $5 million and $7 million. A saying attributed to "Live Oak" George Law was "if it don't make money, it ain't no good." Von Hagen, "Blazing the Trail," 4.

55. Stiles, *First Tycoon*, 175, 207, 373.

56. Evidence of Oliver Charlick, Law's San Francisco shipping agent, in *New York Superior Court, William Heilman v. Marshall O. Roberts*, 125, 138; *Evening Post*, March 26, 1850.

57. *Chicago Tribune*, October 11, 1868, quoted by Stiles, *First Tycoon*, 474.

58. Stiles, *First Tycoon*, 176.

59. May, *Manifest Destiny's Underworld*, 174.

60. The estimated cost of the canal, to be completed within twelve years, was $20 million. *Littell's Living Age* 27, no. 337 (November 2, 1850): 194–195.

2. A FALSE START

1. The Chagres, Panama's largest river, empties into the Caribbean at the port of Chagres. The river served as an improvised artery of communication prior to the advent of the railroad.

2. *Memorial of PRC, 1849*, 24, 12.

3. Panama Railroad Company. Minutes of the Meetings of the Executive and Finance Committee of the Board of Directors, July 11, 25; August 9, 29 (hereafter cited as Minutes, E & F Comm.); Panama Railroad Company. Letters from G. M. Totten (1849–1853). Totten to G. P. Adams, April 11, 1849 (hereafter cited as Totten to recipient).

4. *Panama Star*, November 10, 1849. *American Whig Review* 12, no. 34 (October 1850): 437 reported the cost to be between $400,000 and $1 million.

5. Minutes, E. & F Comm., October 12; November 27, 1849. The minutes provide little information about the contract.

6. Totten to Adams, April 11, 1849.

7. *American Railroad Journal* 5, no. 43 (October 27, 1849): 678; *Memorial of PRC 1849*, 11. In Panama, the wet or rainy season lasts for about two-thirds of the year, from April to December.

8. According to Gisborne, *Isthmus of Darien*, 58, the contractor failed, and the works were left incomplete.

9. Laborers on the canal received thirty cents per day, which was considered a good wage locally. *American Railroad Journal*, 5, no. 43 (October 27, 1849): 678; 8, no. 16 (April 17, 1852): 241.

10. Robinson, *Panama*, 33.

11. Brief biographical details can be found at "Col George Muirson Totten," Find a Grave, accessed April 6, 2020, http://findagrave.com/memorial/22990218/george-muirson-totten.

12. Wolmar, *Blood, Iron and Gold*, 132.

13. Robinson, *Panama*, 37–38.

14. February 12, 1851; Pim, *Gate of the Pacific*, 216.

15. See *American Architect and Building News* 14, no. 405 (September 29, 1883): 145, for Trautwine's obituary.

16. The company had advanced him a letter of credit to hire men. Minutes, E & F Comm., February 6, 1850.

17. Griswold, *Isthmus of Panama*, 113–114; Totten to Ludlow, February 13, 1850.

18. Wheelwright, *Observations on the Isthmus of Panama*, 29.

19. Minutes, E & F Comm., March 12, September 6, 1850.

20. Mack, *Land Divided*, 151. See also Bennett, *History of the Panama Canal*, 88; Kemble, *Panama Route*, 184–185.

21. Minutes, E & F Comm., September 6, 1850; *American Railroad Journal* 6, no. 35 (August 31, 1850): 522; 7, no.2 (January 11, 1851): 28.

22. *Panama Star*, September 26, October 21, 1851.

23. *American Railroad Journal* 6, no. 50 (December 14, 1850): 791–792; 7, no. 24 (June 14, 1851): 376.

24. Letter to *American Railroad Journal* 7, no. 2 (January 11, 1851): 28.

25. *New York Tribune*, March 27, 1850; *Daily Picayune*, March 13, 1850; *Louisville Daily Journal*, April 2, 1850.

26. *Times*, July 23, 1850.

27. Following the decision to build an American railroad in Panama, Britain sent a warship to take possession of San Juan del Norte in 1849 to demonstrate its opposition to further U.S. involvement in Central America. The Clayton-Bulmer Treaty of 1850 provided a temporary respite in the confrontation between the two powers. Petras, *Jamaican Labor Migration*, 59.

28. *Times*, July 23, 1850.

29. This bay, where tradition asserts that Columbus first touched the shores of Central America, appeared on nineteenth-century charts under various names: Limon Bay, Navy Bay, Manzanillo Bay, and Man O' War Bay. *Harper's New Monthly Magazine* 16, no. 95 (April 1858): 591.

30. However, a Royal Navy captain who visited the island in 1832 predicted that it "would afford an excellent site for a town." Peacock, *Notes on the Isthmus of Panama*, 30.

31. The two shipping titans eventually agreed in January 1851 that Aspinwall's company would confine itself to the Pacific and Law's to the Atlantic. Law sold his Pacific steamers to Aspinwall's Steamship Company and purchased the latter's

ships on the Atlantic side. *A Sketch of Events in the Life of George Law.*, 44; Wiltsee, *Gold Rush Steamers*, 27, 30, 47; Kemble, *Panama Route*, 50–51.

32. According to *Times-Picayune,* March 17, 1850, Law paid $12,000 for his purchase. Correa Restrepo, "Inversión Extranjera Directa," 141–160, claims that Law acquired the land around Portobelo for only $500, offering to resell it to the railroad for $3 million. See also Howarth, *Golden Isthmus*, 165; Robinson, *Panama:* 4–5; Minter, *Chagres*, 257–258.

33. Perry to Foreign Office, May 23, 1850. FO289/3.

34. Otis, *Illustrated History*, 26–27. The "Indians" were probably local Panamanians.

35. *American Railroad Journal* 6, no. 35 (August 31, 1850): 552; Minutes, E & F Comm., October 5, 1850.

36. *American Railroad Journal* 6, no. 35 (August 31, 1850): 522; no. 36 (September 7, 1850): 567. The United States was not self-sufficient in rail production at this period.

37. Totten to Adams, April 11, 1849; Trautwine, letter to *American Railroad Journal* 7, no. 2, (January 11, 1851): 28.

38. Liot, *Panama, Nicaragua and Tehuantepec*, 25; *Times,* August 16, 1849; *Times-Picayune*, September 12, 1849.

39. *Times-Picayune,* February 23, 1849.

40. Minutes, E & F Comm., May 18, 22, June 19, 1850; *American Whig Review* 12, no. 34 (October 1850): 437.

41. Minutes, E & F Comm., August 25, 1849; *New York Herald*, March 29, 1850; *American Whig Review* 12, no. 34 (October 1850): 437.

42. Grigore, *Influence of the United States Navy*, 31.

43. McGuinness, "Aquellos Tiempos," 145.

44. For references to slave labor on the railroad see *New York Tribune*, April 25, 1850; *Boston Herald*, April 25, 1850; *American Railway Times*, May 2, 1850; *Liberator,* May 10, 1850; and Correa Restrepo, "Inversión Extranjera," 141–160.

45. McGuinness, *Path of Empire*, 59, 87; McGuinness, "Aquellos Tiempos," 144–145; *Liberator*, September 12, 1851.

46. Totten to Stephens, August 25, 1850.

47. Von Hagen, "Blazing the Trail," 4.

48. Rogers, sometimes referred to as Dr. Rogers, was described by the *New York Herald* as "a perfect gentleman and scholar." December 21, 1850.

49. Minutes, E & F Comm., May 30, 1850.

50. Minutes, June 22, 1850. Paradise Lawrason & Co. also acted as New Orleans agents for the U.S. Mail Steamship Company and the Pacific Mail Steamship Company. *Times-Picayune,* June 2, 1850.

51. *Panama Railroad Company Bank Ledger, 1849–1862,* 27, 28 (hereafter cited as PRC Bank Ledger).

52. "Mechanics" were artisans—men skilled in a particular trade or craft.

53. Baker was to receive $5,000 on signing the agreement, $5,000 after fifty days of work and $10,000 in company stock after one hundred days of work. Minutes, E & F Comm., July 24, 1850; *Times-Picayune*, January 6, 1851.

54. PRC Bank Ledger, 23. $2,500 was deducted from Baker's payment because Totten had provided his men with clothing. Baker received $5,000 circa July 1851 as a final settlement. Minutes, E & F Comm., March 18, July 11, 1851.

55. Totten to Ludlow, July 27, 1850.

56. *Evening Post*, August 6, 1850; *Times*, August 29, 1850.

57. *Illustrated History*, 26.

58. Letter to *American Railroad Journal* 7, no. 2 (January 11, 1851): 27–29.

59. Otis, *Illustrated History*, 27–28.

60. Totten to Ludlow, July 27, 1850.

61. *American Railroad Journal* 6, no. 35 (August 31, 1850): 522; 11, no. 8 (January 20, 1855): 36.

62. Otis, *Illustrated History*, 31.

63. McGuinness, *Path of Empire*, 22–23.

64. *Illustrated History*, 22. See also Pfeiffer, *A Lady's Second Journey* 2: 122, on the alleged laziness of Panamanians.

65. He was presumably referring to the trail from Cruces to the capital. Osborne, *Guide to the Madeiras*, 271.

66. *Times*, October 9, 1852, citing an undated report from *Panama Star*.

67. *American Railroad Journal* 8, No. 16 (April 17, 1852): 241. Their "depravity" probably consisted of requesting increased pay or better working conditions.

68. Totten to Ludlow, February 13, 1850.

69. Trautwine, letter to *American Railroad Journal* 7, no. 2 (January 11, 1851): 27–29.

70. Totten to Stephens, August 25, 1850.

71. Ibid.

72. J. W. Hall to Totten, December 17, 1850.

73. *New Orleans Bulletin*, August 1, 1850, cited by *Louisville Daily Journal*, August 10, 1850; *American Whig Review* 12, no. 34 (October 1850): 437.

74. Totten to Stephens, September 9, 1850.

75. Minutes, E & F Comm., October 5, 1850.

76. *Evening Post*, September 21, 1850.

77. *Panama Star*, October 18, November 15, 1850; Kemble, *Panama Route*, 176.

78. *Chambers's Edinburgh Journal* 15–16 (1851): 250.

79. Schott, *Rails*, 67.

80. November 15, 1850. The paper argued for a toll road that would be superseded by the advancing railroad, but its proposals were ignored by the railroad's bosses. *Panama Star*, September 26, October 21, 1851.

81. Totten to Stephens, September 9, 1850.

82. Ibid. The black deserters were most likely laborers from Cartagena or Panama.

83. Totten to Stephens, September 21, 1850. Ague is a shivering fit brought on by malarial fever.

84. Totten to Stephens, December 22, 1850.

85. Letter to *American Railroad Journal* 7, no. 2 (January 11, 1851): 27–29.

86. Minutes, E & F Comm., January 4, 1851.

87. Waters, letter to *Panama Star,* January 14, 1851.

88. Totten to Center, February 2, 1852.

89. Sheldon, "History of Construction," 4.

90. *Evening Post,* August 16, 1850; Totten to Stephens, September 9, 1850.

91. Brooks, *Across the Isthmus,* 34.

92. *Sydney Morning Herald,* October 25, 1858, citing the *Leader* (London), July 31, 1858. The largest piles requested by Totten were forty feet long.

93. Minter, *Chagres,* 263–264.

94. Abbott, *Panama and the Canal,* 59, gave the depth as 185 feet. Sheldon, "History of Construction," 33, stated that the swamp was 100 feet deep.

95. Totten to Stephens, January 6, 1851.

96. *American Railroad Journal* 6, no. 35 (August 31, 1850): 522; 7, no. 52 (December 27, 1851): 817; 11, no. 8 (January 20, 1855): 36.

97. February 10, 1855.

98. *Times,* October 9, 1852, quoting from *Panama Star,* August 23, 1852.

99. Totten to Stephens, January 6, 1851. Lignum vitae was one of the few timber varieties that could resist the impact of Panama's climate and its wood-boring insects for any length of time.

100. As late as 1853, two hundred tons of earth were being dumped daily on Manzanillo Island. "A Pleasure Excursion on the Panama Railway," *Cork Constitution,* January 14, 1854, reprinted from *United Services Magazine,* n.d.

101. Minutes, E & F. Comm., November 19, 1850.

102. Letter to *American Railroad Journal,* 7, no. 2 (January 11, 1851): 27.

103. Cuesta, "Visión y planeamiento estratégico," 96; Somerville, *Aspinwall Empire,* 48.

104. Totten to Stephens, October 27, 1850.

105. Malaria was endemic on the Isthmus, where it went under a variety of names: Panama fever, Isthmus fever, Chagres fever, etc.

106. Bates, *Incidents on Land and Water,* 89.

107. *New York Weekly Herald,* January 11, 1851.

108. Totten to Stephens, December 22, 1850; in May 1851, the company approved a payment of $99 "due to the late Doctor Gage." Minutes, E & F Comm., March 18, May 19, 1851. Gage was paid $256 from September 14, 1850, to January 21, 1851. PRC Bank Ledger, 52.

109. Minutes, E & F Comm., September 6, October 5, 1850.

110. Totten to Stephens, December 11, 22, 1850.

111. Kemble, *Panama Route*, 191.

112. *American Railroad Journal* 6, No. 35 (August 31, 1850): 522.

113. *New York Tribune*, November 27, 1850. *Times-Picayune*, December 10, 1850, gave his name as "Truesdell."

114. Minutes, E & F Comm., October 5, 1850.

115. Rev. Richard Waters, letter to *Panama Star*, January 14, 1851, praising Truesdale's treatment of Irish laborers.

116. Truesdale received $2,883.85 for his services to the company between October 28, 1850, and July 9, 1851. PRC Bank Ledger, 46. *New York Herald*, February 12, 1851, lauded him as "a gentleman of most active habits . . . kind and attentive to the men, unceasing in his efforts to advance their comfort, and in fine is both brother and father to all."

117. Baker (1811–1861) served with distinction in the Mexican War. He represented Illinois in the 29th Congress and later became a senator for Oregon. A friend and colleague of Lincoln, he was killed in action in the Civil War in 1861. *Dictionary of American Biography*, 517–518.

118. Minutes, E & F Comm., October 5, 1850. See Greenfield, "From St. Louis to San Francisco in 1850," 380–390, for an account of dubious accuracy by one of Baker's recruits.

119. Totten to Stephens, December 22, 1850. Cots were simple beds with a wooden framework and a base of stretched canvas.

120. Borland to Totten, December 23, 1850; Peirce to Totten, December 23, 1850.

121. McGuinness, "Aquellos Tiempos," 145.

122. Totten to Stephens, December 24, 1850.

123. PRC Bank Ledger, November 11, 1851, 113.

124. Minter, *Chagres*, 217; *Louisville Daily Journal*, September 23, 1850, citing *New York Journal of Commerce*, n.d.

125. *Evening Post*, January 7, 1851; *Times-Picayune*, January 3, 1851.

126. *New York Herald*, December 21, 1850.

127. Totten to Stephens, December 22, 1850.

3. SLOW PROGRESS

1. *Panama Star*, January 7, 1851; Totten to Stephens, January 23, 1851; Totten to Board of Directors, February 6, 1851.

2. Totten to Stephens, January 6, 1851.

3. Malaria, typhoid fever, smallpox, and dysentery were some endemic diseases. Epidemics of yellow fever and cholera erupted periodically.

4. Totten to Stephens, January 6, 1851.

5. Ibid., February 24, 1851.

6. *Scientific American* 6, no. 20 (February 1, 1851): 153; *New York Weekly Herald*, February 15, 1851.

7. Totten to Stephens, August 9, 1851.

8. Brooks, *Across the Isthmus*, 34.

9. Lidell, "Medical Topography," 243, 253.

10. Ibid., 244.

11. *New York Weekly Herald*, February 15, 1851; *New York Tribune*, March 10, 1851; *Daily Picayune*, July 22, 1851.

12. *Boston Herald*, March 22, 1851.

13. *American Railroad Journal* 6, no. 50 (December 14, 1850): 791.

14. Totten to Spies, June 6, 1851. Francis Spies acted as company secretary from 1849 to 1854.

15. Minutes, E & F Comm., January 4, 1851.

16. In February, for example, Totten asked for five hundred graders, eighty carpenters, ten blacksmiths, and ten foremen, each to bring his own blankets. Totten to Stephens, February 8, 1851. Graders cleared and prepared the ground for track laying.

17. Totten to Spies, March 28, July 9, 1851.

18. Totten to Stephens, January 23, February 8, 1851; *New York Tribune*, February 19, 1851.

19. *New York Tribune*, January 22, 1851.

20. Ibid., March 10, 1851; Kemble, *Panama Route*, 185–6. Sellers shipped his first locomotive late in 1851, and the other two followed in March 1852. By April 1852, the Panama railroad had five 4-4-0 locomotives on hand. Small, *Rails to the Diggings*, 7, 8. According to Delgado, *To California by Sea*, 53, "The first locomotives and cars, built by Niles & Co. of Cincinnati, were brought by ship and reassembled in August 1851."

21. In the 1860s the track was replaced by conventional sections of wrought iron, seventy-pound rail. Small, *Rails to the Diggings*, 8. See also "Panama Railroad: History of the Panama Railroad Part II," accessed May 15, 2020, www.panamarailroad.org/history1b.html; Panama Canal Railway, "History: Construction of the First Transcontinental Railroad," accessed May 15, 2020, www.panarail.com/en/history/index.html.

22. Small, *Rails to the Diggings*, 7–12. According to Scott, *Americans in Panama*, 34, the line in 1912 consisted of Belgian rails on a five-foot gauge. The gauge was changed once more to four feet, eight and a half inches, in 2000.

23. Between 1835 and 1850, the total mileage of U.S. railroads increased from one thousand to nine thousand, mostly in the Northeast. During the 1850s the focus shifted to the plains of the Midwest. Wolmar, *Great Railway Revolution*, 35, 80, 97.

24. Totten to Stephens, February 24, 1851.

25. Wolmar, *Great Railway Revolution*, 50. This recruitment practice was followed by the Union Pacific and Central Pacific railroads in the 1860s. Ambrose, *Nothing Like It*, 118–119.

26. Totten to Stephens, February 8, 1851.

27. Ibid., August 9, 1851.

28. Totten refers to him as Walters, while the priest signed himself Waters in a letter to the *Panama Star*, January 14, 1851.

29. Totten to Stephens, February 24, 1851.

30. Ibid.

31. *Panama Star*, January 14, 1851.

32. This title was accorded to Catholic missionaries working in politically disputed territories such as South and Central America following the collapse of the Spanish and Portuguese empires. Fox, *El Proyecto Macnamara*, 10–11, 69.

33. *Panama Star*, January 14, 1851.

34. Totten to Spies, March 9, 1851.

35. *New York Weekly Herald*, December 6, 1851.

36. Totten to Spies, March 9, 1851.

37. Minutes, E & F Comm., May 19, 1851; *New York Herald*, June 7, 1851.

38. *American Railroad Journal* 7, no. 52 (December 27, 1851): 817; *Daily Picayune*, April 26, 1851; *International Magazine of Literature, Art and Science*, 3, No. 2 (May 1851): 275.

39. *New York Tribune*, June 4, 1851.

40. *New York Herald*, June 7, 1851; Minter, *Chagres*, 269–270, and Schott, *Rails*, 112–113, mistakenly reported that this incident occurred a year later in May 1852. According to Schott the supervisor in question was an Irishman.

41. *New York Tribune*, July 22, 1851.

42. Minutes, E & F Comm., May 30, 1851.

43. *Scientific American* 6, no. 43 (July 12, 1851): 337.

44. *Times*, June 28, 1851; *Times-Picayune*, June 24, 1851.

45. *American Railroad Journal* 7, no. 25 (June 21, 1851): 392; *Boston Herald*, June 16, 1851.

46. Stiles, *First Tycoon*, 207, 633n20; *Sketch of Events*, 46.

47. Griswold, *Isthmus of Panama*, 118.

48. *Panama in 1855*, 100–103.

49. Fabens, *Story of Life on the Isthmus*, 109. See also Marryat, *Mountains and Molehills*, 2, for an equally dismal opinion of the town.

50. The name was disputed, with New Granada's authorities referring to it as Colón (Columbus). I refer to the settlement as Aspinwall as this was the term used in railroad documents and U.S. newspapers up to the 1890s and because the repetitive use of Aspinwall/Colón is cumbersome. My use of Aspinwall should not be taken as indicating a political preference for the American term.

51. *New York Herald*, June 7, 1851.

52. Pim, *Gate of the Pacific*, 200.

53. Gisborne, *Isthmus of Darien*, 160–161. Gisborne had spent the previous ten years improving the navigation and drainage of the River Shannon in Ireland.

54. Totten to Stephens, February 8, 24, 1851; Totten to Spies, March 9, 1851.

55. Kemble, *Panama Route*, 185.

56. Totten to Stephens, July 23, 1851.

57. Ibid., August 9, 25, 1851.

58. Minutes, E & F Comm., July 25, 1851.

59. Totten to Stephens, August 9, 1851.

60. Ibid., September 8, 1851; *New York Herald*, February 12, 1851.

61. *Rails*, 83. Could an ancient firearm still have been capable of working in Panama's wet and humid climate? Schott probably based this account on Minter, *Chagres*, 264–265, who, in turn, may have taken it from Tomes. The latter recounted that when the train carrying dignitaries celebrating the railroad's completion passed through Gatún station in 1855, a white man and his gang of laborers fired off a blunderbuss. *Panama in 1855*, 79.

62. *American Railroad Journal* 7, no. 52 (December 27, 1851): 817. Schott, *Rails*, 83, gave the date as October 1, 1851.

63. *New York Herald*, November 30, 1851.

64. Mack, *Land Divided*, 152–153.

65. Totten to Spies, May 10; Totten to Stephens, July 23, August 9, 1851.

66. Totten to Stephens, August 25, 1851.

67. According to Minter, a new share issue in 1851 failed, and the value of existing shares dropped substantially. *Chagres*, 265.

68. The loan was not secured until the following April. *Times*, October 10, 1851, April 16, 1852.

69. There were close links between the two enterprises. The West Indian Packet Company had purchased Panama railroad bonds worth $150,000 some months previously. James Cavan, one of the shipping company's founders, was the principal partner in Cavan Brothers, the railroad's London agents.

70. *Times*, December 19, 1851.

71. *New York Tribune*, December 22, 1851; *Times*, December 19, 1851.

72. *Times*, January 6, 1852. The company, not anticipating a demand for public transportation at this stage, had neglected to import passenger cars.

73. DuVal, *And the Mountains will Move*, 15, citing *Panama Herald*, March 23, 1852.

74. Gross receipts amounted to over $250,000 in 1852 and $322,000 in 1853. Annual Reports PRC, 1852–1951.

75. Bennett, *History of the Panama Canal*, 89.

76. *American Railroad Journal* 7, no. 50 (December 13, 1851): 795.

77. Otis, *Illustrated History,* 18.

78. *Times-Picayune,* December 11, 1851.

79. The railroad was paid 22 cents per pound of mail carried.

80. Kemble, *Panama Route,* 198.

81. Minutes, E & F Comm., December 24, 1852; Totten to Stephens, August 9, 1851.

82. *New York Tribune,* February 17, 1852.

83. *Sketch of Events,* 72.

84. Totten to Center, February 2, 16, 1852.

85. According to the *Panama Herald,* May 1, 1852, this was "the first death which has resulted from accident since the opening of the rail road."

86. Minter, *Chagres,* 262, 264.

87. There were sixteen hundred men at work in February 1852, and the arrival of fresh workers to replenish the workforce throughout the year suggests that reports of a catastrophic death rate were exaggerated. *Charleston Mercury,* February 23, 1852. Between January and April 1852, almost eight hundred men were reported to have arrived at Aspinwall from New York and Cartagena. Minutes, E & F Comm., December 31, 1851, February 4, April 12, 1852; Totten to Stephens, May 5, 1852.

88. Totten to Spies, May 25, 1852; Totten to Stephens, June 4, 1852; Totten to Center, July 14, 1852.

4. A NEW DEPARTURE

1. *Panama Herald,* March 9, 1852; Kemble, *Panama Route,* 188. I have been unable to find a biography of Story, and his name does not appear in the principal American biographical dictionaries.

2. Story died on September 30, 1856, leaving an estate valued at $200,000. *New York Times,* October 7, 1856.

3. *Daily Picayune,* July 21, 1851; New York Superior Court, *Heilman v. Roberts,* 299.

4. Story was contracted to repair sections of the Erie Canal and proposed Law as surety for his work in December 1851. Story was also one of three entrepreneurs hired to build the Ninth Avenue Railroad in New York City. *New York Times,* December 22, 1852; *New York Herald,* January 13, August 27, 1853.

5. Story sat in the New York State Assembly in 1850 and became chairman of the state's Democratic Republican Party Committee in 1853. He supported Law's political ambitions at the 1856 Philadelphia Know-Nothing Convention, where Law sought the presidential nomination of the Nativist party. Law was unsuccessful. He received fifty-five votes against Millard Fillmore's 118. *New York Times,* July 16, 1853; *New York Herald,* May 19, 1856; *Times-Picayune,* January 4; February 25, 1856.

6. Law, letter to *New York Herald*, February 9, 1852. See also *Panama Herald*, March 9, 1852.

7. Stiles, *First Tycoon*, 216, citing *New York Times*, March 13, 1852.

8. *New York Herald*, August 27, 1853.

9. *Sketch of Events*, 46.

10. Jaén Suárez, *La Población del Istmo de Panamá*, 499, table 4, "Evolución Demográfica de las Ciudades Terminales en los Siglos XIX y XX."

11. During its early years, the port at Aspinwall remained exposed to occasional northern gales.

12. *Times*, May 10, 1852.

13. Ibid.; *Panama Herald*, May 28, 1852. The brothers were bankrupted in 1854 as the result of a share swindle. Stiles, *First Tycoon*, 214, 239, 305, 419.

14. *Times*, October 19, 1852.

15. Minutes, E & F Comm., May 7, 1852.

16. Minutes, Board of Directors, June 1, 1852.

17. *American Railroad Journal* 8, no. 22 (May 29, 1852): 345. *Times-Picayune*, May 25, 1852, claimed that the contract price was $1 million (about $50,000 per mile), before changing the mileage rate to $80,000 on June 1, 1852, a claim repeated by *New Orleans Crescent* of the same date. *Panama Herald*, December 7, 1852, and Minter, *Chagres*, 271, claimed that the contract was worth $3.5 million (about $175,000 per mile), but this seems excessive. The board's decision on May 20, 1852, to authorize a share issue of $1.5 million to finance the building of the remaining twenty-plus miles of track lends support to the figure of $75,000 per mile. Minutes, Board of Directors, June 1, 1852. Existing shareholders had the option of buying one and a half new shares at par for each existing one held. *Times-Picayune*, June 1, 1852.

18. Stiles, *First Tycoon*, 215; *New York Tribune*, May 21, 1852.

19. Law was reported to have recouped $150,000 from this agreement. *Brockport Republic*, December 19, 1856.

20. *American Railroad Journal* 9, No. 38 (September 17, 1853): 602; *Scientific American* 8, no. 7 (October 30, 1852): 54.

21. *Times-Picayune*, July 14, 1852. These speculations were unfounded.

22. June 28, 1852. In July, shares jumped by 16 percent in just three days, from $120.25 to $140. *Times-Picayune*, July 12, 13, 14, 1852.

23. Totten to Stephens, June 4, 1852.

24. *Times*, May 10, 1852; McGuinness, *Path of Empire*, 69–70; *Times Picayune*, January 29, 1853, citing *Panama Star*, n.d.

25. See Totten to Center, July 14, July 20, 1852; Totten to Spies, December 20, 1852; Totten to Young, December 20, 1852.

26. *American Railroad Journal* 8, No. 22 (May 29, 1852): 345. George Law does not appear to have played a discernible role in the project's management over the next fifteen months.

27. *Times*, May 10, 1852.

28. Minutes, E & F Comm., August 17, 1852.

29. *Panama Herald*, June 25, 1852; *Times-Picayune*, February 19, 1853, reported that Story left New York on the *Empire City* for Panama on February 12 with seventy-five mechanics.

30. McGuinness, "Aquellos Tiempos," 146. Story may have switched his attention to his contract to build part of New York's Ninth Avenue railroad. *New York Times*, December 22, 1852.

31. *Times-Picayune*, December 4, 1852; May, *Manifest Destiny*, 231.

32. Minutes, Board of Directors, December 9, 1851.

33. John C. Campbell and James L. Baldwin were appointed assistant engineers, and G. B. Nichols was made superintendent of motive power and machinery. Minutes, E & F Comm., July 20, 1852.

34. Center served as superintendent of the railroad from 1852 to 1860 and again from 1872 to 1874. Robinson, *Panama*, 273.

35. Totten to president and directors of PRC, October 28, 1852.

36. *Times-Picayune*, October 4, 21, 1852.

37. *Harper's New Monthly Magazine* 6, no. 32 (January 1853): 261. For an obituary see *Putnam's Monthly Magazine* 1, no. 1 (January 1853): 64–68.

38. *Panama Herald*, December 7, 1852. Young's tenure as president was brief—September 24, 1852, to October 31, 1853.

39. Totten to Stephens, June 17, 1852.

40. *Times-Picayune*, May 21, 1852. Story appears to have largely ignored the pool of potential laborers available in Jamaica.

41. Totten to Stephens, August 1, 1852.

42. Minutes, E & F Comm., February 4, 1852. For a description of this bridge see *American Railroad Journal* 8, no. 25 (June 19, 1852): 385.

43. PRC Bank Ledger, 80; *Liberator*, May 28, 1852.

44. *Panama Herald*, June 15, 1852; *Daily Picayune*, May 18, 1852. The bridge's design was modified after flood damage in 1853 to one span of two hundred feet and four spans of one hundred feet. *Panama Star and Herald*, October 20, 1855.

45. *Daily Picayune*, November 11, 1852; *New York Tribune*, November 13, 1852; *Times-Picayune*, January 29, 1853.

46. *New York Tribune*, November 13, 1852.

47. The Illinois Central Railroad advertised for four thousand laborers in September 1852. In November, the New Albany and Salem Railroad sought twenty-five hundred laborers. The New Orleans and Great Northern Railroad sought one thousand laborers at a wage of a dollar per day in December 1852. *Louisville Daily Journal*, September 22; November 5, 1852; *New York Herald*, December 21, 1852.

48. *New York Tribune*, July 6, 1853.

49. *Boston Herald*, July 19, 1853.

50. Reprinted in *Cork Examiner*, November 2, 1853.

51. Conniff, *Panama and the United States*, 32.

52. *Times*, December 19, 1851. Vanderbilt's ships docked at Greytown on the Atlantic, from where passengers crossed Nicaragua to San Juan del Sur on the Pacific.

53. *Panama Weekly Star and Herald*, November 20, 1854. See Wiltsee, *Gold Rush Steamers*, 62–68, 108, 232, for references to Vanderbilt's anti-Panama propaganda.

54. *Panama Star*, November 4, 1852. Taboga is an island in the Bay of Panama close to the capital.

55. *Louisville Daily Journal*, February 20, 1852 (one thousand men); *Charleston Mercury*, February 23, 1852 (sixteen hundred); *New York Tribune*, February 20, 1852 (sixteen hundred); *New York Herald*, February 20, 1852 (sixteen hundred); *Daily Picayune*, November 11, 1852 (one thousand); *Maine Farmer*, November 25, 1852 (eight hundred).

56. Totten to Young, December 31, 1852.

57. Ibid., February 17, 1853.

58. *Communication of the Board of Directors*, 1853, 16.

59. *Times*, June 28, 1852.

60. *Times-Picayune*, September 10, 1852.

61. *Daily Picayune*, November 11, 1852.

62. *Times*, October 19, 1852.

63. *New York Weekly Herald*, November 13, 1852, citing *Panama Echo* of October 29; *New York Weekly Herald*, November 20, 1852. See also *New York Tribune*, November 13, 1852; *American Railroad Journal* 8, (December 4, 1852): 770.

64. *New York Weekly Herald*, December 25, 1852.

65. On November 15, 1852, the price stood at $136, rising to $141.50 by November 19. It fell back to $125 by April 16, 1853. *Times-Picayune*, November 22, 27, 1852; April 23, 1853.

66. Totten to Young, December 20, 1852.

67. *Panama Star*, June 14, 1853.

68. *New York Herald*, July 2, 1853.

69. April 19, 1853. The worker concerned was Irish according to *Estrella de Panama*, April 18, 1853.

70. *Panama Star*, December 30, 1852.

71. Ibid., June 7, 8, 1853.

72. *Panama Herald*, June 11, 1853.

73. *Panama Weekly Star*, June 20, 1853.

74. Ibid., May 16, 1853.

75. *National Democrat*, n.d., quoted by *Panama Weekly Star*, May 16, 1853.

76. *Charleston Mercury*, October 11, 1852.

77. Forty passengers died of cholera on the *Philadelphia*, which left Aspinwall on June 22. *Nation*, July 24, 1852. Kemble, *Panama Route*, 163, reported that one-third of the 155 passengers aboard the ship died of the disease.

78. Three people had succumbed to cholera the previous day, and several others displayed symptoms of the disease. Gisborne, *Isthmus of Darien*, 168.

79. *New York Weekly Herald*, July 17, 1852.

80. *Times-Picayune*, July 24, 25; August 10, 1852.

81. Perry to Foreign Office, August 3, 1852. FO289/5.

82. *Manchester Guardian*, August 4, 1852.

83. Alexander Center, letter to *Cork Examiner*, November 2, 1853.

84. Totten to Center, July 14, 1852.

85. Totten to Stephens, August 1, 1852.

86. Totten to Center, July 14, 1852.

87. Parker, *Hell's Gorge*, 246. Many of these crosses marked the graves of men who died while building the French canal in the 1880s.

88. Totten to Stephens, August 1, 1852.

89. McCullough, "Steam Road," 4. Minter, *Chagres*, 270, incorrectly claimed that Stephens, the railroad's president, was among the victims.

90. *Hell's Gorge*, 29.

91. *New York Herald*, August 24, 1852; Kemble, *Panama Route*, p. 194.

92. *New York Tribune*, July 22, 1852. Peter Sweeney, an Irishman who died on board the *Illinois* en route to New York on July 15, 1852, may have been one of these men. *New York Times*, July 16, 1852; *New York Tribune*, July 16, 1852.

93. *Panama Star*, December 19, 1852.

94. He subsequently commanded the Union armies in the Civil War before becoming president (1869–77). See Chernow, *Grant*, 71–75, for an account of the crossing.

95. Perry to Foreign Office, August 3, 1852, FO 289/5; *Times-Picayune*, August 27, 1852, reprint of account from *Panama Herald*, August 17, 1852. See also *New York Herald*, August 15, 1852; *San Francisco Herald*, n.d., reprinted in *Times-Picayune*, November 26, 1852.

96. Perry to Foreign Office, August 3, 1852, FO 289/5; Grant, *Personal Memoirs*, 104. McCullough, "Steam Road," 4, puts the death toll at over 150. Badeau, "General Grant," 153, stated that about seventy-five perished.

97. *New York Times*, October 30, 1852.

5. HOPES DASHED

1. Parker, *Hell's Gorge*, 97. Sutter provides a useful summary of information on yellow fever in "The First Mountain to Be Removed," *Environmental History* 21 (April 2016): 253.

2. *Mountains and Molehills*, 375. Marryat contracted yellow fever but survived.

3. Perry to Foreign Office, January 20, 1853. FO289/5.

4. Buel, "On 'Chagres Fever,'" 7.

5. Perry to Foreign Office, February 21, May 19, July 1, July 18, August 1, 1853. FO289/4. *Panama Daily Star*, December 11, 1853, reprint of letter from J. Rowell to *New York Independent*, n.d.

6. Nineteen died on board the *Tennessee*, twenty-seven on the *Cortes*, and a total of twenty-eight on four other steamers. *New York Herald*, February 14, 22; March 1, 1853; *New York Weekly Herald*, February 19, March 5, 1853.

7. *Mountains and Molehills*, 376, 380.

8. Totten to Young, January 15, 1853.

9. *Panama Herald*, January 21, 1853.

10. Wiltsee, *Gold Rush Steamers*, 108, citing *Alta California*, March 24, 1853. See also 62–68, 93, 107.

11. Totten to Young, January 31, 1853.

12. *Panama Herald*, February 4, 11, 1853; Perry to Foreign Office, May 19, August 1, 1853. FO289/4.

13. *Panama Herald*, February 4, 8, 11, 1853.

14. *Daily Dispatch*, September 23, 1853, citing a report in *New York Herald*, n.d.

15. Totten to Young, December 20, 1852.

16. Track length: December 1851, seven miles; April 1852, sixteen miles; May 1852, seventeen miles; June 1852, twenty miles; July 1852, twenty-two miles; December 1852, twenty-three miles. Minutes, E & F Comm., December 24, 1852.

17. Cole, "To California via Panama in 1852," 163–172.

18. Minutes, Board of Directors, February 22, 1853.

19. Minutes, E & F Comm., February 3, 1853.

20. According to a visitor in 1853, "A more dirty, disagreeable, uncomfortable place to pass a night in, would with difficulty be found in the highway of modern travel." Bidwell, *Isthmus of Panama*, 150. Bidwell served as British vice consul in Panama in the 1860s. Robinson, *Panama*, 210.

21. Minutes, E & F Comm., February 18, 1853.

22. Ibid., April 27, 1853.

23. Totten to Young, March 4, 1853. Some of the bridge builders might have contracted yellow fever.

24. *Panama Star*, February 24, 1853.

25. Totten to Young, February 17, 1853.

26. *Boston Herald*, January 27, February 14, 15, 18, 21, 1853.

27. *New York Herald*, March 2, 5, 8, 10; April 1; May 10, 11, 12, 17, 18, 26, 28; June 17, 18, 19, 1853.

28. Ibid., May 10, 1853.

29. Ibid., May 26, 1853.

30. Fifteen men arrived from New York in early April. Another eight recruits arrived on April 24 and a further three on April 28, while one hundred men returned

to New York on April 27, with another four due to return on May 4. Totten to Young, April 17, 28, 1853.

31. Sixty-eight white men were employed under contract. Twenty-one more were day laborers. Totten to Young, October 29, 1853.

32. *Louisville Daily Journal*, August 19, 1853.

33. *Panama Herald*, June 14, 21, 1853.

34. See chapter 11, "The American Irish."

35. Schott, *Rails*, 122, 146, 148.

36. Minter, *Chagres*, 271. Schott did not include Minter in his bibliography.

37. Tomes, *Panama in 1855*, 112, 114.

38. See chapter 12, "The Men from Cork."

39. Totten to Young, January 31, 1853.

40. Totten to Spies, February 19, 1853; Totten to Center, April 28, 1853.

41. Totten to Young, May 15, 1853; Totten to Spies, August 1, 1853.

42. On January 5, seven machinists and carpenters, one civil engineer, and one bookkeeper sailed for Aspinwall. They were joined over the next few months by masons, carpenters, quarrymen, and other skilled workers. Minutes, E & F Comm., February 3, 11; April 8, 1853.

43. *New York Herald*, January 18, February 1, 1853; *New York Tribune*, January 18, 1853.

44. *New York Tribune*, May 25, 1853.

45. Totten to Spies, June 10, 1853.

46. Totten to Young, June 11, 1853.

47. "Cruces consists of about one hundred huts ranged along a dirty street, crowded with mules and steaming from liquid filth." Blanchard, *Markham in Peru*, 4.

48. Totten to Young, July 19, 1853.

49. Totten to Center, April 28, 1853; Totten to Young, July 2, 1853.

50. Totten to Young, August 19, 1853.

51. *Panama Herald*, August 20, 1853; *Panama Star*, August 20, 1853.

52. *Panama Herald*, September 15, 1853. *Panama Star*, September 25, 1853, reported that $75,000 had been allocated for improving the Cruces road by the government of New Granada, the railroad, and steamship companies.

53. Totten to Young, April 11, 1853.

54. The volume of water could increase from thirteen to three thousand cubic meters per second after heavy rainfall. Nelson, *Five Years at Panama*, 245, 263.

55. *Panama Star*, April 9, 1853.

56. Totten to Miller, May 13, 1853.

57. Totten to Young, May 14, 15, 1853.

58. Ibid., May 26, June 16, 1853.

59. Ibid., July 19, August 1, 1853. Nailers hammered in the nails and bolts holding the bridge together.

60. Minutes, E & F Comm., May 27, 1853; Totten to Young, June 2, 1853.

61. *Sydney Morning Herald*, May 26, 1857, citing *The Builder* (London), n.d.

62. Totten to Young, June 16, 1853.

63. Minutes, E & F Comm., January 31, 1854; *New York Times*, December 1, 1855, citing *Aspinwall Courier*, November 20, 1855.

64. Totten to Young, April 17, 28; June 2, 1853.

65. Ibid., May 26, 1853.

66. Ibid., April 17, 28, 1853; *La Estrella de Panamá*, June 7–8, 1853.

67. Totten to Young, October 29, 1853. One hundred and thirty-six New Granadians and sixty-eight white men were under contract. In addition, 314 New Granadians, 55 Jamaicans, and 21 white men were employed as casual or day laborers. This is the first reference in company documents to the employment of Jamaicans since 1851.

68. *Panama Star*, June 21, 1853.

69. Totten to Young, May 15, 1853.

70. Ibid., May 26, 1853. The chief engineer made no reference to Jamaicans, which suggests that they had not been employed to any considerable extent in the recent past.

71. Totten to Aspinwall, June 3, 1853. The company or the contractor would have to pay a labor or shipping agent $140 for each labourer recruited in China. The purchaser would also be responsible for their monthly pay and the cost of food.

72. Ibid.

73. *Estrella de Panama*, June 9, 24, 1853. There were an estimated twelve thousand Chinese in California in 1852, rising to almost fifty thousand by the end of 1853. *Times*, June 28, 1852; *New York Herald*, December 12, 1853.

74. Totten to Aspinwall, June 3, 1853.

75. Minutes, E & F Comm., June 17, 1853.

76. Minutes, Board of Directors, July 29, 1853.

77. Totten to Hunt, August 17, 1853.

78. Totten to Young, August 19, 1853.

79. Ibid., September 1, 1853; Totten to Spies, September 2, 1853.

80. *Panama Star*, September 22, 1853 quoting *Aspinwall Courier*, September 11, 1853.

81. Totten to Young, September 20, 1853.

82. Ibid., September 24, 1853.

83. Ibid., October 1, 29, 1853; *Communication of the Board of Directors 1853*, 4–5; *Panama Herald*, December 24, 1853.

84. Minutes, Board of Directors, January 4, 1854.

85. PRC Bank Ledger, 226. No details of payments between June and November 1852, if any, were provided.

86. Totten to Young, September 24, October 1, October 29, 1853.

87. The initial estimate of costs was $3–3.5 million. Minutes, Board of Directors, March 4, 1859.

88. In January 1859, the construction account was closed at $8,010,526.53. PRC Bank Ledger, 231; *Scott Report on the Panama Railroad Company, 1897. Panama Railroad Company. Legal and Fiscal Documents, 1848–1916* (hereafter cited as *PRC Legal and Fiscal Documents*).

89. Totten to Young, August 1, 19, 1853. The establishment and operation of this hospital are discussed in chapter 9, "Workers' Amenities."

90. *Times-Picayune*, April 13, and *Panama Star and Herald*, May 4, 1854, citing *Baltimore Sun*, n.d.

91. *Sketch of Events*, 46.

92. Stiles, *First Tycoon*, 250; Kemble, *Panama Route*, 88, mistakenly dates these events to 1853.

93. David Hoadley (1806–1873), vice president of the American Exchange Bank in New York City from 1848, was a business acquaintance of William Aspinwall and Henry Chauncey. He remained president of the Panama Railroad Company until his retirement in 1869 or 1871. www.hoadleyfamily.com. Hoadley "was a man of wealth," and his name "was the synonym of honor." Robinson, *Panama*, 19, 25, 107.

94. *American Railroad Journal* 9, no. 38 (September 17, 1853): 602; no. 40 (October 1, 1853): 632; no. 41 (October 8, 1853): 641.

95. The dividend in 1854 was 7 percent, and in the first half of 1855, it was 6 percent. *American Railroad Journal*, 11, no. 28, (September 1, 1855): 546.

96. Otis, *Illustrated History*, 35.

97. *Panama Star*, November 10, 1853.

6. THE FINAL PUSH

1. Baring Brothers's decision in July 1852 not to invest in the Nicaragua canal sounded the project's death knell. Stiles, *First Tycoon*, 218.

2. Ibid., 208.

3. McCullough, *Path between the Seas*, 38; Kemble, *Panama Route*, 254. McGuinness calculated that in 1853 approximately ten thousand travelers crossed Nicaragua on their way to San Francisco, compared with fifteen thousand by way of Panama. *Path of Empire*, 69. According to the acting British consul, 22,564 passengers crossed the Isthmus in 1853 and 25,080 in 1854. MacDonald to Foreign Office, December 31, 1853, December 31, 1854. FO289/5.

4. *Panama Herald*, March 11, May 31, 1853.

5. *Weekly Panama Star*, August 1, 1853.

6. Ibid., March 28, 1853.

7. *Panama Herald*, November 3, 24, 1853.

8. Minutes, Board of Directors, October 7, 1853. Article 39 of the company's charter provided for a two-year extension to the original six-year completion period should this becomes necessary.

9. *Panama Star,* March 11, 1853, cited by *New York Herald,* March 29, 1853; *New York Herald,* June 9, July 2, August 11, 1853.

10. *Panama Star,* November 10, 1853.

11. *Panama Herald,* December 27, 1853, citing Totten's 1853 report to the president and directors of the PRC.

12. Minutes, E & F Comm., February 11, 1853. "West" in this context meant states to the west of New York.

13. Letter to editor, *Cork Constitution,* October 27, 1853, signed "Patriot."

14. Minutes, Board of Directors, July 1, 1853.

15. Minutes, E & F Comm., July 8, 1853. Minter's claim that the company "chartered cattle boats and sent agents all over the world to recruit labor" is incorrect. *Chagres,* 271.

16. *Estrella de Panama,* August 24, 1853; *Panama Star,* August 25, 1853; ibid., October 4, 1853, citing *New York Herald,* n.d.; Minutes, E & F Comm., September 16, 1853.

17. Totten to Young, September 1, 1853.

18. Ibid.; and Totten to Spies, September 2, 1853.

19. Totten to Young, October 29, 1853.

20. Three hundred and ninety were white employees and twelve hundred were described as "native laborers, Jamaica men and coolies." *Communication of the Board of Directors 1853,* 17; *Panama Herald,* December 27, 1853. *Panama Herald* November 5, 24, 1853, reported a larger workforce: eighteen hundred in early November rising to twenty-five hundred by the end of the month.

21. Totten to Spies, December 22, 1853.

22. *Panama Herald,* December 27, 1853.

23. *Communication of the Board of Directors 1853,* 16–17.

24. Totten to Young, October 2, 1853; *Panama Herald,* October 4, 8, 1853.

25. *Panama Herald,* November 5, 24; December 20, 1853.

26. Howarth, *Golden Isthmus,* 173, quoting *Aspinwall Courier,* n.d.

27. Minter, *Chagres,* 271. This bridge was replaced four years later by a stronger and more durable iron structure. Sheldon, "History of Construction," 8.

28. *Panama Herald,* December 24, 1853.

29. *New York Times,* December 29, 1853, January 4, 1854; Communication of the Board of Directors 1855, 9; Annual Report of the Panama Railroad Company, 1853.

30. *Chambers's Edinburgh Journal* 23, (1855): 251.

31. *Panama Herald,* January 28, 1854.

32. B.T. Crouch, letter to *Panama Star,* March 12, 1853.

33. *Times-Picayune,* January 25, 1854, quoting *Aspinwall Courier,* January 17, 1854.

34. American banks were overextended after making large loans to railroad contractors, while credit from London had dried up because of borrowing by the British and French governments to finance the Crimean War. Stiles, *First Tycoon*, 248.

35. *Panama Herald*, January 12, April 1, 1854; *Panama Star and Herald*, June 6, 1854.

36. About 16,000 Chinese went to Central America, mainly Panama and Costa Rica in the nineteenth century. Another 19,000 migrated to the British West Indies and 142,000 to Cuba. Lai, *Indentured Labor*, 40.

37. *Daily Picayune*, June 22, 1854, citing *Aspinwall Courier*, June 15, 1854.

38. McGuinness, "Aquellos Tiempos," 145, puts the figure at over five thousand. *American Railway Times*, May 22, 1858, stated that seven thousand had been employed, presumably in 1854.

39. *Times-Picayune*, August 8, 1854.

40. Small amounts of explosives may have been used. In 1851 the company sought foremen acquainted with rock blasting. *Times Picayune*, March 26, 1851.

41. *Weekly Panama Star and Herald*, November 6, 20, 1854; *American Railroad Journal* 11, no. 8 (January 20, 1855): 36.

42. *New York Herald*, January 11, 1855, reprinted from *Aspinwall Courier*, December 31, 1854.

43. December 28, 1854, reprinted in *Weekly Panama Star and Herald,* January 1, 1855.

44. *Communication of the Board of Directors 1855*, 9; Annual Report of the Panama Railroad Company, 1854.

45. Peter Bourne and Juan David Morgan provided fictional descriptions of this event in their novels about the railroad: *Golden Road*, 344; *Caballo de Oro*, 11–13.

46. *Daily News*, February 3, 1855, reprinted in *Sydney Morning Herald*, May 16, 1855.

47. *Panama Star and Herald*, January 30, 1855, reprinted in *Weekly Panama Star and Herald*, February 5, 1855.

48. *Times-Picayune*, February 28, 1855.

49. *Panama Star & Herald*, n.d., quoted by Howarth, *Golden Isthmus*, 174.

50. March 17, 1855.

51. Vol. 11, no. 7 (February 17, 1855): 110.

52. *Journal des Debats*, n.d., quoted by *Sydney Morning Herald*, August 13, 1855.

53. Pim, *Gate of the Pacific*, 193.

54. Minutes, Board of Directors, June 27, 1855.

55. Totten to Kemble, November 15, 1854, *New York Journal of Commerce*, n.d., reprinted in *Panama Weekly Star and Herald*, December 25, 1854.

56. Ward to Secretary of State, March 9, 1855. Dispatches from U.S. Consuls in Panama 3 (1854–1855).

7. THE MEN WHO BUILT THE RAILROAD

1. I refer to men from Central America and New Granada as "local workers" and "New Granadians."

2. The term "coolie" was first used by British writers in the seventeenth century to describe an unskilled, cheaply hired laborer or burden carrier in India and China. The term now has derogatory racial implications.

3. Indentured labor: "a system of contract labor which tied the laborer to a specific employer for a fixed term of years under a contractual arrangement that often exposed the laborer to penal sanctions, including imprisonment, in the event of violation of the terms of the contract." Lai, *Indentured Labor*, xi.

4. Robinson, *Panama*, 15; Cohen, "Chinese of the Panama Railroad," 311; Kemble, *Panama Route*, 194.

5. Newton, *Silver Men*, 47, table 9; Mack, *Land Divided*, 156.

6. At the time, it was accepted that the concept of race had biological validity and that there were inborn differences between people of different colors, views that have since been disproved and discredited.

7. McNeill, *Mosquito Empires*, 4, 53–54.

8. Totten to Adams, April 11, 1849; Totten's report to the president and directors of the PRC, *Panama Herald*, December 27, 1853.

9. *Estrella de Panama*, June 24, 1853.

10. PRC Bank Ledger, 204.

11. Totten to Young, September 1, 1853.

12. The size of the total payment to Posada suggests that he could have recruited up to forty-three hundred men.

13. Bidwell, *Isthmus of Panama*, 144.

14. Totten to Young, May 26, 1853.

15. Minutes, E & F Comm., July 8, 1853; Totten to Young, September 1, 1853.

16. Petras, *Jamaican Labor Migration*, 77, suggested that senior railroad employees were accompanied by their womenfolk, who provided "the graces, culture, and comfort of middle-class privileges in the jungle," but I have seen no evidence to confirm this arrangement between 1849 and 1855. It may have taken place in later years.

17. Griswold, *Isthmus of Panama*, 118; *New York Herald*, August 9, 1853, citing a letter from Spies dated August 8, 1853.

18. Hoadley to House of Commons Select Committee, *New York Times*, September 2, 1859. See also *Sydney Morning Herald*, January 14, 1860, quoting *Illustrated London News*, October 29, 1859.

19. See Appendix 2, Passage Account by Date of Ledger Entry, 1850–1855.

20. *New York Times*, February 10, 1859; *Panama Star and Herald*, September 20, 1855; January 19, 1856; *New York Weekly Herald*, February 2, 1856; McCullough, "Steam Road," 5; Kemble, *Panama Route*, 194.

21. *American Railway Times*, May 25, 1854. Because laborers had recently arrived from Ireland, the periodical may have assumed that the railroad's German-speaking employees had been similarly recruited in their homeland.

22. Otis, *Illustrated History*, 35; Totten to Stephens, February 24, 1851; *American Railway Times*, May 22, 1858.

23. *American Railway Times*, May 22, 1858.

24. Frederick, *Colon Man a Come*, 27; Conniff, *Panama and the United States*, 26; Newton, *Silver Men*, 91; O'Reggio, *Between Alienation and Citizenship*, 38; Barima, "Caribbean Migrants," 50.

25. Leonard, *Historical Dictionary of Panama*, 293.

26. Petras, *Jamaican Labor Migration*, 75.

27. Cumpston, *Indians Overseas*, 145.

28. Letter to *New York Herald*, August 9, 1853.

29. *New York Times*, October 9, 1857.

30. Slavery in the British Empire was abolished in 1833. Abolition was gradual and full emancipation was not granted until 1838.

31. Senior, *Dying to Better Themselves*, 41.

32. Barima, "Caribbean Migrants," 44, 45. The islanders' situation was made worse by a cholera outbreak that took twenty thousand to fifty thousand lives between 1850 and 1852. Senior, *Dying to Better Themselves*, 43.

33. Minutes, E & F Comm., September 6, 1850. Wright Armstrong & Co. acted as the railroad's agents in Jamaica between 1850 and 1852.

34. Totten to Stephens, December 11, 1850.

35. Ibid., December 22, 1850; February 8, 1851.

36. Totten to Spies, July 9, 1851.

37. Otis, *Illustrated History*, 104.

38. PRC Bank Ledger, 39.

39. *Daily Picayune*, June 11, 1853. Lewis, *West Indian in Panama*, 35, suggested that the Jamaicans' self-confidence stemmed from the fact they were never a minority in their own island. The fact that they were free men and no longer slaves would also have boosted their self-esteem.

40. Totten made only one reference to Jamaicans working for Story, reporting that he employed fifty-five islanders at the end of his contract period. Totten to Young, October 29, 1853.

41. Newton, *Silver Men*, 78.

42. *Jamaican Labor Migration*, 68.

43. *Kingston Morning Journal*, January 28, 1854, quoted in *Charleston Mercury*, March 4, 1854.

44. *New York Herald*, July 25, 1854.

45. Parker, *Hell's Gorge*, 29; Cumpston, *Indians Overseas*, 145, stated that about two thousand islanders had left by May 1854.

46. *New York Herald*, August 25, 1854; *Weekly Panama Star and Herald*, December 4, 1854, quoting *Aspinwall Courier*, November 25, 1854.

47. However, McNeill, *Mosquito Empires*, 309n13, suggests that the infrequency of yellow fever outbreaks in nineteenth-century Jamaica may have reduced resistance to this disease among the population, although some Jamaicans would have inherited a level of genetic resistance due to their West African ancestry.

48. Newton, *Silver Men*, 124.

49. Frederick, *Colon Man a Come*, 39. Ague is a fit of shivering brought on by malarial fever.

50. Newton, *Silver Men*, 83.

51. Parker, *Hell's Gorge*, 29.

52. *Liberator*, July 30, 1858.

53. The acting consul in Panama City assured London that he would follow this advice. MacDonald to Foreign Office, September 18, 1854. FO289/5.

54. Cowan to MacDonald, September 15, 1854. FO288/7; MacDonald to Cowan, September 28, 1854. FO289/6.

55. Parker, *Hell's Gorge*, 28; Conniff, *Panama and the United States*, 26.

56. Bayoumi, "Moving Beliefs," 58–81.

57. Sixty thousand laborers from various sources were imported into Jamaica, Trinidad, and British Guiana between 1834 and 1847. Most were Indians. Cumpston, *Indians Overseas*, 124n2; Lai, *Indentured Labor*, 116–117; 108, table 5.1.

58. Totten to Young, September 1, 1853.

59. Totten's report to the president and directors of the PRC, *Panama Herald*, December 27, 1853.

60. *New York Herald*, January 30, 1854, citing *Aspinwall Courier*, January 17, 1854.

61. Kip, *Early Days*, 22.

62. *Weekly Panama Star and Herald*, February 12, 1855.

63. *New York Tribune*, March 2, 1855; Tomes, *Panama in 1855*, 59. See also ibid., 44, 73, 80–81. The references to turbans suggest that some of these men may have been Sikhs.

64. Minutes, Board of Directors, April 29, 1852.

65. Mon, "Mecanismo de Adaptación Psicológica," 59; Tam, "Huellas Chinas," 8. Both sources cite British records in Hong Kong. These migrants could have been transshipped from Panama to other destinations that were accepting Chinese workers, such as Peru, California, or Cuba.

66. Totten to Young, May 26, 1853; Totten to Aspinwall, June 3, 1853.

67. Minutes, Board of Directors, July 1, 15, 1853; Minutes, E & F Comm., July 8, 1853. Aspinwall and his cousin William Edgar Howland, a former director of the Panama railroad, were also owners of the Pacific Mail Steamship Company.

68. Minutes, Board of Directors, August 12; August 30, 1853.

69. Coleman, *Passage to America*, 237–238.

70. Of the laborers, 701 were "fine looking men" in good health, 4 were described as invalids, and a further 11 had died during the sixty-one-day passage from China. *Panama Herald*, April 1, 1854.

71. *Panama Star and Herald*, June 6, 1854; *Colonial Land and Emigration Commission*, 50. Howland and Aspinwall were paid for 1,027 men. Scott Report on Panama Railroad Company, 1897; PRC Bank Ledger, 226, 227.

72. *Illustrated History*, 35–36.

73. *New York Times*, April 27, 1854.

74. *New York Herald*, May 27, 1854.

75. May 18, 1854.

76. Minutes, Board of Directors, June 28, 1854.

77. *Panama Star & Herald*, July 25, 1854; *Estrella de Panama*, July 30, August 4, 1854, also referred to the growing problem of Chinese beggars, some of whom were dying in the streets.

78. *Panama Star and Herald*, August 19, 1854.

79. Ibid., August 20, 1854.

80. Minutes, Board of Directors, March 24, 1854. The railroad jointly owned the islands with the Pacific Mail Steamship Company. See Minutes, E. & F. Comm., June 17, 1853, on this purchase.

81. *Panama Star & Herald*, August 23, 1854.

82. *Weekly Panama Star & Herald*, September 4, 1854.

83. *Colonial Land and Emigration Commission, 1855.* Appendix No. 52. *Copy of Journal of the Chinese interpreter, Wang-te-Chang, reporting state of Chinese Immigrants at Panama*, 150.

84. Ibid., 150–151.

85. *Panama in 1855*, 119–121.

86. *Chagres*, 272.

87. *Rails*, 181. Minter, *Chagres*, 290–293, also refers to Sean Donlan. I have not found any reference to him in the company's records or in the press.

88. Chen, "De la China a Panamá," 99–100.

89. *Illustrated History*, 36.

90. Minutes, Board of Directors, August 16, 1854.

91. *Panama Star and Herald*, September 3, 1854.

92. McGuinness, *Path of Empire*, 71.

93. Minutes, Board of Directors, October 2, November 14, 1854; *New York Times*, December 2, 1854.

94. Bryan, "Settlement of Chinese in Jamaica," 15; *Colonial Land and Emigration Commission, 1855*, 50. The £6 ($30) charge per head presumably included purchase price plus transport cost.

95. In 1855, thirty-two Chinese left Panama to work in Costa Rican coffee plantations, but it is not clear whether they had been railroad employees. Chen, "De la China a Panamá," 100–101.

96. Lai, *Indentured Labor*, 94.

97. PRC Bank Ledger, 226–227; Scott Report.

98. *New York Times*, August 30, 1856. The figures mentioned in its report were inaccurate.

99. *Panama Star and Herald*, October 23, 1855.

100. *American Railway Times*, May 22, 1858.

101. Campbell, *Chinese Coolie Emigration*, xviii.

102. Working in teams and taking few breaks, they dug, hacked, and blasted their way through the Sierra Nevada Mountains, defying snow and blizzards and enduring the scorching deserts of Nevada and Utah. Ambrose, *Nothing Like It*, 204–206, 236–237.

103. Zanetti and Garcia, *Sugar and Railroads*, 122.

104. Senior, *Dying to Better Themselves*, 33.

105. Ambrose, *Nothing Like It*, 153, 162.

106. British surgeons on ships bringing Chinese indentured laborers to Havana in 1858 reported that opium smoking was responsible for their feeble constitutions and susceptibility to infection and disease. *Chambers's Edinburgh Journal*, 35–36 (1861): 11.

107. Millions of Chinese had become addicted to opium by 1838, partly as result of British-sponsored opium exports from India. See Platt, *Imperial Twilight*, for a masterly account of this nefarious trade.

108. Lai, *Indentured Labor*, 91.

109. Ibid., 100, citing *British Guiana Commission Report on Chinese Immigrants 1870–71*.

110. Otis, *Illustrated History*, 35–36; Tomes, *Panama in 1855*, 119. Wang made no reference to the company's alleged supply of opium to its Chinese workers.

8. WORKING CONDITIONS

1. Otis, *Illustrated History*, 28.

2. Tomes, *Panama in 1855*, 77.

3. Robinson, *Panama*, 15.

4. McCullough, "Steam Road to El Dorado," 5.

5. *Harper's New Monthly Magazine* 22, no. 132 (May 1861): 843. A combination of diseases including yellow fever, falciparum malaria, dysentery, and possibly

dengue, also contributed to the failure of the settlement. McNeill, *Mosquito Empires*, 119–121.

6. Tomes, *Panama in 1855*, 203.

7. Cited by Parker, *Hell's Gorge*, 265.

8. George Bartholomew, letter to *New York Tribune*, January 22, 1851.

9. I have not seen any references to the use of explosives during construction, but it is possible that small amounts were used where formidable rock formations were encountered.

10. "A Pleasure Excursion on the Panama Railway," *United Services Magazine*, n.d., reprinted in *Cork Constitution*, January 14, 1854; *Panama Star*, June 29, 1853. Trautwine referred to "burning the dense forest" as a method of clearance. Letter to *American Railroad Journal* 7, 2 (January 11, 1851): 27–29.

11. Monkey Hill became the site for the railroad's first cemetery, which was later renamed Mount Hope.

12. Wolmar, *Blood, Iron and Gold*, 127.

13. Totten to Stephens, August 25, 1850.

14. Ibid., February 8, 24, 1851.

15. Gisborne, *Isthmus of Darien*, 75–76. *Maine Farmer*, November 25, 1852, reported that workers from Cartagena were paid between $1.00 and $1.50 per day.

16. Minutes, E & F Comm., October 5, 1850. General laborers in Jamaica earned about $0.42 per day in 1848. Petras, *Jamaican Labor Migration*, 48.

17. Newton, *Silver Men*, 118, 79.

18. Kemble, *Panama Route*, 190.

19. *Panama Star*, September 27, 1850. The Pacific Mail charged thirty dollars to transport laborers in steerage from New York to Chagres and one hundred dollars from Panama City to San Francisco in 1850. Minutes, E &F Comm., October 5, 1850.

20. Minter exaggerated in stating that "thousands of forty-niners got to California by virtue of a stint of railroading in the Chagres valley." *Chagres*, 290.

21. Minutes, E & F Comm., May 19, 1851.

22. Minutes, Board of Directors, July 23, 1850. A minority of Baker's men requested payment in cash in lieu of a free passage.

23. Totten to Spies, March 9, 1851.

24. *New York Times*, July 30, 1853; June 6, 1854.

25. Totten to Stephens, December 22, 1850; Totten to Spies, November 21, 1851; Totten to Center, February 2, 1852.

26. Totten to Spies, November 21, 1851.

27. Ibid., February 19, 1853. Underlined in original.

28. Ibid., May 26, July 18, 1853. The men's names were McKay, McLane, Bradley, and Hall.

29. *Panama Star*, November 17, 1853; *La Estrella de Panamá*, June 7–8, 1853.

30. *New York Herald*, December 21, 1852; *New York Tribune*, July 6, 1853; *Boston Herald*, July 19, 1853.

31. *Panama Herald*, May 28, 1853. See also *New York Times*, April 6, 1855; Maguire, *Irish in America*, 275.

32. Gisborne, *Isthmus of Darien*, 172–3.

33. Fletcher to Secretary of State, November 15, 1854. Dispatches from U.S. Consuls in Colón (1852–1857).

34. Minutes, Board of Directors, July 2, 1849; October 17, 1853.

35. Ibid., July 23, 1850; Minutes, E & F Comm., September 6, 1850.

36. Minutes, E & F Comm., July 25, 1851; Totten to Stephens, August 9, 1851.

37. Minutes, Board of Directors, December 9, 1851; Totten to president and directors of PRC, October 28, 1852.

38. Minutes, Board of Directors, January 5, 1852. This may have been because he was not on the board of directors.

39. Minutes, E & F Comm., July 20, 1852; Minutes, Board of Directors, April 3, November 14, 1854.

40. Minutes, E & F Comm., July 20, 23, 1852; July 15, 1853.

41. Ibid., December 1, 1853. Green, incorrectly described as "Treasurer" of the PRC, temporarily replaced the American consul in Aspinwall in October 1852, while the latter took sick leave. Munro to secretary of state, October 2, 1852. Dispatches from U.S. Consuls in Colón (1852–1857).

42. Totten, memo, September 3, 1852; Fletcher to secretary of state, November 15, 1854; December 31, 1855. Dispatches from U.S. Consuls in Colón (1852–1857).

43. Coincidentally, during the French attempt to build the Panama Canal in the 1880s, at least a third of the workforce was also incapacitated by sickness at any one time. Gorgas, *Sanitation in Panama*, 279.

44. *Irish American*, August 27, 1853, contains the full text of an agreement between a group of laborers and Story. See also *New York Times*, October 13, 1853.

45. In 1851, Bartholomew (Bartley) Monaghan, probably the same man, was secretary of the Quarrymen's Union Protective Society of the City of New York. *New York Herald*, February 28, 1851.

46. *New York Times*, July 30, 1853.

47. Michael Doheny (1805–63) was a founding member of the Irish republican Fenian movement in the United States in 1858 and author of *In The Felon's Track*, an account of the 1848 Rising in Ireland and its aftermath.

48. *New York Tribune*, August 20, 1853.

49. *Irish American*, August 20, 27, 1853; See also *New York Freeman's Journal*, August 20, 1853.

50. August 27, 1853; *Panama Herald*, September 3, 1853.

51. *New York Freeman's Journal*, September 24, 1853.

52. *New York Times*, October 13, 1853. See *New York Freeman's Journal*, October 22, 1853, for a full account of this case.

53. PRC Contracts, Regulations, Timetables and Train Rules.

54. Ibid., "Regulations Established by the Chief Engineer for the Government of the Employees of the Panama Rail-Road Company, on the Isthmus." Italics copied from the original.

55. Somerville, *Aspinwall Empire*, 54.

56. June 11, 1853, reprinted in *Panama Star*, June 14, 1853.

57. *Hell's Gorge*, 30.

58. See also chapter 13, "Railroad-Government Relations," on this issue.

59. *Hell's Gorge*, 30; Conniff, *Panama and the United States*, 28; Schott, *Rails*, 151–152.

60. Tomes, *Panama in 1855*, 122, 124. This claim was repeated by Heald, *Picturesque Panama*, 93.

61. The formation and operation of this body are discussed in more detail in chapter 13, "Railroad-Government Relations."

62. Borland to Totten, December 23, 1850; Pierce to Totten, December 23, 1850; Totten to Stephens, December 24, 1850.

63. *New York Herald*, June 7, 1851.

64. Totten to Center, July 14, 1852.

65. *New York Times*, July 30, 1853; October 13, 1853; *New York Freeman's Journal*, September 24, 1853.

66. *Panama Star*, June 14, 1853.

67. *Times-Picayune*, August 8, 1854, mentioned strikes, along with rain and sickness, as factors delaying progress in 1854 but provided no further details.

68. *Weekly Panama Star and Herald*, January 1, 1855.

69. *New York Times*, October 7, 1868.

70. According to Robinson, Baldwin retired from the railroad for unspecified reasons. He spent several years in the West before returning to work for the company in the 1860s, "greatly changed by dissipation." *Panama*, 22, 114–116.

71. *Aspinwall Courier*, March 3, 1854, reprinted in *New York Times*, March 15, 1854.

72. I have come across only one case brought against the PRC by a former employee. *New York Times*, June 6, 1854.

73. Totten to Stephens, August 26, 1851.

74. *American Railroad Journal* 8, no. 16 (April 17, 1852): 241.

75. Petition from Irish Laborers to the British consul, Panama, 1 February, 1854. FO288/7.

76. Newton, *Silver Men*, 121.

77. *New York Times*, February 11, 1854, reprint of a report in *Panama Herald*, January 24, 1854.

78. Minutes, E & F Comm., November 2, 1855.

79. *Panama Herald*, June 21, 1853; *Estrella de Panamá,* June 25, 1853.

80. *Panama Herald*, June 11, 1853.

81. *Panama Star,* June 14, 1853.

82. *Scientific American* 6, no. 20 (February 1, 1851): 153.

83. *Spirit of the Times*, April 21, 1855.

84. *Panama Star*, November 10, 1853.

85. Ibid., June 14, 1853.

86. *Aspinwall Courier*, March 3, 1854, reprinted in *New York Times*, March 15, 1854.

87. Ibid., August 6, 1854, reprinted in *Panama Star and Herald*, August 12, 1854.

88. Minutes, E & F Comm., May 27, 1853.

89. Griswold, *Isthmus of Panama*, 98.

90. British naval officers, for example, were provided with free passes over the Isthmus. Pim, *Gate of the Pacific*, 217.

9. WORKERS' AMENITIES

1. *Illustrated History*, 27.

2. Totten to Stephens, September 9, 1850.

3. Minutes, E & F Comm., October 5, 1850.

4. *American Railroad Journal* 7, no. 2 (January 11, 1851): 27–29.

5. *Illustrated History*, 31.

6. Totten to Stephens, January 23, 1851.

7. Totten to Spies, March 9, 1851.

8. George Bartholomew, letter to *New York Tribune*, January 22, 1851; *New York Tribune*, June 21, 1851.

9. Totten to Spies, June 6, 1851. The request for secondhand canvas was presumably to keep costs down.

10. *Colonial Land and Emigration Commission. Appendix No. 52. Copy of Journal of Chinese interpreter*, 150.

11. *Times*, December 19, 1851.

12. Minutes, E & F Comm., November 17, 1852; Totten to Young, March 4, 1853.

13. Gisborne, *Isthmus of Darien*, 208. See also Pfeiffer, *A Lady's Second Journey*, 2: 239.

14. *Early Days*, 29.

15. "A Pleasure Excursion on the Panama Railway," *United Services Magazine*, n.d., reprinted in *Cork Constitution*, January 14, 1854.

16. *New York Times*, February 10, 1855.

17. Trollope, *West Indies*, 242.

18. Newton, *Silver Men*, 119.

19. Totten to Stephens, December 22, 1850; Totten to Spies, May 10, 1851.

20. Minutes, E & F Comm., April 12, 1852.

21. Each man was allocated six or seven pounds of bedding straw. *Irish American*, August 20, 27, 1853.

22. Capron, *History of California*, 348.

23. In 1853, Totten requested ten tons of hay and nine hundred bushels of oats to be sent monthly to Panama. Totten to Spies, September 22, 1853.

24. Kemble, *Panama Route*, 195.

25. Totten to Stephens, August 25, 1850. Some of these supplies may have been purchased at Manhattan's Fulton Market.

26. Totten to Stephens, December 6, 11, 1850.

27. Pierce to Totten, December 23, 1850.

28. Totten to Stephens, January 6, 1851.

29. Greenfield, "From St. Louis to San Francisco," 383–384.

30. Ibid., 385, 390. Passengers on ships sailing to California via Cape Horn at this time fared little better in terms of dietary choice. Delgado, *To California by Sea*, 34–35.

31. *Times*, December 19, 1851.

32. Minutes, E & F Comm., April 8, 1853.

33. Totten to Spies, November 14, 1853; December 22, 1853; *New York Times*, May 10, 1854, reported that the *Falcon* had sailed with five hundred half-barrels of beef for the railroad employees.

34. Totten to Spies, July 2, 18, 1853.

35. *American Railroad Journal* 7, no. 52 (December 27, 1851): 817.

36. Totten to Stephens, January 6, 1851.

37. Minutes, E & F Comm., August 16, 1851, November 3, 1852.

38. Newton, *Silver Men*, 121; PRC Contracts, Regulations, Timetables and Train Rules. The railroad may have issued company "scrip" or vouchers to be redeemed in these stores.

39. *Daily Advertiser*, April 18, 1854, quoted in Newton, *Silver Men*, 79; ibid., 121.

40. *Irish American*, August 20, 27, 1853. "Hickory beef" was a euphemism for tough, hard meat.

41. Ibid. Miller was Story's superintendent in Panama.

42. *New York Freeman's Journal*, September 24, 1853.

43. O'Callaghan, letter to *Cork Examiner*, October 21, 1853.

44. Center, letter to *Cork Constitution*, October 27, 1853; Center, letter to *Cork Examiner*, November 2, 1853.

45. Petition from Irish Laborers to the British consul, Panama, February 1, 1854. FO288/7.

46. Roderick Random, *San Francisco Herald*, June 13, 1854, reprinted in *Panama Star and Herald*, July 9, 1854.

47. *Colonial Land and Emigration Commission. Appendix No. 52, Copy of Journal of Chinese interpreter*, 150–151.

48. *Aspinwall Courier*, March 3, 1854, reprinted in *New York Times*, March 15, 1854.

49. *New York Tribune*, June 21, 1851.

50. *Panama Star and Herald*, July 19, 1855.

51. *Scientific American* 4, no. 34 (May 12, 1849): 270; *New York Tribune*, September 23, 1852.

52. Parker, *Hell's Gorge*, 30. Johnson, *Sights in the Gold Region*, 27, 74, referred to food items such as mule steaks, dead pork, iguana pie, and roast monkey.

53. The word *panama* is generally taken to mean "an abundance of fish" in an indigenous language.

54. Johnson, *Sights in the Gold Region*, 47. On the dangers of fruit, see also Tyson, *Diary of a Physician*, 8, 29; Kip, *Early Days*, 41; *Panama Star*, December 19, 1851.

55. Robinson, *Panama*, 27, 229–230; McCullough, "Steam Road," 7.

56. *New York Times*, January 8, 1856.

57. *Panama Star and Herald*, January 15, 1856. Bullbaiting had been outlawed in England only twenty years earlier.

58. Tracy to Roberts, February 24, 1851, in New York Superior Court, *Heilman v. Roberts*, 271.

59. Minter, *Chagres*, 237, 243.

60. McCullough, "Steam Road," 4; Schott, *Rails*, 105, 142.

61. Howarth, *Golden Isthmus*, 164; Conniff, *Panama and the United States*, 30.

62. Totten to Stephens, September 8, 1851.

63. Totten to Hoadley, December 30, 1853. Incidents like this, which brought the company into conflict with the local authorities, are discussed in chapter 13, "Railroad-Government Relations."

64. Ibid., November 12, 1853.

65. Totten to Stephens, August 17, 1852; Totten to Spies, May 26, 1853.

66. "Regulations Established by the Chief Engineer for the Government of the Employees of the Panama Railroad Company," PRC Contracts, Regulations, Timetables and Train Rules.

67. Totten to Stephens, August 25, 1850. Quinine, derived from cinchona bark, was widely used by settlers in America's Midwest suffering from the ague, as malaria was often referred to.

68. *Panama*, 15.

69. While quinine lessened the symptoms of malaria and relieved a victim's suffering, it was not a cure and was only partially effective as a prophylactic. The real cause of the disease was as yet unknown.

70. Greenfield, "From St. Louis to San Francisco," 388.

71. Totten to Stephens, January 6, 1851.

72. See, for example, Minutes, E & F Comm., May 4, July 20, 1852.

73. Totten to Stephens, December 24, 1850.

74. Greenfield, "From St. Louis to San Francisco," 386.

75. Minutes, E & F Comm., September 6; December 18, 1850.

76. *American Railroad Journal* 7, no. 2 (January 11, 1851): 28.

77. Hall to Totten, December 17, 1850.

78. *Panama Star*, October 24, 1851. The mortality rate reportedly reached 75 percent. Ibid., June 17, 1852, January 22, 1853. See letter, signed "J.R.," describing conditions in this hospital in ibid., March 29, 1853. See also Pfeiffer, *Lady's Second Journey*, 2:124, for a critical description of the public hospital.

79. Totten to Stephens, December 6, 1850.

80. Totten to Spies, July 9, 1851.

81. Totten to Stephens, December 22, 1850; Minutes, E & F Comm., March 18, 1851.

82. Dr. Lidell, for example, worked for the railroad from January to May 1851. "Medical Topography," 244, 246.

83. *Chagres*, 262. Minter provided no source for this allegation.

84. *Rails*, 68, 104.

85. *Path Between the Seas*, 37.

86. *Presidents of the Panama Railroad Company*, 158. See also Petras, *Jamaican Labor Migration*, 74.

87. I have found no reference to this ghoulish practice in the surviving records of the company or in the newspapers of the period.

88. Totten to Center, July 14, 1852.

89. *Sanitation in Panama*, 216.

90. *Colonial Land and Emigration Commission. Appendix No. 52. Copy of Journal of Chinese interpreter*, 150–151.

91. *Chagres*, 264.

92. Fletcher to secretary of state, March 8, 1854. Dispatches from U.S. Consuls in Colón (1852–1857). See also *Panama Star*, November 3, 1853.

93. Brooks, *Across the Isthmus*, 38, 41.

94. "A Pleasure Excursion on the Panama Railway," *United Services Magazine*, n.d., reprinted in *Cork Constitution*, January 14, 1854.

95. *Aspinwall Courier*, March 3, 1854, reprinted in *New York Times*, March 15, 1854.

96. Ibid., August 6, 1854, reprinted in *Panama Star and Herald*, August 12, 1854.

97. *Panama Star*, June 14, 1853.

98. Minutes, E & F Comm., November 3, 1852.

99. Bancroft, *California Inter Pocula*, 162.

100. *Times-Picayune*, July 13, 1853. Green, the railroad's agent at the port, acted as hospital treasurer. It was hoped that migrants would make voluntary contributions for the hospital's support.

101. Fletcher to secretary of state, March 8, 1854. Dispatches from U.S. Consuls in Colón (1852–1857).

102. *Harper's New Monthly Magazine* 17, no. 97 (June 1858): 25.

103. PRC Bank Ledger, 172.

104. Minutes, Board of Directors, April 18, May 13, 1854; August 16, 1855.

105. *Panama Star*, December 30, 1852.

106. Ibid., November 7, 1851. Passengers transiting the Isthmus were asked to contribute fifty cents each. See *Panama Herald*, April 20, 1854; *Panama Star and Herald*, May 16, 1854.

107. *Panama Herald*, February 15, 1853. The hospital closed in 1855, its funds being exhausted. *Weekly Panama Star and Herald*, March 5, 1855.

108. *Panama Star*, December 30, 1852.

109. *Panama Herald*, February 11, 1854.

110. Ibid., February 21, 1854.

111. *Colonial Land and Emigration Commission. Appendix No. 52. Copy of Journal of Chinese interpreter*, 150–151.

112. Minutes, Board of Directors, August 16, 1855.

113. Lidell, "Medical Topography," 246.

114. *Panama Herald*, December 27, 1853.

115. The Aspinwall public hospital charged three dollars per day for the first seven days and two dollars daily thereafter. City Hospital, Colón, to Cowan, September 15, 1854. FO288/7; Fletcher to secretary of state, March 8, 1854. Dispatches from U.S. Consuls in Colón (1852–1857).

116. *Irish American*, August 20, 27, 1853.

117. Ships' passengers were divided into three classes: first, second, and steerage.

118. Lidell, "Medical Topography," 244.

119. Walter, "A Panama Riot," 636.

120. Bancroft, *California Inter Pocula*, 146; 127–128. See Tomes, *Panama in 1855*, 28–30, for a more positive view of steerage conditions.

121. Totten to Stephens, February 8, 1851.

122. Ibid., February 24, 1851.

123. Payments of $21 and $28.50 were authorized by the E & F Committee on January 19, 1852. See ibid., July 23, 1852, for payment to Dr. McBean, a ship's doctor, for medicines furnished to sick men.

124. Totten to Stephens, January 6; August 25, 1851; February 24, 1851.

125. Ibid., February 24, 1851.

126. *New York Freeman's Journal*, August 13, 1853.

127. O'Callaghan, letters to *Cork Examiner*, October 21, 31, 1853.

128. Totten to Stephens, September 21, 1850.

129. Ibid., February 24, 1851.

130. *Panama Star*, January 28, 1851.

131. Totten to Stephens, February 24, 1851; December 22, 1850; August 9, 1851.

132. Ibid., July 9, 23, 1851.

133. *Panama Herald*, May 1, 1852.

134. *Panama Star*, April 5, 1853.

135. Thousands of British troops were sent to fight in Russia with little consideration of how they were to be fed, clothed, and cared for. Twenty-five thousand died, mostly from disease.

10. MORTALITY

1. McNeill described the dismal fates of European incursions in *Mosquito Empires*, 101, 119–121, 132, 143, 189, 258.

2. Ibid., 3, 4.

3. Ibid., 62.

4. Ibid., 4, 10, 53–54.

5. *Panama Star and Herald*, September 20, 1855; Hoadley to House of Commons Packets' Contract Committee, August 9, 1859, cited in *New York Times*, September 2, 1859; Espino, *Ésta es mi patria*, 15.

6. *Irish American*, April 30, 1853. Most trackside mounds are unlikely to have been graves, as dead workers were interred in Mount Hope cemetery after it opened in mid-1851.

7. Cited in *Panama Herald*, August 4, 1853.

8. This issue is missing from the New York Public Library's microfilm collection. The physician in question may have been Antisell or Lidell, who had published an article on diseases in Panama in 1852.

9. *New York Herald*, August 8, 1853.

10. Ibid., August 9, 1853.

11. *Panama Herald*, September 29, 1853.

12. Letter, signed "A Patriot," October 27, 1853.

13. Reprinted in *Daily Express*, November 1, 1853.

14. *Times-Picayune*, November 7, 1855; *Home Journal*, November 10, 1855; *Flag of Our Union*, December 1, 1855.

15. *Sydney Morning Herald*, August 29, 1855, reprint of "Across the Isthmus," *Chambers's Edinburgh Journal*, 23 (1855): 251–252. The *Panama Star and Herald*, June 9, 1855, also copied this article, though its version referred to hundreds rather than thousands of fatalities.

16. *Daily Alta California*, May 23, 1856, reprinted in *Sydney Morning Herald*, August 26, 1856.

17. *Chambers's Edinburgh Journal* 37–38 (1862): 96.

18. Bidwell, *Isthmus of Panama*, 219, 144.

19. He claimed that the total number employed during the construction period did not exceed six thousand. *Panama*, 15.

20. Tripler, *Eunice Tripler*, 106.

21. Nelson, *Five Years at Panama*, 115.

22. Abbott, *Panama and the Canal*, 56. Scott, *Americans in Panama*, 33, also gave the death toll as six thousand.

23. *Chagres*, 273. Minter failed to state the source of his "official estimate" or reveal who these "impartial authorities" were.

24. Howarth, *Golden Isthmus*, 165–166; Wolmar, *Blood, Iron and Gold*, 128; Grigore, *Presidents of the Panama Railroad Company*, 156, 219.

25. Schott, *Rails*, 192; McCullough, *Path between the Seas*, 37; McCullough, "Steam Road," 5. Cuesta, "Visión y planeamiento," 97; Petras, *Jamaican Labor Migration*, 73.

26. Conniff, *Panama and the United States*, 27; Leonard, *Historical Dictionary*, 222; Small, *Rails to the Diggings*, 6; Greenfield, "From St. Louis to San Francisco," 390; Senior, *Dying to Better Themselves*, 30; Alfaro, "Ruta del oro," 25; Espino, *Ésta es mi patria*, 15.

27. Johnson, *Four Centuries*, 343.

28. Trautwine, letter to *American Railroad Journal* 7, no. 2 (January 11, 1851): 28.

29. Moore, "Mosquitoes, Malaria and Cold Butter," 4.

30. Frenkel, "Jungle Stories," 317–333.

31. Robinson, *Panama*, 236, 15.

32. September 25, 1853, cited in *Cork Constitution*, October 25, 1853. The figure of 450 was also reported in *Times-Picayune*, September 22, 1853, quoting *Baltimore Sun*, n.d.

33. *New York Weekly Herald*, February 2, 1856.

34. Wyse, *Le Canal de Panamá*, 42. These figures are also cited by DuVal, *Mountains will Move*, 29, and by Correa Restrepo, "Inversión Extranjera Directa," 141–160.

35. Kemble, *Panama Route*, 193, 194; Haskin, *Panama Canal*, 103.

36. Mack, *Land Divided*, 156; DuVal, *Mountains Will Move*, 29.

37. *American Railway Times*, May 22, 1858. This calculation implied a total mortality of about two thousand.

38. Stiles, *First Tycoon*, 208.

39. Somerville, *Aspinwall Empire*, 54; Conniff, *Panama and the United States*, 32.

40. *Saunders's News-Letter*, October 24, 1853. See *Panama Weekly Star and Herald*, November 20, 1854, on the existence of an anti-Panama propaganda campaign.

41. Newton, *Silver Men*, 129.

42. Some documentation of this nature may survive in Colombia's national archives and in parish records in Panama.

43. Totten to Spies, November 21, 1851; January 18, 1852.

44. Totten to Stephens, August 17, 1852; Totten to Spies, February 19, 1853. See ibid., May 26, July 18, 1853, forbidding other workers, deemed unsatisfactory, to return.

45. Letter from Center to Cummins, *Cork Examiner*, November 2, 1853.

46. For references to returning railroad workers see *New York Tribune*, July 22, 1852; *New York Times*, August 12, 1854; *New York Herald*, August 25, December 11, 1854.

47. Gorgas remained in charge of sanitation in the Panama Canal Zone until 1913 and was largely responsible for eradicating yellow fever from the Isthmus. Ireland, "General William C. Gorgas," 53–54.

48. Gorgas, *Population and Deaths from Various Diseases*.

49. A radical turning point in Panama's public health environment took place in 1906 with the eradication of yellow fever.

50. *Jamaican Labor Migration*, 87, 106.

51. Gorgas, *Sanitation in Panama*, 149, 157, 283.

52. Ibid., 149.

53. McNeill, *Mosquito Empires*, 143.

54. Bancroft, *History of Central America*, 3, 498–501. Some were shot by their captors; others perished as a result of forced labor.

55. May, *Manifest Destiny*, 200.

56. Zanetti and Garcia, *Sugar and Railroads*, 122.

57. McNeill, *Mosquito Empires*, 302.

58. The railroad, 227 miles long, cost $30 million. Wolmar, *Blood, Iron and Gold*, 204–205; Small, *Rails to the Diggings*, 6; Werner, "All aboard to nowhere."

59. Letter from Spies to editor, *New York Herald*, August 9, 1853.

60. *Panama Star and Herald*, September 20, 1855; *New York Times*, September 2, 1859. McCullough stated that the company's death toll "was patently absurd," while Howard claimed that its mortality figures "were so low that nobody could believe them." *Path between the Seas*, 37; *Golden Isthmus*, 165–166.

61. Green, *Canal Builders*, 132, citing Michael Conniff, *Black Labor on a White Canal: Panama 1904–1981*, (Pittsburgh: University of Pittsburgh Press, 1985), 30–31.

62. Totten to Spies, July 9, 1851; Totten to Stephens, August 9, 1851.

63. Minutes, E & F Comm., May 19, 1851. The company's ledger contains a "Deceased Men's Account," but the amount involved ($1,477.23 between 1851 and 1854) is small, and details are few. Only fourteen names are listed, five of which may have been Irish. PRC Bank Ledger, 134.

64. See chapter 11, "The American Irish."

65. Miller, *Emigrants*, 317–318. In 1851 nearly 50 percent of Irish people over five years of age could not read or write. McCaffrey, *Irish Catholic Diaspora*, 78. Possibly a quarter to a third of all famine emigrants, amounting to half a million people, spoke Irish. Many members of Irish-American railroad gangs were Irish speakers. Miller, *Emigrants*, 297–298.

66. In 1847, the mortality of Indian laborers on malaria-infested sugar plantations in British Guiana varied between 2.7 percent and 8.1 percent. Mortality on two estates over five years (1838–1843) was 5 percent per annum. Cumpston, *Indians Overseas*, 118n6; 76.

67. McNeill, *Mosquito Empires*, 288.

68. El Niño is a climate cycle associated with a band of warm ocean water in the equatorial regions of the Pacific. In the year of an El Niño event and in the following year—which specialists refer to as "ENSO" (El Niño/Southern Oscillation), and "ENSO + 1"—rainfall in the Central America region is usually heavier and more prolonged than normal. One consequence is a great increase in the mosquito population, a key contributory factor in the spread of yellow fever and malaria.

69. McNeill, *Mosquito Empires*, 59, 148n31, 272n103.

70. Quinn, "El Niño Occurrences," 14449–14461; Barrett, "Reconstructing El Niño," 3131–3152.

71. Howarth, *Golden Isthmus*, 167; Coleman, *Railway Navvies*, 33.

72. Enock, *Panama Canal*, 151.

73. *Littell's Living Age* 47, no. 602 (December 8, 1855): 622.

11. THE AMERICAN IRISH

1. "American Irish" is arguably the best term to describe Irish-born immigrants to the United States regardless of their religious background. "Irish American" has frequently been used to refer to those from a Catholic background. See letter from historian Brian Walker, *Irish Times*, April 3, 2017.

2. Totten to Stephens, February 24, 1851; Totten to Spies, March 9, 1851.

3. Totten to Stephens, December 22, 1850; February 24, 1851.

4. *Panama Herald*, June 16, 1851.

5. Totten to Stephens, August 25, 1851.

6. Fuller also claimed that most of these men were dead at the end of six months. *New York Times*, February 3, 4, 1857.

7. *New York Tribune*, February 24, May 10, 1851; *New York Weekly Herald*, December 6, 1851; *New York Times*, September 12, 1853.

8. The deceased may have been William Gilmore, a railroad employee, reported to have died of delirium tremens on July 23, 1853, during the outward passage of the *Illinois* to Panama. *New York Freeman's Journal*, September 3, 1853; *New York Weekly Herald*, August 13, 1853.

9. *Aspinwall Courier*, December 9, 1853, reprinted in *Panama Star*, December 14, 1853.

10. Minutes, June 21, 1851. The company was responsible for paying the return fare of workers hired in the United States who had completed their contracts.

11. This Irish name is usually spelled "Cavanagh" or "Kavanagh."

12. Totten to Spies, November 21, December 18, 1851; Minutes, E & F Comm., February 3, 1853; Totten to Spies, February 19; August 1, 1853.

13. It is possible that Story may have had Irish connections as a branch of this English family settled in Ireland in earlier centuries, and the name Story or Storey is not uncommon.

14. *Illustrated History*, 34; Trollope, *West Indies*, 246; Schott, *Rails*, 148; Howarth, *Golden Isthmus*, 168–9.

15. For example, Cosgrove, Fagan, Monahan, Murphy, Lyons, Harris, Shaw, Dalton. *New York Times*, July 30, 1853; February 6, 1854; *Irish American*, August 20, 27, 1853.

16. *Panama Herald*, February 18, 1853.

17. *Panama Star*, March 18, 1853.

18. Ibid., April 5, 6, 1853; *Panama Herald*, April 5, 1853.

19. *Panama Herald*, April 12, 1853; *Panama Star*, April 13, 1853.

20. *Panama Herald*, March 11, 1854.

21. Kip, *Early Days*, 26–27.

22. *Panama Weekly Star*, July 18, 1853. Ireland, as part of the United Kingdom, was represented in Panama by the British consul. Samuel Lover's novel, *Rory O'More: A National Romance* (1837) was well-known in literary circles. For other references to Rory O'Moore or O'More, see "Song of the Irish Exile," *Panama Herald*, December 14, 1852; March 4, 1853.

23. *Freeman's Journal*, December 19, 1859.

24. Perry to Totten, January 30, 1855. FO289/6.

25. This doctor was an avid anatomical collector who had amassed a bizarre collection of the skeletons of deceased patients from many parts of the world. Tomes, *Panama in 1855*, 207.

26. Isthmian Historical Society. "Notes on a Trip to Colon," n.p. Minter claimed that the stationmaster was Sean Donlan, "the toughest Irishman on the Isthmus," who lost his post to an American prizefighter called Tom Sharp in a bare-knuckle contest. *Chagres*, 290–293. Robinson listed a Tom Sharp as a respected senior member of the railroad staff and someone, therefore, unlikely to have been a pugilist. *Panama*, 14.

27. McGuinness, "Aquellos Tiempos," 145; Conniff, *Panama and the United States*, 26.

28. *Panama Herald*, December 27, 1853, quoting from Totten's report to the railroad's president and board of directors, November 1853.

29. Virtually all of the railroad's 6,000 white employees embarked for the Isthmus from the ports of New York and New Orleans between 1850 and 1855, with the exception of 360 men who left from Cork, Ireland, in late 1853.

30. This is an estimate based on informal analysis of contemporary newspaper reports and advertisements.

31. *Times-Picayune*, March 24, 1852.

32. If these assumptions are correct, an estimated 3,760 white workers sailed from New York to Panama between 1850 and 1855, with an additional 1,880 leaving from New Orleans.

33. Gabaccia, "Constructing North America," 35, 36.

34. Totten to Spies, September 22, 1853.

35. The *Ohio* "brought out two hundred and sixty fresh emigrants, who had just landed in New York to labor on the Panama Railroad." *Panama Star*, December 30, 1851, reprinted in *New Orleans Crescent*, January 21, 1852. See also letter in *Waterford News*, August 6, 1852, about the recruitment of newly arrived Irish immigrants at New York port.

36. *New York Evangelist*, n.d., cited by *Friends' Intelligencer*, April 21, 1855.

37. Five of these advertisements appeared in *Boston Herald* and fourteen in *New York Herald* between January and June 1853.

38. *Irish American*, April 30, 1853.

39. Miller, *Emigrants and Exiles*, 193.

40. By 1870, 72 percent of the American Irish were concentrated in five eastern and two midwestern states: Massachusetts, Connecticut, New York, New Jersey, Pennsylvania, Ohio, and Illinois. McCaffrey, *Irish Catholic Diaspora*, 67.

41. Ernst, *Immigrant Life*, 188, table 9.

42. Kenny, *American Irish*, 64.

43. Niehaus, *Irish in New Orleans*, 34.

44. Dolan, *Irish Americans*, 43.

45. Miller, *Emigrants and Exiles*, 315.

46. Quoted by Dolan, *Irish Americans*, 43.

47. According to the U.S. Census of 1850, 26 percent of the city's population was Irish born. The New York State Census of 1855 reported that 28 percent had been born in Ireland. Diner, "The Most Irish City in the Union," in Bayor and Meagher, *New York Irish*, 91.

48. Ernst, *Immigrant Life*, 216, table 27; 219, table 29.

49. Dolan, *Irish Americans*, 86–87. See also Ignatiev, *How the Irish Became White*, 110.

50. Ernst, *Immigrant Life*, 69.

51. Ernst, *Immigrant Life*, 73–74. Of the 300 builders and contractors in New York City listed in the 1855 Census, 207 had been born in Ireland. Ibid., 248n15.

52. Out of 229 antebellum labor leaders in the city, 106 were Irish. Ignatiev, *How the Irish*, 116.

53. During the building of the U.S. transcontinental railroad in the 1860s, Irishmen formed the mainstay of Union Pacific's workforce. The Central Pacific also recruited Irish workers, eight of whom laid ten miles of track on April 28, 1869, a record never equaled. Ambrose, *Nothing Like It*, 18, 177, 217, 349–350.

54. Gabaccia, "Constructing North America," 36; *Irish American*, June 21, 1851.

55. There were over fifty thousand Irish-born residents in the city in 1855. Handlin, *Boston's Immigrants*, 52.

56. Ibid., 60; 250–251, table XIII; 253, table XV.

57. Ibid., 71.

58. I have estimated the nationality of the probable 3,760 men who sailed for Panama from New York as follows: Irish, 2,500; Americans, 1,000; Europeans, 260.

59. Niehaus, *Irish in New Orleans*, 46. In 2014, the Hibernian Memorial Park was dedicated to the Irish immigrant laborers who worked and died on this project. *Irish Times*, November 10, 2014.

60. Johnson, review of *Irish in the South, 1815–1877*: 486; Brennan, "Getting Out of Crescent City," 195.

61. Brennan, "Getting Out of Crescent City," 191.

62. Niehaus, *Irish in New Orleans*, 44, 47.

63. *Times-Picayune*, June 11, 1853.

64. Ten percent of the city's population, including four thousand Irish-born residents, died in this outbreak. Brennan, "Getting Out of Crescent City," 195; Niehaus, Irish in New Orleans, 32.

65. "Numbers of acclimated Irish" from New Orleans were suggested as laborers for a proposed canal across Panama's Darien region in the 1850s. Cullen, *Isthmus of Darien*, 26.

66. This was for six foremen on March 26, 1851.

67. Anbinder, *Five Points*, 120.

68. An estimated 2,500 Irish sailed from New York, 800 sailed from New Orleans, and 360 were brought directly to Panama from Cork in 1854. The recruitment and fate of the latter are dealt with in the next chapter.

69. Schott, *Rails*, 178. For references to alleged Irish racism see Newton, *Silver Men*, 119; Murray, "Secret Diasporas," 17–18; Chen, "De la China a Panamá," 98–99.

70. Schott, *Rails*, 178–179.

71. *Colonial Land and Emigration Commission. Appendix No. 52. Copy of Journal of Chinese interpreter*, 150–151.

72. Schott, *Rails*, 179. This claim was repeated by Parker, *Hell's Gorge*, 28. I have not been able to verify the existence of this letter.

73. Totten to Stephens, September 21, 1850.

74. It is also possible that Totten was commenting, in ironic terms, on the possibility of more serious conflict.

75. Relations between the mainly Chinese men of the Central Pacific and the predominantly Irish workers of the Union Pacific became violently antagonistic for a time. Wolmar, *Blood, Iron and Gold*, 139; Ambrose, *Nothing Like It*, 327.

76. Kenny, *American Irish*, 157; Gabaccia, "Constructing North America," 37.

77. Totten to Stephens, September 21, 1850.

78. For the debate on how Irish immigrants in the United States slowly became accepted as "white Americans," see Handlin, *Boston's Immigrants*, 133, 206, 210; Hodges, "Desirable Companions" in Bayor and Meagher, *New York Irish*, 107, 146, 147; Dolan, *Irish Americans*, 54; Kenny, *American Irish*, 246, 260.

79. Ignatiev, *How the Irish Became White*, 2.

80. Parker, *Hell's Gorge*, 123; 132–133; 291, 296.

81. Kenny, *American Irish*, 107; McCaffrey, *Irish Catholic Diaspora*, 72.

82. Anbinder, *Five Points*, 353.

83. Miller, *Emigrants and Exiles*, 319, cited by Ignatiev, *How the Irish*, 117; Handlin, *Boston's Immigrants*, 115.

12. THE MEN FROM CORK

1. Despite the reference to "Great Britain," the committee had Ireland specifically in mind.

2. *Estrella de Panama*, August 24, 1853; *Panama Star*, August 25, 1853; October 4, 1853, reprinted from *New York Herald*, n.d.; *Panama Herald*, August 23, 1853; *New York Times*, September 12, 1853, reprinted from *Panama Herald*, August 30, 1853; *Sydney Morning Herald*, March 18, 1854.

3. Minutes, Board of Directors, September 3, 1853. Spies had earlier complained of overwork. Minutes, E & F Comm., February 3, 1853.

4. Robinson held him in high regard. "No man in any position connected with the road was ever held in more genuine respect." After retiring from the railroad, he became general manager of Wells Fargo's New York office. *Panama*, 34, 131.

5. Minutes, E & F Comm., September 16, 1853.

6. James Cavan (1771–1859), principal partner, was a founder of the Colonial Bank and of the Royal West India Mail Steam Packet Company. He owned sugar plantations in British Guiana and left £500,000 ($2,500,000) on his death. Legacies of British Slave-Ownership, University College London. http://www.ucl.ac.uk/lbs/person/view.

7. N. & J. Cummins, 21 Marlborough Street, Cork, were commission and wine merchants and agents for the East India Company. *Slater's Commercial Directory of Ireland*, 217, 236.

8. A decade later, in 1863, another American railroad, the Alton and Chicago, recruited 250 men in Dublin and paid their fares to the United States. Miller, *Emigrants and Exiles*, 356.

9. *Daily Express*, November 1, 1853. I have not been able to locate this circular in the papers of the Poor Law Commissioners or those of the Cork Board of Guardians.

10. The average weekly cost of maintaining a pauper in an Irish workhouse in 1852–1853 was just over one shilling, about thirty cents. *Chief Secretary's Office. Registered Papers 1854. Sixth Annual Report of Commissioners for Administering Laws for Relief of the Poor.*

11. Cork Union Board of Guardians, Minute Book no. 16. Minutes of meeting, September 21, 1853, (hereafter cited as CUBG Minute Book). Carroll was later appointed lieutenant governor of London's Greenwich Hospital. *Spectator*, August 4, 1855.

12. Fourteen boys were dispatched to Manchester, but their fate was not a happy one. Most eventually ran away. CUBG Minute Book no. 16, September 28, 1853; O'Mahony, *Cork's Poor Law Palace*, 130–131.

13. CUBG Minute Book no. 16, 17. Weekly report of number of able-bodied adult males remaining in the workhouse, October 1, November 26, 1853.

14. *Cork Examiner*, October 14, 17, 19, 21, 24, 26, 1853.

15. O'Callaghan was presumably referring to Juan Grande, one of the stations on the line, close to Barbacoas.

16. *Cork Constitution*, October 20, 1853.

17. *Cork Examiner*, October 21, 1853.

18. *Cork Examiner*, October 24, 1853. Irish newspaper readers would have been aware that yellow fever in New Orleans earlier that summer had killed approximately 10 percent of its population, many of whom were Irish.

19. *Cork Constitution*, October 25, 1853. The number of deaths related to white workers only and had originally appeared in *New York Herald*, August 9, 1853.

20. *Shipping and Mercantile Gazette*, n.d., reprinted in *Cork Constitution*, October 25, 1853; in *Daily Express* (Dublin), November 1; and in *Cork Examiner*, November 2, 1853.

21. *Cork Constitution*, October 25, 1853. The *Delta* provided no source for this figure, nor did it state whether it related to white workers only or to all employees.

22. *Cork Constitution*, October 27, 1853; *Cork Southern Reporter*, October 27, 1853; *Cork Examiner*, October 28, 1853.

23. *Cork Examiner*, October 28, 1853.

24. CUBG Minute Book no. 16, October 26, 1853.

25. *Cork Constitution*, October 27, 1853. This letter was written in Liverpool, where Center was chartering the *Ben Nevis*, to take the workers to Aspinwall.

26. *Cork Constitution*, October 27, 1853.

27. *Cork Examiner*, October 31, 1853.

28. Ibid., November 2, 1853.

29. *Nation*, n.d., copied by *Limerick Examiner*, n.d., and reprinted in *Cork Examiner*, November 2, 1853.

30. *Waterford News*, November 11, 1853.

31. The item was taken from an unnamed New York paper of October 29, which in turn quoted from *Panama Star*, October 17.

32. *Cork Examiner*, November 18, 1853; *Lloyds Register of British and Foreign Shipping, 1854–1855; Illustrated London News* 21, September 4, 1852; *Freeman's Journal*, September 6, 1852.

33. *Cork Constitution*, November 19, 1853.

34. Ibid., November 24, 1853.

35. Ibid.; CUBG Minute Book no. 16, November 23, 1853.

36. *Cork Southern Reporter*, November 29, 1853.

37. *Cork Constitution*, November 29, 1853.

38. The men's names were Hanlan and Sheehan. *Cork Southern Reporter*, November 29, 1853.

39. *Cork Examiner*, December 7, 1853; see correspondence, October 26, 1853, to December 3, 1853, in CUBG, Incoming Letters from the Poor Law Commissioners. Book no. 10.

40. *Cork Examiner*, December 7, 1853. According to *Cork Southern Reporter*, December 6, 1853, the runaway husbands, with one exception, were sentenced to a month's imprisonment.

41. *Cork Examiner*, December 7, 1853.

42. A fifteen-month period was selected because few able-bodied males would have remained in the workhouse for longer than this.

43. Ten were aged between thirty-one and forty; eight between forty-one and fifty; and four between fifty-one and sixty.

44. O'Mahony, *Famine in Cork City*, 107, quoting from John Arnott, *The Investigation into the Condition of the Children in the Cork Workhouse, with an Analysis of the Evidence* (Cork, 1859), 40.

45. *Cork Southern Reporter*, May 21, 1853, cited by O'Mahony, *Cork's Poor Law Palace*, 196.

46. O'Mahony, *Cork's Poor Law Palace*, 183.

47. Ibid., 294.

48. The rate was 1/6 (1 shilling and 6 pence) per day. *Saunders's News-Letter*, October 24, 1853.

49. For a list of average weekly wages in Poor Law Union areas in the south of Ireland in 1854, see Poor Law Commissioners. Reports to the Poor Law Commission by Assistant Commissioner Burke (1849–1855), April 22, 1854.

50. *Cork Examiner,* December 7, 1853, reported that "upwards of 350" had embarked. *Cork Constitution,* February 7, 1854, gave the number as four hundred. According to *Panama Herald,* January 12, 1854, 360 Irish laborers arrived in the *Ben Nevis.*

51. *Cork Examiner,* December 7, 1853. The reference to those in the last category is puzzling. They may have been soldiers of fortune who suppressed a rising in Pernambuco in 1849 that threatened the unity of Pedro II's Brazilian empire, or they could have fought with Garibaldi in Rio Grande do Sud between 1834 and 1845. Herring, *History of Latin America,* 836; Fagg, *Latin America,* 473.

52. *Cork Constitution,* December 6, 1853.

53. *Cork Examiner,* December 7, 1853.

54. Poor Law Commissioners. Letterbooks. Poor Law Commission to Assistant Commissioner Burke, December 13, 1853.

55. *Cork Constitution,* February 7, and *Waterford News,* February 10, 1854, both reported that one man had died during the voyage.

56. *Panama Herald,* January 12, 1854.

57. *Aspinwall Courier,* January 17, 1854, reprinted in *New York Times,* January 30, 1854.

58. Foreign Office. Petition from Irish Laborers, February 1, 1854. FO288/7.

59. *Panama Herald,* n.d., quoted in *New York Times,* February 11, 1854.

60. *Panama Herald,* January 26, 1854, reprinted in *New York Times,* February 11, 1854.

61. Donald MacDonald, William Perry's clerk, deputized for the absent consul from June 1853 to December 1854. MacDonald's reports to the Foreign Office are infrequent, and usually brief, unlike those of Perry.

62. See appendix 5 for the text of this petition. This document is the only one I have found that was written by Irish laborers working on the Panama railroad.

63. Perry was the son of a former editor of the London *Morning Chronicle* and brother of Sir Erskine Perry, MP. His wife was a member of the Anglo-Irish De Courcy family and a sister of Lord Kinsale. Blanchard, *Markham in Peru,* 5. According to Tomes, Perry had gambled away his inherited fortune before being provided with "the snug retreat of the British Consulate at Panama which is said to bring him in the comfortable return of $20,000 per annum." *Panama in 1855,* 219–220.

64. *Panama Star and Herald,* July 9, 1854, quoting Roderick Random, *San Francisco Herald,* June 13, 1854.

65. Tomes, *Panama in 1855,* 121–122.

66. *Panama Herald,* March 14, 1854.

67. Otis, *Illustrated History,* 35–36.

68. *Cork Examiner,* December 7, 1853; *Panama Herald,* January 26, 1854.

69. Kemble, *Panama Route,* 193; *American Railway Times,* May 25, 1854.

70. This hospital, opened in 1848 under the jurisdiction of the Commissioners of Emigration, received immigrants with noncontagious diseases. The Marine Hospital on Staten Island quarantined immigrants with infectious diseases. Ernst, *Immigrant Life*, 26, 231n12.

71. Purcell, "New York Commissioners of Emigration and Irish Immigrants," 36, citing *Annual Reports of the Commissioners of Emigration of the State of New York, May 5, 1847 to 1860, Inclusive* (New York, 1861), 145.

72. This tax was collected by the Commissioners of Emigration, the body responsible for the welfare of immigrants entering the port. Coleman, *Passage to America*, 265–266.

73. Minutes, Board of Directors, March 24, April 18, 28, 1854.

74. *New York Herald*, May 26, 1854. Both men died on the *Illinois*, en route to New York, one from dysentery and the other from "congestive fever."

75. *New York Times*, August 12, 1854.

76. *Cork Examiner*, September 13, 1854. John Brien's name is not on the list of likely workhouse emigrants in Appendix 3.

77. Tomes, "A Trip on the Panama Railroad," *Harper's New Monthly Magazine* 11, no. 65 (October 1855): 616–622.

78. *Cork Examiner*, May 5, 1858; June 27, 1859.

13. RAILROAD-GOVERNMENT RELATIONS

1. Provincial governors were elected every two years prior to the 1863 constitution, though political instability sometimes produced more frequent changes.

2. *Communication of the Board of Directors to Stockholders, 1853.*

3. *Panama Star,* January 28, 1851.

4. Totten to Stephens, February 8, 1851; *New York Tribune,* February 19, 1851.

5. *New York Tribune,* February 24, 1851.

6. *New York Observer and Chronicle,* May 1, 1851.

7. Boyd to secretary of state, December 11, 1854. For another description of grim prison conditions see letter from A. Hunter to Thomas Ward, in Ward to secretary of state, September 11, 1855. Dispatches from U.S. Consuls in Panama 3 (1854–1855).

8. *Panama Star,* November 9, 1852; *New York Tribune,* October 30, November 13, 1852.

9. Letter from José María Urrutia Aniño, governor of the Province of Panama, to the consuls of the United States, England, Denmark, Portugal, Brazil, Peru, and Ecuador. February 15, 1854. Dispatches from U.S. Consuls in Panama 3 (1854–1855).

10. Totten to Stephens, August 9, 1851; Totten to Spies, December 18, 1851; *New York Herald,* July 24, 1854.

11. Totten to Hoadley, November 12, 1853.

12. Ibid.

13. n.d., reprinted in *Times-Picayune*, November 8, 1853.

14. Totten to Hoadley, November 12, December 30, 1853.

15. Ibid., November 12, 1853.

16. Ibid., December 30, 1853.

17. Ibid.

18. Ibid.

19. McGuinness, *Path of Empire*, 82.

20. "The presence of provincial officials at Limón Bay was negligible." Ibid., 72.

21. Totten to Ludlow, August 11, 1850.

22. *Times-Picayune*, July 1, 1852.

23. The power to alter the original names of places and localities is a characteristic feature of imperial rule, a topic dramatized in Brian Friel's acclaimed play, *Translations*, which deals with the implications of imposing English place-names on the original Gaelic ones in nineteenth-century Ireland.

24. Diego Paredes, as secretary of state for foreign affairs, had signed the contract with Stephens in Bogotá, in April 1850, for the construction of a railroad across the Isthmus.

25. DuVal, *And the Mountains will Move*, 13–14; Minter, *Chagres*, 266–267.

26. Perry to O'Leary, HM Chargé d'Affaires, Bogotá, March 15, 1852. FO289/4; Perry to Foreign Office, March 15, 1852. FO289/5.

27. Bancroft, *California Inter Pocula*, 157.

28. Pim, *Gate of the Pacific*, 217.

29. Bidwell, *Isthmus of Panama*, 127, 133.

30. McGuinness, *Path of Empire*, 10; see also ibid., 82.

31. *Times-Picayune*, January 25, 1854; *New York Herald*, March 12, 1854; *Sydney Morning Herald*, April 20, 1854.

32. *Times-Picayune*, June 29, 1856.

33. *Times*, April 18, May 1, 1854; December 16, 1856.

34. Bowlin to Ward, October 11, 1855. Dispatches from U.S. Consuls in Panama 3 (1854–1855).

35. Bancroft, *History of Central America*, 3: 686.

36. McGuinness, *Path of Empire*, 98–99. For details of the income, expenditure, and deficits of the province of Panama from 1856, see Kalmanovitz, "El Federalismo y la fiscalidad del estado soberano de Panamá, 1850–1886," Table 8, 127.

37. Bancroft, *History of Central America*, 3: 519.

38. Perry to Griffith, HM Chargé d'Affaires, Bogotá, September 7, 1850. FO288/6.

39. Perry to Manuel Díaz, Acting Governor of Panama, March 3, 1851. FO289/4.

40. Corwine to secretary of state, November 14, 1851. Dispatches from U.S. Consuls in Panama 2 (1851–1853).

41. Tracy to Roberts, August 8, 1850, in New York Superior Court, *Heilman v. Roberts*, 233. Tracy asked for twelve Colt revolving rifles; twelve pairs of revolving pistols, dragoon size; twelve pairs of revolving pistols, smaller size; twenty-four bowie knives; one case of power and balls; and two buckshot guns.

42. Capron, *History of California*, 356; *Panama Weekly Star*, January 30, 1854.

43. Castillero, "Ran Runnels," 92; Ward to secretary of state, March 12, 1854. Dispatches from U.S. Consuls in Panama 3 (1854–1855). For an engrossing account of Ward's life, see Humphrey, *Peg Leg: the improbable life of a Texas hero*.

44. Hirsch to secretary of state, August 12, 1854. Dispatches from U.S. Consuls in Colón (1852–1857).

45. Rafael Núñez, *El Porvenir*, November 3, 1857, cited by Ardila, "Los Estados Unidos como aliado natural," 249.

46. *Panama Herald*, March 25, 1854; Fletcher to secretary of state, March 30, 1854. Dispatches from U.S. Consuls in Colón (1852–1857). Fletcher hinted that the British consul was wrongly informing Bogotá that the vigilance committee was composed of American mercenaries, or filibusters.

47. *Aspinwall Courier*, June 20, 1854, cited by *Panama Star and Herald*, June 23, 1854.

48. The victim's stomach had been cut open. *Panama Star and Herald*, July 18, 1854.

49. Ironically, Runnels's own office had been broken into earlier, and eighty dollars and a pair of pistols had been stolen. *Weekly Panama Star*, January 9, 1854.

50. *Panama Star and Herald*, July 18, 1854.

51. Under its 1850 agreement with New Granada, the railroad could propose regulations for the policing and security of its property, subject to approval by Bogotá. Article 26, *Contract between the Republic of New Granada and the Panama Rail-road Company*.

52. For biographical details of Runnels, see Humphrey, "Myth of the Hangman," 5–11; Susto, "La personalidad de Ran Runnels," 97, 99; Arauz, "Ran Runnels," 72–74.

53. *Panama Star and Herald*, July 26, 1854; *New York Times*, October 17, 1857.

54. Zachrisson, consul general for Norway and Sweden, had formerly headed Zachrisson, Nelson & Co., the Pacific Mail Steamship Company's first agents in Panama. He died in October 1855. *Times-Picayune*, October 16, 1855. In 1873, Neira became president of the State of Panama, established by the 1863 Colombian constitution. Delpar, *Red Against Blue*, 86, 88.

55. *Panama Star and Herald*, May 9, July 31, 1854.

56. Bancroft, *California Inter Pocula*, 188.

57. Marryat, *Mountains and Molehills*, 8, 15–16.

58. *Panama Star and Herald*, July 31, August 3, 4, 5, 1854.

59. Minutes, Board of Directors, August 16, 1854.

60. Ibid., October 18, November 14, 1854.

61. Ibid., February 12, 1855; Humphrey, "Myth of the Hangman," 11.

62. *Panama Star and Herald*, August 30, 1854; *Weekly Panama Star and Herald*, September 4, 1854.

63. Humphrey, "Myth of the Hangman," 11.

64. *Weekly Panama Star and Herald*, October 16, 1854. Those attending the meeting were members of Panama City's elite. Humphrey, "Myth of the Hangman," 11.

65. *Weekly Panama Star and Herald*, October 9, 1854. Zachrisson was presented with a gold cigarette case, a silver urn, and a washbasin. Castillero, "Ran Runnels," 95.

66. Bancroft, *History of Central America*, 3: 525n58; Castillero, "Ran Runnels," 91.

67. Humphrey, "Myth of the Hangman," 12.

68. *Panama in 1855*, 122–124.

69. *History of Central America* 3, 519n38.

70. Humphrey, "Myth of the Hangman," 12.

71. *Panama*, 209.

72. According to Humphrey, Bell "had only the slimmest regard for factual accuracy." "Myth of the Hangman," 16.

73. *Chagres*, 246. Urrutia Aniño did not become governor until 1854.

74. *"The Derienni," or, Land Pirates of the Isthmus.* This novella does not mention Runnels or mass executions. Panama's newspapers do not appear to have used the term "Derienni" to refer to criminals in the 1850s.

75. Minter, *Chagres*, 248–249.

76. Conniff, *Panama and the United States*, 28.

77. *New York Herald*, January 11, 1855; *Panama Star and Herald*, June 14, 1855.

78. *Weekly Panama Star and Herald*, April 9, 1855.

79. PRC Bank Ledger, 203; Minutes, Board of Directors, November 14, 1854.

80. Robinson, *Panama*, 208–210. This illustrated the close links between the railroad and the U.S. administration.

81. He died of consumption in Rivas, Nicaragua, in 1882, aged fifty-two. Humphrey, "Myth of the Hangman," 5; *Weekly Panama Star and Herald*, August 21, October 9, 1854; *Times-Picayune*, September 17, 1854, April 30, 1859, January 13, 1860; *Panama Star and Herald*, July 22, 1882, cited by Bancroft, *History of Central America* 3, 519n38.

82. Lino de Pombo O'Donnell, New Granada's secretary of state, recalled that when Panama's governor was conversing with the U.S. consul, an American stepped up to the governor and knocked his hat off, exclaiming, "Take off your hat, sir, when you address the American consul." *Times-Picayune*, March 19, 1857.

83. Woodward, *Manifest Destinies*, xii, 103, 189.

84. This remained the situation until 1867, when a new contract was signed between the railroad company and New Granada that was more to Bogotá's advantage. Robinson, *Panama*, 43–46.

85. Scott, review of *Mobility and Modernity*: 881.

14. THE AFTERMATH

1. *Times*, March 6, 1855.

2. Wolmar, *Great Railway Revolution*, 58, 59; Ambrose, *Nothing Like It*, 26.

3. Tomes, *Panama in 1855*, 128, citing *New York Tribune*, March 13, 1855. See also *Panama Star and Herald*, June 14, 1855.

4. Totten's report to the PRC directors in *Panama Star and Herald*, October 23, 1855.

5. Otis, *Illustrated History*, 145; *Panama Star and Herald*, May 10, 1855; June 14, 1855; March 1, 1856; March 6, 1856.

6. Minutes, Board of Directors, June 1, 1855.

7. J. Rogers, president of the Electro-Interoceanic Company of the Isthmus of Panama and G. J. Hubert Sanders were granted a telegraph concession in 1852 but do not appear to have proceeded. *Times-Picayune*, March 10, September 10, 1852.

8. *Panama Star and Herald*, August 14, 1855; *New York Herald*, August 26, 1855. The transcontinental telegraph across the United States was not completed until October 1861.

9. *New York Times*, April 17, 1856.

10. *Times-Picayune*, June 11, 1856.

11. *New York Times*, September 2, 1859, citing Hoadley to House of Commons Select Committee on Packet and Telegraphic Contracts, August 9, 1859.

12. Kemble, *Panama Route*, 193.

13. *New York Times*, May 14, 1858.

14. Sheldon, "History of Construction of the Panama Railroad," 8; Bidwell, *Isthmus of Panama*, 311.

15. LaRosa and Mejia, *United States Discovers Panama*, 10, 36; *Times-Picayune*, June 13, 1857. The bridge had six one-hundred-foot spans. Robinson, *Panama*, 135.

16. "History: Construction of the First Transcontinental Railroad," Panama Canal Railway, accessed May 13, 2020, http://www.panarail.com/en/history/index.html.

17. This building was badly damaged by an explosion while nitroglycerine was being unloaded from a ship in 1866. Robinson, *Panama*, 84.

18. *New York Times*, December 1, 1857.

19. *Times-Picayune*, June 29, 1856.

20. *Waterford News*, June 20, 1856, reported that ten Irish people were killed. See also *New York Times*, May 17, July 10, 1856 and *Maine Farmer*, June 5, 1856 for

the names of some of the deceased; Boyd to the state department, May 7, 19, 1856. Dispatches from U.S. Consuls in Colón (1852–1857). Otis failed to mention this accident in his history of the railroad.

21. In 1853 there were 138 railroad accidents in the United States with 264 people killed and 496 wounded. *New York Herald*, December 30, 1853. *American Railroad Journal* 10, no. 15 (April 15, 1854): 237, reported that 262 people were killed in railroad accidents in the United States and 624 wounded between January 1853 and March 1854.

22. Robinson, *Panama*, 107–108.

23. *New York Times*, July 17, 1858; Robinson, *Panama*, 62–63.

24. *New York Herald*, July 2, 1853; *Communication of the Board of Directors to Stockholders, 1853*, 9.

25. Kemble, *Panama Route*, 187; *Harper's New Monthly Magazine* 10, no. 55 (December 1854): 50.

26. *Panama Star and Herald*, October 23, 1855, citing Totten's report to the railroad's directors in May 1855, stated that the town had a population of two thousand. *Sydney Morning Herald*, March 18, 1854, gave the population in 1853 as three thousand. Tomes, *Panama in 1855*, 55, 58, reported that the town had only one hundred houses and eight hundred inhabitants.

27. Fletcher to secretary of state, January 16, 1856. Dispatches from U.S. Consuls in Colón (1852–1857).

28. Trollope, *West Indies*, 245.

29. Bancroft, *California Inter Pocula*, 159. For more favorable views of Aspinwall, see letters from "L.H.E." in *Times-Picayune*, June 11, 1853, and from "Amigo" in ibid., June 29, 1856.

30. *Panama in 1855*, 64.

31. According to the construction account, expenditure to March 31, 1855, was $5,047,934.52 and rose to $8,010,526.53 by December 20, 1858. PRC Bank Ledger, 126–129; 226–231. According to Minutes, Board of Directors, March 4, 1859, expenditure to January 1855 amounted to $6 million.

32. Between 1850 and 1900, the cost of building railroads throughout the world varied between $15,000 and $40,000 per mile. Grigore, *Presidents of Panama Railroad Company*, 157. Aguirre, *Mobility and Modernity*, 30, claimed that the construction cost would amount to billions of dollars in 2009 terms, but $250 million by 2020 is probably more accurate, taking inflation into account.

33. Johnson, *Sights in the Gold Region*, 48.

34. *New York Times*, April 30, 1855.

35. Ibid., November 6, 1855, citing a report from the London *Morning Chronicle*, n.d.

36. *Sydney Morning Herald*, January 14, 1860.

37. Annual Reports, Panama Railroad Company, 1852–1951; Bidwell, *Isthmus of Panama*, 278.

38. *Rails*, 201–202.

39. *Times*, May 29, 1860.

40. *Annual Report of the Panama Railroad Company, 1868.*

41. Minter, *Chagres*, 282, 288.

42. Edwards, *Panama: the Canal, the Country and the People*, 428.

43. *Sydney Morning Herald*, March 22, 1860.

44. Grigore, *Influence of the United States Navy*, 23, 27; Kemble, *Panama Route*, 196; *A Collection of Pamphlets, Circulars, Newspaper Clippings, Maps, etc., relating to the Panama Railroad Company*, 295.

45. Von Hagen, "Blazing the Trail," 6.

46. J. Finner to David Hoadley, December 17, 1859, *Times-Picayune*, January 15, 1860.

47. *Manchester Guardian*, April 20, 1858; Bidwell, *Isthmus of Panama*, 306. British bondholders had invested £569,800 (approximately $2.85 million) in the railroad by 1868. Rippy, "British Investments in Latin America," 15.

48. *Weekly Panama Star and Herald*, November 27, 1854.

49. Kemble, *Panama Route*, 196; McCullough, "Steam Road," 6.

50. Coal transported by rail across the Isthmus sold in Panama City for seventeen dollars per ton, while coal shipped via Cape Horn cost twenty-five dollars per ton. *Sydney Morning Herald*, July 9, 1856. Robinson claimed that the railroad's failure to purchase sufficient coal cars led to the loss of a $100,000 contract with the Pacific Mail Steamship Company. *Panama*, 39.

51. Stiles, *First Tycoon*, 215.

52. Filibustering was a term used to describe nineteenth-century armed invasions of Latin American territory by American citizens with the hope of annexing those lands to the United States. Gobat, *Confronting the American Dream*, 2, 26, 29–30; Stiles, *First Tycoon*, 271.

53. Stiles, *First Tycoon*, 279.

54. May, *Manifest Destiny*, 202.

55. Members of Walker's forces captured with arms were frequently executed. This was the fate of nineteen men, including five from Ireland, shot at Santa Rosa, Costa Rica, on March 25, 1856. *Waterford News*, May 16, 23, 1856.

56. *Harper's New Monthly Magazine* 14, no. 84 (May 1857): 837.

57. May, *Manifest Destiny*, 244. See also Trollope, *West Indies*, 356.

58. Kemble, *Panama Route*, Appendix II, Number of Passengers via Nicaragua, 254.

59. Stiles, *First Tycoon*, 315.

60. *Panama Star and Herald*, August 23, 1855.

61. May, *Manifest Destiny*, 19, 46–47, 312n61.

62. Robinson, *Panama*, 24. Passenger fares in the United States in the 1850s varied from 2.5 cents to 5 cents per mile. Wolmar, *Blood, Iron and Gold*, 85.

63. *New York Tribune*, February 26, 1855; *New York Herald*, February 28, 1855.

64. *New York Times*, May 17, 1858. The railroad was 47.5 miles long.

65. *Weekly Panama Star & Herald*, March 26, 1855; Kemble, *Panama Route*, 199. There was a shortage of coinage in California until the opening in San Francisco of the U.S. Mint in 1854. Specie had to be brought in from eastern states via Panama. Delgado, *To California by Sea*, 66.

66. The firm of Zachrisson and Nelson charged over $5,000 for delivering one shipment of $2 million in specie across the Isthmus in 1850. New York Superior Court, Heilman v. Roberts, 230.

67. *Panama Star*, February 26, 1853.

68. The United States, United Kingdom, France, Sweden, Norway, Belgium, Denmark, Portugal, Brazil, Chile, Peru, Ecuador, and Mexico.

69. *Weekly Panama Star and Herald*, January 22, 1855; *Panama Star and Herald*, September 4, 1855.

70. *New York Times*, September 13, 1855.

71. *Panama Star and Herald*, December 29, 1855.

72. *Weekly Panama Star and Herald*, March 26, 1855.

73. Ward to secretary of state, October 2, 1855. Dispatches from US Consuls in Panama 3 (1854–1855).

74. According to Bell, Oliver was "a drunken, turbulent Irishman, who had given considerable trouble in the steerage of the New York steamer." *Reminiscences of a Ranger*, 360. Humphrey questioned Bell's reliability. "Myth of the Hangman," 16.

75. For a comprehensive analysis of these events and the background to them, see McGuinness, *Path of Empire*, 126–151. *Harper's New Monthly Magazine* 13, no. 73 (June 1856): 118–119, provided a succinct account of the incident.

76. October 7, 1856.

77. *New York Times*, September 23, 1856.

78. *Times-Picayune*, March 19, 1857. Colombia eventually paid over $412,000 in reparations to the American government for the deaths, injuries, and damages caused to its citizens and their property. Minter, *Chagres*, 253; McGuinness, "Aquellos Tiempos," 155; Grigore, *Influence of the United States Navy*, 27.

79. Ambrose provides an account of this unprecedented engineering feat in *Nothing Like It in the World*.

80. *New York Times*, December 4, 1892, provided a summary of the railroad's history from 1855 to 1892.

81. *Panama*, 33–34, 107. Robinson was accused in 1874 of misappropriating company funds. He blamed a bookkeeper for not keeping proper accounts and was exonerated from all charges by the board of directors. *A Collection of Pamphlets*, 268; Robinson, *Panama*, 131.

82. *Panama Star and Herald*, June 14, 1855.

83. *New York Times*, June 6, 1869.

84. Edwards, *Panama*, 428; Robinson, *Panama*, 54–58.

85. A rail ticket across the United States in 1869 cost $173. Wiltsee, *Gold Rush Steamers*, 312. The advertised cost later dropped to $70 while the price of a passage from New York to San Francisco via Panama was only $50. *A Collection of Pamphlets*, 99, 187.

86. Wolmar, *Great Railway Revolution*, 220. Passengers had to purchase multiple tickets for use on different company lines and were obliged to change trains several times. The United States did not establish a national rail company for another century.

87. Robinson, *Panama*, 43–46.

88. McCullough, *Path Between the Seas*, 136. The railroad's office continued to be located in New York City during the period of French ownership.

89. The following year the American government purchased the remaining railroad shares from private owners.

90. The breeding sites of the *aedes aegypti* mosquito, the yellow fever vector, were eliminated in much of the Isthmus thanks to the sanitation work of American expert Dr. William Gorgas. McNeill, *Mosquito Empires*, 308–312.

91. McCullough, "Steam Road," 7.

92. Moore, "Mosquitoes, Malaria and Cold Butter," 11.

93. McCullough, "Steam Road," 8.

94. An attempt to resurrect the railroad in the 1990s forms the basis of a novel by Michael Conniff entitled *The Great Panama Railroad Caper* (2020).

CONCLUSION

1. Cuba, with 359 miles of track, largely servicing the sugar industry, was exceptional in the Central American and Caribbean region. *Littell's Living Age* 44, no. 566 (March 31, 1855): 789.

2. Canned foods had been in existence for several decades, but I have found no record of their use by the railroad in the 1850s.

3. *Friends' Intelligencer*, April 21, 1855. British and French armies laid siege to the Crimean stronghold of Sevastopol in September 1854, and the Russian fortress fell one year later.

4. There was considerable historical justification for these views. McNeill, *Mosquito Empires*, 101, 119–121, 132, 143, 189.

5. Elder and Shaughnessy, *Greatest Events*, 33.

6. Kemble, *Panama Route*, 148.

7. Ibid., 207–208; Somerville, *Aspinwall Empire*, 76.

8. Ambrose, *Nothing Like It*, 19, 301. Less urgent construction material was shipped around Cape Horn, a cheaper though slower supply route.

9. Wolmar, *Blood, Iron and Gold*, 126.

10. Ibid., 129.

11. Scott, *Americans in Panama*, 35; *U.S. Interstate Committee. Report of Subcommittee on PRC*, 131–132; Meditz and Hanratty, *Panama: A Country Study*, 19; Robinson, *Panama*, 112.

12. Somerville, *Aspinwall Empire*, 105.

13. Bidwell, *Isthmus of Panama*, 84.

14. Ibid., 100–101, 308.

15. Pim, *Gate of the Pacific*, 4, 7.

16. Johnson, *Sights in the Gold Region*, 78. The decline in Britain's political power in Central America was counterbalanced by its considerable economic and commercial influence arising from growing trade and investments in the region.

17. Between 1856 and 1903, the U.S. military intervened fourteen times in Panama. Greene, *Canal Builders*, 313.

18. In terms of its legal status, the present railroad is regarded as a contiguous in-bond corridor where cargo can be transshipped duty-free from coast to coast. See "Freight Service: In-Bond Railway Corridor," Panama Canal Railway, accessed May 13, 2020, http://www.panarail.com/en/cargo.

19. The expansion of the Panama Canal, completed in 2016, has given birth to a new class of larger ships called New Panamax or Neo-Panamax vessels, up to 427 meters long, capable of passing through the Panama Canal's locks. Super-Panamax ships are even larger. They constitute about a fifth of the world's container fleet but carry half of all shipping cargo. On the Canal expansion, see Conniff and Bigler, *Modern Panama*, 200–201, 222–229, 317–319.

20. Bishop, *Panama Gateway*, 47.

21. Otis, *Illustrated History*, 32.

22. Heald, *Picturesque Panama*, 90.

APPENDIX 2

1. This amount probably includes passages undertaken throughout the twenty-month period from January 1850 to August 1851.

2. This figure was arrived at by deducting the 360 workers from Cork from the overall estimate of 6,000 white railroad employees.

APPENDIX 4

1. Gorgas, *Population and Deaths from Various Diseases*. Gorgas was in charge of sanitation during the U.S. canal construction period.

2. The 1885–89 death rate in Aspinwall (Colón) on the unhealthier Caribbean coast was estimated at 96.5 per thousand. Maurer and Yu, "What Roosevelt Took," 39, table 15.

3. Simmons, *Malaria in Panama*, 15.

4. This is a more-or-less informed guess based on the limited statistical data available.

5. Jaén Suárez, *La Población del Istmo de Panamá*, 505, table 15, arrived at an average mortality rate of 60.73 per thousand for 1881–1889.

6. McCullough, *Path between the Seas*, 610; Parker, *Hell's Gorge*, xvii, 376; Gibson, *Physician to the World*, 191; Ireland, "Gorgas," 54; McNeill, *Mosquito Empires*, 309.

7. Conniff, *Panama and the United States*, 210n26; Parker, *Hell's Gorge*, 118.

8. McCullough, quoting the *New York Tribune*, reported a hospital mortality rate of 75 percent. *Path between the Seas*, 172.

9. Enock, *Panama Canal*, 150.

10. McNeill, *Mosquito Empires*, 309.

11. Bunau-Varilla, *Panama*, 44.

APPENDIX 5

1. This is almost certainly John Twomey, forty-six, described as an able-bodied mendicant in the Cork workhouse records, who sailed for Panama in the *Ben Nevis* in December 1853.

2. Foreign Office. Petition from Irish Laborers, February 1, 1854. FO288/7.

Bibliography

Manuscript and Archival Sources

WASHINGTON, DC

U.S. National Archives and Records Administration

Panama Railroad Company: Record Group 0185.

Annual Reports of the Panama Railroad Company. 1852–1951.

Letters from G. M. Totten. 1849–1853.

Minutes of the Meetings of the Board of Directors of the Panama Railroad Company. June 7, 1849–June 24, 1861.

Minutes of the Meetings of the Executive and Finance Committee of the Board of Directors of the Panama Railroad Company. July 9, 1849–June 1906.

Scott Report on the Panama Railroad Company. 1897. Panama Railroad Company. Legal and Fiscal Documents. 1848–1916.

United States Department of State. Dispatches from United States Consuls in Panama. 1823–1906: Microfilm M139, boxes 1–3.

Vol. 1. April 7, 1823–December 20, 1850.

Vol. 2. January 1, 1851–December 17, 1853.

Vol. 3. January 10, 1854–December 15, 1855.

Dispatches from United States Consuls in Colón: Microfilm T193, roll 1. July 10, 1852–December 19, 1857.

Library of Congress. Manuscript Division

Panama Collection of the Canal Zone Library-Museum.

Isthmian Historical Society. "Notes on a Trip to Colon." Container 26.

Panama Railroad Company. Contracts, Regulations, Timetables and Train Rules. Container 31.

Panama Railroad Company. Bank Ledger, 1849–1862. Container 32.

Library of Congress

Miscellaneous Pamphlets AC901 M5 Vol. 325.

NEW YORK

New York Public Library

A Collection of Pamphlets, Circulars, Newspaper Clippings, Maps, etc., relating to the Panama Railroad Company, the Shipping in the West Indies, and the Pacific Mail Company, mounted in One Scrapbook. 1849 to 1893.

LONDON

U.K. National Archives (Kew)

Foreign Office. Consulate, Panama.
General Correspondence. 1840–1854. FO288/5.
General Correspondence. 1845–1850. FO288/6.
General Correspondence. 1852–1854. FO288/7.
Letter Books. 1838–1851. FO289/3.
Letter Books. Miscellaneous. 1850–1854. FO289/4.
Letter Books. Miscellaneous. 1851–1854. FO289/5.
Letter Books. Miscellaneous. 1854–1856. FO289/6.

DUBLIN

National Archives of Ireland

Chief Secretary's Office Registered Papers 1853. Vol. 105.
Chief Secretary's Office Registered Papers 1854/5080.
Poor Law Commissioners. Letterbooks. Poor Law Commission to Assistant Commissioner Burke. 1852–1855. Ref. no. 244043.
Poor Law Commissioners. Reports to the Poor Law Commission by Assistant Commissioner Burke. 1849–1855. Ref. no. 244046.

CORK

Cork City and County Archives

Cork Union Board of Guardians.
General Ledgers. BG/69/CA.
No. 9. March 25, 1853–March 25, 1855.
Minute Books. BG/69/A.
No. 16. June 22, 1853–November 30, 1853.
No. 17. December 7, 1853–May 17, 1854.

Indoor Relief Registers. BG/69/G. Microfilm.

No. 7. February 25, 1852–March 25, 1853.

No. 8. March 26, 1853–November 13, 1854.

Index Books to Indoor Relief Registers. BG/69/GX

No. 8. March 25, 1853–November 13, 1854.

Incoming Letters from the Poor Law Commissioners and Local Government
    Board. BG/69/BC

Book No. 10. January 3, 1853–December 30, 1853.

Book No. 11. January 7, 1854–December 30, 1854.

Board of Guardians Outgoing Letter Books. BG/69/B

No. 1. June 19, 1839–April 6, 1854.

Visiting Committee Report Books. BG/69/FM

No. 1. November 8, 1847–July 19, 1865.

Newspapers, Journals, Periodicals, Magazines
PANAMA

Panama Star
Daily Panama Star
Weekly Panama Star
Panama Herald
Daily Panama Star and Herald
Weekly Panama Star and Herald
La Estrella de Panama (Spanish language supplement of *Daily Panama Star and
    Herald*)

IRELAND

Cork Constitution
Cork Examiner
Cork Southern Reporter
Daily Express
Freeman's Journal
Nation
Saunders's News-Letter and Daily Advertiser
Waterford News

GREAT BRITAIN AND COLONIES

Chambers's Edinburgh Journal
Illustrated London News
Manchester Guardian
Observer
Spectator
Sydney Morning Herald
Times

UNITED STATES

American Architect and Building News
American Railroad Journal
American Railway Times
American Whig Review
Boston Herald
Brockport Republic
Charleston Mercury
Daily Dispatch
Daily Picayune
Evening Post
Flag of Our Union
Friends' Intelligencer
Harper's New Monthly Magazine
Home Journal
International Magazine of Literature, Art and Science
Irish American
Liberator
Littell's Living Age
Louisville Daily Journal
Maine Farmer
New Orleans Crescent
New York Freeman's Journal and Catholic Register
New York Herald
New York Observer and Chronicle
New York Times
New York Tribune
New York Weekly Herald
Putnam's Monthly Magazine of American Literature, Science and Art

Scientific American: The Advocate of Industry, and Journal of Scientific, Mechanical and Other Improvements
Spirit of the Times
Times-Picayune

Printed Primary Sources

Abbott, Willis J. *Panama and the Canal in Picture and Prose*. London & New York: Syndicate Publishing, 1913.

A Sketch of Events in the Life of George Law Published in Advance of His Biography. Also Extracts from the Public Journals. New York: J. C. Derby, 1855.

Badeau, Adam. "General Grant." *The Century: A Popular Quarterly* 30, no. 1 (May 1885): 151–163.

Bancroft, Hubert Howe. *History of Central America. Vol. 3, 1801–1887*. San Francisco: History Company, 1887.

———. *California Inter Pocula. The Works of Hubert Howe Bancroft*. Vol. 35. San Francisco: The History Company, 1888.

Barker, Charles Albro, ed., *Memoirs of Elisha Oscar Crosby. Reminiscences of California and Guatemala from 1849 to 1864*. San Marino, CA: Huntington Library, 1945.

Bates, D. B. *Incidents on Land and Water. Four Years on the Pacific Coast*. 8th ed. Boston: published by the author, 1860.

Bell, Horace. *Reminiscences of a Ranger, or Early Times in Southern California*. Los Angeles: Yarnell, Caystile and Mathes, Printers, 1881.

Bennett, Ira E. *History of the Panama Canal, Its Construction and Builders*. Washington, DC: Historical Publishing Company, 1915.

Bidwell, Charles Toll. *The Isthmus of Panama*. London: Chapman & Hall, 1865.

Bishop, Joseph Bucklin. *The Panama Gateway*. New York: Charles Scribner's Sons, 1913.

Blanchard, Peter, ed. *Markham in Peru. The Travels of Clements R. Markham, 1852–1853*. Austin: University of Texas Press, 1991.

Brooks, Sarah Merriam. *Across the isthmus to California in '52*. San Francisco, CA: Murdock & Co., 1894.

Buel, William P. "On 'Chagres Fever' and some of the other diseases to which Californian emigrants are liable." *American Journal of the Medical Sciences* 62 (April 1856).

Bunau-Varilla, Philippe. *Panama: The Creation, Destruction and Resurrection*. New York: McBride, Nast & Co, 1914.

Capron, E. S. *History of California from its Discovery to the Present Time*. Boston: John P. Jewett & Co., 1854.

Cole, Cornelius. "To California via Panama in 1852." *Annual Publication of the Historical Society of Southern California* 9, no. 3 (1914): 163–172.

Colonial Land and Emigration Commission, 1855. Fifteenth general report of the Colonial Land and Emigration Commissioners. Session 1854–55. Command Paper no. 1953. London: Eyre & Spottiswoode for HMSO, 1855.

Communication of the Board of Directors of the Panama Railroad Company to the Stockholders together with the Report of the Chief Engineer to the Directors. New York: John F. Trow, Printer, 1853.

Communication of the Board of Directors of the Panama Railroad Company to the Stockholders. New York, 1855.

Contract between the Republic of New Granada and the Panama Rail-Road Company, embracing the amendments applied for by the company, and adopted by the Act of Congress at Bogota, of June 4th 1850. New York: Lambert and Lane, stationers and printers, 1850.

Cullen, Edward. *The Isthmus of Darien Ship Canal.* London: Effingham Wilson, 1852.

Edwards, Albert. *Panama: The Canal, the Country and the People.* New York: Macmillan, 1911.

Enock, C. Reginald. *The Panama Canal: Its Past, Present and Future.* London & Glasgow: Collins, n.d. [1914].

Fabens, Joseph W. *A Story of Life on the Isthmus.* New York: George P. Putnam & Co., 1853.

Foreign Office List Containing Diplomatic and Consular Appointments, etc., January 1858. London: Harrison & Son, 1858.

Gisborne, Lionel. *The Isthmus of Darien in 1852. Journal of the Expedition of Inquiry for the Junction of the Atlantic and Pacific Oceans.* London: Saunders and Stanford, 1853.

Gorgas, William Crawford. *Population and Deaths from Various Diseases in the City of Panama, by Months and Years, from November, 1883, to August 1906. Number of Employees and Deaths from Various Diseases Among Employees of the French Canal Companies, by Months and Years, from January, 1881, to April, 1904.* Washington: Government Printing Office, 1906.

———. *Sanitation in Panama.* New York & London: D. Appleton & Co., 1915.

Grant, Ulysses S. *Personal Memoirs of U.S. Grant.* New York: Penguin, 1999. First published in the United States in two volumes, 1885 and 1886.

Greenfield, Mary C. "'From St. Louis to San Francisco in 1850,' by J. E. Clark." *Historical Society of Southern California* 1, no. 5 (1890): 27–32, reprinted in *Southern California Quarterly* 95, no. 4 (Winter 2013): 380–390.

Griswold, C. D. *The Isthmus of Panama and What I Saw There.* New York: Dewitt and Davenport, 1852.

Haskin, Frederick J. *The Panama Canal*. Garden City, New York: Doubleday Page & Company, 1913.

Heald, Jean Sadler. *Picturesque Panama. The Panama Railroad. The Panama Canal*. Panama: Maduro, 1928.

Johnson, Theodore Taylor. *Sights in the Gold Region and Scenes by the Way*. 2nd ed. New York: Baker & Scribner, 1850.

Johnson, Willis Fletcher. *Four Centuries of the Panama Canal*. New York: Henry Holt & Company, 1906.

Kip, William Ingraham. *The Early Days of My Episcopate*. New York: Thomas Whittaker, 1892.

Lidell, John A. "Upon the Medical Topography and Diseases of the Isthmus of Panama." *New York Journal of Medicine and Collateral Sciences* 8, no. 2 (March 1852): 242–259.

Liot, W. B. *Panama, Nicaragua and Tehuantepec; or Considerations upon the Question of Communication between the Atlantic and Pacific Oceans*. London: Simpkin & Marshall, 1849.

Lloyd, John Augustus. "Account of Levellings carried across the Isthmus of Panama, to ascertain the relative height of the Pacific Ocean at Panama and of the Atlantic at the mouth of the river Chagres; accompanied by Geographical and Topographical Notices of the Isthmus. Read, November 26, 1829." *Philosophical Transactions of the Royal Society of London* 120, (1830): 59–68. http://royalsocietypublishing.org/doi/10.1098/rstl.1830.0004.

Lloyds Register of British and Foreign Shipping from 1st July, 1854 to the 30th June, 1855. London: Cox & Wyman, 1854.

Maguire, John Francis. *The Irish in America*. London: Longmans, Green, 1868. Reprinted New York: Arno Press & The New York Times, 1969.

Manning, William R. *Diplomatic Correspondence of the United States. Inter-American Affairs 1831–1860*. Vol. 3, *Central America 1831–1850. Documents 723–995*. Vol. 4, *Central America 1851–1860. Documents 996–1578*. Washington, DC: Carnegie Endowment for International Peace, 1933–34.

Marryat, Frank. *Mountains and Molehills or Recollections of a Burnt Journal*. London: Longman, Brown, Green & Longmans, 1855.

Memorial of the Panama Rail-Road Company to the Congress of the United States, 10th December, 1849. Appendix. Memorial of Messrs. Aspinwall, Stephens & Chauncey, presented at the last session of Congress. New York: Van Norden & Amerman, Printers, 1850.

Nelson, Wolfred. *Five Years at Panama. The Trans-Isthmian Canal*. London: Sampson Low, Marston, Searle & Rivington, 1891.

New York, Superior Court. *William Heilman v. Marshall O. Roberts*. New York: Wynkoop, Hallenbeck & Thomas, Printers, 1861.

Notes Respecting the Isthmus of Panama. Communicated by J.A. Lloyd. n.p., 1831. Library of Congress Miscellaneous Pamphlets AC901M5, Vol. 325.

Osborne, John. *Guide to the Madeiras, Azores, British and Foreign West Indies, Mexico, and Northern South-America, etc.* 5th ed. London: Walton & Mitchell Printers, 1847.

Otis, F. N. *Illustrated History of the Panama Railroad.* 2nd ed. New York: Harper & Brothers, 1862.

Peacock, George. *Notes on the Isthmus of Panama and Darien, also on the River St. Juan, Lakes of Nicaragua with reference to a railroad and canal for joining the Atlantic and Pacific Oceans.* Exeter: W. Pollard, 1879.

Pfeiffer, Ida. *A Lady's Second Journey Round the World.* Vol. 2. London: Longman, Brown, Green & Longmans, 1855.

Pim, Bedford. *The Gate of the Pacific.* London: Lovell Reeve & Co., 1863.

Richards, Benjamin B., ed. *California Gold Rush Merchant. The Journal of Stephen Chapin Davis.* San Marino, CA: Huntington Library, 1956.

Robinson, Tracy. *Panama: A Personal Record of Forty-Six Years, 1861–1907.* New York and Panama: Star and Herald Company, 1907. Reprinted, Kessingers, n.d.

Scott, William R. *The Americans in Panama.* New York: Statler Publishing Co., 1912.

Sixth Annual Report of the Commissioners for Administering the Laws for Relief of the Poor in Ireland. Dublin: Alexander Thom, printer, May 1853.

Slater's Royal National Commercial Directory of Ireland. Manchester & London: Isaac Slater, 1856.

Taylor, Bayard. *Eldorado; or Adventures in the Path of Empire.* Vol. 1. London: Richard Bentley, 1850.

"*The Derienni,*" *or, Land Pirates of the Isthmus.* New Orleans: A. R. Orton, 1853.

Tomes, Robert. *Panama in 1855. An account of the Panama railroad, of the cities of Panama and Aspinwall, with sketches of life and character on the Isthmus.* New York: Harper & Brothers, 1855. The Michigan Historical Reprint Series. Scholarly Publishing Office of the University of Michigan University Library, n.d.

Tripler, Eunice. *Eunice Tripler. Some Notes of Her Personal Recollections.* New York: Grafton, 1910.

Trollope, Anthony. *The West Indies and the Spanish Main.* New York: Harper & Brothers, 1860.

Tyson, James L. *Diary of a Physician in California; Being the Results of Actual Experience, including Notes of the Journey by Land and Water and Observations on the Climate, Soil, Resources of the Country, etc.* New York: D. Appleton & Co., 1850.

United States Interstate and Foreign Commerce Committee. *Report of Subcommittee of Committee on Interstate and Foreign Commerce on Investigation of Affairs of Panama Railroad Company. 384303.* Washington, DC: Government Printing Office, 1905.

Walter, Carrie Stevens. "A Panama Riot." *Overland Monthly and Out West Magazine* 4, no. 24 (December 1884): 635–640.

Wheelwright, William. *Observations on the Isthmus of Panama; as comprised in a paper read at a meeting of the Royal Geographical Society on the evening of the 12th February 1844*. London: John Weale, 1844.

Wyse, Lucien Napoleon Bonaparte. *Le Canal de Panama. L'Isthme Americain. Explorations; Comparaison des Traces Etudies; Negociations; Etat des Travaux*. Paris: Hachette, 1886.

Secondary Sources

Aguirre, Robert D. *Mobility and Modernity: Panama in the Nineteenth-Century Anglo-American Imagination*. Columbus: Ohio State University Press, 2017.

Alfaro, Ana. "La ruta del oro." *Istmo* (Panama) I, no. 1 (August–September 2004): 22–26.

Ambrose, Stephen E. *Nothing Like It in the World. The Men Who Built the Transcontinental Railroad 1863–1869*. New York: Simon & Schuster, 2000.

Anbinder, Tyler. *Five Points: the 19th-century New York City neighborhood that invented tap dance, stole elections and became the world's most notorious slum*. New York: Free Press, 2010.

Arauz, Celestino Andrés. "El ferrocarril transísmico durante la fiebre de oro." *Ellas* (Panamá), no. 594 (June 8, 2001).

———. "Ran Runnels y el bandolerismo en Panamá." *Ellas*, no. 598 (July 6, 2001).

Ardila, Daniel Gutierrez. "Los Estados Unidos como aliado natural y como aliado peligroso de la Nueva Granada (1810–1865)." *Co-herencia: Revista de Humanidades* 13, no. 25 (July–December 2016): 231–260.

Barima, Kofi Boukman. "Caribbean Migrants in Panama and Cuba, 1851–1927: The Struggles, Opposition and Resistance of Jamaicans of African Ancestry." *Journal of Pan African Studies* 5, no. 9 (March 2013): 43–62.

Barrett, Hannah G., Julie M. Jones, and Grant R. Bigg. "Reconstructing El Niño Southern Oscillation using data from ships' logbooks, 1815–1854." Part II. *Climate Dynamics* 50, no. 9–10 (May 2018): 3131–3152.

Bayor, Ronald H. and Timothy J. Meagher, eds. *The New York Irish*. Baltimore & London: Johns Hopkins University Press, 1997.

Bayoumi, Moustafa. "Moving Beliefs. The Panama Manuscript of Sheikh Sana See and African Diasporic Islam." *Interventions: International Journal of Postcolonial Studies* 5, no. 1 (January 2003): 58–81.

Bourne, Peter. *The Golden Road*. New York: G. P. Putnam's Sons, 1951.

Brehony, Margaret. "Irish Railroad Workers in Cuba: Towards a Research Agenda." *Irish Migration Studies in Latin America* 5, no. 3 (November 2007): 183–188.

Brennan, Patrick. "Getting Out of Crescent City: Irish Immigration and the Yellow Fever Epidemic of 1853." *Louisiana History: Journal of the Louisiana Historical Association* 52, no. 2 (Spring 2011): 189–205.

Bryan, Patrick. "The Settlement of the Chinese in Jamaica: 1854–c. 1970." *Caribbean Quarterly* 50, no. 2 (June 2004):15–25.

Campbell, Malcolm. *Ireland's New Worlds: Immigrants, Politics and Society in the United States and Australia, 1815–1922.* Madison: University of Wisconsin Press, 2008.

Campbell, Persia Crawford. *Chinese Coolie Emigration to Countries within the British Empire.* London: P. S. King & Son, 1923.

Castillero R., Ernesto J. *El Ferrocarril de Panamá y su Historia.* Panamá: Imprenta Nacional, 1932.

———. "Ran Runnels en la ruta de 'El Dorado.'" *Revista Lotería* (Panamá), no. 23 (October 1957): 88–96.

Chen P., Berta Alicia "De la China a Panamá." *Revista Cultural Lotería* (Panamá), no. 459 (March–April 2005): 87–120.

Chernow, Ron. *Grant.* London: Head of Zeus, 2018.

Cohen, Lucy M. "The Chinese of the Panama Railroad: Preliminary Notes on the Migrants of 1854 Who 'Failed.'" *Ethnohistory* 18, no. 4 (Autumn 1971): 309–320.

Coleman, Terry. *Passage to America. A History of Emigrants from Great Britain and Ireland to America in the Mid-Nineteenth Century.* Harmondsworth, Middlesex: Penguin Books, 1974.

———. *The Railway Navvies. A History of the Men Who Made the Railways.* London: Pimlico, 2000.

Conniff, Michael L. *Panama and the United States: The End of the Alliance.* 3rd ed. Athens: University of Georgia Press, 2012.

———. *The Great Panama Railroad Caper.* Self-published, 2020.

Conniff, Michael L., and Gene E. Bigler, *Modern Panama: From Occupation to Crossroads of the Americas.* New York: Cambridge University Press, 2019.

Correa Restrepo, Juan Santiago. "Inversión Extranjera Directa y Construcción de Ferrocarriles en Colombia: El Caso del Ferrocarril de Panamá (1849–1869)." *Estudios Gerenciales*, 26, no. 115 (April–June 2010): 141–160.

Cuesta, Eduardo Martín. "Visión y planeamiento estratégico para unir dos océanos a través de Panamá. El caso del William Henry Aspinwall y la Panamá Rail Road Company (1847–1861)." *Revista de Historia Industrial* 24, no. 1 (2015): 87–109.

Cumpston, I. M. *Indians Overseas in British Territories 1834–1854.* London: Dawsons of Pall Mall, 1969.

Delgado, James P. *To California by Sea: A Maritime History of the California Gold Rush.* Columbia: University of South Carolina Press, 1990.

Delpar, Helen. *Red Against Blue: The Liberal Party in Colombian Politics 1863–1899.* Tuscaloosa: University of Alabama Press, 1981.

Dictionary of American Biography. New York: Charles Scribner's Sons, 1964.

Dolan, Jay P. *The Irish Americans. A History*. New York: Bloomsbury, 2008.

DuVal, Miles Percy, Jr. *And the Mountains will Move*. Stanford: Stanford University Press, 1947.

Elder III, Donald, and Shaughnessy, Michael F. *The Greatest Events in American History*. Newcastle upon Tyne: Cambridge Scholars Publishing, 2018.

Ernst, Robert. *Immigrant Life in New York City 1825–1863*. New York, 1949. Reprint, New York: Octagon Books, 1979.

Espino, Rodrigo. *Ésta es mi patria*. Panamá: Edición Centenario, 2003.

Fagg, John Edwin, *Latin America: A General History*, 2nd ed. London: Collier-Macmillan, 1969.

Fanning, Tim. *Paisanos: The Forgotten Irish Who Changed the Face of Latin America*. Dublin: Gill Books, 2016.

"Fessenden Nott Otis, M.D." *British Medical Journal* 1, no. 2060 (June 23, 1900): 1566.

Fox, John. *El Proyecto Macnamara. The Maverick Irish Priest and the Race to seize California, 1844–1846*. Sallins, Co. Kildare: Merrion, 2014.

Frederick, Rhonda D. "Colon Man a Come." *Mythographies of Panama Canal Migration*. Lanham, MD: Lexington, 2005.

Frenkel, Stephen. "Jungle Stories: North American Representations of Tropical Panama." *Geographical Review* 86, no. 3 (July 1996): 317–333.

Gabaccia, Donna R. "Constructing North America. Railroad Building and the Rise of Continental Migrations, 1850–1914." Chapter 3 in *Repositioning North American Migration History: New Directions in Modern Continental Migration, Citizenship and Community*, edited by Marc S. Rodriguez. Rochester, New York: University of Rochester Press, 2004.

Gibson, John M. *Physician to the World. The Life of General William C. Gorgas*. Durham, NC: Duke University Press, 1950.

Glazier, Michael, ed. *The Encyclopedia of the Irish in America*. Notre Dame, IN: University of Notre Dame Press, 1999.

Gobat, Michel. *Confronting the American Dream: Nicaragua under U.S. Imperial Rule*. Durham and London: Duke University Press, 2005.

Greene, Julie. *The Canal Builders: Making America's Empire at the Panama Canal*. New York: Penguin, 2009.

Grigore, Julius. *The Influence of the United States Navy upon the Beginnings of the Panama Railroad*. Balboa, Panama: Balboa Press, n.d.

———. *Presidents of the Panama Railroad Company, 1849 to 1916*. Balboa, Panama: published by the author, 2001.

Guerron-Montero, Carla. "Racial Democracy and Nationalism in Panama." *Ethnology* 45, no. 3 (Summer 2006): 209–228.

Handlin, Oscar. *Boston's Immigrants 1790–1880. A Study in Acculturation*. Rev. ed. Cambridge, MA: Belknap, 1979.

Harding, Robert C. *The History of Panama*. Greenwood Histories of the Modern Nations. Westport, CT: Greenwood, 2006.

Hauberg, C. A. Review of *Rails Across Panama. The Story of the Building of the Panama Railroad 1849–1855*, by Joseph L. Schott. *Hispanic American Historical Review* 48, no. 2 (May 1968): 314–315.

Herring, Hubert. *A History of Latin America from the Beginnings to the Present*, 3rd ed. London: Jonathan Cape, 1968.

Howarth, David. *The Golden Isthmus*. London: Collins, 1966.

Humphrey, David C. *Peg Leg: the improbable life of a Texas hero, Thomas William Ward, 1807–1872*. Denton: Texas State Historical Association, 2009.

———. "The Myth of the Hangman: Ran Runnels, the Isthmus Guard, and the Suppression of Crime in Mid-Nineteenth-Century Panama." *Latin Americanist* 59, no. 4 (December 2015): 3–24.

Ignatiev, Noel. *How the Irish Became White*. New York & London: Routledge, 1995.

Ireland, M. W. "General William C. Gorgas." *Science* (July 16, 1920): 53–54.

Jaén Suárez, Omar. *La Población del Istmo de Panamá*. Madrid: Agencia Española de Cooperación Internacional, 1998.

Johnson, Jerah. Review of *The Irish in the South, 1815–1877*, by David T. Gleeson. *Louisiana History: Journal of the Louisiana Historical Association* 44, no. 4 (Fall 2003): 486.

Kalmanovitz, Salomón. "El Federalismo y la fiscalidad del estado soberano de Panamá, 1850–1886." *Revista de Economía Institucional* 14, 27 (2012): 99–145.

Kemble, John Haskell. *The Panama Route, 1848–1869*. Columbia, SC: University of South Carolina, 1990. First published 1943 by University of California Press, Berkeley.

———. "The Gold Rush by Panama, 1848–1851." In Caughey, John Walton, ed., *Rushing for Gold*. Berkeley and Los Angeles: University of California Press, 1949: 45–56. Pacific Coast Branch of the American Historical Association Special Publication No. 1. Reprinted from the *Pacific Historical Review* 18, no. 1 (February 1949).

Kenny, Kevin. *The American Irish. A History*. Harlow, Essex: Longman, 2000.

Lai, Walton Look. *Indentured Labor, Caribbean Sugar: Chinese and Indian Migrants to the British West Indies, 1838–1918*. Baltimore and London: Johns Hopkins University Press, 1993.

LaRosa, Michael, and German Mejia, eds. *The United States Discovers Panama. The Writings of Soldiers, Scholars, Scientists and Scoundrels, 1850–1905*. Lanham, MD: Rowman and Littlefield, 2004.

Leonard, Thomas M. *Historical Dictionary of Panama*. Lanham, MD: Rowman & Littlefield, 2015.

Lewis, Lancelot S. *The West Indian in Panama: Black Labor in Panama, 1850–1914*. Washington, DC: University Press of America, 1980.

Mack, Gerstle. *The Land Divided. A History of the Panama Canal and Other Isthmian Canal Projects*. New York: Alfred Knopf, 1944.

Maurer, Noel, and Carlos Yu. "What Roosevelt Took: The Economic Impact of the Panama Canal, 1903–37." Working Paper 06–041, Harvard Business School, 2006.

May, Robert E. *Manifest Destiny's Underworld: Filibustering in Antebellum America*. Chapel Hill & London: University of North Carolina Press, 2002.

McCaffrey, Lawrence J. *The Irish Catholic Diaspora in America*. Rev. ed. Washington, DC: Catholic University of America Press, 1997.

McCullough, David. "Steam Road to El Dorado." *American Heritage Magazine* 27, no. 4 (June 1976).

———. *The Path Between the Seas. The Creation of the Panama Canal 1870–1914*. New York: Simon & Schuster, 1977.

McGuinness, Aims. "Aquellos Tiempos de California: el ferrocarril de Panamá y la transformación de la zona de tránsito durante la Fiebre del Oro." In *Historia General de Panamá*. Vol. 2, *El Siglo XIX*, (141–159), edited by Alfredo Castillero Calvo. Panamá: Comité Nacional del Centenario de la República, 2004.

———. *Path of Empire: Panama and the California Gold Rush*. Ithaca and London: Cornell University Press, 2008.

McNeill, J. R. *Mosquito Empires: Ecology and War in the Greater Caribbean, 1620–1914*. New York: Cambridge University Press, 2010.

Meditz, Sandra W. and Dennis M. Hanratty, eds. *Panama: A Country Study*. Area Handbook Series DA Pam 550–46. Washington, DC: Department of the Army, 1989.

Miller, Kerby A. *Emigrants and Exiles. Ireland and the Irish Exodus to North America*. New York & Oxford: Oxford University Press, 1985.

Minter, John Easter. *The Chagres: River of Westward Passage*. New York & Toronto: Rinehart & Co., 1948.

Mon P., Ramón A. "Mecanismo de Adaptación Psicológica y Procesos de Integración de los Inmigrantes Chinos." *Revista Cultural Lotería* (Panama), no. 459 (March–April 2005): 56–62.

Moore, Sarah J. "Mosquitoes, Malaria, and Cold Butter: Discourses of Hygiene and Health in the Panama Canal Zone in the Early Twentieth Century." *Panorama: Journal of the Association of Historians of American Art* 3, no. 2 (Fall 2017): 1–27.

Morgan, Juan David. *El Caballo de Oro: La Gran Aventura de la Construcción del Ferrocarril de Panamá*. Barcelona: Ediciones B, 2005.

Murray, Edmundo. "Ireland and Latin America: A Cultural History." DPhil diss., University of Zurich, 2010.

———. "Secret Diasporas: the Irish in Latin America and the Caribbean." *History Ireland* 16, no. 4 (July–August 2008):15–19.

———. "The Irish in Latin America and Iberia: A Bibliography." Last modified May 7, 2009. http://www.irlandeses.org/bibliography.htm.

Newton, Velma. *The Silver Men. West Indian Labor Migration to Panama 1850–1914*. Kingston, Jamaica: Institute of Social and Economic Research, 1984.

Niehaus, Earl F. *The Irish in New Orleans 1800–1860*. Baton Rouge: Louisiana State University Press, 1965.

O'Mahony, Colman. *Cork's Poor Law Palace. Workhouse Life 1838–1890*. Cork: Rosmathun, 2005.

O'Mahony, Michelle. *Famine in Cork City. Famine Life at Cork Union Workhouse*. Cork: Mercier, 2005.

O'Reggio, Trevor. *Between Alienation and Citizenship. The Evolution of Black West Indian Society in Panama 1914–1964*. Lanham, MD: University Press of America, 2006.

Parker, Matthew. *Hell's Gorge: The Battle to Build the Panama Canal*. London: Arrow, 2008.

Perez-Venero, Alex. *Before the Five Frontiers. Panama from 1821–1903*. New York: AMS, 1978.

Petras, Elizabeth McLean. *Jamaican Labor Migration: White Capital and Black Labor, 1850–1930*. Boulder: Westview, 1988.

Platt, Stephen. *Imperial Twilight: The Opium War and the End of China's Last Golden Age*. London: Atlantic Books, 2018.

Purcell, Richard J. "The New York Commissioners of Emigration and Irish Immigrants: 1847–1860." *Studies: An Irish Quarterly Review* 37, no. 145 (March 1948): 29–42.

Quinn, William H., Victor T. Neal, and Santiago E. Antunez de Mayolo. "El Niño Occurrences Over the Past Four and a Half Centuries." *Journal of Geophysical Research* 92, no. C13 (December 1987): 14449–14461.

Rippy, J. Fred. "British Investments in Latin America, End 1876." *Pacific Historical Review* 17, no. 1 (February 1948): 11–18.

Rosenwaike, Ira. *Population History of New York City*. Syracuse, NY: Syracuse University Press, 1972.

Schott, Joseph L. *Rails Across Panama. The Story of the Building of the Panama Railroad 1849–1855*. Indianapolis: Bobbs-Merrill, 1967.

Scott, Blake C. Review of *Mobility and Modernity: Panama in the Nineteenth Century Anglo-American Imagination* by Robert D. Aguirre, *Journal of British Studies* 57, no. 4 (October 2018): 881–882.

Senior, Olive. *Dying to Better Themselves. West Indians and the Building of the Panama Canal*. Kingston: University of the West Indies Press, 2014.

Sheldon, R. C. "A History of Construction, Operation, and Maintenance of the Panama Railroad." Thesis, Ohio Northern University, 1933.

Simmons, James Stevens. *Malaria in Panama*. The American Journal of Hygiene Monographic Series No. 13. Baltimore: Johns Hopkins Press, 1939.

Small, Charles S. *Rails to the Diggings: Construction Railroads of the Panama Canal*. United States: Railroad Monographs, 1981.

Somerville, Duncan S. *The Aspinwall Empire*. Mystic, Connecticut: Mystic Seaport Museum, 1983.

Stiles, T. J. *The First Tycoon. The Epic Life of Cornelius Vanderbilt*. New York: Vintage, 2010.

Susto, Juan Antonio. "La personalidad de Ran Runnels." *Revista Lotería* (Panamá) 2, no. 23 (October 1957): 97–99.

Sutter, Paul S. "'The First Mountain to Be Removed': Yellow Fever Control and the Construction of the Panama Canal." *Environmental History* 21 (April 2016): 250–259.

Tam, Juan. "Huellas Chinas en Panamá." *Revista Cultural Lotería* (Panamá), no. 459 (March–April 2005):7–45.

Von Hagen, Victor Wolfgang. "Blazing the Trail for the Panama Canal." *Travel*, December 1946. 11 pp.

Ward, Christopher, and Richard J. Junkins. "Panamanian Historical Sources." *Latin American Research Review*, 21, no. 3 (1986): 129–136.

Werner, Louis. "All Aboard to Nowhere." *Americas* 42, 4 (July 1990).

Westerman, George W. "Historical Notes on West Indians on the Isthmus of Panama." *Phylon* 22, no. 4 (1961): 340–350.

Wiltsee, Ernest A. *Gold Rush Steamers of the Pacific*. San Francisco: Grabhorn, 1938.

Wolmar, Christian. *Blood, Iron and Gold. How the Railways Transformed the World*. London: Atlantic, 2010.

———. *The Great Railway Revolution. The Epic Story of the American Railroad*. London: Atlantic, 2012.

Woodworth, Steven E. *Manifest Destinies. America's Westward Expansion and the Road to the Civil War*. New York: Vintage, 2011.

Zanetti, Oscar, and Alejandro Garcia. *Sugar and Railroads; A Cuban History, 1837–1959*. Chapel Hill: University of North Carolina Press, 1998.

Internet Resources

American Heritage: https://www.americanheritage.com

British Newspaper Archive: https://www.britishnewspaperarchive.co.uk

California Digital Newspaper Collection: http://cdnc.ucr.edu

Cornell University Library. Making of America Digital Collection: http://ebooks.library.cornell.edu/m/moa

Find a Grave: https://findagrave.com/memorial/22990218/george-muirson-totten

Google Books: https://books.google.co.uk

Hathi Trust Digital Library: https://www.hathitrust.org

Historical Newspapers: https://www.newspapers.com

Hoadley Family: http://www.hoadleyfamily.com

Indiana University Library: https://www.iucat.iu.edu

Internet Archive Digital Library: https://archive.org

Legacies of British Slave-Ownership, University College London: https://www
.ucl.ac.uk/lbs/person/view

Library of Congress. Chronicling America. Historic American Newspapers:
https://chroniclingamerica.loc.gov

New York State Historic Newspapers: https://www.nyshistoricnewspapers.org

New York Times: https://www.nytimes.com

Panama Canal Authority: http://www.pancanal.com

Panama Canal Railway Company: http://www.panarail.com

Panama Railroad: http://www.panamarailroad.org

The Political Graveyard: http://politicalgraveyard.com

ProQuest Databases: https://www.proquest.com/libraries/academic/databases

The Silver People Heritage Foundation: https://www.thesilverpeopleheritage
.wordpress.com

Society for Irish Latin American Studies (SILAS): https://www.irlandeses.org

Spectator Archive: https://archive.spectator.co.uk

Washington Post: https://www.washingtonpost.com

Index

Page numbers in italics refer to illustrations.

PETER PYNE was born in 1941 in Dublin, Ireland. He studied at University College Dublin and Glasgow University. Until his retirement some years ago, he lectured at Magee University College of the University of Ulster. He is the author of a number of articles on Irish and Latin American history and politics. With his wife, Joan, he currently runs a guesthouse in Derry, Northern Ireland.

9 780253 052070